INSTRUCTIONAL
MODELS
IN
READING

INSTRUCTIONAL MODELS IN READING

Edited by

STEVEN A. STAHL
DAVID A. HAYES
The University of Georgia, Athens

LEA LAWRENCE ERLBAUM ASSOCIATES, PUBLISHERS
1997 Mahwah, New Jersey

Lawrence Erlbaum Associates, Inc., Publishers
10 Industrial Avenue
Mahwah, New Jersey 07430

Cover design by Kristin L. Alfano

Library of Congress Cataloging-in-Publication Data

Instructional models in reading / edited by Steven A. Stahl, David A.
Hayes.
    p.   cm.
    Includes bibliographical references and indexes.
    ISBN 0-8058-1459-0 (cloth : alk. paper). — ISBN 0-8058-2286-0
(paper : alk. paper).
    1. Reading. I. Stahl, Steven A. II. Hayes, David A.
LB1050.I45 1996
428.4'071—dc20   96-29111
                                       CIP

Books published by Lawrence Erlbaum Associates are printed on acid-free paper,
and their bindings are chosen for strength and durability.

Printed in the United States of America
10 9 8 7 6 5 4 3

Contents

Preface

This volume started with a simple idea—to examine models of reading instruction that have emerged over the past 20 years or so. These models span a wide range of instruction representing a continuum from highly structured, task analytic instruction to child-centered and holistic instruction. Each model has its own epistemology or views on how "reading" and how "instruction" are to be defined. The different epistemologies indicate different principles of instruction, which, in turn, indicate different practices in the classroom. Each model is also supported by a different research base. Our goal in putting this book together was to get leading proponents of these different models to discuss their ideas about reading instruction and to assemble these discussions into one volume so that readers could make their own comparisons and contrasts.

We thought of these as *models* rather than *approaches* or *methods* in that they represented constructs of what the authors think "reading instruction" might be. The first appearance in writing of the word *model* occurred in Germany during the 16th century to denote an object replicated in the manufacture of a product. Model is a word whose sound and meaning were close to the Italian word *modello,* an object that stood before an artist for imitation or representation. The words *model* and *modello* derive ultimately from the Indo-European *med* meaning a measure or to measure or to take a measure. From *med* came the Latin *modo,* meaning form. The diminutive of *modo, modello,* served as an architectural term referring to one half the diameter of a column. Its meaning generalized first from modo, meaning form, to refer to an object to be imitated, as a model imitated or represented by an artist, then to denote an object to be replicated in the manufacture of a product. From tangible object of imitation its meaning eventually generalized to refer to a notion or idea that could guide the implementation of a course of action. A *conceptual model* provides a way of thinking that incorporates specific instances within a common system of categories having a structure or form governed by a set of assumptions. In this respect a conceptual model is like a theory, but a conceptual model differs from a theory in that it cannot allow proposing formal causal explanations.

Our hypothesis was that proponents of different models view "reading" in different ways and that each would be relatively effective in producing reading outcomes consistent with the way that proponents of that model instantiated reading. For example, whereas proponents of instruction that views reading as a concatenation of skills should be relatively effective in helping children master subskills of reading (such as decoding words with short vowels), proponents of instruction that views *reading* more holistically and *instruction* as getting children interested in reading would be expected to produce motivated readers. Having such a notion of models of reading instruction, researchers could examine the strong hypothesis that instruction in accordance with a particular model would have an outcome that is part of its epistemology and also examine aspects of reading incidental to its view of reading. Further, as interest or "general motivation for reading" becomes more important to a teacher, one would expect to find a concomitant increase in the importance of holistic instructional constructs. As "skills" become more important, so should the importance of instructional principles related to teaching skills.

From an instructional viewpoint, one could postulate that, because reading is a multifaceted concept, then the "ideal" reading instruction would also be multifaceted, drawing from the range of reading instructional models. As Stahl (this volume) suggests, eclectic instruction would draw from these models as needed to meet the different needs of different learners at different stages of their development.

We began the project by soliciting chapters from scholars whom we believed hold a clear perspective on reading instruction. We asked them to (a) describe their instructional model, (b) discuss the "epistemology" of that model or how it defined reading and instruction, (c) describe what a classroom using this model would look like, (d) discuss research supporting this model, and (e) discuss future research that is needed. As would be expected, the chapters they produced differed in emphasis placed on each of the points we asked them to address. Because we wanted to present a variety of voices in this book, we restrained our editing so that the voices of the authors remained distinctively their own.

As the chapters came in, our perspectives on the different reading models changed. Our basic assumption holds that there are identifiable models of reading instruction and that these models do differ in terms of epistemology and practice. However, there is much more blending between models, especially as we get closer to practice. The authors of these chapters seem to adopt this eclectic approach, to some greater or lesser extent, incorporating aspects of other models into their instruction as they see other goals. Thus, models of reading instruction are complex. Further complicating matters is the fact that teachers hold their own models of reading, as discussed by Hayes (this volume), which may or may not be congruent with those discussed here. Although academically developed models influence college preservice and inservice instruction, teachers' own models of reading filter the information that they take from what they learn from these perspectives.

We originally planned to have sections corresponding to what we thought were the major classes of models of reading instruction. However, we found that we were unable to categorize the chapters so neatly. And, indeed, most models are complex enough to defy simple categorization. We have put the two overview chapters (one by each of us) in the beginning. All but one of the other chapters constitute the main body of the book. Duffy's chapter serves as a final word since his journey from a direct instruction orientation to a more holistic orientation seems to represent the movement of our field.

We are not only satisfied that the authors make clear their perspectives on reading instruction but believe that they present their ideas quite cogently. As the chapters came in, we learned from them. Examining their ideas again and again as a task of this kind demands we have gained a strong appreciation for the complexity of reading instruction. Our hope is that this book makes a contribution toward disciplined inquiry into what it means to teach reading.

Steven A. Stahl
David A. Hayes

CHAPTER ONE

Instructional Models in Reading: An Introduction

Steven A. Stahl
The University of Georgia, Athens

In the 1950s, there was basically one approach to teaching reading. Basal readers dominated instruction. According to Austin and Morrison's (1963) survey, 95% of all teachers used a basal reader to teach. Basal readers all used Betts' (1946) Directed Reading Activity: background building and vocabulary development prior to reading, guided silent reading followed by questions and oral rereading, and a series of postquestions. This was how reading was to be taught, and the basic model was not questioned. "Reading" was thought to consist of accurate word recognition and the ability to answer questions about what was read. "Instruction" was what was done to facilitate word recognition and question answering. According to Durkin's (1974) observations, teachers' manuals in the basal reading program were followed closely, if not slavishly. There were dissenters to this point of view (see Y. Goodman, 1989), but they were far outnumbered by those who used basals.

In the 1990s, there are many competing models of reading instruction. The whole-language movement (K. Goodman, 1986) has had a pervasive influence in elementary classes. Direct instruction has a strong influence in special education, but is reemerging in regular education as well. Sociocultural models have a strong influence, especially in schools with multicultural populations. Response-oriented reading approaches are seen more often in secondary English classes, and emergent-literacy models are used to guide kindergartners' development.

Our models of reading instruction guide our research and serve as a filter for us to view practice. This chapter reviews several widely held models, examining both how they view reading instruction and how they define *reading*. Then it discusses how these different models fit into a specific model of reading development (Stahl, 1992a). Finally, it suggests that effective instruction involves a melding of the different models. Because reading instruction involves multiple goals, different approaches are best to reach different goals.

MODELS OF READING INSTRUCTION

Garcia and Pearson (1991) divided competing approaches to reading instruction into four general approaches: direct instruction, explicit explanation, cognitive apprenticeship, and whole language. These are distinctly different from conventional, basal instruction. Taken as a group, these four approaches represent a continuum from highly teacher-directed, task-analytic approaches to more student-directed, holistic approaches—from the reliance on contrived materials designed for specific instructional purposes to the use of "natural" materials written primarily for an audience of young readers. They should not be thought of as discrete approaches, but as points on that continuum.

Direct Instruction

Although direct-instruction approaches can trace their lineage back to behavioral analyses of decoding tasks and process–product analyses of teaching (see Rosenshine & Stevens, 1984), more recent work in the direct-instruction paradigm has been directed toward teaching more complex skills. Such approaches begin with a task analysis of the target behavior, which is used to design the instruction. Students are taught each component, both singly and in combination with the other components. Teachers model the desired behavior, provide ample practice and feedback at each step, and assess whether reteaching is necessary. Unlike earlier versions of direct instruction, current use of the model also includes metacognitive explanation of the importance of the strategy; how, when, and where it is to be used; and when its use is inappropriate.

The direct-instruction model makes clear assumptions about learning, based on behavioral roots. Direct-instruction proponents assume that reading can be decomposed into identifiable subskills that, when taught directly, will improve children's reading ability. These subskills are to be taught using a specified set of teacher behaviors. A direct-instruction phonics lesson might begin with the introduction of a letter sound, discrimination of that sound and previously taught sounds, blending that sound into words, and so on. At its most extreme, direct instruction tends to view teachers as interchangeable dispensers of instruction. By attempting to specify the exact behaviors (e.g., hand signals, pointing) that teachers perform, as well as the exact words that they say, direct-instruction proponents try to make the curriculum "teacher proof." Many teachers resist this programming, either subverting the program by their actions or abandoning the program as soon as they have a chance (Shannon, 1987).

Direct-instruction approaches: (a) break language down into components that are taught in isolation, not in a meaningful context; (b) are highly teacher directed, allowing students little choice in what is to be learned and how it is to be learned; and (c) view the acquisition of literacy as highly "unnatural," requiring systematic instruction, rather than absorption. This need not be so. Research shows that direct-instruction programs are most effective when combined with wide reading in tradebooks (Meyer, 1983). Indeed, direct instruction in one aspect of reading is not incompatible with allowing self-selection in other aspects of a reading curriculum (see Cunningham, 1991).

Explicit Explanation

Explicit explanation is similar to direct instruction in that they both involve explicit definitions of cognitive strategies used in reading, including discussions of their usefulness, as well as modeling and practice. In explicit-explanation lessons, there is greater emphasis on practicing the strategy in the context of reading text, although the strategy may be introduced using specially constructed materials. In explicit explanation, there is also greater concern with gradually releasing the responsibility for the execution of a strategy. In direct instruction, it is assumed that, as readers become more proficient at using a strategy, they will automatically use that strategy while reading. In explicit explanation, there is greater emphasis on leading students to make that transfer. In the beginning of the explicit-explanation instruction, the responsibility for using a strategy lies largely with the teacher; by the end, the student executes the strategy independently.

An example of an explicit-explanation program is Raphael's work in teaching children to answer questions strategically using a question–answer relationship taxonomy (e.g., Raphael & Wonnacott, 1985). In these lessons, students are taught about the relationship between questions and their answers. After an initial exposition of the taxonomy, students are shown a passage and given questions with their answers. As a class, the students discuss the relationship between the question and the answer. In succeeding lessons, students answer questions given the relationship, provide the answer and the relationship, and generate their own questions, providing both answers and relationships. Thus, the students gradually assert "ownership" of the strategy.

Explicit explanation has been used to teach a variety of reading strategies—from using context to identify unknown words (Duffy et al., 1986) to making inferences during reading (Hansen & Pearson, 1983). It also has been used as a model for an entire school's curriculum, involving the explicit integration of strategies in all subject matter learning from primary- to middle-school grades (Gaskins & Elliot, 1991).

Because it is so new, it is difficult to draw conclusions about the effectiveness of explicit explanation. There are some indications that, when teaching skills such as using context to identify words (e.g., skills that might have been mastered through children's oral language development), explicit explanation makes children better able to discuss what they are doing, but does not directly improve their reading achievement (Duffy et al., 1986). Duffy et al. asserted that this greater awareness will eventually translate into higher achievement, but did not present evidence that it does. Because skills are best performed automatically, without conscious application, it is not clear that explicit explanation would be useful. For strategies such as summarization, which is applied deliberately, such explicit explanation may be highly effective.

Explicit-explanation instruction also presents a clear contrast to whole language. Although both approaches stress the importance of reading natural text for authentic purposes, explicit instruction involves isolation and instruction of subskills, and complete teacher control of the purposes of the lesson, at least in the beginning. These would be anathema to a whole-language advocate.

Cognitive Apprenticeship

A third alternative to whole language is a cognitive-apprenticeship approach. Cognitive-apprenticeship approaches attempt to set up a master–apprentice relationship between student and teacher. The teacher's role is to scaffold the learning, withdrawing support as students are able to proceed on their own. Just as an apprentice first watches the master as the master does a skilled craft, so does the student initially observe the teacher as the teacher models the processes of comprehension. Gradually, the teacher gives more and more responsibility to the student, until it is the teacher who watches the student perform comprehension tasks.

Those who advocate the use of cognitive apprenticeships view reading as the orchestration of complex processes. Teaching these processes skill by skill creates a distorted view of reading (Brown, Collins, & Duguid, 1989). Citing Vygotsky, Brown et al. argued that cognition is socially situated—that all cognitive acts take place within a sociocultural context, and that the larger context can either support or impede cognitive activities, such as those involved in reading. This new view of cognition has been called *situated cognition,* or *socially constructed knowledge.* From this view, researchers suggest that an apprenticeship model is more appropriate for teaching than the transmittal model of direct instruction. Through the process of interacting with the knowledgeable other, students learn how an expert orchestrates the processes involved in comprehension (Garcia & Pearson, 1991).

In cognitive apprenticeships, teacher and students work together to comprehend increasingly complex text. In contrast to direct instruction, instruction is performed using authentic texts for authentic purposes. Teacher and students might read a text together, with the teacher providing as much support as necessary for the students to successfully work through the text.

The cognitive-apprenticeship model emphasizes constructing the meaning of a text through social interactions, and usually involves a reorganization of the basic organization of the class. Instead of a teacher-dominated class structure, cognitive-apprenticeship models usually involve small groups working together. Cooperative learning (Stevens, Madden, Slavin, & Farnish, 1987), reciprocal teaching (Palincsar & Brown, 1984), collaborative problem solving (Palincsar, David, Winn, & Stevens, 1991), and conversational discussion groups (O'Flahaven, 1990) all use group dynamics to scaffold or support children's learning. For example, in reciprocal teaching, small groups of students work together with the teacher to read a text. Each person in the group takes a turn being the "teacher." As the "teacher," a child uses four teaching behaviors: questioning, summarizing, clarifying, and predicting. Unlike many of the training approaches discussed so far, reciprocal teaching usually takes place over a period of weeks or months, not a single class period. Initiation of reciprocal teaching might begin with direct instruction of the four teaching operations, followed by direct teacher modeling. In the early stages of reciprocal teaching, the teacher takes a dominant role, modeling the operations during his or her turn and prompting students during theirs. Such prompts might include, What is the main idea of this paragraph? or Could you make it into a question? Over time, the prompts become more general. Also, over time, students take over the groups, acting more and more like expert teachers.

By having students act as a teacher, reciprocal teaching requires students to externalize the operations of comprehension. Through this externalization, the teacher and other students are able to scaffold the development of each student's comprehension. The learning that occurs in conversational discussion groups, where groups of students respond to stories (O'Flahaven, 1989), or cooperative learning groups, which have been used for a great many learning situations (e.g., Stevens, Madden, Slavin, & Farnish, 1987), involves similar scaffolding through group dynamic processes.

As with explicit explanation, cognitive apprenticeships are too recent to have been fully evaluated. Rosenshine and Meister (1991) performed a meta-analysis of studies evaluating reciprocal teaching, and found that reciprocal teaching was most effective when combined with direct teaching of cognitive strategies. Brown and Palincsar (1989; cited in Prawat, 1991) compared reciprocal teaching with a peer-collaboration approach (which appears to be analogous to whole language, but directed specifically toward science learning), and found that a peer-collaborative approach, combined with text materials rewritten for conceptual coherence, produced the highest quality of student discourse about science and evidence of higher level thinking in writing samples. This line of research was continued by Brown and her colleagues (Brown, 1992). Brown and Palincsar (1989; cited in Prawat, 1991) suggested that the original reciprocal-teaching approach was successful in getting poor readers to focus on comprehension, but that its structure may not be necessary for accomplished readers to develop deeper understanding of content materials.

Whole Language

As Gunderson (chap. 10, this volume) points out, *whole language* is difficult to define. In recent years, at least three professional journal articles (Altwerger, Edelsky, & Flores, 1987; Bergeron, 1990; Watson, 1989) and three books (Edelsky, Altwerger, & Flores, 1991; K. Goodman, 1986; Newman, 1985) have been essentially devoted to the topic of defining whole language. However, the definitions have been rather hazy. Bergeron (1990) examined articles that used the term to examine commonalities among definitions. She found that "whole language was defined differently in each of the 64 articles reviewed," and that "little consistency was also found in the descriptions of those attributes thought to be the focus of whole language" (p. 312).

In the case of whole language, this lack of an objective definition seems deliberate. Even adherents refuse to define *whole language*, arguing that to do so would disempower practitioners. For example, Watson (1989) cited several different definitions of *whole language*, and then said: "These definitions may lack sameness, but they never go outside the boundaries of an acceptable definition of some dimension of whole language. The definitions are diverse because the personal and professional histories of the authors are different. This variety frees those who have studied and practiced whole language to generate their own definitions, then to revise their definitions again and again" (p. 132). Edelsky (1990), however, argued that the freedom to create one's own definition is limited only to those who accept whole-language principles. Edelsky took McKenna, Robinson, and Miller (1990) to task for not understanding what whole language was, and suggested that they could not understand it unless they believed in it. Further, Edelsky argued that McKenna et al. could not propose a research agenda to evaluate whole language because they were outsiders.

Even if one cannot precisely define *whole language*, there are beliefs that are shared by most whole-language practitioners. Among these are that language (oral and written) is used for authentic purposes, including communication, information, and so on (K. Goodman & Y. Goodman, 1979), and that children will learn language best if it is learned for authentic purposes. In the classroom, this involves: using authentic reading and writing tasks using whole texts, not looking at parts of language (e.g., sound–symbol correspondences) for their own sake, and not using artificial tasks such as work sheets or specially adapted stories found in basal reading programs. There is also a belief in child-centered learning—in empowering children to direct their own learning. Instruction should occur not when the teacher or curriculum developer plans it, but in response to students' needs as they are attempting to use language for communication. There are activities found in many whole-language classrooms, such as choral reading of Big Books (Holdaway, 1979), teachers' reading aloud to children, sustained silent reading, use of process writing (Graves, 1983), and use of the "author's chair" (Graves & Hansen, 1983). But these activities do not define *whole language*. Instead, these activities are practical ways to implement a whole-language philosophy. These activities can be used in classes holding a number of different philosophies. Whole-language theorists make it clear that whole language is not a "method" or collection of activities, but a philosophy underlying all the teacher's instructional decisions.

As Gunderson (chap. 10, this volume) points out, the term *whole language* is an intertext—it is defined by the people who use it. Because each person constructs his or her own meaning, the term means something slightly different (but related) to each person who uses it. In this book, there are a number of approaches that are similar, but not identical to, whole language, including Pappas' (chap. 12) integrated-language perspective, Labbo and Teale's (chap. 11) emergent-literacy perspective, Klein, Kelly, and Pinnell's (chap. 7) Reading Recovery, and Galda and Guice's (chap. 13) and Faust's (chap. 14) description of response-oriented reading instruction. We think that these notions bear this "family resemblance" with each other, but also recognize that the notions of reading and its instruction in these chapters are significantly different from each other.

SORTING OUT THE ALTERNATIVES

Each of these instruction alternatives, as well as the conventional basal instruction to which they have been compared, stem from different views of the reading process. Each of these views is limited and ultimately incomplete when advocates attempt to extrapolate it beyond the problem it was designed to solve. Discussing the limitations in these different world views may bring a way out of the impasse, and may suggest a more complex model of instruction, which will better serve the multiple aims of reading instruction.

The Epistemology of Objective-Based Basal Reading Program and Direct Instruction

Basically, each of these approaches is a solution to a different problem in reading. Each approach was originally developed to deal with a specific aspect of reading, and was later extended to encompass the whole of reading instruction. In the process of extension, educators developed a view of reading rooted in their analysis of the original problem. For example, direct-instruction approaches were originally developed to teach decoding, and did so through a task analysis. When these approaches were extended to other areas of reading, the same task-analysis approach was applied to areas such as comprehension and problem solving. Thus, direct-instruction proponents view "reading" as a process composed of isolated subprocesses or subskills, and "reading instruction" as using a set of procedures to teach students each of these subprocesses. These views are rooted in behaviorist psychology, in which complex tasks are broken down and each component is taught, using contingency management until it is mastered. These components are chained to get the larger behavior (Kameenui, Simmons, Chard, & Dickson, chap. 3, this volume). However, in the beginning, the behaviorist approach was developed to teach motor skills to animals such as pigeons and rats. In a classic critique that heralded the end of the behaviorist and the beginning of the cognitive era in psychology, Chomsky (1957) rejected the validity of behaviorist explanations for language learning. If behaviorism is applicable to reading, it would be applicable in relatively mechanical aspects, such as decoding. When behaviorist principles have been applied to more complex reading processes, such as critical evaluation of arguments (Patching, Kameenui, Carnine, Gersten, & Colvin, 1983), they have tended to reduce the complex phenomena to a simple algorithm, losing the applicability to a broad set of problems. However, Kameenui, Simmons, Chard, and Dickson (chap. 3, this volume) dispute this, arguing that "big ideas" that apply to a wide variety of problems can be taught directly.

Similarly, basal reading programs, at least those based on the objective-oriented models developed in the 1970s (e.g., Otto & Askov, 1972), tend to view reading as a concatenation of skills. These early objective-based programs were initially designed to break the domain of decoding into manageable chunks, but they were soon extended to text comprehension. Prior to the use of objectives, comprehension was synonymous with question answering. By breaking reading into distinct subskills, it was hoped that the teacher could teach children *how* to comprehend, rather than merely assess the product of that comprehension. Scope and sequence charts have been developed, dividing the reading process into a sequenced series of skills and subskills. These skills are taught and reviewed—through direct teaching and workbook practice—every lesson, bracketing each story. Observers have found that up to 75% of "reading" time is spent on workbook practice, in which children read no more than a word or a sentence at a time (Anderson, Hiebert, Wilkinson, & Scott, 1985). These skills are tested using criterion-referenced tests, whose results are used for evaluation or reteaching. The implicit assumption in these programs is that reading instruction involves the mastery of all the skills taught—often 300 or more.

In contrast to direct instruction, most basal reading instruction consists of what Durkin (1979–1980) called "mentioning" the skills enough to provide direction for students to complete the work sheets assigned and going on to another skill. Although there seems to be more instruction provided in the more recent basals than in the 1970s' basals, which Durkin observed, this is still a predominant pattern in the schools I observed. Thus, the belief behind objective-based basals, at least in terms of comprehension and de-coding instruction, is that students will learn skillful reading behaviors through (a) exposure to those skills practiced in isolation in workbooks, and (b) through their reading of stories in the book. A number of studies (e.g., Haynes & Jenkins, 1986; Leinhardt, Zigmond, & Cooley, 1981) have found that the amount of time spent doing workbook pages had no relation to children's reading achievement.

Explicit-Explanation and Cognitive-Apprenticeship Views of Reading

It does not appear that the whole of reading can be decomposed into a discrete set of skills. As is discussed later, there are processes used in reading (i.e., skills and strategies), and many students can benefit from learning them. However, reading is not merely the processes that are amenable to instruction, but involves something more. Reading involves the flexible use of processes to meet different purposes, the integration of text information with the reader's knowledge, and so on. If processes are used during reading, a number of processes may be executed simultaneously, and processes will be executed flexibly. The simultaneous and flexible use of processes is not encouraged by the use of work sheets, in which skills are practiced one at a time, with specially constructed material designed for clear applicability of the taught skill. Instead, many authors have argued that reading instruction should stress the use of multiple processes in real text for real aims. Ex-plicit-explanation and cognitive-apprenticeship approaches grew out of the desire to apply direct teaching to authentic reading tasks.

Explicit explanation developed as an amalgam between the direct-instruc-tion technologies discussed earlier and the concepts of informed instruction and metacognition, as discussed by Brown, Campione, and Day (1981) and Paris, Lipson, and Wixson (1984). Developers of these explicit-explanation approaches, which they often called "direct-instruction" approaches (e.g.,

Rinehart, Stahl, & Erickson, 1986), attempted to teach comprehension strategies in a manner that would transfer to "real" reading tasks. In addition to providing explicit instruction in the use of a comprehensive strategy, they informed children explicitly about why the instruction was being taught and where it could be used in ordinary comprehension.

The content of this instruction was single strategies, such as summarization (Day, 1986; Rinehart et al., 1986), question answering (Raphael, 1984), and so on. The assumption was made that children need to learn the target strategy as an end in itself so that it can be evoked at an appropriate time during reading. This contrasts with decoding instruction, whose goal is that the strategy be overlearned so that it can be executed automatically. Strategies are taught singly, but are carefully brought into a larger reading context over the course of instruction. For example, Rinehart et al. began by teaching sixth graders to summarize short paragraphs, gradually lengthening the material used until the students were writing summaries from their social studies textbooks.

Explicit-explanation approaches typically focus on a single strategy at a time, assuming that the strategy will be used, along with other strategies, when reading. Even when multiple strategies are taught, they are taught one at a time (e.g., Gaskins & Elliot, 1991). In contrast, cognitive-apprenticeship models teach multiple strategies simultaneously. In reciprocal teaching (Palincsar & Brown, 1984), for example, groups of students are taught to summarize, question, predict, and clarify while reading.

Cognitive-apprenticeship models also transfer responsibility for learning from teacher to student, but do so using social interaction as a mediator. The importance of social mediation is rooted in a social constructivist view of knowledge. The classic explication of this view is the following quotation from Vygotsky (cited in Wertsch, 1985):

> Any function in the child's cultural development appears twice, or on two planes. First it appears on the social plane, and then on the psychological plane. First it appears between people as an interpsychological category and then within the child as an intrapsychological category. This is equally true with regard to voluntary attention, logical memory, the formation of concepts, and the development of volition. . . . [I]t goes without saying that the internalization transforms the process itself and changes its structure and functions. Social relations or relations among people genetically underlie all higher functions and their relationships. (pp. 60–61)

Peers' interactions are used to develop strategic comprehension (Palincsar & Brown, 1987; Palincsar et al., 1991) as well as critical thinking in reading (Commeyras, 1991) and literary response (O'Flahaven, 1990). In Vygotsky's model, "higher level thought" is a form of internal speech—a dialogue with oneself (see Wertsch, 1985). This dialogue is modeled after dialogues one has with others. These groups, by discussing the text in sophisticated terms (strategically, critically, or with an emotional response), provide a model for the development of this internal speech.

Cognitive apprenticeships are based on two root beliefs. The first is that skilled reading involves the complex interactions between the reader's strategies and knowledge, and the information presented in the text. Proponents believe that students may not integrate strategies that have been taught one at a time into their repertoire of reading behaviors. Explicit-explanation advocates explicitly provide for that integration, but cognitive-apprenticeship advocates argue that isolating a strategy distorts it, making it difficult to use in "real" reading. In cognitive apprenticeships, texts are treated as wholes, using all appropriate strategies simultaneously. The task difficulty is lessened by the teacher, who initially provides a great deal of scaffolding, and then gradually transfers control to the learner over the course of instruction (in a manner similar to that used in explicit explanation).

In practice, cognitive-apprenticeship models share many components with whole-language instruction. First, they both treat the task of reading holistically—they do not break it down into subskills, nor do they teach subskills in isolation. Second, they both stress the "higher levels" of thinking. If decoding and literal comprehension are dealt with, they are dealt with in the context of higher levels of comprehension, such as literary response or critical evaluation. Third, they both use social interaction as a model for desired comprehension behaviors, with both groups relying on Vygotsky for theoretical support.

The Epistemology of Whole Language

Whole-language theorists have clearly explicated their views of reading and reading instruction. Basically, they view reading as one of many manifestations of language ability in general, with written language as a form parallel to oral language, differing only in mode. Written language is viewed as having the same functions as all other forms of language. K. Goodman and Y. Goodman (1979) used Halliday's (e.g., 1973) description of language functions, and described how written language can be used to inform, regulate, interact with others, question and learn about the world, and so on, just as oral language can be.

Whole-language theorists postulate that oral language is learned without direct instruction because it serves a purpose for the learner. Young children learn to talk and understand talk because they can see that talk fulfills a function for them. If written language is seen as functional, then children will learn to produce and understand it. Whole-language theorists see the teacher's role as providing an environment in which language—oral and written—is functional. This environment would contain circumstances in which children would be reading and writing, as well as speaking and listening, in order to learn together (K. Goodman & Y. Goodman, 1979). The teacher's role is twofold: to create an environment in which children would be interested in using reading and writing (i.e., to create "invitations" to learn; Newman, 1985), and to support children's learning about reading and writing (i.e., to enable children to join the "literacy club"; Smith, 1992). Teaching in a whole-language setting involves observing children as they work through problems in reading and writing, and providing assistance when they need it. Children are not expected to "learn through osmosis" in a whole-language classroom, but instead are helped and supported in their efforts to learn (Smith, 1992).

Whole-language advocates view reading as a problem-solving activity (Y. Goodman, 1989); they view the reader as actively building concepts through problem solving. A great deal of reference is paid to the notions of discovery and risk taking. This is similar to the way Piaget described children developing language concepts (Y. Goodman, 1989). Whole-language theory also draws on Vygotsky, especially on the notion that cognitive processes are first developed through social interactions (see Wertsch, 1985). Thus, in whole-language classes, children work together to read a book or write a story (see Newman, 1985). The purpose of these interactions is to develop socially constructed cognitions about the reading process.

Learning in a whole-language classroom begins from the whole, the discourse, and the context in which the discourse is set; it may proceed to an analysis of the parts of language, but only if necessary. Thus, if the task is to write a letter to a friend and the child needs to know how a word is spelled, the teacher might ask the child to remember words that resemble the needed word, or ask the child to think of words that begin similarly. This phonics lesson would be assistance to the child's writing of the letter. A whole-language teacher might also include minilessons on different topics. In both cases, the instruction would be in response to children's needs to use written language. This view of instruction is in clear contrast to direct instruction and objective-based instruction, which rely on the fragmentation of written language into subskills and systematic, preplanned instruction to teach these subskills. Whole-language theorists suggest that children may not see the purpose of such preplanned instruction, leading to a view of reading as purposeless.

The major difference between cognitive apprenticeships and whole language is philosophical: Whole-language theorists reject the *master–apprentice* metaphor. In some such apprenticeships, there is a great deal of teacher planning and control, at least initially. In reciprocal teaching, for example, the teacher initially is in control of the lesson's direction, modeling what the teacher as expert feels are appropriate reading strategies. The teacher displays the strategies that the students are expected to learn. In whole-language lessons, students would direct the emphasis of the lesson from the beginning, with the teacher's role to be to "lead from behind" (Newman, 1985). In whole-language lessons, students learn strategies that they feel they will need to accomplish a desired literacy goal. For example, students may want to learn how to summarize because they have decided to learn about a particular topic and present that information to another. For this purpose, they may ask the teacher for hints in how to summarize. The teacher's role is to present interesting material to the students—to "invite" them to learn (again in Newman's [1986] terminology).

The activity-based model of learning in a whole-language classroom harkens back to a number of sources, including the language-experience movement in reading, as well as the work of educators Donald Holdaway, Marie Clay, and Sylvia Ashton-Warner in New Zealand. On the base of activity-based literacy education, they added influences from literary response theory and composition. From psychology, they draw on the developmental psychology of both Piaget and Vygotsky. This area is reviewed well by Y. Goodman (1989), who also drew on her personal history as a first-grade teacher (see also Gunderson, chap. 10, this volume).

WHAT IS READING?

Theoretically, all one needs to do is find the best match between the epistemology of an approach and our best understanding of the nature of reading and its instruction to choose the "best" method of teaching reading. Unfortunately, it is not that simple. Aside from the fact that educators differ in their understandings of what reading is, and even in their approaches to looking for that understanding, our search for the "best" approach to teaching reading is hindered by the fact that reading is really many different things. Gough and Tumner (1986) argued that decoding and general language comprehension are separable components of reading comprehension. Stahl (1992a) added a strategic knowledge component to this model, and broke each of those components into subcomponents. To complicate matters further, the type of reading that Gough/Tumner and Stahl discussed is what Rosenblatt (1985) called *efferent reading*, or reading to get information from text. One also needs to consider *aesthetic reading*, or affective responding to literature and expository prose to get a complete picture of reading.

The next section outlines decoding, comprehension, and aesthetic reading, and reviews how they are developed. First, I define the terms *skills*, *strategies*, and *knowledge*. Confusion among these terms has led to confusion about how to teach these different aspects of reading.

Skills, Strategies, and Knowledge

An elemental problem with the objective-based views of reading (and those approaches that contrast themselves with objective-based instruction) is a confusion among knowledge, skills, and strategies. Readers employ skills and strategies to act on their knowledge during reading. Following Paris, Lipson, and Wixson (1983), *skills* are cognitive processes that are executed automatically, without the reader's conscious attention or choice. In contrast, *strategies* are deliberately chosen and applied to a reading situation. Conventionally, a skill is a cognitive process that is executed without conscious attention. A strategy is executed deliberately, at least on some level, as when a reader chooses to make notes when studying or looks away from the text when reading to puzzle out an ambiguous sentence. As Paris et al. (1984) stated, "strategies are skills under consideration" (p. 295).

Objective-based programs seem to attach equal weight and equivalent pedagogy to these three aspects of cognition. The "rule of silent *e*" is taught as a strategy, or that "when you see a word with an *e* at the end of it, you try the long sound for the vowel." Actually, the "rule of silent *e*" reflects knowledge that readers have, not a skill or strategy that they apply—namely, that *CVCe* is a common pattern in English orthography. This knowledge is learned through multiple encounters with words with that pattern, and hence is used automatically. The amount of practice given in the brief teacher introduction and work sheets may not be adequate for children to internalize the knowledge to the automatic level. Instead, they need exposure to words with the same pattern in connected text (Juel & Roper/Schneider, 1985). Many reading programs do not coordinate their instruction and the text; thus, readers get a lesson on one phonic pattern, but do not see it in the ensuing story (Adams, 1990).

Skills, Strategies, and Knowledge in Decoding

Skills, strategies, and knowledge interact differently in decoding and comprehension. In decoding, skilled readers know that certain letters tend to be closely associated with other letters. They have gained this knowledge through their experience with words, and through their careful consideration of letters within those words. For example, the letter *t* is more likely to be followed by an *b* than by an *n* or a *q*. Readers use this knowledge in recognizing words rapidly and automatically (Adams, 1990).

Readers also have generalized skill in recognizing words. This skill is used automatically, and is not available for conscious inspection. It may involve the automatic translation of letters to a phonologically based code, or it may involve the translation of orthographic patterns directly to word meanings, or both translations occurring in parallel (Adams, 1990). Readers also have strategies they can use to decode unknown words if they do not recognize them automatically. One strategy might be "sounding out" or producing a sound for each letter or letter cluster, and then blending the sounds together to make a word. It is more likely that proficient readers use an analogy strategy, in which they compare an unknown word, or parts of an unknown word, to analogous words they know (Cunningham, 1991). These strategies can be taught to children. Proficient readers rarely evoke their strategies; young readers may use them more often.

The task for a reader learning to decode written language to its oral form is as follows. First, the reader needs to get a general concept of what decoding involves. This general concept is based on an understanding that spoken words can be divided into phonemes, and that letters can represent those phonemes. Researchers have found that this awareness of phonemes in spoken words is the strongest predictor of children's eventual success or failure in reading (Adams, 1990). It is also based on a reader's knowledge about print and its conventions, such as the concept of what a "word" is, that print starts at the left side of the page and progresses across to the right, and so on. Second, the reader needs to develop strategies for attacking words. These strategies can be learned through direct instruction, as in the direct-instruction or objective-based models, or through the process of reading and writing, as in whole-language approaches. These strategies may or may not translate directly to skill in decoding. Third, the reader needs to develop knowledge of letter patterns. This knowledge can be developed only through exposure to and examination of words.

The Nature of Word Recognition

The various approaches to reading view the process of decoding differently. Direct-instruction advocates see decoding as an automatic response to a stimulus. To get to this automatic level of response, students are given multiple repetitions of sound–symbol relationships. Objective-based reading programs have a similar approach, but do not provide as many repetitions, and may not achieve the automaticity of response. Explicit-explanation and cognitive-apprenticeship approaches view the process of decoding as a strategic process, with the teacher providing an explicit explanation of decoding strategies as the reader is attempting to decode text. Whole-language approaches have a similar view of decoding, but tend to place an equal stress on the strategic use of context to decode words and the use of phonic cues.

Research indicates that good readers tend to decode words automatically, through the recognition of orthographic patterns within words (Adams, 1990). Good readers do not rely heavily on context to identify words (see Stanovich, 1980, for review). The reason for this is efficiency: It takes a competent reader significantly longer to predict a word's meaning from context—even in a highly constraining context where the word is highly predictable—than it takes to recognize the word using orthographic cues. In most contexts, however, individual words are not easily predicted (Shatz & Baldwin, 1986). Thus, a hypothesis-driven model of decoding, such as that posited by whole-language theorists, would fail much of the time.[1] If decoding were in fact a strategic process, whole-language approaches might be effective in teaching children to decode. However, good readers do not decode words strategically because stopping and applying a strategy interrupts the ongoing process of comprehension. Instead, good readers rely on automatic word recognition (Samuels, 1985). Such automaticity is dependent on practice.

Stages of the Development of Word Recognition. However, more than practice alone is involved in learning to decode. Readers seem to go through three stages as they develop efficient word-recognition abilities.[2] In the first stage, awareness, readers develop a conceptual knowledge of the nature of written language and its relationship to speech. This involves learning how print functions—that it can tell stories, inform, direct, and so on. This stage also involves learning the conventions of print, such as directionality—that sentences begin with capital letters and end with periods, and the concept of what a "word" is in both written and spoken language. It involves learning about the form of print, including the letters of the alphabet. During this stage, children also learn that spoken words can be broken down into phonemes—a key insight for learning the relationships between letters and sounds. These four aspects of the written language–oral language relationship (e.g., functions, conventions, form of print, and awareness of phonemes) form the conceptual foundation on which reading knowledge is built. Children who lack any or all of these concepts have difficulty learning to read—a difficulty that is magnified as they progress through the grades (Stanovich, 1986).

In the second stage, accuracy, readers learn to accurately decode words. Children in this stage are "fixed" on the print, placing emphasis on accurate decoding of words. At this point, children's emphasis is on acquiring knowledge of words and sound–symbol correspondences, and strategically applying that knowledge to unlock simple texts. Chall (1983) called this stage "grunting and groaning" because children often hesitantly go through a text calling words aloud.

The accuracy stage is short-lived, and gives way to the third stage, automaticity. At this point, children begin to develop automatic word-recognition

---

[1]Context is used to choose between meanings of words once they are identified. For example, a reader can identify *lead* in the absence of context, but cannot determine a meaning.

[2]A number of authors have posited similar sets of stages of learning to recognize words, including Biemiller (1970), Chall (1983), Frith (1985), Lomax and McGee (1987), and McCormick and Mason (1986).

skills, so that the process of recognizing words is transparent and the reader can concentrate fully on the text (Samuels, 1985). Because humans are limited-capacity information processors (i.e., they can only attend to a certain amount of information at any given time), devoting attention to word recognition would take cognitive resources away from processes needed to comprehend text. Thus, slow word recognition interferes with comprehension.

The transition from accurate to automatic word recognition occurs over a number of years, conventionally from the end of first grade to the end of third grade. Following the model of Adams (1990), as children are exposed to more and more words and devote attention to their patterns, they build up a network of relations among letters. This network contains knowledge of which letters typically appear with others. Thus, we know that *t* and *h* frequently occur together, as do *a* and *t* and thousands of other patterns. According to Adams, when one letter is recognized, it primes other letters in the network, with the strength of priming being related to the probability of the letters co-occurring. In other words, when *t* is recognized, its priming may spread to *h, a, n,* and many others, but not to letters such as *q* and *x,* which rarely co-occur with *t*. This accounts, in part, for the fact that orthographically regular nonwords are recognized nearly as well as real words in a variety of tasks, at least by proficient readers.

Thus, beyond the conceptual stage, it seems that all one needs to develop word recognition is exposure to written words. This exposure can occur in whole-language classes, as well as other types of classes. Indeed, many children go through these stages in whole-language classes. However, for many children, mere exposure might not be enough. Adams (1990) speculated that the process of sounding words out draws attention to the orderings of individual letters, hastening the formation of networks. By examining each letter, one at a time, to sound a word out, Adams suggested, children devote more attention to individual letters, instead of using external cues to identify the word. Excessive use of context may impair children's development of orthographic knowledge.

Exposure to more words of a particular pattern may also hasten the development of automaticity. Juel and Roper/Schneider (1985) compared the word-recognition skills of two groups of first graders, both taught with a synthetic-phonics approach. One group read materials containing multiple instances of taught patterns from stories using a phonically controlled vocabulary. The other group read materials from a conventional basal series, using a vocabulary controlled by word frequency. They found that the phonically controlled materials seemed to induce earlier use of letter–sound relations in recognizing words than did the other materials. Students in the conventional basal series seemed to rely on distinctive letter cues, such as *ight*, to identify words.

Matching Word-Recognition Development With Instruction. Try-ing to match these phases of word recognition to instruction, it would seem that whole-language approaches might be most effective in developing the conceptual base about reading instruction. The social interactions around a text, both student–teacher and student–student, mirror those found in households with a high literacy press (e.g., Snow & Ninio, 1986). In those households, parents and children read together, shifting their focus to dif-ferent aspects of print as the need arises. Through these interactions, around Big Books or experience charts, children in whole-language classes can develop a sound foundation for formal reading instruction. Indeed, Stahl and Miller (1989) found that whole-language approaches are significantly more effective in kindergarten than in first grade, where their effects were somewhat smaller than or approximately equal to objective-based formal reading approaches.

Many children make the transition from the conceptual stage to accuracy and automaticity without any help. Durkin (1974) documented the growth of many "natural" readers, who learned to read at home without any formal instruction in phonics or other aspects of reading. Others will make that transition in a whole-language classroom by benefit of ample experiences with print. Others, including siblings of the children in Durkin's study, need some direct instruction.

For those who need more instruction, approaches should (a) stress the importance of sounding words out to force children to attend to the order of letters in words, and (b) give children ample practice reading phonically patterned words. These conditions would seem to be satisfied by direct-in-struction programs, such as Distar (Engelmann & Bruner, 1969), which seem to be highly effective in teaching children to recognize words. However, these programs contain a great deal of extraneous baggage that may not be necessary to accomplish this purpose. Some of this baggage is philosophical, relating to the relation of the teacher to the materials (see Shannon, 1987)— problems that may impair the acceptance of this approach by teachers. Some of the baggage is pedagogical. Distar materials use an artificial orthography, which might not be needed. Either way, some form of direct teaching, rather than a regimented direct-instruction approach, may be all that is needed, at least for the accuracy phase.

Pointing out orthographic features and providing practice in reading words would seem to be antithetical to the insistence of whole-language theorists—that teachers keep focused on meaning and not break language into parts. However, it is this area that teachers who profess a whole-lan-guage philosophy most often break with that philosophy. One teacher whom we interviewed said that, although she believed in whole language, she felt her students, from homes without many literacy resources, needed direct instruction in phonics (Stahl, Osborn, Winsor, & Pearson, 1994).

To develop automaticity, children need to read as much as possible. Such reading need not contain a vocabulary controlled by phonic elements. Instead, children need to read materials at an appropriate instructional level. This has been traditionally defined as a 95%–99% accuracy rate (Wixson & Lipson, 1991). But there are some indications that children benefit from reading text with as low as a 90% accuracy rate or lower in some circumstances (see Stahl, Heubach, & Cramond, 1994).

These conditions can be met in whole-language classes, as well as other types of classes. There are some indications that children in whole-language classes may not read as much at an appropriate instructional level as one might think. First, some research suggests that there is more time devoted to talk in Whole Language/Language Experience Approach (WL/LEA) classes, and less time spent on reading connected text (Stahl & Miller, 1989). This finding is based on older research, so it may not be generalizable to more modern formulations of whole language. Second, informal observations suggest that children in many whole-language classes, given their ability to choose materials they want by interest rather than instructional level, may spend more time reading materials that are either very easy or too difficult. These readers spend time looking at pictures in the difficult materials, not attempting the difficult text (E. Hiebert, personal communication, December 1991). In an ethnographic study of four Chapter I classes using whole-language principles, Shanklin (1990) found the greatest achievement gain in the two classes that most closely monitored the difficulty of children's reading materials.

However, there is no reason that whole-language classes cannot provide appropriate level connected text reading, which is needed to move from accuracy to automaticity; indeed, many such teachers do provide those opportunities. Problems emerge when children have not gone through the accuracy stage, and thus have less knowledge to practice during connected text reading. This is the case in a few first-grade classes we observed (Stahl et al., 1994). Both of these studies involved observations and comparisons of achievement between different variations of "whole-language" and "traditional" classes. In the whole-language classes, we observed a greater range of abilities, with more children significantly reading below grade level or nonreaders. One interpretation of the larger number of lower ability children in these classes is that, without a prerequisite amount of print knowledge, students cannot take full advantage of the reading opportunities provided in a whole-language class. Those with greater ability can take advantage and make larger gains in that environment than they would in a more traditional class.

In terms of decoding, concept building is important in the early stages of learning, where the student needs to develop a clear concept of how reading functions. Children develop a concept of how print functions and phoneme awareness in whole-language classes (Freppon & Dahl, 1990). Yet after these concepts are fully formed, further problem solving may be counterproductive. Being strategic at decoding can impair comprehension if reader concentrates on the strategy. They may lose track of the meaning (Samuels, 1985). After a child develops a concept of what decoding is, he or she needs to practice with more and different orthographic patterns to develop automaticity. Beyond the beginning stages, further discovery is not needed. Discovering each new pattern, as in a whole-language approach, is less efficient than simply being told about various patterns, as in a more structured phonics approach. This might explain why whole-language approaches appear markedly less effective in first grade, when compared with a traditional basal instruction, than they seem to be in kindergarten, when compared with a traditional "readiness" program (Stahl & Miller, 1989).

Learning to Comprehend

Difficulties in learning to comprehend are rooted in the differences and similarities between oral and written language. Oral and written language share a common vocabulary, syntax, structure, and so on. When children learn to read, they use what they know about oral language to comprehend written language. The skills that children ordinarily use in oral language need minimal instruction to transfer to written language. For example, even young children can make inferences about familiar content (Paris & Lindauer, 1976). Getting children to make inferences during reading involves little more than encouragement. Teaching specific inferencing strategies may be unnecessary. Hansen (1981) found that increasing the percentage of inferential questions asked during a lesson was just as effective in improving children's ability to answer inference questions as a direct-instruction inference-training program. Similar results have been found with teaching children to use a story grammar in recalling stories, to get the meanings of unknown words from context, and sentence comprehension.

However, oral and written language do differ in several essential aspects. First, oral language makes assumptions about its audience that written language does not. Oral conversation assumes a shared knowledge base between speaker and listener, so that much content can be implied. Written language cannot make use of that assumption because authors write for audiences unknown to them. Thus, written language tends to be autonomous, whereas oral language tends to be context-bound (Olson, 1977). These differences in voice may create difficulties for some children; thus, teachers and texts attempt to make a transition between the context-bound oral language spoken by children and autonomous texts typical of school (Baker & Freebody, 1989). Learning about the schoollike language of texts can also take place through exposure to storybooks, or through parents or teachers reading aloud.

Second, there are strategies specifically used in comprehension of written texts that are not relied on in comprehending comprehension. Dole, Duffy, Roehler, and Pearson (1991) suggested four such strategies: determining importance, summarization, self-questioning, and comprehension monitoring.[3] They suggested that these strategies be taught directly as part of a comprehension curriculum, and cited research showing that such instruction leads to overall improvement in comprehension.

The distinctions among skills, strategies, and knowledge are important. Teaching a skill as if it were a strategy (as suggested by Duffy & Roehler, 1987) is counterproductive. Human minds can attend to a limited number of processes at one time. *Skills* are supposed to be executed automatically, without conscious attention, thus minimizing the drain on attentional resources. *Strategies* require attentional resources. Transforming a skill into a strategy may interfere with the normal reading process because it encourages readers to attend to processes that should happen automatically.

Objective-based and direct-instruction programs treat skills such as "getting the main idea" or "learning word meanings from context," which are part of students' general language behaviors. These behaviors are used automatically in oral language comprehension, as are strategies such as summarization, complex study approaches, and so on, which are specific to written language and new to the student. Skills that students already use proficiently in their language comprehension may be best taught through minimal instruction, such as asking questions that require the skill (see Stahl, 1992a, for review). The Duffy et al. (1986) program of research—having teachers transform the skills taught in objective-based basal reading programs into strategies—was not effective in raising student achievement (although students were better at articulating what they were doing during reading). Teaching a strategy, especially one that students do not use in any other context, may require more complex instruction. One cannot simply teach the knowledge needed in reading, or the skills and strategies that act on that knowledge, as if they were all the same.

As in the area of decoding, whole-language advocates' insistence on children discovering their own strategies as they need them creates "winners" and "losers" in the classroom. Some children will figure out effective, generalizable strategies that aid them in their growth as learners, such as those discussed earlier. Others will choose strategies that get them through an assignment or work with one particular class, but are not generalizable. In our reading clinic, we find many children who have figured out strategies to cope with particular classes, such as skimming through the text to find stems that match study guide questions, looking bold-faced vocabulary items

---

[3]They also suggested a fifth—making inferences—which I feel is part of ordinary language comprehension and probably does not need to be taught directly.

up in the glossary, trying to memorize the chapter, and so on. These strategies might be useful as part of a study plan, but are maladaptive when they are the only strategies a child has.

Instead, strategies should be taught through the scaffolding provided by explicit-explanation and cognitive-apprenticeship approaches. Explicit explanation may be most effective when the strategy involved can be used singly. An example is Raphael's (Raphael & Wonnacott, 1985) program of teaching question–answer relationships. Cognitive-apprenticeship approaches might be most effective for processes that work in orchestration with other processes, such as those taught in reciprocal teaching (Palincsar & Brown, 1984; Rosenshine & Meister, 1991).

Responding to Literature

We have been discussing what Rosenblatt (1985) called *efferent reading*. Efferent reading is centered on information to be acquired after reading a text, such as what is learned from a history text or from a set of directions. In contrast, *aesthetic reading* involves the reader's empathetic response to the work of art. Aesthetic reading is idiosyncratic—the same text may activate different responses in each reader, given different life experiences and affective makeups.

Response-oriented curricula based on reader-response theories were developed for high school and college literature classes (Faust, chap. 14, this volume) as an alternative to the plot memorization found in many high school classes. Such a facts-only approach has been criticized rightly as dulling and denying children the joy of literature. Response-oriented classes, in which students are encouraged to discuss their individual reactions to what they have read, are a bracing alternative.

Transporting a response-oriented approach to literature down to the early grades creates a new set of problems (Galda & Guice, chap. 13, this volume). First, texts used in the early grades are simpler than those used in high school. Although many of these texts are well written and evocative, many cannot bear the weight of individual response. Excessive response to a pleasant, but not richly evocative, text may be as numbing as excessive questioning on minute details. Second, responding to a work of literature presupposes that one can read the work. In his work with avid readers, Nell (1988) found that basic reading comprehension was a prerequisite for aesthetic reading. This presupposition is more likely to be valid with able high school students than with children in the earlier grades. I have seen children who do not understand what they have read fake their way through a discussion of what they like about the book.

Third, many of these discussions begin with a teacher reading a book to the children, rather than the children reading on their own. In the whole-language philosophy, reading is just one aspect of language, along with writing, speaking, and listening. Reading to children is one way to expose children to more complex works of literature, thus enriching their literary experiences. The effects of adult story reading are problematic, however. Meyer, Stahl, Wardrop, and Linn (1994) examined observational data in kindergarten and first grade. They found that the amount of adult story reading had an effect on children's listening comprehension, but had no effect on a variety of reading measures. It was the *amount* of interactions by children with print, however, that had the strongest effects on children's reading skill. Just discussing a heard text may not improve children's ability to read other texts. Even if children read the text themselves, long discussions may take away time from more practice in reading. Harris and Serwer (1966) found that children in language-experience classes spent less time actually reading and more time discussing what they read than children in traditional classes. This discussion time was negatively correlated with achievement. Some time spent discussing what is read might be useful, but an excessive amount of time may displace other important interactions with text.

This is not to say that children should not be encouraged to respond aesthetically to texts in the early grades. Such responses are an integral part of understanding literary works, even simple works. Rather, I argue that such responses should not be the *only* way that texts are handled in classes— that some guidance through the text should also be included to ensure that children have comprehended it. Such guidance might be withdrawn over the years as children become better comprehenders, but it seems necessary in the beginning.

Describing the Elephant

When put side by side, these instructional models remind me of the story of the blind men describing the elephant. Each of the blind men felt a different part of the elephant, and extrapolated it to a mistaken sense of the whole. Similarly, each of these approaches to reading education was designed to solve a different problem in reading.

Whole language originated from two roots: as a developmentally appropriate approach to developing a secure print concept in kindergarten and first grade, and as an approach to developing higher level critical abilities and creative response to literature. The earliest discussions of whole language emerged from the amalgam of Y. Goodman's observations of children's emerging notions of literacy and K. Goodman's "top–down" model of word recognition (K. Goodman & Y. Goodman, 1979). Although the whole-language movement has broader aims, through its adoption of response-oriented literature curricula and the extension of its ideas to other curricular areas (Harste, 1989; Pahl & Monson, 1992), its epistemology is rooted in early reading, tending to view other grades and curricula as extrapolations of developmentally appropriate preschools. In such preschools, children work on projects of their own choosing, being free to explore a rich environment.

Since its beginnings, whole language has absorbed ideas from reader-response theorists (e.g., Rosenblatt, 1985). Reader-response-oriented curricula were developed to help secondary-school students develop affective and individual responses to literature. These have been extrapolated down to earlier grades, thus there is even discussion of kindergartners developing individual responses to literature.

In contrast, direct-instruction and objective-based instruction were developed to teach decoding accuracy. The roots of direct instruction are in the deficit models, such as those used by Bereiter and Engelmann (1966) to develop their preschool and Distar reading program, and in the early attempts to decompose the task of reading into skills, which can be taught (Otto & Askov, 1974). The assumptions that reading can be task analyzed into a set of skills, that these skills can be practiced until mastery, and that such practice will lead to improved reading are rooted in behaviorist notions of psychology (which, in turn, are rooted in even older notions; see Bartine, 1989). Although the behaviorist model is not often used in reading, these instructional models did prove effective in teaching children how to decode (Gersten & Keating, 1987). Whether their effectiveness is due to the direct instruction or their provision of a great deal of concentrated practice with orthographic patterns is not clear. However, direct-instruction and objective-based instruction have been less successful in extrapolating their methods to other aspects of reading. In terms of teaching skills or strategies, their success has been limited.

Explicit explanation was developed to teach specific reading-comprehension strategies in a manner that would transfer to general reading skill. Cognitive-apprenticeship approaches were developed from the viewpoint that reading was a product of the complex interaction between readers' strategies/knowledge, and the information provided by the text. Both of these approaches have been effective in teaching comprehension strategies, showing that the use of such strategies can be transferred from the instructional setting to become part of children's comprehension repertoire. Explicit-explanation approaches seem to work well for discrete strategies, which are appropriate when used singly. The most obvious example is question answering (see Raphael & Wonnacott, 1985), but there are others as well. Summarization and note taking work well as studying strategies when taught through explicit explanation (Rinehart et al., 1986), as does self-questioning (Davey & McBride, 1986). However, these strategies seem to work best when they are taught together as part of a cognitive-apprenticeship approach (Palincsar, 1985). In ordinary comprehension, one uses a variety of strategies, as dictated by the task and the reader's ongoing understanding of the text. For such a task, an integrated approach, such as those provided by cognitive apprenticeships, may be more appropriate. Other more complex reading activities, such as critical evaluation and creative response to literature, require social interaction, as provided in cognitive-apprenticeship and whole-language classes. These approaches have not been extrapolated to decoding instruction, nor does there seem to be a need to do so.

It should be obvious by now that none of these approaches is "best"—that under certain circumstances, reading is every one of these things. Although reading is not decoding, certainly decoding is an integral part of reading, and children should master decoding as part of learning to read. As a part of learning to decode, children need to develop a secure print concept, which the whole-language approach seems to provide quite well. After such concepts are established, children need to learn about the different orthographic patterns in English. For this, some form of direct teaching, if not full-blown direct instruction, seems to work most effectively. To develop automaticity in word recognition, practice in reading connected text is desirable. This practice can be provided in classes with any of the philosophies discussed earlier.

It should be clear from this exploration that all of these instructional approaches have their place in a reading curriculum. Designing such a curriculum would seem to require two tasks: (a) to meld these different approaches so they can be used to achieve different goals in the same classroom, but not provide mixed instructional messages; and (b) to analyze children's needs at different stages of learning to read to clarify the goals of reading instruction at different times. For example, we need to know how much emphasis should be placed on the goals of comprehension and response in the early grades, and how those emphases should change as children grow in their ability to comprehend more complex text.

This principled eclecticism is what good teachers have always done. This eclecticism is not just "a little of this and a little of that," nor is it the result of teachers' failure to firmly commit to a particular philosophy. Instead, teachers are confronted with children day in and day out, and are charged with meeting a variety of reading goals. The teachers whom we interviewed (Stahl et al., 1994) had multiple goals for their children. Of the six first-grade teachers we interviewed about their goals for their children, five mentioned fluent and accurate reading, five mentioned comprehension, and all six mentioned enjoyment. Success in meeting these goals simultaneously involves using different instructional procedures. Over time, through trial and error, and through the influence of inservice instruction and reading in professional journals, successful teachers evolve their classroom reading program by incorporating ideas from a number of different instructional philosophies.

The question of what approach is best should change into Best for what? or Best for whom? because each of these approaches is effective for teaching one aspect of reading or another. It is the spirit of Best for what? and Best for whom? that we encourage as the chapters in this volume are read. The task before us should be to determine which aspects of reading should be emphasized when, and amalgamate our instruction so that we can meet students' changing needs, rather than picking one best approach to use throughout the curriculum.

REFERENCES

Adams, M. J. (1990). *Beginning to read: Thinking and learning about print.* Cambridge, MA: MIT Press.

Altwerger, B., Edelsky, C., & Flores, B. M. (1987). Whole language: What's new? *The Reading Teacher, 41,* 144–155.

Anderson, R. C., Hiebert, E. F., Wilkinson, I. A. G., & Scott, J. (1985). *Becoming a nation of readers.* Champaign, IL: National Academy of Education and Center for the Study of Reading.

Austin, M. C., & Morrison, C. (1963). *The first R: The Harvard report on reading in elementary schools.* New York: Macmillan.

Baker, C. D., & Freebody, P. (1989). *Children's first school books.* Oxford, England: Basil Blackwell.

Bartine, D. E. (1989). *Early English reading theory: Origins of current debate.* Columbia, SC: University of South Carolina Press.

Bereiter, C., & Engelmann, S. (1966). *Teaching disadvantaged children in the preschool.* Englewood Cliffs, NJ: Prentice-Hall.

Bergeron, B. S. (1990). What does the term whole language mean? Constructing a definition from the literature. *Journal of Reading Behavior, 22,* 301–330.

Betts, E. A. (1946). *Foundations of reading instruction.* New York: American Books.

Biemiller, A. (1970). The development of the use of graphic and contextual information as children learn to read. *Reading Research Quarterly, 6,* 75–96.

Brown, A. L., Chair (1992, April). *Learning and thinking in a community of learners.* Symposium presented at the annual meeting of the American Educational Research Association, San Francisco, CA.

Brown, A. L., Campione, J. C., & Day, J. D. (1981). Learning to learn: On training students to learn from texts. *Educational Researcher, 10,* 10–21.

Brown, J. S., Collins, A., & Duguid, P. (1989). Situated cognition and the culture of learning. *Educational Researcher, 18*(1), 32–42.

Chall, J. S. (1983). *Stages of reading development.* New York: McGraw-Hill.

Chomsky, N. (1957). *Syntactic structures.* The Hague, Netherlands: Mouton.

Commeyras, M. (1991). *Dialogical-thinking reading lessons: Promoting critical thinking among "learning disabled" students.* Unpublished doctoral dissertation, University of Illinois at Urbana–Champaign.

Cunningham, P. M. (1991). *Phonics they use.* New York: HarperCollins.

Davey, B., & McBride, S. (1986). Effects of question-generation training on reading comprehension. *Journal of Educational Psychology, 78,* 256–262.

Day, J. D. (1986). Teaching summarization skills: Influences of student ability level and strategy difficulty. *Cognition and Instruction, 3,* 193–210.

Dole, J. A., Duffy, G. G., Roehler, L. R., & Pearson, P. D. (1991). Moving from the old to the new: Research on reading comprehension instruction. *Review of Educational Research, 61*, 239–264.

Duffy, G. G., & Roehler, L. R. (1987). Teaching skills as strategies. *The Reading Teacher, 40*, 414–419.

Duffy, G. G., Roehler, L. R., Meloth, M., Vavrus, L., Book, C., Putnam, J., & Wesselman, R. (1986). The relationship between explicit verbal explanation during reading skill instruction and student awareness and achievement: A study of reading teacher effects. *Reading Research Quarterly, 21*, 237–252.

Durkin, D. (1974). A six-year study of children who learned to read in school at the age of four. *Reading Research Quarterly, 10*, 9–61.

Durkin, D. (1978–1979). What classroom observations reveal about reading comprehension instruction. *Reading Research Quarterly, 14*, 481–533.

Edelsky, C. (1990). Whose agenda is this anyway? A response to McKenna, Robinson & Miller. *Educational Researcher, 19*, 7–11.

Edelsky, C., Altwerger, B., & Flores, B. M. (1991). *Whole language, what's new?* Portsmouth, NH: Heinemann.

Engelmann, S., & Bruner, E. (1969). *Distar reading program.* Chicago: SRA.

Freppon, P. A., & Dahl, K. L. (1991). Learning about phonics in a whole language classroom. *Language Arts, 68*, 190–197.

Frith, U. (1985). Beneath the surface of developmental dyslexia. In K. E. Patterson, J. C. Marshall, & M. Colheart (Eds.), *Surface dyslexia: Neuropsychological and cognitive studies of phonological reading* (pp. 301–330). Hillsdale, NJ: Lawrence Erlbaum Associates.

Garcia, G. E., & Pearson, P. D. (1991). Modifying reading instruction to maximize its effectiveness for all students. In M. S. Knapp & P. M. Shields (Eds.), *Better schooling for the children of poverty* (pp. 31–60). Berkeley, CA: McCutcheon.

Gaskins, I. W., & Elliot, T. (1991). *Implementing cognitive strategy training across the school: The Benchmark manual for teachers.* Brookline, MA: Brookline Books.

Gaskins, R. W., Gaskins, J. C., & Gaskins, I. W. (1992). Using what you know to figure out what you don't know: An analogy approach to decoding. *Reading and Writing Quarterly: Overcoming Learning Difficulties, 8*, 197–221.

Gersten, R., & Keating, T. (1987). Long-term benefits from direct instruction. *Educational Leadership, 54*(3), 28–31.

Goodman, K. S. (1967). Reading—A psycholinguistic guessing game. *Journal of the Reading Specialist, 6*, 126–135.

Goodman, K. S. (1986). *What's whole in whole language?* Portsmouth, NH: Heinemann.

Goodman, K. S., & Goodman, Y. M. (1979). Learning to read is natural. In L. B. Resnick & P. A. Weaver (Eds.), *Theory and practice of early reading* (Vol. 1, pp. 137–154). Hillsdale, NJ: Lawrence Erlbaum Associates.

Goodman, Y. M. (1989). Roots of the whole-language movement. *Elementary School Journal, 90*, 113–127.

Gough, P. B., & Tumner, W. E. (1986). Decoding, reading, and reading disability. *Remedial and Special Education, 7*, 6–10.

Graves, D., & Hansen, J. (1983). The Author's Chair. *Language Arts, 60*, 176–183.

Graves, D. H. (1983). *Writing: Teachers and children at work.* Portsmouth, NH: Heinemann.

Halliday, M. A. K. (1973). *Explorations in the functions of language.* London: Edward Arnold.

Hansen, J. (1981). The effects of inferences training and practice on young children's reading comprehension. *Reading Research Quarterly, 16*, 391–417.

Hansen, J., & Pearson, P. D. (1983). An instructional study: Improving the inferential comprehension of fourth grade good and poor readers. *Journal of Educational Psychology, 75*, 821–829.

Harris, A. J., & Serwer, B. L. (1966). The CRAFT project: Instructional time in reading research. *Reading Research Quarterly, 2,* 27–57.

Harste, J. C. (1989). The future of whole language. *Elementary School Journal, 90,* 243–249.

Haynes, M. C., & Jenkins, J. R. (1986). Reading instruction in special education resource rooms. *American Educational Research Journal, 23,* 161–190.

Holdaway, D. (1979). *The foundations of literacy.* Sydney: Ashton-Scholastic.

Juel, C., & Roper/Schneider, D. (1985). The influence of basal readers on first grade reading. *Reading Research Quarterly, 20,* 134–152.

Leinhardt, G., Zigmond, N., & Cooley, W. (1981). Reading instruction and its effects. *American Educational Research Journal, 18,* 343–361.

Lomax, R. G., & McGee, L. M. (1987). Young children's concepts about print and reading: Toward a model of reading acquisition. *Reading Research Quarterly, 22,* 237–256.

McCormick, C. E., & Mason, J. M. (1986). Intervention procedures for increasing preschool children's interest in and knowledge about reading. In W. H. Teale & E. Sulzby (Eds.), *Emergent literacy: Writing and reading* (pp. 90–115). Norwood, NJ: Ablex.

McKenna, M. C., Robinson, R. D., & Miller, J. W. (1990). Whole language: A research agenda for the nineties. *Educational Researcher, 19,* 3–6.

Meyer, L. A. (1983). Increased student achievement in reading: One district's strategies. *Research in Rural Education, 1,* 47–51.

Meyer, L. A., Stahl, S. A., Wardrup, J., & Linn, R. (1994). Effects of reading storybooks aloud to children. *Journal of Educational Research, 88,* 69–85.

Nell, V. (1988). *Lost in a book: The psychology of reading for pleasure.* New Haven, CT: Yale University Press.

Newman, J. (1985). *Whole language.* Portsmouth, NH: Heinemann.

O'Flahaven, J. O. (1989). *Second graders' social, intellectual, and affective development in varied group discussions about narrative texts: An exploration of participation structures.* Unpublished doctoral dissertation, University of Illinois at Urbana–Champaign.

Olson, D. R. (1977). From utterance to text: The bias of language in speech and writing. *Harvard Educational Review, 47,* 257–281.

Otto, W., & Askov, E. (1974). *Rationale and guidelines: The Wisconsin design for reading skill development.* Minneapolis, MN: National Computer Systems.

Pahl, M. M., & Monson, R. J. (1992). In search of whole language: Transforming curriculum and instruction. *Journal of Reading, 35,* 518–525.

Palincsar, A. S. (1985, April). *"Unpacking" multicomponent, metacognitive training packages.* Paper presented at the annual meeting of the American Educational Research Association, Chicago, IL.

Palincsar, A. S., & Brown, A. L. (1984). Reciprocal teaching of comprehension-fostering and comprehension-monitoring activities. *Cognition and Instruction, 2,* 117–175.

Palincsar, A. S., David, Y. M., Winn, J. A., & Stevens, D. D. (1991). Examining the context of strategy instruction. *RASE, 12*(3), 43–53.

Paris, S. G., & Lindauer, B. K. (1976). The role of inference in children's comprehension and memory for sentences. *Cognitive Psychology, 8,* 217–227.

Paris, S. G., Lipson, M. Y., & Wixson, K. K. (1983). Becoming a strategic reader. *Contemporary Educational Psychology, 8,* 293–316.

Patching, W., Kameenui, E. J., Carnine, D., Gersten, R., & Colvin, G. (1983). Direct instruction in critical reading skills. *Reading Research Quarterly, 18,* 406–418.

Prawat, R. S. (1991). The value of ideas: The immersion approach to the development of thinking. *Educational Researcher, 20*(2), 3–10.

Raphael, T. E. (1984). Teaching learners about sources of information for answering comprehension questions. *Journal of Reading, 27*(4), 303–311.

Raphael, T. E., & Wonnacott, C. A. (1985). Heightening fourth-grade students' sensitivity to sources of information for answering comprehension questions. *Reading Research Quarterly, 20*(3), 282–296.

Rinehart, S. D., Stahl, S. A., & Erickson, L. G. (1986). Some effects of summarization training on reading and studying. *Reading Research Quarterly, 21*(4), 422–438.

Rosenblatt, L. M. (1985). The transactional theory of the literary work: Implications for research. In C. R. Cooper (Ed.), *Researching response to literature and the teaching of literature: Points of departure* (pp. 33–53). Norwood, NJ: Ablex.

Rosenshine, B. V., & Meister, C. (1991, April). *Reciprocal teaching: A review of nineteen experimental studies.* Paper presented at the annual meeting of the American Educational Research Association, Chicago, IL.

Rosenshine, B. V., & Stevens, R. (1984). Classroom instruction in reading. In R. Barr, P. D. Pearson, M. L. Kamil, & P. Mosenthal (Eds.), *Handbook of research in reading* (pp. 745–798). White Plains, NY: Longman.

Samuels, S. J. (1985). Automaticity and repeated reading. In J. Osborn, P. T. Wilson, & R. C. Anderson (Eds.), *Reading education: Foundations for a literate America* (pp. 215–230). Lexington, MA: Lexington Books.

Schatz, E. K., & Baldwin, R. S. (1986). Context clues are unreliable predictors of word meaning. *Reading Research Quarterly, 21*, 439–453.

Shanklin, N. L. (1990). Improving the comprehension of at-risk readers: An ethnographic study of four Chapter I teachers, Grades 4–6. *Reading, Writing, and Learning Disabilities, 6*, 137–148.

Shannon, P. (1987). Commercial reading materials, a technological ideology, and the deskilling of teachers. *Elementary School Journal, 87*, 307–329.

Smith, F. (1971). *Understanding reading.* New York: Holt, Rinehart & Winston.

Smith, F. (1992). Learning to read: The never-ending debate. *Phi Delta Kappan, 73*(6), 432–435.

Snow, C. E., & Ninio, A. (1986). The contracts of literacy: What children learn from learning to read books. In W. H. Teale & E. Sulzby (Eds.), *Emergent literacy: Writing and reading* (pp. 116–138). Norwood, NJ: Ablex.

Stahl, S. A. (1992a). *The state of the art of reading instruction.* Paris, France: International Institute of Educational Planning.

Stahl, S. A. (1992b). Saying the "p" word: Nine guidelines for exemplary phonics instruction. *The Reading Teacher, 45*, 618–625.

Stahl, S. A., Heubach, K., & Cramond, B. (1994, December). *Fluency oriented reading instruction: A second year evaluation.* Paper presented at annual meeting, National Reading Conference, San Diego, CA.

Stahl, S. A., & Miller, P. D. (1989). Whole language and language experience approaches for beginning reading: A quantitative research synthesis. *Review of Educational Research, 59*(1), 87–116.

Stahl, S. A., Osborn, J., Winsor, P., & Pearson, P. D. (1994). *Six teachers in their classrooms: Looking closely at beginning reading* (Tech. Rep. No. 606). Champaign, IL: Center for the Study of Reading, University of Illinois at Urbana–Champaign.

Stanovich, K. E. (1980). Toward an interactive-compensatory model of individual differences in the development of reading fluency. *Reading Research Quarterly, 16*, 32–71.

Stanovich, K. E. (1986). Matthew effects in reading: Some consequences of individual differences in the acquisition of literacy. *Reading Research Quarterly, 21*, 360–407.

Stevens, R. J., Madden, N. A., Slavin, R. E., & Farnish, A. M. (1987). Cooperative Integrated Reading and Composition: Two field experiments. *Reading Research Quarterly, 22*, 433–454.

Watson, D. (1989). Defining and describing whole language. *Elementary School Journal, 90*, 129–142.

Wertsch, J. (1985). *Vygotsky and the social formation of mind.* Cambridge, MA: Harvard University Press.

Wixson, K. K., & Lipson, M. Y. (1991). *Reading disability.* New York: HarperCollins.

CHAPTER TWO

Models of Professional Practice in Teacher Thinking

David A. Hayes
The University of Georgia, Athens

Teaching is a thought-driven endeavor. Teachers think about what they teach and why they teach what they do. They think about what they have to do to elicit thinking and learning in others. They think about the effect of their practices. Teachers think about these things with one or another idea in mind about what it is that teachers do. Whatever idea they may hold, it is likely to be dominated by notions about the purposes of teaching and the role teachers play in fulfilling those purposes. It is certain to be infused with ideal images and general imperatives for guiding practice; it is one open to be shaped through experience and study. The range of ideas of teaching is wide in level of development and degree of sophistication. Ideas of teaching may amount to little more than a loose collection of metaphors and rules for teaching; or they may be ideas composed of values and standards of practice that are more or less consistently and coherently linked with another. Some dominant ideas are sufficiently developed that they provide a systematic, principled approach to reasoning about the aims and practices of teaching.

Such ideas are represented in the chapters of this volume as models for teaching reading. The authors of these chapters present the details of the models they espouse, and in the introductory chapter my colleague Steven Stahl comments on the significance of the ideas they present. Here I discuss the role that models play in teachers' thinking about teaching. I briefly explain the purposes served by models, propose a conceptual model general to all professional practice, and describe professional teaching as an instance of

31

professional practice that fits that general model. I point out that, within the overall scheme of professional teaching, practices vary according to teachers' dominant idea of teaching, and that such ideas that provide for coherent and principled action are, in effect, what we mean by *models* of teaching. I discuss models of teaching as structures for organizing knowledge about teaching. I argue that models implicit in teachers' thinking serve not only as designs for guiding professional practice, but also as ideas for fostering professional change and development—and that those ideas change and develop as teachers gain experience and insight into their work.

CONCEPTUAL MODELS OF PROFESSIONAL PRACTICE

In every profession, practice proceeds in accordance with some dominant idea of what the profession does. Teaching is no exception. All teaching takes place in light of some idea about what teaching is, what needs to be taught, and what needs to be done to teach it. Teachers have in mind some idea of teaching when they select content and skills to be taught, when they structure activities so that teaching is likely to result in the learning they have in mind for learners, and when they make decisions about what to say and do in carrying out those activities. It is by some idea of teaching that they situate themselves vis-à-vis learners, the subject, and the curriculum in some certain environment. They may even do so by an idea that serves them paradigmatically (i.e., by one that suggests goals, standards, and criteria for planning and carrying out courses of action, and that provides them rationale for those actions and their work in general). Such an idea serves as a model by which they can measure themselves and what they do.

In the most general sense, a model is an image, pattern, or design to be followed to produce some desired outcome. Models of professional practice are conceptual models. Models of this sort have been described by philosophers and systems theorists (Decker & Saunders, 1976; Diesing, 1971; Moore, 1970) as providing a framework for organizing practitioners' thoughts about processes and activities that are directed toward the goals of their work. The framework serves as an overall plan for thinking about professional practice. It allows the translation of large quantities of data relevant to the model into manageable form. In such form, the data can rationally be described, interpreted, and evaluated.

A General Model of Professional Practice

Figure 2.1 illustrates a way to think about the structures of professional practice in general. Professional practice in specific areas would elaborate these structures in their own ways, but the figure does capture the essential

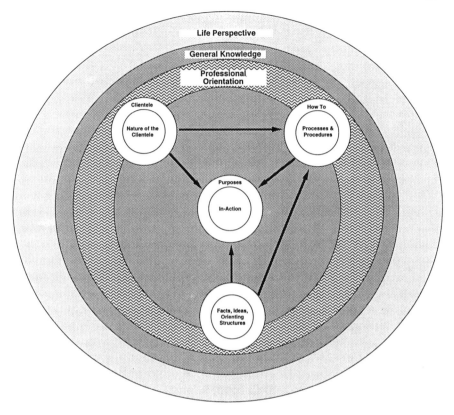

FIG. 2.1.   General model of professional practice.

nature of any professional practice: All professional practitioners serve clients by setting into motion a series of actions that apply a domain of knowledge in which they are expert. In providing that service, they ascertain purposes toward which they are to work, and, with particular clients with particular needs, deploy procedures that they deem will bring to bear knowledge appropriate to serving their clients' needs. Surrounding this service are areas of knowledge on which practitioners draw: knowledge of clientele, knowledge of the field, and knowledge of vehicles for getting things done. *Knowledge of clientele* includes classes of information and ideas about the population they serve. *Knowledge of the field* refers to the fund of conceptual and factual knowledge that constitutes the professional specialty. *Knowledge of "how to"* is made up of ways and means of delivering service. These areas of knowledge are significantly influenced by a basic professional orientation, or core of professional values, by which professional values are determined, questions of ethical propriety are handled, and general approach to practice is taken. All professional knowledge exists within a larger frame of knowledge acquired through life experience and is influenced to some degree by overall outlook on life.

Many examples of professional practice come to mind, but two that are most familiar are the dentist and the lawyer. My dentist examines my teeth, paradigmatically commits her thinking to conditions she sees in my mouth, and acts in accordance with her knowledge of oral health and dental procedure. My lawyer listens to the problem I relate to him, sorts from it the content having legal significance, and responds to my problem as his knowledge of law and contingencies attendant to the adjudication process indicates. Although my dentist and lawyer have only preliminary information, their models of practice allow them to place that information cognitively, and to conjecture about the consequences of different courses of action. They are able to do this because the models of professional practice by which they operate provide stable structures for sorting information—in ways that allow making smart hunches about what the information is insufficient to show for sure. Given the variation of information usually encountered in practice, professionals can infer the presence of other information and occurrences that tend to be correlated with the information given. Their models of professional practice serve the organization of the data of practice so that they can take reasonable actions, make accurate predictions, and offer responsible recommendations.

Within the framework of a model of professional practice, a system of categories facilitates the management of certain general kinds of thought and action (but not specific thoughts and actions). The system sets rules for selecting the kinds of arguments, logic, and actions that are allowable, and restricts the ways by which arguments are formulated, reasoning is set forth, and actions are taken. These rules of argument, logic, and action are assigned to categories within the model, and their relations are defined within and across categories. When the rules are brought to bear in specific circumstances, the system restricts their focus, controls the intensity of their application, and indicates how the particulars of the circumstances are to be arranged, ordered, directed, and so on for disposition. If my dentist observes a problem and decides a procedure is needed, she initially invokes general categories of her thinking—about patients like me, with dental conditions like mine—that suggest a certain sequence of certain actions. As she proceeds, she takes this step and that step as the data of the unfolding procedure suggest (e.g., for this step, knowledge related to anesthesia is needed; for that step, a mix of explicit and tacit knowledge about using chemicals and manipulating instruments is needed). The knowledge summoned for taking each step of the procedure is multifaceted, with each facet having its own system of specific kinds of knowledge (e.g., of varieties of anesthesia, their methods of administration, their indications and contraindications, etc.) and connecting with other facets of knowledge (e.g., of oral anatomy, of physiology, etc.) in ways the data indicate. My lawyer sees me as a certain type of client in a certain legal situation. Thus, he begins his response to my legal problem with a course of action in mind common to cases like mine, and files standard documents with the court and other interested parties. As he sees me through the legal process, he advises me about the legal implications of these parts of the problem and possible consequences of those parts of the problem: that these parts are interpretable according to a variety of legal principles and in light of facts and evidence, whereas those parts are dealt with in terms of presumptions about which no amount of facts and evidence will matter. He soft pedals some arguments on my behalf, whereas he drives hard on others. To the extent that my dentist and lawyer take actions in accordance with the rules of a conceptual model of their respective professions, their actions are systematic. To the extent that the model provides a system that is rational, actions they take may be justified as rational.

Professional Development Through Recognition of Pattern and Structure

In reasonably stable situations, similar patterns in conditions and events may appear again and again. These patterns may lead to similar outcomes or be associated with certain other conditions that are alike. In such situations, professional practitioners are expected to see these similarities and recognize them as examples of more or less the same thing that occurs in many different situations (Argyris, 1982; Margolis, 1993; Moore, 1970; Schön, 1983). If every situation were approached as if it were without similarities to other situations, as if it were in all respects unique, operating within those situations would have less to do with the application of professional knowledge than with getting by through trial and error. Any management of difficulties or solutions to problems that might prove satisfactory would be accidental, rather than the result of actions taken on the basis of recognition of parallels in the difficulties and problems with others. Practitioners find enormous advantage in operating on the basis of patterns of intuition that work reasonably well across a wide range of situations (i.e., they find advantage in making paradigmatic connections between professional knowledge and practice). Because it is general in its applicability, a conceptual model not only expands the options for practitioners who use it but fosters their continued professional development.

When practitioners apprehend the correspondence between a set of events or questions and the form of a proposition in a model for dealing with such events or questions, they find in it a useful source of self-consciousness. They find a tool for intellectual development, as well as for making decisions and taking actions. Bruner (1966) commented on the development of models in professional practitioners' thinking: "I suspect that much of growth starts out by our turning around on our own traces and recoding in new forms what we have been doing or seeing and then going on to new modes of organization with the new products that have been formed by these recodings" (p. 21). Practitioners progress from experiences of "A-ha, I get it now . . . that's an instance of . . . which can be handled by . . ." to structuring their thoughts into instruments for translating experiences into more powerful systems of thinking for guiding professional practice. Information is more than information itself. It is a member of a class of information, which is a member still of a larger class, and so on. It is in a network of information belonging to such and such category, which is governed by such and such principle, and is therefore subject to the applications of that principle. As practitioners gain experience with models and grow to rely on them more and more, their models become increasingly powerful for representing a multitude of situations in their professional practice. Conceptual models not only expand practitioners' options, but foster the continued professional development of those practitioners.

MODELS OF TEACHING

The conceptual models of interest here are models for guiding the practice of classroom teaching. Models of teaching are not different from other kinds of conceptual models. They offer classroom teachers a framework for going about their work (i.e., for thinking about and taking action toward the learning outcomes they have in mind for their students). Joyce, Weil, and Showers (1992) put it this way: "A model of teaching is a plan or pattern of thinking that we can use to design face-to-face teaching in classrooms or tutorial settings and to shape instructional materials. . . . Each model guides us as we design instruction to help students achieve various objectives" (p. 4).

Thus, models of teaching afford teachers rational ways to describe and interpret their classroom circumstances, and to evaluate and justify their instructional actions. With the growth of public education during the past century, curriculum decisions have increasingly reflected the influences of diverse social orientations and competing political ideals. These influences are incorporated into various conceptions of curriculum, common to which are certain core curricular justifications. Expressed as goals, these core justifications provide the basis on which curricular decisions are typically based: to transmit the cultural heritage; to equip citizens with the practical skills for living and earning a living; to ameliorate injustice, improve society, and deepen individuals' sense of humanity and connection with others; and to provide for individuals' personal development and enhancement of their capacity for living a satisfying life (Eisner & Vallance, 1974; Kliebard, 1992; Liston & Zeichner, 1991). Aligned more or less with these curricular justifications are different orientations toward the way intellectual development is thought to take place: through acquisition of ideas and cultivation of the mind, through association of experiences, through intuitive insights that accompany stages of maturation, and through reflection on conflict and perplexity (Bigge, 1992; Rich, 1992).

Together, curricular justifications and ideas about intellectual development provide important orienting ideas about how teaching should proceed. However, it would be a mistake to assume, as many have (as Lamm, 1976, has pointed out), that ideas about curriculum and learning can somehow substitute for ideas about teaching—and that, because they are equivalent to ideas about teaching, ideas about curriculum and learning can serve as reference points for in-action teaching practices. Ideas about curriculum and learning are different from ideas about teaching. They are different in both nature and purpose. Ideas about curriculum and learning are essentially descriptive in nature, whereas ideas about teaching tend to be prescriptive. Ideas about curriculum and learning allow making inferences about the significance of instructional practice, whereas ideas about instructional practice are about taking actions. Models of teaching provide for taking actions consistent with certain justifications about goals of instruction and about certain understandings of the way learning happens. Although orienting ideas of curriculum and learning cannot serve as models for teaching practice, they can, and in fact do, imply certain ways of teaching.

Table 2.1 shows how different ideas about teaching may be aligned more or less with certain perspectives on curriculum. At another level, it shows how these may be aligned with certain epistemological and psychological perspectives on the way intellectual development occurs. The alignments shown between curricular justifications and associated orientations to learning and teaching are only approximations. In reality, teachers are not so committed to a particular approach to teaching that they do not draw on ideas and practices ordinarily associated with other approaches (Stahl, chap. 1, this volume). Certainly, teachers do not adhere strictly to their espoused beliefs in their actual classroom practices (Deford, 1985; Richardson, Anders, Tidwell, & Lloyd, 1991). Nonetheless, teachers' expressed beliefs about teaching and their classroom practices are closely intertwined (Anders & Evans, 1994).

Models of teaching may be conceived of either in terms of goals to be achieved or, more generally, the kinds of knowledge teachers bring to bear in teaching. Models of the first sort are represented in the work of Joyce and his colleagues (Joyce, Soltis, & Weil, 1974; Joyce, Weil, & Showers, 1992; Weil, Joyce, & Kluwin, 1978). Their descriptions of teaching models have well-defined educational missions or goals (e.g., to develop inductive

TABLE 2.1

Curricular Justifications and Associated Orientations to Learning and Teaching

Curricular Justification	Dominant Conception of Learning	Emphasis in Teaching	Approach to Teaching Reading
Transmission of cultural heritage	Structuralism (J. Herbart, E. D. Hirsch, M. Adler, W. Bennett)	Explain generalizations, laws, principles, rules, theories Teacher-centered	Direct Instruction, Explicit Explanation
Social efficiency	Stimulus–Response Connectionism (E. L. Thorndike, A. I. Gates, C. Hull, B. F. Skinner)	Train mind/modify behavior through practice in applying skills Teacher-centered	Direct Instruction
Social reconstruction	Social Constructionism (L. Vygotsky, P. Freire, H. Giroux)	Engage students in raising, reflecting on, and managing/solving problems Teacher-centered (can be student-centered)	Cognitive Apprenticeship
Human development	Romantic Naturalism (J. J. Rosseau, J. Dewey, J. Piaget, J. Holt)	Respond to what students do to promote intuitive awareness of self and own natural abilities, without coercion or prescription Student-centered	Reader Response, Whole Language

reasoning, to teach skills for participating in democratic processes, to develop creativity and creative problem solving, etc.). These models find application in teacher education efforts aimed at developing proficiency and creativity related to particular curricular agendas. Models of the second sort are represented in the work of several educational theorists (e.g., Cruickshank, 1984; Dunkin & Biddle, 1974; Grossman, 1990; Shulman, 1987). These teaching models are concerned with developing and relating areas of knowledge generally thought to be needed in teaching. Largely because of their generality, these models provide highly useful points of reference in planning and evaluating teacher education programs in institutions that serve teachers and students with diverse needs.

Models of teachers' knowledge are rooted in a long tradition of scholarly inquiry into the qualities of effective teachers (Kratz, 1896; Ruediger & Strayer, 1910; Ryans, 1947, 1960; Tomlinson, 1955) and the models of effective teaching developed from that scholarship (Biddle, 1964; Ryans, 1960; Smith, 1960; Strasser, 1967). Among these models, Biddle's conceptualization is notable for representing effective teaching in terms of four large classes of variables previously suggested by Mitzel (1960): (a) presage (e.g., teachers' personal characteristics, such as their formative experiences, training, attitudes, etc.), (b) context (e.g., school and community, materials available, age and ethnicity of students, etc.), (c) process (e.g., student behavior, teacher–student interactions, etc.), and (d) product (e.g., short-term learning and attitudes, long-term effects on personality and occupational skills, etc.). In models of teachers' knowledge (Colton & Sparks-Langer, 1993; Cruickshank, 1984; Doyle, 1977; Elbaz, 1983; McDonald & Elias, 1976; Reinsmith, 1992; Shulman, 1986, 1987), these four classes of effective teaching variables are reframed as areas of teachers' knowledge. Shulman (1986, 1987) and his colleagues (Grossman, Wilson, & Shulman, 1989; Gudmundsdottir & Shulman, 1987; Wilson, Shulman, & Richert, 1987) gave emphasis to what they called *pedagogical content knowledge*, which is knowledge of process by which teachers make subject matter accessible to students. Grossman (1990) highlighted the central importance of pedagogical content knowledge in a model whose components are reminiscent of the four broad classes of teacher effectiveness variables proposed by Mitzel (1960) and represented by Biddle (1964).

A Model of Teachers' Knowledge

Figure 2.2 fits teachers' knowledge proposed by others (especially Shulman, 1987; Grossman, 1990) into a general model of professional practice. At the center of the model is teachers' in-action knowledge, which is fed by other areas of professional knowledge. These are embedded in a field of general knowledge gained from life experiences, and are bounded and ultimately

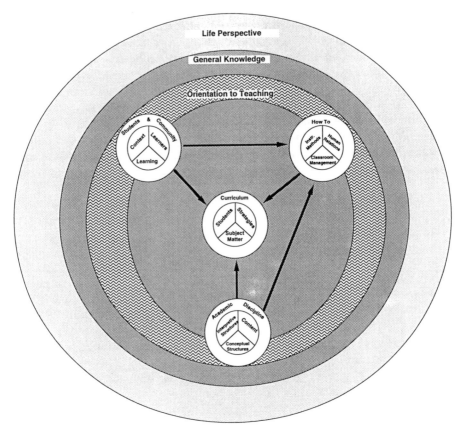

FIG. 2.2. Model of teacher knowledge.

biased by overall life perspective. These areas of knowledge are bounded and biased more directly by teachers' basic orientation to teaching—what Lyons (1990) called teachers' *epistemological stance*. It is by this orientation, or epistemological stance, that teachers make value judgments related to teaching and educational issues in general, confront ethical dilemmas in their work, and interpret all aspects of professional knowledge.

In-Action Knowledge

In-action knowledge is like Shulman's *pedagogical content knowledge*. It is governed primarily by curricular purposes, and is created directly from what teachers know about the students present, the subject matter taught, and strategies for making that subject matter accessible to students. Curricular purposes that govern in-action knowledge concern ideas both within and outside the academic content area. Curricular purposes within the academic content area are comprehended as the discourse structures of that content area; curricular purposes outside the academic content area are concerned with fostering responsibility for personal actions, increasing sensitivity to others' feelings, developing understandings needed for participating in a free society, and so on. Teachers' in-action knowledge of students present takes account of the latter's beliefs, conceptions, misconceptions, motivations, languages, ages, abilities, aptitudes, interests, and so on. In-action knowledge of the subject matter provides for selecting material from the academic content area that fits with curricular purposes, interpreting and adapting the material to student characteristics, and structuring and sequencing it so as to make it accessible to students. In-action knowledge of strategies for making subject matter accessible to students includes managing classroom interactions (e.g., assignments, group work, give-and-take procedures, questioning, discipline) and deploying representational devices (e.g., analogies, metaphors, examples, explanations). Curricular purposes and elements of in-action knowledge draw from areas of knowledge about learners (clientele), academic content areas (domain of expertise), and how to take action (how to).

Knowledge About Learners

Teachers' classroom practices tend to be congruent with their assumptions about students (McCarthey et al., 1994; Rosenthal, 1968). Knowledge about learners includes knowledge of: developmental characteristics typical of students of the age they are teaching, contexts from which learners come, and psychology of learning. Developmental characteristics especially salient in teachers' minds are those related to learners' physical, emotional, intellectual, moral, and social development. It is by this knowledge that teachers adjust their sights on what is possible and desirable for children to learn, and thus trim their actions and interactions with them. For example, teachers of primary-grade children remain sensitive to the feelings of individual children whenever taking measures to teach or socialize them into the school culture, whereas teachers of middle- and secondary-grade students are considerably less likely to be concerned with the feelings that individual students may have about efforts to teach them subject matter or attend to their social adjustment. Teachers' knowledge of context takes account of situations that affect learners' ways of seeing the world and that suggest kinds of learning expected of those learners; these are situations learners encounter in the school, the community, and the religious and social groups to which learners belong. For example, in a community where a particular industry is vital to the economy (e.g., submarine building), students are likely to come to school with biases favorable to the preservation of that industry, and teachers would be expected to foster the community's prevailing pro-Navy, strong defense ethos in the curricular decisions they make and the classroom actions they take. This does not always happen, of course. Delpit (1988) observed that progressive White teachers often take a whole-language approach to reading instruction clearly in conflict with African-American parents' expectations that children be taught skills of reading through direct instruction. Knowledge by which teachers explain how learning occurs is also important in the mix of knowledge about learners. It is this knowledge that predisposes teachers to adopt certain instructional positions and reject others. Teachers who view learning behavioristically (i.e., as the mastery of subject matter through the establishment of connections in information as a result of responding to it under circumstances favorable to reinforcing those connections) are inclined to set hierarchically organized curricular goals, and to take sequences of instructional actions that are carefully paced and punctuated with reinforcers for desired responses. Teachers who see learning humanistically (i.e., as the discovery of personal meaning in ideas and information) are likely to set learning goals that promote insight and to perform instructional actions that confront learners with problems that have them restructure their ways of seeing the world and themselves in it.

Knowledge of Academic Content Area

Another broad area of knowledge on which teachers draw for setting purposes and taking instructional actions is knowledge of the academic content areas they teach. This includes knowledge of content areas beyond facts and ideas. Content area knowledge includes knowledge of the ways in which ideas and information are structured, and of various ways in which the facts and ideas would be structured if considered from different perspectives (Schwab, 1964). Literature teachers know more facts and ideas related to literature study than they actually teach. They know many facts and ideas about a great many written works, about the enterprise of expressing thoughts and feelings in writing, and about language in general. Yet for teaching, they choose facts and ideas that suit their own theories about the nature and purpose of literature, reading and writing, and language.

A common conceptual structure that literature teachers use to structure knowledge of their field is genre (e.g., novel, fable, short story, poetry, etc.). Within each genre, further substructures are found (e.g., epic poetry, dramatic poetry, lyric poetry, and their substructures). The field's interpretive structures determine how the content within conceptual structures is studied (indeed, whether even to allow certain conceptual structures; e.g., a notion of genre), the questions pursued, the interpretations offered, and so on. To continue with the example of literature, teachers might take a New Critical approach to literary study, whereby close reading of literary works alone is called for (to detect symbol, metaphor, theme, hidden meanings, etc.) without distraction or contamination which would creep into interpretation by any consideration of the circumstances of any literary work's creation or any intentions of authors. Teachers might take a semiotic approach to literary study, whereby a hypothetical model reader deals interpretively with texts in the same way that authors deal with them generatively. Teachers might take any number of other interpretive approaches to the study of literature, just as teachers across the academic disciplines may take any number of interpretive approaches available to them in their fields of study. Knowledge of perspectives and canons of evidence in a field of study is important. Such knowledge influences which facts and ideas teachers select for teaching, and which vehicles they use for teaching them.

Knowledge of How to Take Action

A third area of knowledge from which teachers draw is knowledge of how to take action. This is an area of knowledge that draws on knowledge of learners and content areas. Knowledge of how to take action comprises three kinds of knowledge that work together in classroom teaching: a repertoire of instructional methods, a set of classroom management routines, and some understanding of human relations. How these kinds of knowledge become activated depends on immediate demands of teaching, as well as teachers' conceptions of content area knowledge and their understandings with respect to learners. For example, teachers who take a humanistic view of learners and learning would likely select subject matter consistent with humankind's basic goodness and perfectibility; they would likely use permissive classroom management routines and teaching methods that place more emphasis on having students take different angles on the subject matter and take risks with it than mastering it fact by fact and idea by idea. Teachers who take a behavioristic view of learners and learning would likely accept the challenge of teaching subject matter as prescribed in a curriculum—to be taught at its presumed optimum place in a sequence of instruction—and do that teaching in a classroom in which the teacher prescribes, directs, and exercises close control of students' behavior.

This depiction of teachers' knowledge provides an admittedly rough analysis of the knowledge that goes into teachers' thinking. However, it does offer a way to organize thought and discussion about teachers' professional thinking—a way to place the code structures for thinking about and discussing what teachers know. It is necessarily a fiction. Nothing about mental life could ever be so neatly compartmentalized and sealed off from the rest of its content, not even aspects of highly specialized professional thought. All areas of professional knowledge are permeated by feelings, images, biases, and knowledge acquired from life experiences. And those residual mental consequences of life experience are themselves biased by some overall way of seeing things. This is not to say that teachers give conscious thought to overall life perspective as they act professionally. It would be hard to imagine that teachers deliberate on epistemological principles as they think and act. Yet as teachers gain professional experience and develop intellectually, their overall way of seeing things tends to become increasingly clear, articulable, and useful in setting conscious criteria for thinking and acting. Personal perspective and professional knowledge become increasingly coherent, consistent, and integrated.

Belief and Evidence in Models of Teaching

Teachers operate within models of teaching for reasons having mostly to do with their overall life perspective and beliefs about teaching, not because they are convinced by evidence regarding their effectiveness (Fenstermacher, 1986; Peterson, 1994; Richardson et al., 1991). Teachers who explore ideas and information primarily for the sake of developing students' insights about themselves and their connection with humanity do so because they have a romantic perspective on teaching, not because they are acting on the basis of research on teaching to develop insights. Teachers concerned with ideas and information primarily for the sake of equipping students with skills for ferreting out ideas and information independently, and for using it to their own ends, do so because they have a pragmatic perspective on teaching, not because they have read the research literature on academic skill development. Still, prominent models of teaching are not inconsistent with researchers' conclusions in the areas of teacher knowledge, belief, and action, which form the basis of those models. Models vary in the way they identify essential influences on teaching and learning, and they reflect different perspectives on these influences and the ways in which they are related to one another. However, they are sufficiently alike in the essential features of teaching they propose—that it is possible to identify categories of those features in the teaching variables examined by researchers and to find patterns of empirical research that fit those categories.

Indeed, using such an approach, Medley (1982) found patterns in the research on effective teaching that coincide with the structural features of models of teaching that appear in the literature. Taking an approach called "triangular design," Medley established patterns of research findings by interrelating researchers' criteria for evaluating teachers (e.g., preexisting teacher characteristics, competencies, performance, learning experiences, pupil learning outcomes) with variables that affect the outcomes of teaching, but are not affected by the teacher (e.g., features of teacher training, resources available, characteristics of the school and community, and influences on teacher behavior such as class size and student characteristics). The variables were interrelated on the basis of their position in a logically constructed scheme for explaining the direction of variables' influence on other variables. Teacher evaluation variables were positioned such that preexisting teacher characteristics were assumed to affect teacher competencies, which in turn were assumed to affect teacher performances, which in turn affect pupil learning experiences, and so on. Interrelating ("triangulating") these directionally determined variables with variables not affected by the teacher resulted in the identification of categories of research on essential influences on teaching and learning. These categories can be used as constructs in the formulation of models of effective teaching.

Models of Teaching as Code Structures

Although models of teaching tend to be normative and lawlike in their function, it would be a mistake to think of any model of teaching as a truth structure, in terms that would impute truth values or certain validity to its categories, or in terms that would see necessary discreteness between its categories. At best, models of teaching are discursive structures. They supply codes for deploying knowledge about teaching (i.e., the terms for thinking about and discussing teaching). In other words, they are sources of language and rules for putting knowledge about teaching into play coherently and productively.

Petrosky (1994) emphasized this point in his recent portrayal of teachers' knowledge. Drawing on Foucault's (1972 cited in Petrosky, 1994) conception of knowledge as discourse produced in response to problems, Petrosky argued that teachers' knowledge about teaching can be usefully conceived as the discourse they produce in responding to a variety of open-ended problems. It is discourse of which they are the object and by which they create themselves as teachers. According to Petrosky's application of Foucault's epistemology to teaching, teachers "create knowledge with language and within a particular educational discourse in response to the various kinds of open-ended problems they solve, and they are also created as teachers and thinkers by the language they use within that particular educational discourse" (p. 25). The discourse they produce is exterior to themselves, yet it is discourse that includes them as an integral subject. In other words, it is a fabric into which they weave themselves and thereby position themselves on the loom of their work, and in particular on the loom of their area of teaching.

The rules for forming the discourse in teachers' minds operate more or less uniformly within the profession as discursive structures for responding to problems typically encountered in the profession. Formative elements of the discourse vary among individual teachers and privilege certain discursive practices and structures over others. In other words, thinking about knowledge as discourse locates knowledge in language, and specifically knowledge about teaching of a certain sort, in the language of that teaching. Thinking about knowledge as discourse allows knowledge to operate as language (i.e., orderly and controlled, yet ongoing and developing), rather than exist as an aggregation of facts and truths—discrete and listable—that can be compared to some ideal set of valid and acceptable facts and truths. It allows teachers to speak and know in ways different from one another, to hold contrary opinions, and to act idiosyncratically while sharing an understanding of what it means to teach their subject. By this perspective, knowledge of teaching is seen not as a matter of facts and truths about teaching, but as a matter of how teachers represent the discourse of their discipline and its pedagogy, and how they put those representations into play.

Taking the view that knowledge of teaching operates discursively allows teaching models to be seen as personal representations that develop with experience. To regard them as other than personal and formative would be mistaken: It would see them as existing outside teachers' own thinking as static instruments conceived by authorities and researchers to be applied by teachers as they need them. Certainly, professional teachers inform themselves of knowledge produced by authorities and researchers, and they do make use of that knowledge in formulating their own ideas about teaching. But teacher's models of teaching are not simply fixed cognitive instruments for guiding teaching. To be sure, models are instrumental in guiding teaching, but the guidance they provide is in the orientation they provide. Their code structures represent certain kinds of knowledge in certain ways, thereby favoring thinking about certain things over other things and in certain ways rather than in other ways. In this way, teaching models structure the ways in which teachers think about their work; by this thinking, teachers take certain actions and not others. The code structures vary and develop as teachers think and act from one situation to another. With specific instances of teaching, or of merely thinking about teaching, code structures are subject to modification to accommodate variations from what previous belief or experience would have suggested. By these modifications, the model becomes more useful in particular circumstances of teaching; by the variations encountered in practice, the content of thought becomes increasingly specialized. Although teaching models provide guidance insofar as they provide structures of knowledge and principles for thinking about teaching, the structures they provide develop and vary idiosyncratically as teachers think about the situations they encounter in their practice.

Development and Modification of Models of Teaching

Situational influences on the development of structures for thinking about professional practice become increasingly significant as teachers gain experience (Jordell, 1987). When novice teachers start out, they operate, by and large, on the basis of cultural knowledge of teaching acquired from their experiences as a student. But that knowledge gives way to practical knowledge that is developed in professional practice. Their thinking is shaped by classroom situations, as well as the contexts of school, community, and society at large (Liston & Zeichner, 1991; Ross, 1987; Zeichner & Tabachnick, 1991). All of these contexts call for certain ways of thinking and acting; all create pressures to conform to norms of language, practice, and institutional operations; all limit options of thinking and acting (Zeichner & Gore, 1990). Teachers deal with situational demands by bringing themselves into conformity with their immediate situational and larger contextual demands, or by redefining those demands (Ross, 1992). When teachers comply with situational demands, they either make internal adjustments and accept the demands as right and appropriate, or they comply while retaining personal reservations. When teachers attempt to redefine situational demands, they aim to widen the range of acceptable ways of meeting them. For example, when schools establish institutional expectations of teachers and their practices, and teachers accept these expectations, teachers' conceptions of teaching become shaped accordingly; even their conceptions of subject matter become shaped by institutional expectations (Grossman, 1991; Stodolsky, 1993; Zancanella, 1991). Teachers' actions that fit with their guiding model are planned and carried out. But as McCutcheon (1988, 1992) observed, contemplated actions that would fall outside the model are either revised so they fall within the model or are discarded altogether. When schools direct teachers to implement curricula and make available materials that are incompatible with the teaching model within which teachers work, teachers either modify the curricular content and materials so that they agree with their model, or they find reasons for setting aside nonconforming activities and materials (e.g., "That's something for parents to teach," "That objective was met in another lesson," "This set of materials is not appropriate for kids who live around here," etc.).

Clearly, how teachers think and act is conditioned by their circumstances. Whatever model or dominant idea of teaching they hold, it is shaped by the way things are and the pressures exerted by the way things are to lead their practices in certain directions. As paths of thinking are established to accommodate the way things are, the dominant idea evolves to accommodate those paths of thinking. The paths of thinking currently in use serve to facilitate some extensions or variants of the dominant idea, and at the same time block others. Behind all of this are tendencies to do what is satisfying, strengthen ways of thinking that get desirable results, and extinguish those that are in some way punishing (Dennett, 1975). Margolis (1993) argued that these tendencies turn on two complementary points: *propensity to comfort* and *propensity to economy.*

An idea feels comfortable if it fits with existing patterns of experience. It is comfortable if what it implies is also implied by an existing state of knowledge. But if what it implies is not implied by other things observed and believed, it feels uncomfortable. If an idea makes sense with what is already accepted, it also appeals to the sense of economy. What makes an idea economical is its efficiency in the service it performs. An idea is economical if the additional things that have to be accepted to make it work are few relative to the inferences that can be made with it. So it is with updating, modifying, or shedding aspects of existing ideas. If there is an alteration to an idea in the offing, the alteration is effected if it fits with the rest of the idea and serves the idea efficiently. Otherwise, it is rejected.

In professional teaching, there is an ongoing tension between accepting and rejecting ideas or adaptations of ideas. Teachers are forced to weigh the risks of accepting an idea or its adaptation that is mistaken against rejecting an idea or its adaptation that turns out to be a good one. The propensity to comfort offers some protection against making errors of the first type—of accepting a mistaken idea: What obviously does not sort with what is already known and believed is rejected. The assertion that the best science teaching engages students in science texts is likely to be rejected by hands-on teachers who do not use texts. The propensity to economy offers some protection against errors of the second type—of failing to accept what is sound: What seems obviously too reasonable to be wrong is accepted. Science teachers who are satisfied that science learning is best facilitated by hands-on instruction will concur with counsel that, where science subject matter is concerned, direct experience is the best teacher. Where there is no conflict between the two propensities in accepting or amending an idea, (e.g., where science teachers are satisfied with the results of hands-on teaching and they are advised that hands-on teaching is the best approach to teaching science), there is clearly a good fit with the way things are.

Still, there can arise compelling reasons to see things differently. Hands-on science teachers may have occasion to face some unsettling facts: (a) that the science they teach is fundamentally a literature of science; (b) that even though a hands-on approach has been effective for teaching specific lessons, students have not been taught how to learn further science material on their own through reading; and (c) that there is a lack of persuasive evidence that hands-on instruction is most effective for students' overall education in science. In cases where an idea or its modification runs counter to existing knowledge and belief, comfort and economy can only evolve over time, if at all, as knowledge and belief change to allow an accommodation. In such cases, economy comes gradually as pieces of a candidate idea are fitted into a larger familiar pattern as if they were integral to it. Hands-on science teachers begin to accommodate by incorporating reading into instruction when they see value in having students refer to texts as they undertake hands-on activities. They further the accommodation when they see value in extending the amount of reading they assign relative to the time devoted to hands-on activity. They complete the accommodation when they see texts as essential instructional tools that hands-on activities serve to augment. Comfort comes as the larger pattern of knowledge and belief is reshaped as the result of normal change with the passage of time or favorable experience with a candidate idea or modification. Comfort with students learning science from their texts comes as teachers gain experience teaching the literature of their subject and witness its positive results.

MODELS OF TEACHING IN TEACHERS' THINKING

Insofar as teachers' thinking is consistent with a developed set of interrelated principles of teaching, their thinking may be said to be theoretical or model based. But it cannot be said that teachers' thinking of any sort or caliber is ever in any strict sense theoretically deductive. The guiding principles in teachers' thinking never amount to a formal model or theory, as one ordinarily conceives of a scientific model or theory. The constructs that make up teachers' dominant ideas of teaching are not deduced from a set of basic postulates, they are not derived from other components, and they are not hierarchical or interdependent. Rather, any idea that dominates teachers' thinking takes the form of a "holist" concept, which, as described by Diesing (1971) and Kaplan (1964), exists as a concatenation of relatively independent parts loosely connected. The parts of that idea are developed more or less independently of one another, and can operate in teachers' minds without necessary linkage to one another. Each of the parts comprises, in turn, several relatively independent subparts associated with it. When teachers' thinking conforms to a model of teaching, the model's different parts may illuminate different aspects of a situation and may indicate directions of action. Together, the model's parts may offer multifaceted illumination and guidance in particular situations.

What teacher thinking do models offer illumination and guidance? What kinds of things do teachers think about when they think about their work? As the size of the literature on teaching suggests, the kinds and objects of teacher thinking are many and varied in their manifestations. I limit the naming of the content and processes of teachers' thinking here to those highlighted in a review of research on teachers' thinking by Clark and Peterson (1986). Roughly following their organizational scheme for discussing research on teachers' thinking, I briefly summarize the content and processes of teachers' thinking that would affect and be affected by models of teaching: (a) planful thinking in advance of teaching, (b) thinking during teaching, and (c) thinking related to theories and beliefs about teaching.

Thinking in Advance of Teaching

Teachers' thinking about upcoming teaching moves from some general, even vague, idea about that teaching to thinking through a succession of increasingly detailed visualizations and rehearsals (Clark & Yinger, 1979; Yinger & Clark, 1982; cited in Clark & Peterson, 1986). Framing their thinking within an imagined instructional setting, usually a familiar one, they formulate mental pictures of the teaching they will do, imagining sequences of activities and speculating about probable responses by students. The most prominent concern in planning is students' needs, abilities, and interests (Taylor, 1970; Zahorik, 1975; cited in Clark & Peterson, 1986). Taking these into account, teachers set subject matter goals and consider instructional situations and procedures likely to engage their students productively. Remembering previous teaching experiences (Clark & Elmore, 1979; Yinger, 1977; cited in Clark & Peterson, 1986) and making judgments about materials (Clark & Elmore, 1981; cited in Clark & Peterson, 1986) to be used, they determine the task demands of teaching the content or skills and adjust the sequence and pace of activity accordingly. Thinking planfully, then, teachers think ahead about (a) how they will manage the instructional situation, (b) what strategies they will deploy, and (c) how their interactions will affect learners and learners' interactions will affect one another. They think about this in ways consistent with their overall orientation to teaching. They project themselves imaginatively into upcoming events of teaching in ways provided for by the code structures of their overall orientation to teaching.

Thinking During Teaching

During instruction, teachers continually interpret the events surrounding their interactions with learners. Attaching subjective meaning to what they see and hear, they speculate about what is likely to come up in the lesson. Reflecting on the action, they think about how events or aspects of the lesson might have developed in ways other than they actually did (Clark & Peterson, 1986). Their thinking concerns several variables always present during instruction: learners, subject matter, materials, procedures, and time (Clark & Peterson, 1986). Of these, they typically devote most of their thinking to learners: about their attitudes and abilities, and about what can be expected of them, and about how to communicate with them (Colker, 1982; Marx & Peterson, 1981; McNair, 1978; Semmel, 1977; cited in Clark & Peterson, 1986). During teaching, teachers think about and deal with matters of classroom management, social roles, and instructional routines, many of them more or less simultaneously. How teachers think about and deal with these matters ultimately depends on their overall orientation to teaching, as well as the structures of thinking and acting suggested for achieving their goals (Clark & Peterson, 1986). Thus, as Grossman (1992) pointed out, classroom practice is never entirely neutral, but "carries within it its own implicit theory of instruction."

Thinking Related to Theories and Beliefs

Teachers bring in their theories and beliefs when they plan for teaching and when they attempt to understand and interpret classroom events. In their thinking about these things, teachers draw on their general knowledge, as well as their knowledge more specifically related to teaching. Much of their knowledge is structured and represented as beliefs. Included in knowledge related to teaching are beliefs about their role as teacher, about the nature of learners and learning, and about rules and principles of practice. Thinking about their role as teacher, teachers attend to establishing and maintaining an atmosphere in which students are committed to participating in classroom activities cooperatively (Duffy, 1977; Conners, 1978; Marland, 1977; cited in Clark & Peterson, 1986). Even though teachers may hold clear ideas about what they teach and have strong beliefs consistent with those ideas about how they should teach, their thinking is dominated by concerns about how to conduct themselves in order to manage the classroom. Monitoring themselves, they consciously suppress emotions that would compromise their authority as teacher, lead to disruption, or make them appear unfair. They consciously exhibit feelings intended to prompt harmonious student interactions and smoothness in the flow of classroom activities.

Thinking about learners and learning, teachers explain to themselves what accounts for students' performance (Weiner et al., 1971; Freige, 1976; Bar Tal & Darom, 1979; cited in Clark & Peterson, 1986). Teachers may explain students' performance either as a result of responding (or failing to respond) to their actions as teacher or as a consequence of students' own abilities and efforts. Another way that teachers think about causes of students' performance is to take account of students' abilities and efforts as part of a larger mental construction of classroom events. Thinking about rules and principles of practice, teachers concern themselves with the social dynamics of instruction and what they might do to bring coherence to instructional events (Janesick, 1977; Munby, 1982; cited in Clark & Peterson, 1986).

In this vein, thinking about the social dynamics of instruction is not so much about managing the classroom as it is about teaching and learning; it is thinking about how to involve students productively in classroom activity and how to respond to their attempts to learn. To bring coherence to instruction, teachers think about how they might link different parts of its content effectively, how they might integrate them with the larger body of instruction, and how they might bring closure to instructional events.

If anything can be said about teachers' thinking, it is that it is contextual and empirical. That is, it is thinking that takes account of the contingencies of particular situations of teaching and that makes reference to familiar situations resembling the immediate situation on which thinking focuses. To the extent that teachers' thinking proceeds along the lines of a model of teaching, the particulars of an instructional situation can be fitted into a comprehensible framework, comparison across like situations can be made in terms of the model's code structures, and an implicit analysis of the situation can be effected so as to allow reducing it to manageable interpretations that can be acted on sensibly. It is thinking in which meaning continually undergoes change and enrichment as new situations are encountered.

MODELS IN REFLECTIVE PRACTICE

Teachers face many situations that could be approached in a number of ways by a range of measures. To each situation or problem, teachers bring ways of thinking and acting consistent with some dominant idea. With this idea in mind, they keep their focus on their instructional intentions, gather their feelings about the learners involved, and proceed on the basis that the course of action they take will likely accomplish its purposes in ways sensitive to the learners present. The dominant ideas they bring to teaching situations are general ideas. They are executive designs. Being general ideas, they do not prescribe specific actions for specific situations. The value of such ideas is that they help teachers cope with situations in which their knowledge is limited. Although teachers have to deal with situations without highly detailed prescriptions, the general executive designs they do have can be sufficient nonetheless to suggest strategies for confronting particular contingencies and give them confidence for carrying them out.

Strategic Reflection

Executive designs indicate directions in which instructional actions might be taken, but do not specify how actions might be carried out. Taking a direction that would be indicated by this or that general design still requires the accommodation of contextual specifics. For this, teachers are largely without algorithms. Within each novel situation, skillful teachers act in ways that resemble the actions Argyris (1982) believed all skillful professionals take. They act in ways that allow learning from those novel situations; they approach such situations and problems as occasions for creating and interpreting knowledge about their professional practices. Argyris argued that smart professionals learn from their work by designing their unawareness. More exactly, he argued that unawareness is a kind of action professionals can design, and that skillful professionals are skillful because they are skillful in managing their unawareness. They know how to be unaware productively.

They remain alert to the possibility that they may be unaware; when they detect instances of unawareness, they take measures to learn from them. According to Argyris, the measures they take are designed in ways that set up a mental connection between the novel situation in which the unawareness presents itself and the dominant professional idea or model. This allows deficiencies in knowledge to come to the forefront of their thinking. The setup identifies specific gaps in their knowledge so that they can attend to and close them.

Strategies described in the literature on classroom management and teaching exemplify making a connection between immediate situation and dominant idea. Teachers are portrayed as consciously setting the pace and flow of instruction on the basis of what they see students do and what they hear students say (Corno, 1981). By putting into play highly familiar routines at certain junctures in instruction, teachers free themselves to become acquainted with students and the school situation. As they do, they fine tune the instruction and classroom management (Doyle, 1977; Joyce, 1978, 1980). Where they are certain to devote attention is to departures from the expected and the usual, and it is in dealing with those departures that teachers refine their practice.

Teachers encounter certain types of situations again and again. As they experience variations within these situation types, they become increasingly adept at handling them. They develop sets of expectations, images, and techniques. They learn what needs their attention and what can be ignored, and, as they do, they learn how to respond. As long as they encounter more or less the same types of situations, they are seldom surprised, and thus teaching remains stable for them. Their practical knowledge about how to act in certain situations becomes increasingly tacit. Accordingly, their actions become more and more spontaneous. The positive result for students is that they become beneficiary to practices polished by experience. There can be a negative side to expertise, however. Tacit practical knowledge for handling routine situations spontaneously can also be knowledge for handling those situations automatically without thinking. As teaching becomes routine, aspects of it can become grindingly repetitive. If teachers learn to screen out information that does not fit their routine ways of thinking, they may become disinterested and inattentive, and may even find themselves caught in a tangle of mistakes. Just as students can be beneficiary to spontaneous and polished teaching, so too can they fall victim to automatic and uninteresting teaching.

Constructive Reflection and Its Limitations

Argyris (1982) and Schön (1983) argued that problems stemming from overly routine situations can be headed off through practices consciously reflective in character. By applying this kind of preventive reflection to teaching, teachers can bring to light and examine the tacit understandings that have gathered around routine practices; they can come to fresh understanding of what may have struck them as odd or puzzling. If they are faced with a problem, they can turn to the principles by which they work for guidance in taking steps to manage the problem. If they cannot manage it as they understand it, they can reset the problem by reframing their understanding of it. Perhaps they can reassign the particulars of the problem to different categories of thought, or they can apply different ways of reasoning through it. Still, there are limits to gains in understanding through experience alone. Some understandings about teaching are not necessarily reached through experience alone. In a number of case studies, Grossman (1990) found that teachers relied principally on their experience as students, but hardly at all on their experience as teachers. Grossman also found that even when certain practices were ineffective, and teachers were aware of their ineffectiveness, teachers did not always consider alternative practices. The teachers she observed tended to explain away ineffectiveness of their instructional practices without considering the instructional practices themselves, notably without considering the need to rethink the subject matter so as to make it more accessible to students.

Of course there are limitations on the power of deliberation. Teachers' deliberation on a problem entails a description of the situation and the actions they have taken intuitively, yet their ability to describe the content of their teaching nearly always falls short in portraying what they do on the basis of what they know intuitively. Teachers' tacit ways of representing what they are doing at the moment they are teaching are much richer than their ways of describing how they do it. Another factor that limits deliberation is that teachers cannot deliberate on their acts of teaching moment by moment during the throes of teaching. What teachers do cognitively when they think about their actions is different from what they do when they act. By attempting to deliberate on their actions in progress, they may recognize complexity that, although easily managed unconsciously, may interfere with the smooth flow of action, and may even be paralyzing if brought to consciousness. Reflection in teaching, as in any other professional practice, is bounded by what Schön (1983) called the "action-present," which he defined as "the zone of time in which action can still make a difference." The action-present may be a span of minutes, or it could extend from hours to days, or even weeks or months, depending on the activity.

Whenever constructive reflection occurs, it is connected paradigmatically to professional knowledge. It connects with what Elbaz (1983) called the "practical knowledge" of teaching: of self, in the situation, conducting some procedure to teach some skill or subject matter in implementation of the curriculum. By this connection, teachers see themselves and what they do as agents in implementing curriuculm; they see themselves in instructional relationships with learners, and consider the dynamics of those relationships. Connected with a dominant idea of teaching, the actions teachers take can be considered in light of principles and criteria indicated by that idea. That is the purpose of paradigmatic ideas. They provide rationale, and suggest goals, standards, and criteria for planning and carrying out courses of action. With them may be seen strategic possibilities for pursuing educational missions and achieving certain outcomes.

SUMMARY AND CONCLUSION

Models of teaching propose one or another comprehensive set of knowledge needed in teaching. More exactly, they provide code structures for representing ideas about teaching. They name skills and understandings essential to classroom practice. By this naming, they provide ways to think about teaching, about what to consider, and about what, in general terms, happens or should happen in teaching. They suggest criteria for inclusion (and exclusion) of certain kinds of practices, and for judgments about the appropriateness and desirability of certain educational outcomes. Models of teaching reflect different points of view about purposes of education and the nature of learning and teaching, incorporating tenets of curriculum and learning theories with which they are aligned.

Models of teaching provide frameworks for organizing professional practice and learning from it. Indeed, Shulman (1987) described teaching as a professional practice by which teachers continually learn. In teaching, there is an ongoing interplay between reasoning and doing. What teachers plan and do they plan and do in light of what they know and think about their subject matter, their students, and their situation. What they actually do builds their knowledge for further planning and doing. When teachers plan, they rehearse different imaginary lesson scripts and anticipate possible consequences of one course of action they might take rather than another—how a lesson might play out among students, how individual students might think about and act on what is proposed for teaching, and what might have to be done in response to students' reactions. In actually working with students, teachers process the ongoing action, continually judge the flow of the activity, weigh alternatives, and shift direction and emphasis as they deem the situation indicates. Following these instructional events, teachers reflect on the action and their in-process thinking about that action. In this reflection, they go over aspects of their teaching that stand out in their mind. They evaluate their own performance as well as the responses of students, and they evaluate outcomes or conclusions reached and any products that may have been generated. As teachers teach, they gain insight about the effects of their practices, and so modify certain practices; as experience builds, so does understanding of teaching.

To the extent that teachers think and act in conformity with a paradigmatic idea of teaching that can work in their particular circumstances, they stand to bring reasonableness and coherence to their work. No less important, they position themselves to learn from their practices about their practices.

REFERENCES

Anders, P. L., & Evans, K. S. (1994). Relationship between teachers' beliefs and their instructional practice in reading. In R. Garner & P. A. Alexander (Eds.), *Beliefs about text and instruction with text* (pp. 137–153). Hillsdale, NJ: Lawrence Erlbaum Associates.

Argyris, C. (1982). *Reasoning, learning, and action.* San Francisco: Jossey-Bass.

Biddle, B. J. (1964). The integration of teacher effectiveness research. In B. J. Biddle & W. J. Ellena (Eds.), *Contemporary research on teacher effectiveness* (pp. 1–40). New York: Holt, Rinehart & Winston.

Bigge, M. L. (1992). *Learning theories for teachers* (5th ed.). New York: HarperCollins.

Bruner, J. S. (1966). *Toward a theory of instruction.* Cambridge: The Belknap Press of Harvard University Press.

Clark, C. M., & Peterson, P. L. (1986). Teachers' thought processes. In M. C. Wittrock (Ed.), *Handbook of research on teaching* (pp. 255–296). New York: Macmillan.

Colton, A. B., & Sparks-Langer, G. M. (1993). A conceptual framework to guide the development of teacher reflection and decision making. *The Journal of Teacher Education, 44,* 45–54.

Corno, L. (1981). Cognitive organizing in classrooms. *Curriculum Inquiry, 11,* 359–377.

Cruickshank, D. R. (1984). Toward a model to guide inquiry in preservice teacher education. *The Journal of Teacher Education, 35,* 43–48.

Decker, C., & Saunders, F. (1976). *A model for models.* Tucson, AZ: C. S. Decker and T. F. Saunders.

Deford, D. (1985). Validating the construct of theoretical orientation in reading instruction. *Reading Research Quarterly, 20,* 351–367.

Delpit, L. D. (1988). The silenced dialogue: Power and pedagogy in educating other people's children. *Harvard Educational Review, 58,* 280–298.

Dennett, D. (1975). Why the law of effect will not go away. *Journal of the Theory of Social Behavior, 3,* 169–180.

Diesing, P. (1971). *Patterns of discovery in the social sciences.* New York: Aldine.

Doyle, W. (1977). *Paradigms for research on teacher effectiveness.* Itaska, IL: F. E. Peacock.

Dunkin, M. J., & Biddle, B. J. (1974). *The study of teaching.* New York: Holt, Rinehart & Winston.

Eisner, E. W., & Vallance, E. (1974). Five conceptions of curriculum: Their roots and implications for curriculum planning. In E. W. Eisner and E. Vallance (Eds.), *Conflicting conceptions of curriculum* (pp. 1–18). Berkeley, CA: McCutchan.

Elbaz, F. (1983). *Teacher thinking: A study of practical knowledge.* New York: Nichols.

Fenstermacher, G. D. (1986). A philosophy of research on teaching: Three aspects. In M. C. Wittrock (Ed.), *Handbook of research on teaching* (pp. 37–49). New York: Macmillan.

Grossman, P. L. (1990). *The making of a teacher: Teacher knowledge & teacher education.* New York: Teachers College Press.

Grossman, P. L. (1991). The selection and organization of content for secondary English: Sources of teachers' knowledge. *English Education, 23,* 39–53.

Grossman, P. L. (1992). Why models matter: An alternative view on professional growth in teaching. *Review of Educational Research, 62,* 171–179.

Grossman, P. L., Wilson, S., & Shulman, L. (1989). Teachers of substance: Subject matter knowledge for teaching. In M. Reynolds (Ed.), *Knowledge base for the beginning teacher* (pp. 23–36). New York: Pergamon.

Gudmundsdottir, S., & Shulman, L. (1987). Pedagogical content knowledge in social studies. *Scandinavian Journal of Education Research, 31,* 59–70.

Jordell, K. (1987). Structural and personal influences in the socialization of beginning teachers. *Teaching and Teacher Education, 3,* 165–177.

Joyce, B. R. (1978). Toward a theory of information processing in teaching. *Educational Research Quarterly, 3,* 66–77.

Joyce, B. R. (1980). *Toward a theory of information processing in teaching.* East Lansing, MI: Michigan State University Institute for Research on Teaching.

Joyce, B. R., Soltis, J. F., & Weil, M. (1974). *Performance-based teacher education design alternatives: The concept of unity.* Washington, DC: American Association of Colleges for Teacher Education.

Joyce, B. R., Weil, M., & Showers, B. (1992). *Models of teaching.* Boston: Allyn & Bacon.

Kaplan, A. (1964). *The conduct of inquiry.* San Francisco: Chandler.

Kliebard, H. (1992). *Forging the American curriculum: Essays in curriculum history and theory.* New York: Routledge.

Kratz, H. E. (1896). Characteristics of the best teachers as recognized by children. *Pedagogical Seminary, 3,* 413–418.

Lamm, Z. (1976). *Conflicting theories of instruction.* Berkeley, CA: McCutchan.

Liston, D. P., & Zeichner, K. M. (1991). *Teacher education and the social conditions of schooling.* New York: Routledge.

Lyons, N. (1990). Dilemmas of knowing: Ethical and epistemological dimensions of teachers' work and development. *Harvard Educational Review, 60,* 159–180.

Margolis, H. (1993). *Paradigms and barriers: How habits of mind govern scientific beliefs.* Chicago: The University of Chicago Press.

McCarthey, S. J., Hoffman, J. V., Stahle, D., Matherne, D., Elliott, B., Dressman, M., & Abbott, J. (1994, December). *"Very sweet, but very, very slow": How teachers' ways of knowing are reflected in their assumptions about students.* Paper presented at the annual meeting of the National Reading Conference, Charleston, SC.

McCutcheon, G. (1988). Curriculum and the work of teachers. In M. Apple & L. Beyers (Eds.), *Curriculum problems, politics and possibilites* (pp. 191–203). Albany, NY: State University of New York Press.

McCutcheon, G. (1992). Facilitating teacher personal theorizing. In E. W. Ross, J. W. Cornett, & G. McCutcheon (Eds.), *Teacher personal theorizing: Connecting curriculum practice, theory and research* (pp. 191–205). Albany, NY: State University of New York Press.

McDonald, F. J., & Elias, P. (1976). A report on the results of phase two of the beginning teacher evaluation study. *Journal of Teacher Education, 27,* 315–316.

Medley, D. (1982). Teacher effectiveness. In H. Mitzel (Ed.), *Encyclopedia of educational research* (5th ed., pp. 1894–1903). New York: The Free Press.

Mitzel, H. (1960). Teacher effectiveness. In C. W. Harris (Ed.), *Encyclopedia of educational research* (3rd ed., pp. 1481–1486). New York: Macmillan.

Moore, W. E. (1970). *The professions: Roles and rules.* New York: Russell Sage Foundation.

Peterson, P. L. (1994). *Research studies as texts: Sites for exploring the beliefs and learning of researchers and teachers.* Hillsdale, NJ: Lawrence Erlbaum Associates.

Petrosky, A. (1994). Producing and assessing knowledge: Beginning to understand teachers' knowledge through the work of four theorists. In T. Shanahan (Ed.), *Teachers thinking, teachers knowing* (pp. 23–38). Urbana, IL: National Council of Teachers of English.

Reinsmith, W. A. (1992). *Archetypal forms in teaching: A continuum.* Westport, CT: Greenwood.

Rich, J. M. (1992). *Foundations of education: Perspectives on American education.* New York: Macmillan.

Richardson, V., Anders, P. L., Tidwell, D., & Lloyd, C. V. (1991). The relationship between teachers' beliefs and practices in reading comprehension instruction. *American Educational Research Journal, 28,* 559–586.

Rosenthal, R. (1968). *Pygmalion in the classroom: Teacher expectation and intellectual development.* New York: Holt, Rinehart & Winston.

Ross, E. W. (1987). Teacher perspective development: A study of preservice social studies teachers. *Theory and Research in Social Education, 15,* 225–243.

Ross, E. W. (1992). Teacher personal theorizing and reflective practice in teacher education. In E. W. Ross, J. W. Cornett, & G. McCutcheon (Eds.), *Teacher personal theorizing: Connecting curriculum practice, theory, and research* (pp. 179–190). Albany, NY: State University of New York Press.

Ruediger, W. C., & Strayer, G. D. (1910). The qualities of merit in teachers. *The Journal of Educational Psychology, 1,* 272–278.

Ryans, D. G. (1947). Appraising teacher personnel: A report of the activities of the American Council on Education's Committee on Teacher Examinations and analysis of the results of the Eighth Annual Teacher Examination Program. *Journal of Experimental Education, 16,* 1–30.

Ryans, D. G. (1960). *Characteristics of teachers: Their description, comparison, and appraisal.* Washington, DC: American Council on Education.

Schön, D. A. (1983). *The reflective practitioner.* New York: Basic Books.

Schwab, J. J. (1964). The structure of the disciplines: Meanings and significances. In G. W. Ford & L. Pugno (Eds.), *The structure of knowledge and the curriculum* (pp. 1–30). Chicago: Rand McNally.

Shulman, L. (1986). *Paradigms and research programs in the study of teaching.* New York: Macmillan.

Shulman, L. (1987). Knowledge and teaching: Foundations of the new reform. *Harvard Educational Review, 57,* 1–22.

Smith, B. O. (1960). A concept of teaching. *Teachers College Record, 61,* 229–241.

Stodolsky, S. S. (1993). A framework for subject matter comparisons in high schools. *Teaching and Teacher Education, 9,* 333–346.

Strasser, B. (1967). A conceptual model of instruction. *The Journal of Teacher Education, 18,* 63–74.

Tomlinson, L. R. (1955). Pioneer studies in the evaluation of teaching. *Educational Research Bulletin, 34,* 63–71.

Weil, M., Joyce, B., & Kluwin, B. (1978). *Personal models of teaching.* Englewood Cliffs, NJ: Prentice-Hall.

Wilson, S., Shulman, L., & Richert, A. (1987). 150 ways of knowing: Representations of knowledge in teaching. In J. Calderhead (Ed.), *Exploring teachers thinking* (pp. 104–124). London: Cassell.

Zancanella, D. (1991). Teachers reading/reading teachers: Five teachers' personal approaches to literature and their teaching of literature. *Research in the Teaching of English, 25,* 5–32.

Zeichner, K. M., & Gore, J. M. (1990). Teacher socialization. In W. R. Houston (Ed.), *Handbook of research on teacher education* (pp. 329–348). New York: Macmillan.

Zeichner, K. M., & Tabachnick, B. R. (1991). Reflections on reflective teaching. In K. M. Zeichner & B. R. Tabachnick (Eds.), *Issues and practices in inquiry-oriented teacher education* (pp. 1–21). New York: Falmer.

CHAPTER THREE

Direct-Instruction Reading

Edward J. Kameenui
Deborah C. Simmons
University of Oregon, Eugene

David Chard
Boston University

Shirley Dickson
Northern Illinois University

Words are very peculiar creatures (Anderson & Nagy, 1991; Baumann & Kameenui, 1991; Bryson, 1990). They serve to inspire and enrage, clarify and confuse, comfort and cudgel, obscure and occupy; the possibilities are endless. Were he to offer his uncanny wisdom to the discussion, Yogi Berra, that legendary wordsmith of baseball slurs, would probably add: "There are words and there are words." Indeed there are.

In the world of reading, literacy, and language, few words incite, inspire, and obscure more than *Direct Instruction* (Kameenui & Shannon, 1988). To those who are inspired, Direct Instruction represents "a comprehensive system that integrates curriculum design with teaching techniques to produce instructional programs in language, reading, mathematics, spelling, written expression, and science" (Tarver, 1992, p. 141). Interestingly, but not surprisingly, the same words that inspire some serve to incite others, such as Shannon (1988), who stated:

> Explicit in Carnegie's remarks—and implicit in those of direct instruction advocates—is the assumption that the poor, however defined, do not have the wherewithal to make sense of their lives or texts without direct aid from their betters.
>
> Of course, the form that this aid takes varies according to the specific type of direct instruction one selects. Clearly, the aid with the most strings of dependence for both teachers and students comes from the University of Oregon's Direct Instruction Model because it makes the teacher rely completely on curriculum programmers; it ignores the experience and knowledge of

students altogether with its standardization of methods, making students dependent on lessons to learn to read; and it analyzes actual acts of literacy use into numerous preliteracy skills, having students wait to use literacy for their own purposes. (pp. 36–37)

Words. They inspire and incite, but, more often than we would like to admit, they obscure. Bryson (1990) pointed out that the same word can have contradictory meanings. He called these words *contronyms*. For example, the word *sanction* "can either signify permission to do something or a measure forbidding it to be done. *Cleave* can mean cut in half or stick together . . ." (p. 70). Sometimes how a word is used and what it means in public (or pedagogical) discourse is so unstable and wobbly that the word is best characterized by another word, *eonomine*, which means, roughly, something "called by that name."[1]

The words *Direct Instruction* are both eonomine and contronym; that is, their meaning in public discourse is so contradictory (e.g., Kameenui, 1988; Shannon, 1988) that the words are best rendered as obscure, unstable, and perhaps even unsafe for general public use. The ambiguity and contradiction incited by *Direct Instruction* in the context of reading and literacy are interesting and worthy of analysis. One needs to clarify the features that render Direct Instruction unique, as well as what the educational community, in general, and the reading community, in particular, value as worthy of imitation, replication, and celebration.

In this chapter, we examine the historical, theoretical, and empirical bases of Direct-Instruction reading. The chapter is organized into three sections. In the first, the historical context of Direct Instruction and its various pedagogical inflections are examined to clarify how these terms are used or misused. The theoretical basis of Direct-Instruction reading is reviewed, and particular attention is given to theories on information as communication (Campbell, 1982), instructional design (Bruner, 1966; Gagne, 1965; Tennyson & Cochiarella, 1986), and sameness analysis (Engelmann & Carnine, 1982; Kameenui & Simmons, 1990). This section is concluded with a descriptive analysis of the particulars that distinguish the Direct-Instruction approach to teaching reading.

In the second section, the research on Direct-Instruction reading is described. The results of Project Follow Through are briefly examined, whereas a three-strand program of instructional research on the teaching of beginning reading and reading comprehension from a Direct-Instruction perspective is described in depth. In the final section of the chapter, the status and future of Direct-Instruction reading are examined. Direct-Instruction reading

---

[1]The first author wants to thank Moddy McKeown, University of Pittsburgh, for bringing this word to his attention.

is reviewed in the context of three criteria for the design of quality programs: efficacy, parsimony, and sustainability.

A HISTORICAL PERSPECTIVE
OF DIRECT-INSTRUCTION READING

One cannot glance at or casually study the words *Direct Instruction* and walk away with a clear and full rendering of what they mean. However, the problem of discerning what is meant by Direct Instruction or "direct instruction" is not necessarily an etymological artifact of Direct Instruction (or direct instruction). Instead, it reflects a general malady (i.e., a chronic and deep-seated problem) that appears to affect many, if not most, educational terms. For example, take heed of the terms *learning, teaching, education, ability, disability, learning disability, gifted and talented, at risk, whole language, literacy, authentic assessment, educational reform, inclusion,* and so on. The list is endless, indeed with ample and passionate argument surrounding each term.

Most, if not all, educational terms are context-bound, and the meaning becomes transparent, or less opaque, only in the context of other words. The galaxy of meanings assigned to Direct Instruction has been great and unwieldy, and the remedy to understanding what Direct Instruction really means is best captured by the poignant exchange between Alice and Humpty Dumpty in Lewis Carroll's (1990) *Through the Looking Glass*: "The question is," said Alice, "whether you can make words mean so many different things." "The question is," said Humpty Dumpty, "which is to be master—that's all" (p. 253).

To determine which meaning of Direct Instruction is "master," it is necessary to turn to the originators of the approach (i.e., those who inspired and incited its original authentic meaning).

Siegfried Engelmann and Direct Instruction

Direct Instruction is often and conveniently distinguished from other similar approaches (e.g., "direct instruction") by the emphasis given the icons DI (i.e., "big D" for *D*irect and "big I" for *I*nstruction). However, Direct Instruction is made distinctive, pedagogically and philosophically, by its originator, Siegfried Engelmann, and the 40 or so curriculum programs that he and his colleagues have authored over the past 25 years. It is Engelmann's uncompromising intellect and passionate voice that gives Direct-Instruction curriculum programs their distinct tone, delivery, and pedagogical markings. It is simply not possible to speak of Direct Instruction accurately or meaningfully without giving attention to the assumptions on which the Direct-Instruction curriculum programs are based. The following assumptions were gleaned from Engelmann's writings:

1. The premise from which all the procedures derive—either directly or indirectly—is that the teacher is responsible for the learning and performance of the children. (1969, p. 39)
2. The first and most important step in cause finding is to discover *what* the child has failed to learn. (1969, p. 8; italics original)
3. There are individual differences between children, but these differences must be expressed in such a way that the teacher can do something about them. (1969, p. 23)
4. A further teaching assumption is that the more carefully skills are taught, the greater the possibility that the child will learn them. (1969, p. 25)
5. Teach children in a way that provides maximum feedback on what they are learning and where they are having difficulty. (1969, p. 43)
6. The point is this: there is no such thing as "memory" or "perception" or "learning speed" apart from specific tasks. And a child's performance on a given task is predictable if you know something about the *experiences* he has had. He doesn't merely *learn*; he learns specific facts and relations. (Engelmann & Engelmann, 1966, p. 62; italics original)

The statements by Engelmann point to a basic principle of Direct Instruction—children's failure to learn is unacceptable and unnecessary if we understand what we want to teach and design the teaching carefully, strategically, and with full consideration of the learner. The passion behind this basic principle of Direct Instruction gains its force from a commitment to children who have failed year after year—disabled students, slow readers, disadvantaged learners, students with diverse learning and curricular needs, poor students, and atypical learners—through no fault of their own. Moreover, the tenets espoused by Engelmann almost 25 years ago persist today and serve to shape the continued development of Direct Instruction (Engelmann & Carnine, 1982; Kameenui & Simmons, 1990).

RESEARCH ON DIRECT INSTRUCTION

Direct Instruction is also distinguished from other educational approaches by the extensive research base supporting its effectiveness in improving students' academic performance. Throughout this chapter, we refer to this program as the University of Oregon Direct Instruction Program (Carnine,

1979). Our review and analysis focus exclusively on this form of Direct Instruction.

The research evidence for the effectiveness of the University of Oregon Direct Instruction Program as a comprehensive educational model comes in numerous forms, and is derived from a range of research programs (e.g., longitudinal, experimental, quasiexperimental) conducted over the last 30 years. In fact, one could persuasively argue that the Direct-Instruction model enjoys a more substantive, extensive, validated, and elaborate empirical basis than most educational approaches to teaching and learning.

National Follow Through Project: University of Oregon Direct Instruction

The most prominent, largest, and longest independent evaluation of Direct-Instruction reading was conducted in the context of Project Follow Through, a federally funded program in the late 1960s and early 1970s designed initially to sustain and extend Head Start into the elementary grades. However, as Becker (1977) pointed out, ". . . in the wake of major funding cutback . . . Follow Through shifted its aim from service to research" and was ". . . deliberately organized to select, test, and evaluate promising, but different, educational programs for disadvantaged youngsters in the first three grades" (p. 519). McDaniels (cited in Becker, 1977) called the program the "largest and most expensive social experiment ever launched" (p. 520). Follow Through continues as a federally funded program of research today. However, between 1968–1978, Follow Through found its way into 180 communities and served 75,000 low-income children per year through 20 educational models or sponsors.

For all practical purposes, Follow Through pitted pedagogy against pedagogy, practitioner against practitioner, and instructional philosophy against instructional philosophy. This pedagogical horse race included nine major sponsors, five of whom derived ". . . their practices from the subjective theories of Piaget, Freud, and Dewey. They have in common: (1) individualized approaches to instruction, (2) goals which focus on the whole person, and (3) encouragement of child-initiated activities" (Becker & Carnine, 1980, p. 430). These models included the Open Education Model sponsored by the Education Development Center (EDC); the Tucson Early Education Model (TEEM), which relied on a language-experience approach; the Cognitively Oriented Curriculum, which was sponsored by the High/Scope Educational Research Foundation and built on Piaget's stages of learning; the Response Education Model, which was sponsored by Far West Laboratory and drew from a variety of materials and procedures; and the Bank Street College Model, which incorporated strands of philosophy from Dewey, Piaget, and Freud (Becker & Carnine, 1980).

Two other models that were different in orientation from those described previously were also included in Project Follow Through. The models included the Florida Parent Education Model, which trained parent educators to teach parents; and the Language Development (Bilingual) Model, which was sponsored by the Southwest Educational Development Laboratory (SEDL) and relied on systematic programs for teaching English and Spanish.

In contrast to these models, two emphasized student skill development: the University of Kansas Behavior Analysis Model and the University of Oregon Direct Instruction Model. The Kansas model relied on ". . . the systematic and precise use of positive reinforcement to induce mastery in reading, arithmetic, handwriting, and spelling" (Becker & Carnine, 1980, p. 432).

The University of Oregon Direct Instruction Model is best described by Becker and Carnine (1980):

> The Direct Instruction Model emphasizes the use of small-group, face-to-face instruction by teachers and aides using carefully sequenced lessons in reading, arithmetic, and language. . . . They utilize advanced programming strategies which are consistent with current behavior theory, but which go beyond current research on task analysis and stimulus control. . . . The model also emphasizes careful quality control of training procedures, teaching processes, and child progress. . . . Key assumptions of the model are: (1) that all children can be taught (the teacher is responsible); (2) that to "catch up," low-performing students must be taught *more*, not less; and (3) that the task of teaching more requires a careful use of educational technology and of *time*. (p. 433)

The data from Project Follow Through were analyzed by Stanford Research Institute (SRI) and Abt Associates (Stebbins, St. Pierre, Proper, Anderson, & Cerva, 1977) for the U.S. Department of Education. The reports on Project Follow Through have been extensive, and, in some cases, controversial (Becker, 1977; Becker, Engelmann, Carnine, & Rhine, 1981; Gersten, Becker, Heiry, & White, 1984; Guthrie, 1977; House, Glass, McLean, & Walker, 1978). A full and detailed discussion of the results of Follow Through are beyond the scope of this chapter, but a brief summary is in order.

The SRI and Abt Associates' longitudinal evaluation examined the impact of the nine different instructional models by comparing Follow Through (FT) model sites with non-Follow Through (NFT) comparison sites. As Becker and Carnine (1980) noted, the analysis included 9,255 FT children and 6,485 NFT children, with the nine major sponsors represented in 111 of the 139 sites studied. In general, the national evaluation of Project Follow Through found that the Direct-Instruction model had a beneficial effect on the achievement of low-income students who participated for 4 years (kindergarten through third grade). At the end of third grade, students taught using the Direct-Instruction programs performed at, near, or above the national median in math, language, and spelling. In reading, performance corresponded to the 41st percentile—9 percentile points below the median. In summary, the Direct-Instruction model succeeded in bridging the gap between low-income students and their middle-income peers.

In a secondary analysis of the achievement data from Project Follow Through, Gersten et al. (1984) examined the yearly achievement test profiles of students who entered with IQs of 70 or below on the Slosson Intelligence Test. These researchers found that low-IQ students who began at the 5th percentile on the Wide Range Achievement Test (WRAT) were virtually at norm levels (47th percentile) by the end of kindergarten, and continued to make slow but steady growth. By the end of third grade, reading word-identification performance was at the 70th percentile, or at a 4.3 grade level.

The results of Project Follow Through revealed that the Direct-Instruction approach produced greater gains in basic skills (i.e., word identification, mathematics computation, spelling), cognitive problem solving (e.g., reading comprehension, mathematical reasoning), and affective learning (e.g., self-esteem, locus of control) than other educational models. Less effective were several nondirective instructional approaches, such as an Open Classroom model, a Piagetian Cognitively Oriented Curriculum Model, a Tucson Early Education Model (language experience approach), and a Bank Street Model.

The results of Project Follow Through provide direct support for the effectiveness of Direct-Instruction curriculum programs in language, reading, spelling, and mathematics. The results also offer indirect support for various features of the curriculum programs, including their design, delivery, organization, and administration. However, substantive empirical support for these features has been provided by an extensive program of applied instructional research conducted by Carnine and colleagues during the last 20 years.

Research on Teacher Effectiveness: Convergence in the Early Years

The National Evaluation of Project Follow Through and the success of the University of Oregon Direct Instruction Model (Carnine, 1979) coincided with Rosenshine's (1976) review of research on teaching effectiveness. Direct Instruction and various inflections of "instructional" approaches were prominent educational forces that converged around the important relations between classroom variables (e.g., academic engaged time, content coverage) and achievement for students low in economic status and verbal ability (Rosenshine, 1976). This pedagogical, theoretical, and empirical convergence was evidenced by the widespread adoption and promotion of teaching innovations nominally identified as *direct instruction* (Kameenui, 1985), or direct, explicit teaching (e.g., Baumann, 1988; Pearson, 1984).

In fact, it has been argued that Rosenshine's (1976) summary of elements of the Direct-Instruction model, coupled with the results of the Follow

Through Project (Becker & Carnine, 1981), set the stage for an extraordinary range of teaching innovations that embraced the term *direct instruction* in the 1980s (Kameenui, 1985). These conceptualizations of direct instruction ranged from Zahorik and Kritek's (1983) notion of direct instruction as 21 elements including "available materials," "lecturing," and "warm climate," to Baumann's (1983) notion that, in direct instruction, the teacher is "in command of the learning situation and leads the lesson" (p. 287). In another definition, Baumann (1984) stated, "In direct instruction, the teacher, in a face-to-face, reasonably formal manner, tells, shows, models, demonstrates, teaches the skill to be learned. The key word here is teacher, for it is the teacher who is in command . . . as opposed to having instruction 'directed' by a worksheet, learning center, or workbook" (p. 287). According to Duffy and Roehler (1982), *direct instruction* meant "an academic focus, precise sequencing of content, high pupil engagement, careful teaching monitoring, and specific corrective feedback to students" (p. 35). Roehler and Duffy (1984) later defined *direct instruction* as "little more than efficient management of materials, activities, and pupils" (p. 265).

Rosenshine (1976) referred to direct instruction as a *model*, but later characterized it as a *method*. Similarly, Berliner (1984) called it both a *concept* and a *syndrome*. Roehler and Duffy (1982) viewed direct instruction as a *form*, and Baumann (1983) called it a *paradigm*. Not only was there ambiguity about the critical features of direct instruction, but also uncertainty about what direct instruction represented as a pedagogical or theoretical approach or package. Was it a model, concept, syndrome, form, system, or paradigm? What is prominent and telling about all these terms is that they referred to a pattern or representation that was worthy of imitation—something to be reproduced or copied.

·The cluster of attributes referenced by various researchers suggests that what was worthy of reproducing at the time was a dynamic set of teacher-directed actions. These actions generally centered on academic activities, and involved the teacher communicating information to students directly and in ways that used instructional time deliberately and efficiently. As learning progressed, the teacher gradually released responsibility to students. During this guided practice and "scaffolded" phase, instruction was less direct than the initial phase of teacher-guided instruction. Clearly, direct instruction, like Direct Instruction, is teacher guided, academically oriented, goal directed, and highly intentional.

[handwritten margin note: as a method, not a program]

Research on the Delivery of Direct Instruction

The programs of Direct Instruction tested in the context of Project Follow Through, and the features of "direct instruction" derived in the teacher-effectiveness research (Brophy & Evertson, 1976; Rosenshine, 1976), tell only part of the story. The theme of this part of the story is that Direct Instruction is about teacher delivery and organizational variables, such as teacher pacing (Carnine, 1976b; Darch & Gersten, 1986), unison oral responding, small-group instruction (Fink & Carnine, 1975; Fink & Sandall, 1978), scripted teaching formats (Gersten, Carnine, & Williams, 1982), strategic correction procedures (Carnine, 1976a, 1980c; Gersten, Carnine, & Williams, 1982), teacher signals (Carnine, 1981; Cowart, Carnine, & Becker, 1976), and systematic teacher feedback and monitoring of student performance (Brophy & Evertson, 1976; Carnine & Fink, 1978). Research on the effectiveness of these teacher delivery and organizational techniques has been documented extensively, and is reviewed and summarized by Carnine, Silbert, and Kameenui (1990) in *Direct Instruction Reading*.

According to Tarver (1992), the other part of the Direct Instruction story is what distinguishes it from other inflections of direct instruction. As Tarver noted, what separates Direct Instruction from other direct teaching approaches is "not easily distinguishable on the basis of teaching techniques" (p. 143). As Tarver noted, the teaching approaches are "easily distinguishable on the basis of curriculum components" (p. 143). Kameenui (1985) argued the same point: "Finally, the way the information is 'packaged' *before* teacher delivery and the form in which it is made available to the learner serve as the basis for Direct Instruction" (p. 257).

Research on the Design of Direct Instruction

The curriculum or instructional design feature of Direct Instruction is perhaps its best kept secret, ostensibly because it is the most embedded and, therefore, elusive feature (Carnine, 1979; Kameenui, 1985). For all practical purposes, the instructional design of Direct-Instruction programs refers to the architecture of the information to be communicated to the learner. *Instructional design* refers to the "systematic process of translating principles of learning and instruction into plans for instructional materials and activities" (Smith & Ragan, 1993, p. 3). Instructional design is also concerned with "initially preparing instruction that (a) has a high probability of preventing learner errors and/or misconceptions and misrules" (Tennyson & Christensen, 1986, p. 4).

The design or architecture of the information is predicated on the assumption that the structure of the information to be taught is of paramount importance in the communication. That is, structure dictates, in part, how the information is communicated, sent, or delivered to the receiver or learner. If the structure is complex (e.g., historical events that shaped the development of the U.S. Constitution), the communication (e.g., the number and sequence of examples the teacher presents to the learner) is potentially complex and messy, and the information to be communicated requires careful packaging before it is delivered. If the structure is simple (e.g., communicating the name of the capital of Oregon—Salem), the communication of the information is likely to be straightforward.

The Direct-Instruction approach to instructional design in reading has embraced Tennyson and Christensen's probabilistic model—that initial instruction should have a "high probability of preventing learner errors and/or misconceptions and misrules" (Tennyson & Christensen, 1986, p. 4). Such a model is consistent with Direct Instruction's commitment to preventing learner failure, as discussed previously. In their text *Theory of Instruction: Principles and Applications*, Engelmann and Carnine (1982) provided an exhaustive analysis and prescription for designing instruction that has a "high probability of preventing learner errors" (p. 4).

According to Moore (1986), common to definitions of *instructional design* is "a focus on the prescription of instructional procedures to achieve particular changes in learner behaviour" (p. 202). Bruner (cited in Moore, 1986) proposed four features of instructional design: (a) description of the experiences necessary for learning, (b) analysis of the structure and forms of knowledge, (c) specification of sequences in which to present the materials to be learned, and (d) system for monitoring and rewarding student performance during the instructional process. Engelmann and Carnine's three-part design of instruction analysis of cognitive learning aligns with Bruner's theory. However, of particular importance to the design of Direct Instruction are what Engelmann and Carnine (1982) referred to as (a) the analysis of the knowledge systems, and (b) the analysis of the communications. Simply put, the design of what teachers teach depends, in part, on the complexity of *what* is taught and *how* it is communicated to the learner.

The design of Direct Instruction is concerned with "*transforming the structure of information* in a way that the intended message is communicated clearly, unambiguously, and efficiently" (Kameenui, 1992, p. 254; italics original). For all practical purposes, a lesson's design should maximize the clarity of a message and minimize the noise in that message (Kameenui, 1992). This approach to instruction is rooted in information and communication theory. As Campbell (1982) stated, "In communications parlance, noise is anything which corrupts the integrity of a message: static in a radio set, garbling in a printed text, distortion of the picture on a television screen" (p. 26). To be clearly received, the message must be clearly communicated.

Research on the design of Direct-Instruction reading has been extensive and varied in both focus and methodology, but the primary thrust has been on the "integrity" of the message (e.g., teaching main idea comprehension or the meaning of the word *contronym*), as noted by Campbell (1982). The program of research on beginning reading and concept development conducted by Carnine in the early 1970s, coupled with the program of research in reading comprehension conducted by Carnine and Kameenui and their colleagues in the mid-1970s and 1980s, provided the empirical support for the design of instruction features of Direct-Instruction reading.

The research on the design of Direct-Instruction reading is best examined as three separate, yet interrelated, strands of inquiry: (a) Strand 1: Materials Analysis, (b) Strand 2: Stimulus Variation, and (c) Strand 3: Instructional Intervention. The conceptual and theoretical foci of these strands are on the structural features of reading tasks and experiences. In addition, special attention is given to the intricacies of what is taught and how it is designed to communicate a clear and unambiguous message to learners, especially those whose ability and capacity to receive, retain, rehearse, and appreciate information has been threatened by social, familial, or cognitive factors. The three-strand program of research on Direct-Instruction reading begins with the inspection of a rather static context (i.e., print materials in reading), proceeds to an analysis of the structural features of texts, and culminates with the analysis of the most dynamic research context—that of teaching children in real-world classrooms.

Strand 1: Research on the Analysis of Materials and Tools. The purpose of the research on materials or instructional tools was to examine school-based print materials in reading and language arts used to promote student learning and literacy. This research follows the Durkin (1981) tradition. It involves the descriptive analysis of information: how it is packaged and prescribed for delivery to the learner. The analysis relies on taxonomy of knowledge models, such as those developed by Gagne (1985), Markle and Tiemann (1969), Bruner (1966), and Tennyson and his colleagues (Tennyson & Christensen, 1986; Tennyson & Cochiarella, 1986; Tennyson & Park, 1984), to provide logical and organizational analyses of the featural and structural dimensions of knowledge. The materials research methodology involves analyzing and evaluating the congruence between what is prescribed in target materials (e.g., a lesson on teaching main idea comprehension in a third-grade basal text) and a particular model of knowledge organization and structure. The analysis reveals the extent to which the structure of information, as developed in the curriculum program, deviates from how knowledge forms *should be* designed to communicate a message clearly and with little or no noise.

For example, Jitendra and Kameenui (1988) studied the analysis of concept teaching procedures in five basal language programs. Design of instruction guidelines for the teaching of concepts was derived from three empirically based models (i.e., Engelmann & Carnine, 1982; Gagne, 1985; Tennyson & Cochiarella, 1986). Teaching sequences for five of the same concepts taught in five different basal language programs and five different concepts selected at random from the same programs were analyzed. Congruence between the actual and "ideal" concept teaching sequences derived from the models was judged and documented. Jitendra and Kameenui (1988) found substantial "discrepancies" in the five basal language programs. The basal concept teaching lessons violated every basic "design" principle derived from the models. For example, all three models prescribed the use of negative examples, but every lesson failed to include negative examples in concept teaching. Simply put, the gap between the "ideal" and "real" design of concept teaching lessons was expansive.

A recent analysis of five kindergarten-level commercial reading programs revealed numerous inadequacies in the instructional recommendations for phonological awareness, a skill of empirically validated importance to early reading success (Adams, 1990; Simmons et al., 1995; Wagner & Torgesen, 1987). Specifically, programs were analyzed to determine the quantity and quality of phonological awareness activities in teachers' manuals accompanying basal reading programs. Preliminary analyses indicated that, based on current curricular materials, beginning readers may encounter difficulty acquiring fundamental phonological awareness skills particularly in the areas of phonemic blending and segmenting. Analyses revealed that existing commercial programs do include activities designated to address phonological awareness; however, the instruction (a) allocates insufficient attention to this important skill area, (b) is seldom explicit, (c) leaves much to the learner to make the connections between phonological awareness and alphabetic understanding, and (d) focuses on dimensions of phonological awareness such as rhyming and word matching that are not most highly correlated to subsequent reading acquisition.

Armbruster and Gudbrandsen (1986) examined five social studies programs at the fourth- and sixth-grade levels through similar methodology. They wanted to determine how much and what kind of reading comprehension was provided in student textbooks and teacher editions. They found "direct instruction" to be rare. Duncan-Malone and Kameenui (1987) replicated this study with fourth- and fifth-grade social studies basal programs.

Another study in the materials research strand was an analysis of word problem-solving skills in basal mathematics programs (Kameenui & Griffin, 1989). More recently, descriptive analyses of materials have been conducted to determine teachers' perceptions of the importance and adequacy of commercial curricula for students with and without disabilities (Simmons & Kameenui, 1993). General ($n = 28$) and special educators ($n = 14$) reviewed lessons from popular language arts programs, and rated lesson adequacy along 10 dimensions of instructional design (e.g., number and sequence of examples in a lesson, range of examples selected). Results indicate that both groups perceived commercial language arts lessons insufficient to meet the needs of students with learning disabilities.

The descriptive analysis of existing curriculum materials is essential to a program of research whose primary feature is the design of instructional materials. Carnine and Kameenui (1993) considered it a necessary and indispensable activity for the National Center to Improve the Tools of Educators (NCITE), which they currently direct. NCITE's mission is to assist publishers, authors, and developers of educational tools in their efforts to "design" high-quality educational tools (e.g., print materials, electronic media, and software). One level of this assistance is to provide publishers with information on teachers' perceptions of high-quality educational tools. To this end, Baker, Simmons, Kameenui, and Carnine (1995) asked general education teachers ($n = 21$) to examine the qualities and weaknesses of commercial reading and mathematics instructional materials, media, and technology. Six focus groups were conducted nationwide, and content analyses of group responses reflected teachers' general discontent with the quality of commercial materials. Teachers illuminated specific considerations for improving instructional tools, with particular emphasis focused on (a) strengthening the alignment between the curriculum and learner needs, (b) improving the design of instructional tools, and (c) ensuring the relevance and accuracy of curriculum content.

Although few studies are formally published in this research strand, the methodology is employed frequently and consistently as a first step to the conceptualization of an instructional intervention. However, the results of a materials analysis study often serve to isolate a particular instructional design feature or variable that could prove influential for students with diverse learning and curricular needs.

Strand 2: Stimulus Variation Research. Once a problematic design of instruction is identified through descriptive analysis, a study or series of studies is designed to examine the influence of the feature on student performance. The purpose of stimulus variation research is to investigate the extent to which experimental variation of a "stimulus feature" (e.g., the presence or absence of anaphora in narrative text) affects the acquisition, recall, generalization, and maintenance of information by learners of diverse learning backgrounds (e.g., learning disabled vs. nonlearning disabled) or grade levels. For example, to examine fourth graders' comprehension of pronoun constructions, Kameenui and Carnine (1982) varied the presence or absence of pronouns in two types of text: narrative and expository. After reading a series of narrative and expository passages, in which pronouns were either included or omitted, children answered both general and pronoun-specific comprehension questions. Kameenui and Carnine found that fourth-grade students had greater difficulty answering comprehension questions that required knowledge of anaphora in expository passages than they did answering comprehension questions specific to anaphora in narrative passages.

Numerous studies have examined the effects of instructional design along a range of reading stimuli. Examples of selected studies that examined variables in reading comprehension include:

1. Type of inferential information (i.e., negation, antonym) in contrived narrative texts was varied, and fourth-, fifth-, and sixth-grade students' comprehension was assessed (Carnine, Kameenui, & Woolfson, 1982).

2. Form of contextual clues (i.e., contrast, synonym) and proximity to a target word (i.e., close or separated) were varied in contrived narrative texts, and fourth-, fifth-, and sixth-grade students' comprehension was assessed (Carnine, Kameenui, & Coyle, 1984; Study 1). This study was replicated with students with learning disabilities (Simmons, Kameenui, & Darch, 1988).

3. Fables in which characters' apparent and actual motives were varied (i.e., made textually explicit, textually implicit, or scriptally implicit) were used, and the comprehension and recall of characters' motives by second-, fourth-, and sixth-grade students were assessed (Shannon, Kameenui, & Baumann, 1988).

4. Different forms of vocabulary tasks (i.e., production vs. choice-selection response of word meanings) and two levels of teacher support (i.e., prompted vs. unprompted) were varied, and the performances of students with and without learning disabilities were compared (Simmons & Kameenui, 1990).

5. The proximity of essential and nonessential information in contrived narrative texts was varied, and the metacognitive strategies of elementary-age students with learning disabilities were assessed (Simmons, Kameenui, & Darch, 1988).

In addition to these studies on reading comprehension, Carnine conducted a program of experimental research that examined a range of instruction design variables, such as the range of examples used to teach a concept (Carnine, 1980a; Williams & Carnine, 1981), visual and auditory similarity of examples (Carnine, 1976a, 1980b, 1980c; Granzin & Carnine, 1977), and the most effective schedule for presenting examples (Kryzanowski & Carnine, 1980).

Results of studies in the stimulus variation strand set the stage for the design and development of studies in the instructional intervention strand. By identifying the "stimulus" features that were consequential in a particular design of instruction context, the differential effects of selected instructional interventions to simplify the contexts of learning could be experimentally examined.

Strand 3: Instructional Interventions Research. This strand represents the primary focus of the Direct-Instruction program of applied, instructional research. All the studies in this strand were designed to investigate explicitly the differential effectiveness of a range of instructional procedures and strategies in reading. Early studies were conducted with normal achieving elementary-age children in Grades 1–6. More recently, the focus of this research has been on students with identified learning disabilities.

Instructional intervention research involves experimentally examining the intricate requirements of teaching complex instructional tasks. Studies are designed by: (a) identifying component tasks, responses, or knowledge forms that comprise a complex cognitive operation; (b) selecting and sequencing examples of the component tasks or knowledge forms; (c) constructing and testing procedures for teaching the component tasks or knowledge forms separately; and (d) linking the teaching procedures of the component tasks or knowledge forms into a systematically integrated teaching sequence. *Study by:*

Many studies in the instructional interventions research strand were conceptualized in conjunction with studies in the stimulus variation strand. For example, Carnine, Kameenui, and Coyle (1984; Study 2) based their investigation of the effectiveness of three different instructional strategies for comprehending contextual clues on a descriptive study (Carnine, Kameenui, & Coyle, 1984; Study 1), in which different forms (e.g., contrast, synonym) of contextual information were manipulated and placed in close or separated proximity to a target word in contrived narrative texts. In another example, Dommes, Gersten, and Carnine (1984) designed a study to examine instructional procedures for increasing fourth graders' comprehension of pronoun constructions based on the descriptive study by Kameenui and Carnine (1982). It is important to note that Kameenui and Carnine examined the influence of pronoun constructions on comprehension because an elementary classroom teacher lamented the problems his students were having understanding anaphora in expository texts. Other studies were conceptualized and developed in response to various influences. For example, a study was conceptualized and designed to address a thorny theoretical problem in the research on vocabulary learning and reading comprehension (Kameenui, Carnine, & Freschi, 1982): Is knowledge of word meanings instrumental in comprehension of texts?

Studies that comprise this research strand are extensive in number, focus, and reading content. Examples of selected studies follow:

1. Kameenui, Carnine, and Maggs (1980) examined instructional procedures for teaching students with mild disabilities to simplify and comprehend complex clause constructions.

2. Kameenui, Carnine, and Freschi (1982) investigated five instructional strategies for teaching the meanings of unfamiliar vocabulary words to fourth-, fifth-, and sixth-grade students.

3. Carnine, Stevens, Clement, and Kameenui (1982) selected fourth-, fifth, and sixth-grade students, and compared three instructional strategies for identifying and comprehending actual and apparent motives of characters in fables.

4. Adams, Carnine, and Gersten (1982) compared three conditions—an SQ3R (i.e., Survey, Question, Read, Recite, Review) method, systematic in-

struction, and no instruction—in teaching study skill strategies to fifth-grade students who had adequate decoding skills, but lacked study skill strategies.

5. Patching, Kameenui, Carnine, Gersten, and Colvin (1983) taught fifth-grade students three instructional strategies for applying three critical reading skills; this study was replicated with elementary-age students with learning disabilities (Darch & Kameenui, 1987).

6. Carnine and Kinder (1985) compared a schema-based comprehension strategy with a generative-based comprehension strategy in teaching a full range of students (e.g., remedial, special education, normal achieving) in Grades 4, 5, and 6.

7. Kameenui and colleagues conducted a series of studies on the differential effectiveness of instruction involving graphic organizers for comprehending content-area texts in science with normal achieving students (Darch, Carnine, & Kameenui, 1986; Simmons, Griffin, & Kameenui, 1988) and students with learning disabilities (Griffin, Simmons, & Kameenui, 1991), and in social studies (Griffin, Duncan-Malone, & Kameenui, 1993).

8. Johnson, Gersten, and Carnine (1987) selected high school students with identified learning disabilities and compared two computer-assisted instructional (CAI) vocabulary programs, in which the size of the word sets and the procedures for review of word meanings were varied. Several studies involving CAI have examined experimentally specific design of instruction features (Collins & Carnine, 1988; Collins, Carnine, & Gersten, 1987; Woodward & Carnine, 1988).

9. Several studies have also examined the effectiveness of instructional strategies for teaching beginning reading skills (Kameenui, Stein, Carnine, & Maggs, 1981) and complex rules (Carnine, Kameenui, & Maggs, 1982; Fielding, Kameenui, & Gersten, 1983).

10. Simmons, Kameenui, Dickson, Chard, Gunn, and Baker (1994), in a study of middle-school students' narrative comprehension and composition, found that instructional design strategies including the incremental introduction of story grammar elements, strategic review, scaffolded writing materials, and explicit instruction significantly increased the number and quality of story grammar elements in narrative compositions.

The general results of the studies comparing instructional interventions support the Direct-Instruction approach to teaching reading comprehension and beginning reading. Instructional strategies that incorporated the delivery and design of instruction principles were more likely to enhance students' performance on reading tasks than a range of "control" strategies, which included practice only, the use of traditional basal reading materials strategies, and general, non-Direct-Instruction approaches.

The research on the delivery of instruction reviewed earlier, and the design of instruction, coupled with the results of Project Follow Through, provide

Direct-Instruction reading with one of the most comprehensive and substantial empirical foundations in reading. In fact, Project Follow Through offers a logical and empirical confirmation of the instructional intervention research strand because of its planned comparisons of curriculum programs or instructional approaches, albeit in a longitudinal, large-scale, quasiexperimental design.

THE STATUS AND FUTURE
OF DIRECT-INSTRUCTION READING

Perhaps the strongest impact that research evidence can have is to persuade an individual to change practice. The empirical evidence of Direct-Instruction reading—corroborated through multiple strands of research, with various learners, and across a range of literacy dimensions—has, for all practical purposes, not changed practice. In fact, Direct-Instruction interventions frequently encounter radical resistance (Kameenui, 1988; Shannon, 1988).

Such resistance cannot be explained rationally, given the body of empirical evidence grounded in materials analyses and validated through stimulus variation and instructional intervention research, and longitudinally planned variation educational experiments such as Project Follow Through. More likely, the resistance and lack of transfer from research to practice can be explained by a (a) basic theoretical difference in what constitutes quality reading instruction and literacy experiences, or (b) fundamental misunderstanding of the critical dimensions of Direct-Instruction programs and practices. The debates surrounding reading theory have polarized the reading community (Kameenui, 1993), and are not within the purview of this chapter. Rather, we focused on identifying those underlying dimensions that distinguish Direct Instruction from direct instruction and other instructional inflections "called by that name."

Direct Instruction as Eonomine

As previously discussed, Direct Instruction involves both the design and delivery of information. Plausibly, the strongest weakness of Direct-Instruction reading methods is the active, teacher-directed interaction that separates it from more contemporary child-centered or teacher-facilitated literacy models. It is a weakness because many perceive the signature of Direct Instruction as a briskly paced, teacher-orchestrated delivery and exchange of information. In fact, this feature has become so commonly associated with the term *Direct Instruction* that, for some, it defines "direct instruction." The strength of teacher-directed academic, engaged time is clear (e.g., Rosenshine, 1983; Sindelar, Smith, Harriman, Hale, & Wilson, 1986). Future efforts must continue to clarify and make known the central, but insufficient, role of delivery in Direct-Instruction reading.

Moreover, researchers who contrast Direct Instruction with other instructional interventions must maintain treatment integrity, being careful not to obscure the salient design features by highlighting only the delivery dimensions of Direct Instruction. Specifically, to proclaim that teacher presentation and rote rehearsal of word meanings constitutes Direct Instruction is fundamentally wrong and misleading. To neglect the systemic design of Direct-Instruction programs reflects a basic misconception, if not malevolence, on the part of researchers. If the intent is to compare the potency of Direct-Instruction reading, then fair comparisons must be set up at the outset. Otherwise, interventions or practices that extract selected features of Direct Instruction should be called by another name. Such levels of specification and clarification are essential if educational research is to move toward higher theoretical and procedural grounds—where the variables and conditions responsible for change can be clearly articulated.

Designing Quality: Criteria
for Future Reading Instruction

Accepting that today's children's learning problems are serious and beyond debate (Hodgkinson, 1991; Kameenui, 1993), we argue that quality Direct-Instruction reading has at least three characteristics: (a) efficacy, (b) parsimony, and (c) sustainability. Moreover, we contend that quality instruction is best achieved through attention to instructional design, and specifically to these criteria. First, quality reading instruction must be effective, which means it produces measurably greater achievement than would be otherwise achieved through alternate methods. Second, instruction must be parsimonious to ensure that what is taught is essential and allows students to learn more in less time (Kameenui & Simmons, 1990). Parsimony is essential for students who are behind and face the "tyranny of time" (Kameenui, 1993) in attempting to keep pace with their school-age peers. Third, quality reading instruction must produce maximum, long-term, generalizable effects. In essence, outcomes must be sustainable. This criterion does not suggest that practitioners should endorse the seemingly least costly method. For example, cognitive science research indicates that teaching word recognition via the direct pathway is appealing and, on its face, most efficient. In actuality, the long-term instructional requirements exceed those of the phonological-mediated path (e.g., Carr & Posner, 1992).

Putting Direct Instruction into Practice:
Principles of Quality Instructional Curricula

We believe, and our beliefs are corroborated through empirical evidence, that the design of Direct-Instruction reading programs and methods uniquely meet these criteria. However, efficacy, parsimony, and sustainability are necessary, but not sufficient, criteria for designing quality instructional programs. What is also needed is a strategy that will communicate the design features of Direct-Instruction reading and increase the likelihood of its appearance in the design and development of educational tools. Despite best efforts, the model of dissemination has not informed practitioners, researchers, or the publishers and developers of educational tools. What is needed is a set of critical principles that communicate the essence of Direct Instruction effectively and parsimoniously.

In recent years, researchers have identified critical principles of quality instruction (Dixon, Carnine, & Kameenui, 1992)—principles that transcend specific programs, theory, and practice, and that affect student achievement. These principles serve to expand our thinking beyond the best way to teach to a more comprehensive focus on the design of what we teach. In this final section, we summarize those principles, their relation to the proposed criteria for evaluating reading instruction, and our expectations for putting quality instruction into practice.

Big Ideas. Dixon, Carnine, and Kameenui (1992) defined *big ideas* as concepts or principles within a content area that have the greatest potential for enabling students to apply what they learn in varied situations. For example, in the areas of reading comprehension and written composition, text structure represents a consummate example of a big idea. Sometimes as many as 25 different text structures are "covered" in a single level of a language arts program, including summary, story, theme, fable newspaper reports, invitations, and persuasive writing (Dixon et al., 1992). Therefore, to increase efficacy, parsimony, and sustainability, it is important to identify those text structures that provide the greatest application. Narrative text structure, or story grammar elements, represents a generalizable big idea.

Integration. A second curriculum design principle is based on the concept of integration. In a comprehensive examination of research, including studies with large and small numbers of subjects and subject ages ranging from preschool through college, Tierney and Shanahan (1991) found consistent support for integrated reading and writing instruction. Specifically, they concluded that integrating reading and writing appears to engage learners in a greater variety of reasoning operations than when writing or reading is taught separately, or when students perform a variety of other tasks in conjunction with their reading, thus addressing the efficacy criterion. The NCITE investigated (Simmons et al., 1993) the efficacy, parsimony, and sustainability of integrated reading and writing. In the integrated curriculum, students first learn a text structure (big idea) through reading stories with predictable story grammar elements. They next summarize stories using the text structure as an organizing framework. Following explicitly designed and delivered instruction, students then generate their own stories using the familiar text structure.

Strategy. The third curriculum design principle that frames Direct-Instruction curricula is the use of "medium-range" strategies. A *strategy* is defined as an organized set of actions designed to accomplish a task or activity. To be optimally effective, strategies must be sufficiently broad, but not overly narrow or prescriptive (Dixon et al., 1992). Well-designed strategies can be particularly cost-efficient: Once learned, the component rules and processes can be applied to novel instances. Such instructional routines minimize instructional time and optimize opportunities for independent learning.

Scaffolds. The fourth curriculum design principle, scaffolded instruction, is particularly critical for students who fail to keep pace with traditionally sequenced and structured curricula, thus addressing the parsimony criterion. The purpose of scaffolding is to provide the learner with support during the developmental phases of learning. Once structures are firm and the learner can apply strategies and big ideas independently, these external supports are gradually removed. Scaffolds help bridge the gap between a learner's current ability and the intended goal. Consequently, scaffolding varies as a function of ability.

For example, in basal and computer-based education programs, students are frequently introduced to new material through some form of demonstration/tutorial/model, and are then expected to apply the skills independently. For many students, such rapid jumps to independence are overwhelming and unrealistic (Dixon et al., 1992). Such practice not only violates the efficacy criterion because little has been learned, but further compromises the economy criterion because necessary reteaching reduces available time for more advanced instruction.

Review. The fifth and final curriculum design principle focuses on review. Unfortunately, many curricular materials lack well-designed review (Carnine, 1992), which poses particular hazards for students with learning problems. Research suggests that effective review is (a) distributed over time, (b) cumulative, and (c) varied (Dixon et al., 1992). Specifically, review must be distributed over time, with sufficient opportunities to practice previously taught skills and strategies. Review must be cumulative, which is achieved by integrating skills and strategies, and providing review opportunities over an extended time. Although this sequence may appear costly in terms of instructional time, it is economic because it prevents extensive reteaching. Finally, review must be varied (Dixon et al., 1992). As skills and strategies for improving reading comprehension and writing are introduced, a firming cycle (Kameenui & Simmons, 1990) that offers numerous opportunities for students to practice newly taught skills and strategies should be utilized.

CONCLUSION

Too many students fail to acquire the reading skills and literacy knowledge that will allow them to function effectively in and out of schools (Hodgkinson, 1991). Moreover, empirically validated interventions and programs to address today's learners' reading difficulties do not readily or systematically find their way into classrooms.

Direct-Instruction researchers, through almost three decades of systematic descriptive and experimental research, have identified principles to guide and expand future applications of Direct Instruction. The research described in this chapter offers a legacy of evidence about reading instruction that works. This legacy, by any etymological or empirical standard, is neither contronym nor eonomine. As Humpty Dumpty noted in his rejoinder to Alice's assertion that words can be made to mean many different things, "The question is, which is to be master—that's all."

REFERENCES

Adams, A., Carnine, D., & Gersten, R. (1982). Instructional strategies for studying content area texts in the intermediate grades. *Reading Research Quarterly, 17*(1), 27–55.

Adams, M. (1990). *Beginning to read: Thinking and learning about print.* Cambridge, MA: MIT Press.

Anderson, R. C., & Nagy, W. E. (1991). Word meanings. In R. Barr, M. L. Kamil, P. Mosenthal, & P. D. Pearson (Eds.), *Handbook of reading research* (Vol. 2, pp. 690–724). New York: Longman.

Armbruster, B. B., & Gudbrandsen, B. (1986). Reading comprehension instruction in social studies programs. *Reading Research Quarterly, 21*(1), 36–48.

Baker, S., Simmons, D. C., Kameenui, E. J., & Carnine, D. (1995). *General education teacher perceptions of educational tools in elementary grades.* Manuscript submitted for publication.

Baumann, J. F. (1983). A generic comprehension instructional strategy. *Reading World, 23,* 284–294.

Baumann, J. F. (1984, December). *The systematic, intensive instruction of reading comprehension skills.* Paper presented at the annual meeting of the National Reading Conference, St. Petersburg, FL.

Baumann, J. F. (1988). Teaching third-grade students to comprehend anaphoric relationships: The application of a direct instruction model. *Reading Research Quarterly, 21*(1), 70–90.

Baumann, J. F., & Kameenui, E. J. (1991). Vocabulary instruction: Ode to Voltaire. In J. Flood, J. Jensen, D. Lapp, & J. R. Squire (Eds.), *Handbook of research on teaching the English language arts* (pp. 604–632). New York: Macmillan.

Becker, W. C. (1977). Teaching reading and language to the disadvantaged—What we have learned from field research. *Harvard Educational Review, 47,* 518–543.

Becker, W. C., & Carnine, D. W. (1980). Direct instruction: An effective approach to educational intervention with the disadvantaged and low performers. In B. B. Lahey & A. E. Kazdin (Eds.), *Advances in clinical and child psychology* (Vol. 3, pp. 429–473). New York: Plenum.

Becker, W. C., & Carnine, D. W. (1981). Direct instruction: A behavior theory model for comprehensive educational intervention with the disadvantages. In S. Bijou (Ed.), *Contributions of behavior modification in education* (pp. 1–106). Hillsdale, NJ: Lawrence Erlbaum Associates.

Becker, W. C., Engelmann, S., Carnine, D. W., & Rhine, R. (1981). The Direct Instruction model. In R. Rhine (Ed.), *Encouraging change in America's schools: A decade of experimentation* (pp. 95–154). New York: Academic Press.

Berliner, D. (1984). The half-full glass: A review of research on teaching. In P. Hosford (Ed.), *Using what we know about teaching* (pp. 61–77). Alexandria, VA: Association for Supervision and Curriculum Development.

Brophy, J. E., & Evertson, C. N. (1976). *Learning from teaching*. Boston: Allyn & Bacon.

Bruner, J. S. (1966). *Toward a theory of instruction*. Cambridge, MA: Belknap Press of Harvard University.

Bryson, B. (1990). *The mother tongue: English and how it got that way*. New York: Morrow.

Campbell, J. (1982). *Grammatical man: Information entropy, language, and life*. New York: Simon & Schuster.

Carnine, D. W. (1979). Direct instruction: A successful system for educationally high-risk children. *Journal of Curriculum Studies, 11*(1), 29–45.

Carnine, D. W., & Kameenui, E. J. (1993, Winter). NCITE's mission: To advance the quality of technology, media, and materials for students with diverse learning needs. *The NCITE Network*, p. 1.

Carnine, D. W., & Kinder, D. (1985). Teaching low-performing students to apply generative and schema strategies to narrative and expository material. *Remedial and Special Education, 6*(1), 20–30.

Carnine, D. W. (1976a). Similar sound separation and cumulative introduction in learning letter-sound correspondences. *Journal of Educational Research, 69,* 368–372.

Carnine, D. W. (1976b). *Conditions under which children learn the relevant attribute of negative instances rather than the essential characteristic of positive instances.* Unpublished manuscript, Follow Through Project, University of Oregon.

Carnine, D. W. (1980a). Relationships between stimulus variation and the formation of misconceptions. *Journal of Educational Research, 74,* 106–110.

Carnine, D. W. (1980b). Three procedures for presenting minimally different positive and negative instances. *Journal of Educational Psychology, 72,* 452–456.

Carnine, D. W. (1980c). Two-letter discrimination sequences: High-confusion alternatives versus low-confusion alternatives first. *Journal of Reading Behavior, 12*(1), 41–47.

Carnine, D. W. (1981). Reducing training problems associated with visually and auditorily similar correspondences. *Journal of Learning Disabilities, 14,* 276–279.

Carnine, D. W. (1992). Introduction. In D. Carnine & E. J. Kameenui (Eds.), *Higher order thinking: Designing curriculum for mainstreamed students* (pp. 1–22). Austin, TX: Pro-Ed.

Carnine, D. W., & Fink, W. T. (1978). Increasing the rate of presentation and use of signals in elementary classroom teachers. *Journal of Applied Behavior Analysis, 11*(1), 35–46.

Carnine, D. W., Kameenui, E. J., & Coyle, G. (1984). Utilization of contextual information in determining the meaning of unfamiliar words. *Reading Research Quarterly, 19,* 188–204.

Carnine, D. W., Kameenui, E. J., & Maggs, A. (1982). Components of analytic assistance: Statement saying, concept training and strategy training. *Journal of Educational Research, 75,* 374–377.

Carnine, D. W., Kameenui, E. J., & Woolfson, N. (1982). Training textual dimensions related to text-based inferences. *Journal of Reading Behavior, 14,* 335–340.

Carnine, D. W., Silbert, J., & Kameenui, E. J. (1990). *Direct instruction reading.* (2nd ed.). Columbus, OH: Merrill.

Carnine, D. W., Stevens, C., Clement, J., & Kameenui, E. J. (1982). Effects of facilitative questions and practice on intermediate students' understanding of character motives. *Journal of Reading Behavior, 14,* 179–190.

Carr, T. H., & Posner, M. I. (1992). *The impact of learning to read on the functional anatomy of language processing* (Tech. Rep. No. 92-1). Eugene: University of Oregon, Institute of Cognitive & Decision Sciences.

Carroll, L. (1990). *More annotated Alice.* New York: Random House.

Collins, M., & Carnine, D. (1988). Evaluating the field test revision process by comparing two versions of a reasoning skills CAI program. *Journal of Learning Disabilities, 21,* 375–379.

Collins, M., Carnine, D. W., & Gersten, R. (1987). Elaborated corrective feedback and the acquisition of reasoning skills: A study of computer-assisted instruction. *Exceptional Children, 54,* 254–262.

Cowart, J. B., Carnine, D. W., & Becker, W. C. (1976). The effects of signals on child behaviors during Distar instruction. In W. C. Becker & S. E. Engelmann (Eds.), *Analysis of achievement data on six cohorts of low-income children from 20 school districts in the University of Oregon Direct Instruction Follow Through model* (Tech. Rep. No. 76-1, Appendix A). Eugene: University of Oregon Press.

Darch, C., Carnine, D. W., & Kameenui, E. (1986). The role of visual displays and social structure in content-area instruction. *Journal of Reading Behavior, 18,* 275–295.

Darch, C., & Gersten, R. (1986). Direction-setting activities in reading comprehension: A comparison of two approaches. *Learning Disabilities Quarterly, 9,* 235–243.

Darch, C., & Kameenui, E. J. (1987). Teaching critical reading skills to learning disabled children. *Learning Disabilities Quarterly, 10,* 82–92.

Dixon, R., Carnine, D. W., & Kameenui, E. J. (1992). Math curriculum guidelines for diverse learners. *Curriculum/Technology Quarterly, 3*(3), 1–3.

Dommes, P., Gersten, R., & Carnine, D. W. (1984). Instructional procedures for increasing skill-deficient fourth-graders' comprehension of syntactic structures. *Educational Psychology, 4,* 155–165.

Duffy, G. G., & Roehler, L. F. (1982). Direct instruction of comprehension: What does it really mean? *Reading Horizons, 23*(1), 35–40.

Duncan-Malone, L., & Kameenui, E. J. (1987). *Social studies text analysis.* Unpublished manuscript.

Durkin, D. (1981). Reading comprehension instruction in five basal reader series. *Reading Research Quarterly, 26,* 515–544.

Engelmann, S. (1969). *Preventing failure in the primary grades.* Chicago: Science Research Associates.

Engelmann, S., & Carnine, D. W. (1982). *Theory of instruction: Principles and applications.* New York: Irvington.

Engelmann, S., & Engelmann, T. (1966). *Give your child a superior mind.* New York: Simon & Schuster.

Fielding, G. D., Kameenui, E. J., & Gersten, R. (1983). A comparison of an inquiry and a direct instruction approach to teaching legal concepts and applications to secondary school students. *Journal of Educational Research, 76,* 287–293.

Fink, W. T., & Carnine, D. W. (1975). Control of arithmetic errors using informational feedback and graphing. *Journal of Applied Behavior Analysis, 8,* 461.

Fink, W. T., & Sandall, S. R. (1978). One-to-one vs. group academic instruction with handicapped and nonhandicapped preschool children. *Mental Retardation, 16,* 236–240.

Gagne, R. M. (1965). *The conditions of learning and theory of instruction.* New York: Holt, Rinehart & Winston.

Gagne, R. M. (1985). *The conditions of learning and theory of instruction* (4th ed.). New York: Holt, Rinehart & Winston.

Gersten, R., Becker, W. C., Heiry, T. J., & White, W. A. (1984). Entry IQ and yearly growth of children in Direct Instruction programs: A longitudinal study of low SES children. *Educational Evaluation and Policy Analysis, 6,* 109–121.

Gersten, R., Carnine, D. W., & Williams, P. (1982). Measuring implementation of a structured educational model in an urban school district: An observational approach. *Educational Evaluation and Policy Analysis, 4,* 67–79.

Granzin, A. C., & Carnine, D. (1977). Child performance on discrimination tasks: Effects of amount of stimulus variation. *Journal of Experimental Child Psychology, 24,* 332–342.

Griffin, C. C., Duncan-Malone, L., & Kameenui, E. J. (1993). *Effects of graphic organizer instruction on fifth grade students' comprehension, recall, and transfer of social studies texts.* Manuscript submitted for publication.

Griffin, C. C., Simmons, D. C., & Kameenui, E. J. (1991). Investigating the effectiveness of graphic organizer instruction on the comprehension and recall of science content by students with learning disabilities. *The Journal of Reading, Writing, and Learning Disabilities International, 7,* 355–376.

Guthrie, J. T. (1977). Research views—Follow Through: A compensatory education experiment. *Reading Teacher, 3,* 240–244.

Hodgkinson, H. (1991). Reform versus reality. *Phi Delta Kappan, 73,* 9–16.

House, E. R., Glass, G. V., McLean, L. D., & Walker, D. F. (1978). No simple answer: Critique of the "Follow Through" evaluation. *Harvard Educational Review, 28,* 128–160.

Jitendra, A., & Kameenui, E. J. (1988). A design of instruction analysis of concept teaching in five basal language programs: Violations from the bottom up. *Journal of Special Education, 22,* 199–219.

Johnson, G., Gersten, R., & Carnine, D. (1987). Effects of instructional design variables on vocabulary acquisition of LD students: A study of computer-assisted instruction. *Journal of Learning Disabilities, 20,* 206–213.

Kameenui, E. J. (1985). Direct instruction of reading comprehension: Beyond teacher performance variables to the design-of-instruction. In J. Niles & R. Lalik (Eds.), *Thirty-fourth yearbook of the National Reading Conference, issues in literacy: A research perspective* (pp. 257–262). Rochester, NY: National Reading Conference.

Kameenui, E. J. (1988). Direct instruction and the Great Twitch: Why DI or di is not the issue. In J. R. Readence & S. Baldwin (Eds.), *Dialogues in literacy research: Thirty-seventh yearbook of the National Reading Conference* (pp. 39–45). Chicago, IL: National Reading Conference.

Kameenui, E. J. (1992). Toward a scientific pedagogy: A sameness in the message. In D. W. Carnine & E. J. Kameenui (Eds.), *Higher order thinking: Designing curriculum for all students* (pp. 247–267). Austin, TX: PRO-ED.

Kameenui, E. J. (1993). Diverse learners and the tyranny of time: Don't fix blame; fix the leaky roof. *The Reading Teacher, 46,* 376–383.

Kameenui, E., & Carnine, D. W. (1982). An investigation of fourth-graders' comprehension of pronoun constructions in ecologically valid texts. *Reading Research Quarterly, 17,* 556–580.

Kameenui, E. J., Carnine, D. W., & Freschi, R. (1982). Effects of text construction and instructional procedures for teaching word meanings on comprehension of contrived passages. *Reading Research Quarterly, 17,* 367–388.

Kameenui, E. J., Carnine, D. W., & Maggs, A. (1980). Instructional procedures for teaching reversible passive-voice and clause constructions to three mildly handicapped children. *The Exceptional Child, 27*(1), 27–40.

Kameenui, E. J., & Griffin, C. (1989). The national crisis in verbal problem solving in mathematics: A proposal for examining the role of basal mathematics programs. *Elementary School Journal, 89,* 575–593.

Kameenui, E. J., & Shannon, P. (1988). Point/counterpoint: Direct instruction reconsidered. In J. R. Readence & S. Baldwin (Eds.), *Dialogues in literacy research: Thirty-seventh yearbook of the National Reading Conference* (pp. 35–37). Chicago, IL: National Reading Conference.

Kameenui, E. J., & Simmons, D. C. (1990). *Designing instructional strategies: The prevention of academic learning problems.* Columbus, OH: Merrill.

Kameenui, E., Stein, M., Carnine, D., & Maggs, A. (1981). Primary level word-attack skills based on isolated word discrimination list and rule application training. *Reading Education, 6*(2), 46–55.

Kryzanowski, J., & Carnine, D. W. (1980). Effects of massed versus spaced formats in teaching sound/symbol correspondences to young children. *Journal of Reading Behavior, 12,* 225–230.

Markle, S. M., & Tiemann, P. W. (1969). *Really understanding concepts: Or in frumious pursuit of the jabberwock.* Champaign, IL: Stipes.

McConkie, G. W., & Rayner, K. (1976). Asymmetry of the perceptual span in reading. *Bulletin of the Psychonomic Society, 8,* 365–368.

Moore, J. (1986). Direct Instruction: A model of instructional design. *Educational Psychology, 6,* 201–229.

Patching, W., Kameenui, E., Carnine, D. W., Gersten, R., & Colvin, G. (1983). Direct instruction in critical reading skills. *Reading Research Quarterly, 18,* 406–418.

Pearson, D. P. (1984, December). *Direct explicit teaching of reading comprehension.* Paper presented at the annual meeting of the National Reading Conference, St. Petersburg, FL.

Roehler, L., & Duffy, G. (1982). Matching direct instruction to reading outcomes. *Language Arts, 59,* 476–480.

Roehler, L., & Duffy, G. (1984). Direct explanation of comprehension processes. In G. G. Duffy, L. R. Roehler, & J. Mason (Eds.), *Comprehension instruction: Perspectives and suggestions* (pp. 265–280). New York: Longman.

Rosenshine, B. (1976). Classroom instruction. In N. L. Gage (Ed.), *The psychology of teaching methods: The 75th yearbook of the National Society for the Study of Education, Part I* (pp. 335–371). Chicago: University of Chicago Press.

Rosenshine, B. V. (1983). Teaching functions in instructional programs. *Elementary School Journal, 83,* 335–351.

Shannon, P. (1988). Can we directly instruct students to be independent in reading? In J. R. Readence & S. Baldwin (Eds.), *Dialogues in literacy research: Thirty-seventh yearbook of the National Reading Conference* (pp. 36–39). Chicago, IL: National Reading Conference.

Shannon, P., Kameenui, E. J., & Baumann, J. (1988). An investigation of children's ability to comprehend character motives. *American Educational Research Journal, 25,* 441–462.

Simmons, D. C., Chard, D., Dickson, S., Gunn, B., Landsom, D., & Kameenui, E. J. (1993). Integrating reading comprehension and writing: Applications of curriculum design principles. In G. Tindal & G. Sugai (Eds.), *Oregon Conference Monograph* (pp. 1–10). Eugene: University of Oregon Press.

Simmons, D., Gleason, M., Smith, S., Chard, D., Gunn, B., Sprick, M., Thomas, C., Baker, S., Peineido, R., & Placencia-Peineido, J., & Kameenui, E. J. (1995). *Phonological awareness: Is there evidence of translation of research into practice?* Manuscript submitted for publication.

Simmons, D. C., Griffin, C. C., & Kameenui, E. J. (1988). Effects of teacher-constructed pre- and post-graphic organizer instruction on sixth-grade science students' comprehension and recall. *Journal of Educational Research, 82*(1), 15–21.

Simmons, D. C., & Kameenui, E. J. (1990). The effect of task alternatives on vocabulary knowledge: A comparison of students with learning disabilities and students of normal achievement. *Journal of Learning Disabilities, 23,* 291–297.

Simmons, D., & Kameenui, E. J. (1993, April). *A curriculum-based examination of the adequacy of instruction for students with reading disabilities.* Paper presented at the annual meeting of the American Educational Research Association, Atlanta, GA.

Simmons, D. C., Kameenui, E. J., & Darch, C. (1988). The effect of textual proximity on fourth- and fifth-grade LD students' metacognitive awareness and strategic comprehension behavior. *Learning Disabilities Quarterly, 11,* 380–395.

Simmons, D., Kameenui, E. J., Dickson, S., Chard, D., Gunn, B., & Baker, S. (1994). Integrating narrative reading and writing instruction for all learners. *Yearbook of the National Reading Council, 43,* 572–582.

Sindelar, P. T., Smith, M. A., Harriman, N. E., Hale, R. L., & Wilson, R. J. (1986). Teacher effectiveness in special education programs. *Journal of Special Education, 20,* 195–207.

Smith, P. L., & Ragan, T. J. (1993). *Instructional design.* New York: Macmillan.

Stebbins, L. B., St. Pierre, R. G., Proper, E. C., Anderson, R. B., & Cerva, T. R. (1977). *Education as experimentation: A planned variation model (Vols. 4A, 4C). An evaluation of Follow Through.* Cambridge, MA: Abt.

Tarver, S. G. (1992). Direct Instruction. In W. Stainback & S. Stainback (Eds.), *Controversial issues confronting special education: Divergent perspectives* (pp. 141–152). Boston: Allyn & Bacon.

Tennyson, R., & Christensen, D. L. (1986, April). *Memory theory and design of intelligent learning systems.* Paper presented at the annual meeting of the American Educational Research Association, San Francisco, CA.

Tennyson, R. D., & Cochiarella, M. J. (1986). An empirically based instructional design theory for teaching concepts. *Review of Educational Research, 56,* 40–71.

Tennyson, R. D., & Park, S. I. (1984). Process learning time as an adaptive design variable in concept learning using computer-based instruction. *Journal of Educational Psychology, 76,* 452–465.

Tierney, R. J., & Shanahan, T. (1991). Research on the reading-writing relationships: Interactions, actions, and outcomes. In R. Barr, M. Kamil, P. B. Mosenthal, & P. D. Pearson (Eds.), *Handbook of reading research* (Vol. 2, pp. 246–280). New York: Longman.

Wagner, R., & Torgesen, J. (1987). The nature of phonological processing and its causal role in the acquisition of reading skills. *Psychological Bulletin, 101,* 192–212.

Williams, P. B., & Carnine, D. (1981). Relationship between range of examples and of instruction and attention in concept attainment. *Journal of Educational Research, 74,* 144–148.

Woodward, J. P., & Carnine, D. W. (1988). Antecedent knowledge and intelligent computer assisted instruction. *Journal of Learning Disabilities, 21,* 131–139.

Zahorik, J. A., & Kritek, W. J. (1983, April). *Using direct instruction.* Paper presented at the annual meeting of the American Educational Research Association, Montreal, Canada.

CHAPTER FOUR

Cognitive Strategy Instruction in Reading

Barak Rosenshine
Carla Meister
University of Illinois at Urbana

This article is about the instructional procedures that have been developed since 1980 to help teach cognitive strategies to students. Cognitive strategies are guiding procedures that students can use to help them complete less-structured tasks such as those in reading comprehension and writing.

It is possible to place academic tasks (Doyle, 1983) on a continuum from well-structured to less structured tasks. Well-structured tasks are tasks that can be broken down into a fixed sequence of steps that consistently lead to the same goal. There is a specific, predictable algorithm that can be followed, one that enables students to obtain the same results each time they perform the algorithmic operations. These well-structured tasks are taught by teaching each step of the algorithm to students. The research on teaching effects (Brophy & Good, 1986; Rosenshine & Stevens, 1986) is best seen as research that has helped us learn how to teach skills to students that they can use to complete well-structured tasks.

In contrast, reading comprehension, writing, and study skills are examples of less-structured tasks. These tasks cannot be broken down into a fixed sequence of subtasks that consistently and unfailingly lead to the goal. Because these tasks are less-structured and difficult, they have also been called higher-level tasks. These types of tasks do not have the fixed sequence that is part of well-structured tasks. One cannot develop algorithms that students can use to complete these tasks.

Until the late 1970s, students were seldom provided with any help in completing less-structured tasks. In a classic observational study of reading comprehension instruction, Durkin (1979) noted that of the 4,469 minutes she observed in reading instruction in grade 4, only 20 minutes were spent in comprehension instruction by the teacher. Durkin noted that teachers spent almost all of the instructional time asking students questions, but they spent little time teaching students *comprehension strategies* they could use to answer the questions. Duffy, Lanier, and Roehler (1980) noted a similar lack of comprehension instruction in elementary classrooms. They wrote that:

> There is little evidence of instruction of any kind. Teachers spend most of their time assigning activities, monitoring to be sure the pupils are on task, directing recitation sessions to assess how well children are doing and providing corrective feedback in response to pupil errors. Seldom does one observe teaching in which a teacher presents a skill, a strategy, or a process to pupils, shows them how to do it, provides assistance as they initiate attempts to perform the task and assures that they can be successful. (Duffy et al., 1980, p. 4)

As a result of these astonishing findings, and as a result of emerging research on cognition and information processing, investigators began to develop and validate procedures that students might use to aid their reading comprehension. In the field of reading, the procedures have consisted of teaching students specific cognitive strategies, that students could use to help perform higher-level operations in reading. This paper is about those cognitive strategies and how they might be taught to students.

Cognitive strategies are heuristics. A cognitive strategy is not a direct procedure; it is not an algorithm to be precisely followed. Rather, a cognitive strategy is a heuristic that serves to support or facilitate the learner as she or he develops internal procedures that enable them to perform the higher level operations. Teaching students to generate questions about their reading is an example of a cognitive strategy. Generating questions does not directly lead, in a step-by-step manner to comprehension. Rather, in the process of generating questions, students need to search the text and combine information, and these processes serve to help students comprehend what they read.

The distinction between using providing students with algorithms to help them complete well-structured tasks and providing them with cognitive strategies to help them complete less-structured tasks is illustrated in Fig. 4.1. The first line illustrates the procedures for helping students learn to complete well-structured tasks such as map reading. The teacher teaches students an algorithm, and the students then apply the algorithm to complete well-structured tasks. The complete lines connecting the boxes for teaching well-structured tasks indicates that, in those cases, the teacher teaches the algorithmic directly to the student and then the student directly uses the algorithm to complete the well-structured task.

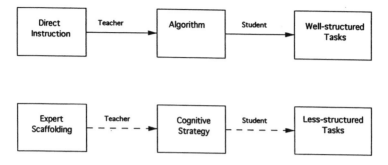

FIG. 4.1. Procedures for teaching well-structured and less-structured tasks. The complete lines indicate that the teacher teaches the algorithm directly to the student and the student directly applies the algorithm to complete the well-structured task. The dashed lines indicate that the teacher uses scaffolds to support the student as the student learns the cognitive strategy, and then the cognitive strategy supports the student as the student attempts to complete the less-structured task.

The second line illustrates the procedures for helping students learn to complete less-structured tasks such as reading comprehension. The teacher teaches students a cognitive strategy and the students then apply the cognitive strategy to help them complete the less-structured task. The dashed lines connecting the boxes indicate that the teacher and student are less direct when they work on less-structured tasks. Here, the teacher uses scaffolds to support the student as the student learns the cognitive strategy, and then the cognitive strategy supports the student as the student attempts to complete the less-structured task.

Although it is convenient to talk of well-structured and less-structured tasks, many tasks are a mixture of well-structured and less-structured parts. Long division, for example, is primarily a well-structured task, but the step of estimating the divisor is less-structured than the other steps. Many areas of grammar are well-structured tasks, but some areas, such decisions on when to use a comma, are less-structured. Although textbook examples of restrictive and nonrestrictive clauses are quite clear, in practice there are many examples where the rules cannot be confidently applied. We would recommend that students be taught cognitive strategies to use for the less-structured parts of well-structured tasks.

Cognitive strategies have been developed and taught in a number of subject areas. These include reading (Paris, Wixson, & Palincsar, 1986; Pearson & Dole, 1987; Pressley, Burkell, Cariglia-Bull, Lysynchuk, McGoldrick, Schneider, Symons, & Woloshyn, 1990), retention of expository text (Alvermann, 1991; Dansereau, Collins, McDonald, Halley, Garland, Diekkoff, & Evans, 1979), and writing (Englert & Raphael, 1989; Scadramalia, Bereiter, & Steinbach, 1985). Students have been taught specific cognitive strategies to assist them in mathematics problem-solving (Schoenfeld, 1985), and physics problem-solving (Larkin & Reif, 1976).

The teaching of cognitive strategies is an example of working in a child's zone of proximal development. Vygotsky (1978) observed that a child has two developmental levels. One is the "actual developmental level," the level at which children can independently deal with tasks, and the other is the "level of potential development," the level at which a child can solve a problem with the assistance of a teacher or in collaboration with other children. The zone of proximal development is the distance between the level of potential development and the actual developmental level of the child (Vygotsky, 1978). The concept of a zone of proximal development means that one does not have to wait until a child is "developmentally ready" before beginning instruction, rather, Vygotsky (1962) emphasized the role of instruction in fostering development:

> In the child's development, imitation and instruction play a major role. . . . Therefore, the only good kind of instruction is that which marches ahead of development and leads it. (p. 104)

Although Vygotsky did not provide much information on how one might instruct children in their zone of proximal development (Palincsar, David, Winn, Snyder, & Stevens, 1989) other investigators have developed instructional procedures. Those procedures are the focus of this chapter.

TEACHING COGNITIVE STRATEGIES

How does one teach cognitive strategies? As noted, one cannot develop an algorithm to teach cognitive strategies. Rather, cognitive strategies have been taught by providing students with scaffolds to help them learn the strategies. *Scaffolds* are forms of support provided by the teacher (or another student) to help students bridge the gap between their current abilities and the intended goal (Palincsar & Brown, 1984; Paris, Wixson, & Palincsar, 1986; Tobias, 1982; Wood, Bruner, & Ross, 1976). "The metaphor of a scaffold captures the idea of an adjustable and temporary support that can be removed when no longer necessary" (Brown & Palincsar, 1989, p. 411).

A scaffold allows the learners "to participate at an ever-increasing level of competence" (Palincsar & Brown, 1984, p. 122). Scaffolding procedures reduce the complexities of problems, breaking them down into manageable chunks that the child has a real chance of solving (Bickhard, 1992). Examples of teachers' scaffolds include (a) providing simplified problems, (b) modeling of the procedures, (c) and thinking aloud as they solve the problem. Scaffolds may also be tools, such as cue cards or checklists. Scaffolds are gradually withdrawn or faded as learners become more independent, although students may continue to rely on scaffolds or periodically request them when they encounter particularly difficult problems.

The first use of scaffolding was by Wood, Bruner, and Ross (1976). They used the term to refer to the instructional process, whereby an adult controls "those elements of the task that are initially beyond the learner's capacity, thus permitting the learner to concentrate upon and complete only those elements that are within his range of competence" (Wood et al., 1976, p. 90). Several scaffolding procedures identified by Wood et al. include (a) reducing the complexity of the task to manageable limits, (b) maintaining student interest, marking critical features, and (c) demonstrating solutions when the learner can recognize them.

Although scaffolds can be applied to the teaching of all skills, they are particularly useful, and often indispensable, for teaching higher-level cognitive strategies, where many of the steps or procedures necessary to carry out these strategies cannot be specified. Instead of providing explicit steps, one supports, or scaffolds, the students as they learn the skill. As illustrated in Fig. 4.1, one cannot teach less-structured tasks as algorithms. Instead, one uses scaffolds to support the learner while the learner is creating internal structures.

This article is about the variety of instructional procedures and scaffolds that have been developed to help students to learn and apply cognitive strategies. In order to develop this knowledge, we first located 50 intervention studies in which cognitive strategies were taught to students in an effort to improve their reading comprehension. At the end of the study, the comprehension scores of students in the experimental group was compared with the scores of students in the experimental group. We studied the methods section of these studies, and abstracted from them the instructional procedures and scaffolds that were used to teach the cognitive strategy. We grouped the scaffolds and instruction found in these studies into seven instructional procedures as shown in Table 4.1.

Develop and Present a Procedural Prompt

In the studies we reviewed, the first step in teaching a cognitive strategy was the development of a procedural prompt. Procedural prompts are scaffolds that are specific to the cognitive strategy. These prompts are concrete references on which students can rely for support as they learn to apply the cognitive strategy. Two of the main cognitive strategies in reading comprehension have been teaching students to generate questions and teaching students to summarize passages. A number of specific procedural prompts that were used in intervention studies to help students learn these two cognitive strategies, and these prompts are described in detail here. They are provided in order to (a) illustrate specific procedural prompts that teach-

TABLE 4.1
Components for Teaching Higher-Order Cognitive Strategies

1. Develop and present a procedural prompt.
2. Demonstrate the use of the prompt through modeling and thinking aloud.
   a. Model the process of using the procedural prompt.
   b. Think aloud as choices are being made.
3. Guide students through initial practice using techniques that reduce the difficulty of the task.
   a) Start with simplified material and gradually increase the complexity of the task.
   b) Complete part of the task for the students.
   c) Provide cue cards.
   d) Present the new material in small steps.
   e) Anticipate student errors and difficult areas.
4. Provide for student practice.
   a) Provide teacher-led practice.
   b) Engage in reciprocal teaching.
   c) Have students work in small groups.
5. Provide for feedback and self-checking.
   a) Offer teacher-led feedback.
   b) Provide checklists.
   c) Provide models of expert work.
   d) Suggest fix-up strategies.
6. Increase the students' responsibility as they master the strategy.
   a) Diminish prompts and models.
   b) Gradually increase the complexity and difficulty of the material.
   c) Diminish the support provided to students.
   d) Provide for consolidation activities.
   e) Check for student mastery.
7. Provide independent practice with new examples.
   a) Provide extensive practice.
   b) Facilitate application to new examples.
   Caution: This list offers only suggestions for consideration when teaching cognitive strategies. It is not intended to be used as a tool for evaluation.

ers might use in their own instruction and (b) to illustrate the concept of procedural prompts by providing a number of examples.

Three different procedural prompts have been used in intervention studies to help students learn the cognitive strategy of generating questions. In some studies, the investigators gave the students "question words" (e.g. who, what, when, where, why, and how) and taught them to use these words as prompts. These six simple question words were the procedural prompt.

Another set of procedural prompts comes from a study by King (1990), where students were provided with and taught to use a list of question stems that served to help the students form questions about a particular passage:

How are _____ and _____ alike?
What is the main idea of _____?
What do you think would happen if _____?

What are the strengths and weakness of _____ ?
In what way is _____ related to _____ ?
How does _____ affect ____?
Compare _____ and _____ with regard to _____.
What do you think causes _____?
How does _____ tie in with what we have learned before?
Which one is the best _____ and why?
What are some possible solutions for the problem of ____?
Do you agree or disagree with this statement: _____? Support your answer.
What do I (you) still not understand about . . . ? (p. 667).

Procedural prompts have also been developed to help students generate questions about narrative text. One approach has been to provide students with questioning prompts that focus on a story's "grammar," namely, questions such as:

What is the setting?
Who are the main characters?
What problem did the main character face?
What attempts were made to resolve the problem?
How was the problem finally resolved?
What is the theme of the story?

Each of the three procedural prompts described above was used in at least three studies that obtained significant results.

Two different procedural prompts have also been developed to help teach students the cognitive strategy of summarizing. Baumann (1984) and Taylor (1985) used the following prompt:

1. Identify the topic.
2. Write two or three words that reflect the topic.
3. Use these words as a prompt to help figure out the main idea of the paragraph.
4. Select two details that elaborate on the main idea and are important to remember.
5. Write two or three sentences that best incorporate these important ideas.

Palincsar (1987) used a different procedural prompt for teaching summarizing:

Step 1: Identify the topic sentence.
Step 2: If there is not a topic sentence, identify the topic and the most important information about that topic.

Rule 1: Leave out unimportant information.
Rule 2: Give steps or lists a title.
Rule 3: Cross out information that is redundant/repeated.

Prompts used in both the question-generation and the summarization strategies were developed so they could be applied flexibly to most expository text, particularly in the areas of social studies and science.

Other investigators developed specific procedural prompts to help students improve their writing. For example, Englert, Raphael, Anderson, Anthony, and Stevens (1991) provided "Plan Sheets" that cued students to consider their audience (e.g., "Who am I writing for?", "Why am I writing this?"), and "Organize Sheets" that helped students sort their ideas into categories (e.g., "How can I group these ideas?", "What is being explained?", "What are the steps?").

To assist students during the writing process, Scardamalia, Bereiter, and Steinbach (1984) offered students cues to stimulate their thinking about the planning of compositions. These cues took the form of introductory phrases, and were grouped according to the function they served: planning a new idea, improving, elaborating, goal setting, and putting it all together. Students first determined the type of cue needed, then chose a particular cue to incorporate into the silent planning monologue. The cues found to be helpful when planning opinion essays are given here:

Elaborate

An even better idea is . . .
An example of this . . .
An important point I haven't considered yet is . . .
This is true, but it's not sufficient so . . .
My own feelings about this are . . .
A better argument would be . . .
I'll change this a little by . . .
A different aspect would be . . .
The reason I think so . . .
A whole new way to think of this topic is . . .
Another reason that's good . . .
I could develop this idea by adding . . .
No one will have thought of . . .
Another way to put it would be . . .

Improve

A good point on the other side of the argument is . . .

I'm not being very clear about what I just said so . . .

Goals

I could make my main point clearer . . .
A goal I think I could write is . . .
A criticism I should deal with in my paper is . . .
My purpose . . .

I really think this isn't necessary because . . .

Putting It Together

I'm getting off topic so . . .
If I want to start off with my strongest idea, I'll . . .
I can tie this together by . . .
My main point is . . .

The purpose of this section was to illustrate the concept of procedural prompts by giving examples of those that have been developed and used in intervention studies that obtained significant results. Some prompts were derived from studying the strategies used by experts, and other prompts were simply invented by the investigators.

Demonstrate the Use of the Prompt Through Modeling and Thinking Aloud

After finding or developing a procedural prompt, the next step is to help students learn to use the prompt. Two overlapping procedures have been used by the teacher in these studies to help teach the students how to use and apply the procedural prompts: modeling and thinking aloud.

Model the Process of Using the Procedural Prompt. The instruction would begin with the teacher introducing, explaining, and demonstrating the utility of the procedural prompt. Then the teacher would model its application as the students observed. Thus, when students were taught to generate questions, the teacher modeled how to use the cues to think of questions related to a particular passage. When teaching students to write a summary, the teacher identified the details of a paragraph or passage, used the details to form a main idea, and stated the details in the summary. In writing an explanation paper, the teacher used the planning cues in a self-talk or inner dialogue style. The teacher modeled how to use the Plan Sheet as a way to record ideas and thoughts about the topic.

The teacher gradually diminished this modeling as students began to take on more of the responsibility for completing the task. The teacher continued to model only the part(s) of the process that students were unable to complete at that particular time. Often during the transitional stage, when the students were ready to take on another part of the task, the teacher continued to model, but requested hints or suggestions from the students regarding how to complete the next step in the task. Several studies also relied on more capable students to provide the modeling.

A number of researchers have used a combination of both modeling and labeling of the procedures that were used (Manning, 1988; Meichenbaum & Goodman, 1971; Raphael & Pearson, 1985) and then gradually and systematically shifting responsibility for the completion of the task from the teacher to the student. Under this process, the teacher first does all the steps and provides the labels. Then the students are gradually asked to provide the labels. Then the students take on more of the task. An example of this process is described here:

1. Teacher models the use of the strategy while talking aloud, labeling, and/or describing his or her actions and thoughts.
2. Teacher models the use of the strategy as the student provides the labels or gives directives to the teacher.
3. Student models the use of the strategy as the teacher provides the labels or directives.
4. Student models the use of the strategy while overtly instructing self, labeling and/or describing actions and thoughts.
5. Student models the use of the strategy, providing self-guidance through covert inner speech.

As the students practice, the teacher also describes typical scenarios in which the strategy would be helpful.

__Think Aloud as Choices Are Being Made.__   Another scaffold, similar to modeling, is the vocalization of the internal thought processes one goes through when using the cognitive strategy. For example, when teaching students to generate questions, the teacher describes the thought processes that occur as a question word is selected and integrated with text information to form a question. A teacher might think aloud while summarizing a paragraph, illustrating the thought processes that occur as the topic of the passage is determined and then used to generate a summary sentence.

Anderson (1991) provided illustrations of thinking aloud for several cognitive strategies in reading:

1. For clarifying difficult statements or concepts: I don't get this. It says that things that are dark look smaller. I know that a white dog looks smaller than a black elephant, so this rule must only work for things that are about

the same size. Maybe black shoes would make your feet look smaller than white ones would.

2. For summarizing important information: I'll summarize this part of the article. So far, it tells where the Spanish started in North America and what parts they explored. Since the title is "The Spanish in California," the part about California must be important. I'd sum up by saying that Spanish explorers from Mexico discovered California. They didn't stay in California, but lived in other parts of America. These are the most important ideas so far.

3. For thinking ahead: So far this has told me that Columbus is poor, the trip will be expensive, and everyone's laughing at his plan. I'd predict that Columbus will have trouble getting the money he needs for his exploration.

As individual students accepted more responsibility in the completion of a task, they often modeled and thought aloud for their less capable classmates. Not only did student modeling and think alouds involve the students actively in the process, but it allowed the teacher to better assess student progress in the use of the strategy. Thinking aloud by the teacher and more capable students provided novice learners with a way to observe "expert thinking" which is usually hidden from the student. Indeed, identifying the hidden strategies of experts so that they can become available to learners has become a useful area of research (Collins et al., 1989).

Guide Students Through Initial Practice Using Techniques That Reduce the Difficulty of the Task

Guided practice, as described in the teacher effects research (Rosenshine & Stevens, 1986), consists of the teacher dividing the task into smaller parts and helping the students as they first learn each part and then consolidate the parts into a unified whole. This division into smaller parts is a way to regulate the difficulty of the task. In the studies that taught cognitive strategies, a number of scaffolds were used to regulate the difficulty of the task and guide student practice. These scaffolds are described next.

Start With Simplified Material. In order to help the learner, many investigators began with simple exercises and then gradually increased the difficulty of the task. This allowed the learner to begin participating early in the process. For example, in a study by Palincsar (1987), the task of generating questions was first simplified to that of practicing how to generate questions about a single sentence. The teacher first modeled how to generate questions and this was followed by student practice. Then the complexity of the task was increased to the teacher generating questions after reading a paragraph, followed by the student practice. Finally, the teacher modeled and the class practiced generating questions after reading an entire passage.

When learning the strategy of summarizing, students in the study by Dermody (1988) first learned how to write summary statements on single paragraphs. After students received guided practice on this task, teachers showed them how to combine several summary statements to produce a single summary for a longer passage, and had them practice this more difficult task. Thus, in the study by Palincsar (1987), the task of processing a paragraph was first reduced to processing a sentence; in the study by Dermody (1988) the task of processing a passage was first reduced to processing a paragraph.

Another form of regulating the difficulty is to begin with simpler materials, materials that do not cause as much cognitive strain. Such simplification occurred when teaching summarization, where the investigator located materials that were one or two years below the students' reading level and used these materials during initial instruction (Lonberger, 1988). As the students became more proficient, the level of the materials was increased.

Complete Part of the Task for the Students.   In many of the studies, instruction on the cognitive strategy began with the teacher completing most or all of the task through modeling and thinking aloud. The teacher continued to carry out the parts of the task not yet introduced to the students, or those parts that students were unable to complete at the time. Sometimes the students' participation began at a very simple level. For example, as the teacher modeled the strategy, the students were asked to provide the label, or students were requested to state the next step in the process the teacher needed to model. As student involvement increased, teacher involvement was decreased. Teachers provided hints, prompts, suggestions, and feedback when students encountered difficulty in their attempts to complete part of the task. Sometimes these difficulties required the temporary increase of teacher involvement until students were able to overcome the difficulty.

Provide Cue Cards.   In some of these studies, students received cue cards containing the procedural prompts they had been taught. Having a cue card relieved the strain on the limited working memory by "downloading" the task from the working memory to the card (Perkins, Simmons, & Tishman, 1989). Students could look at the cue card to recall the procedural prompt instead of having to hold the prompt in their limited working memory. This allowed the student to expend more effort and thought into the actual application of the prompt. For example, in the study by Billingsley and Wildman (1984), the teacher gave students a card containing the list of question words (e.g., who, what, and why) they could use to generate questions. Singer and Donlon (1982) taught students to use the elements of story grammar (e.g., leading character, goal, obstacles, outcomes, and theme) as prompts to generate questions, and gave them lists of these story elements for reference.

Wong and Jones (1982) provided each student with cue cards that were printed with the following procedural prompts. The students were instructed to use these prompts to help them generate questions on the main idea of the passage:

1. Why are you studying this passage? (So you can answer some questions you will be given later.)
2. Find the main idea/ideas in the paragraph and underline it/them.
3. Think of a question about the main idea you have underlined. Remember what a good question should be like.
4. Learn the answer to your question.
5. Always look back at the questions and answers to see how each successive question and answer provide you with more information.

Eventually, the cue cards were removed, and students were asked to formulate questions or write summaries without them. Cue cards were used in studies at all levels—from third grade through college.

Present the New Material in Small Steps. When presenting a procedural prompt with several steps or component parts, the difficulty can be regulated by "teaching in small steps," that is, first teaching one step or part and then providing for student practice before teaching the next part. In this way, students deal with manageable, yet meaningful, bits. In a study (Blaha, 1979) in which students were taught a strategy for summarizing paragraphs, the teacher explained and modeled the first step, identifying the topic of a paragraph, and provided student practice on new paragraphs. Then she taught the second step, the concept of main idea, and students practiced both finding the topic and locating the main idea together. Following this, she taught students the third step, identifying the supporting details, and the students practiced that part of the task. Finally, the students practiced doing all three steps of the strategy.

Anticipate Student Errors. Another way to regulate the difficulty of learning a new cognitive strategy is to anticipate and discuss potential student errors. When teaching students the cognitive strategy of summarization, one teacher anticipated errors in summarizing by presenting a summary with a poorly written topic sentence and asking students to state the problem. In another study (Brady, 1990), the investigator noticed that students had a tendency to produce summary statements that were too broad, often providing only the general topic of the passage (e.g., "This paragraph was about toads"). To help students avoid this error, Brady developed a simple, yet successful, procedural prompt. He suggested students begin their summary statements with the phrase, "This paragraph tells us that _____." This prompt significantly improved the quality of summary statements.

When teaching students to generate questions, the teacher showed questions that were inappropriate because they were about a minor detail, and then asked students to state why they were inappropriate. The teacher also showed questions that were too broad to be answered from the text, and asked students to explain why the questions were inappropriate. The students then used these hints and suggestions as they generated their questions.

One characteristic of expert teachers is the ability to anticipate student errors prior to instruction. One teacher stated, "With experience, you can pinpoint mistakes students make ahead of time. The more you teach, the more you realize where the pitfalls are" (Borko & Livingston, 1990, p. 490).

Provide for Student Practice

Students in most studies practiced the application of cognitive strategies in one or more of the three different contexts: teacher-guided practice, reciprocal teaching, and work in small groups.

Teacher-Guided Practice. When teaching cognitive strategies, the teachers guided students by providing hints, reminders of the procedural prompts, reminders of what was overlooked, and suggestions on how something could be improved. Students participated by giving answers and deciding upon the correctness of other students' answers. Where appropriate, students were called upon to justify their procedures by explaining their thinking. Through this process, students' "oversimplified and naive conceptions are revealed" (Brown & Campione, 1986). Such dialogue may also aid in understanding. As Brown and Palincsar (1986) wrote, "Understanding is more likely to occur when a student is required to explain, elaborate, or defend his or her position to others; the burden of explanation is often the push needed to make him or her evaluate, integrate, and elaborate knowledge in new ways" (p. 395).

Reciprocal Teaching. In some studies, guided practice took place in the context of a dialogue among teacher and students—reciprocal teaching (Palincsar & Brown, 1984)—with students and teacher rotating the role of teacher. This allowed for shifting of responsibility to the students and gradual internalization of the cognitive strategies. As a student took on the role of the teacher in the process of applying the strategies to a text, the teacher was able to evaluate the student's progress and provide feedback or assistance.

Collaborative social dialogue was also emphasized in the Englert et al. (1991) Cognitive Strategy Instruction in Writing. During guided practice, students were invited to participate in a dialogue about a class writing project. Students and teacher collaborated to generate self-questions, apply the new cognitive strategies, and carry on the dialogue to complete a class paper. The students progressively took on more responsibility for completing the writing task. Englert et al. (1991) contend that, as students accept more responsibility in the exchange that takes place during the instructional dialogues, they begin to internalize the dialogue. This inner dialogue allows students to (a) talk to themselves about their own writing, (b) hear what their own writing has to say, and (c) talk to others about their writing (Englert et al., 1991).

Work in Small Groups.   In some studies, notably those conducted with high school and college students, the students practiced the task in small groups without the teacher. For example, King (1990) reported that, after hearing a lecture, students met in small groups and practiced using the prompts to generate questions. Schoenfeld (1985) suggested that small group work facilitates the learning process in four ways. First, it provides an opportunity for the teacher to assess students and to then provide support and assistance as students actively engage in problem solving. Second, group decision-making facilitates the articulation of knowledge and reasoning as students justify to group members their reasons for choosing alternative solutions. Third, students receive practice in collaboration, a skill required in real-life problem-solving. Fourth, students who are insecure about their abilities to solve problems have the opportunity to see more capable peers struggle over difficult problems. These insecure students come to realize that problem solving is not always easy for others, and that even the more capable students can have difficulty understanding and solving problems.

Provide for Feedback and Self-Checking

Feedback is important in teaching cognitive strategies, as it is for all forms of learning. Four types of feedback appeared in these studies: traditional teacher feedback, use of checklists, use of models of expert responses, and use of fix-up strategies.

Teacher-Led Feedback.   Traditional feedback from teachers and other students on the correctness of their responses took place throughout the lessons on cognitive strategies.

Checklists.   In several studies, the teacher provided self-checking procedures to increase student independence. For example, as part of their instruction in teaching students to summarize a passage, Rinehart, Stahl, and

Erickson (1986) had students use the following list of questions to check their summaries:

Have I found the overall idea that the passage is about?

Have I found the most important information that tells me more about the overall idea?

Have I used any information that is not directly about the main idea?

Have I used any information more than once?

Davey and McBride (1986) provided students with a checklist to refer to after they had generated questions:

Did my "think" question use different words from the text?

Did I use good signal words?

Checklists for writing programs ranged from checklists on punctuation (e.g., Does every sentence start with a capital?) to checklists on style elements. For example, students being taught to write explanatory material were also taught to ask, "Did I tell what materials you need?", "Did I make the steps clear?" (Englert et al., 1991). Teachers usually presented these checklists at the end of guided practice. The teacher modeled the use of the checklist, and provided students with guidance as they began to use the checklists.

Models of Expert Work.   In some studies, students were provided with expert models to which they could compare their work. For example, where students were taught to generate questions, they could compare their questions with those generated by the teacher. Similarly, when learning to write summaries, students could compare their summaries on a passage with those generated by an expert.

Fix-Up Strategies.   Fix-up strategies are the other side of checklists. They refer to strategies that students can use when they realize, through the use of checklists or metacognitive processes, that their comprehension is not proceeding well. One example of fix-up strategies (Lonberger, 1988) consists of four possible steps:

a) Reread the difficult portion of the text.
b) Read ahead to see if the problems clear up.
c) Consult an expert source such as a teacher or a parent.
d) Ask a friend for help. (p. 89).

Bereiter and Bird (1985) analyzed protocols of adult expert readers thinking aloud while reading difficult text. They identified online fix-up strategies used by skilled readers when they encountered difficulty in comprehension of text during initial reading. From these identified strategies used by expert readers, Bereiter and Bird selected four particular strategies that met the following criteria: (a) the strategy must accurately represent how expert readers addressed comprehension difficulties, and (b) the strategy must be teachable, in that the strategy implies a set of conditions to be met and a set of actions to be taken. The four main comprehension fix-up strategies selected by Bereiter and Bird included the following:

1. Restatement of confusing text in simpler or more familiar terms
2. Backtracking for rereading
3. Demanding relationships between sections of the text
4. Formulating the difficulty as a problem

Students who received instruction in these strategies—instruction that identified, modeled, and explained the strategies, and provided students with practice in identifying and applying the strategies—significantly increased their use of these strategies and made significant gains in reading comprehension.

Increase the Students' Responsibility as They Master the Strategy

Just as it is important to simplify material and provide support for students in the initial stages of learning a cognitive strategy, it is also important to diminish the number of prompts and provide students with practice using more complex material. Thus, responsibility for learning shifts from the teacher to the student. This gradual decrease in prompts and supports, and gradual increase in student responsibility, have been described as a shift in the teacher's role from that of coach to that of supportive and sympathetic audience (Palincsar & Brown, 1984).

Diminish Prompts and Models. After the students in the study by Wong and Jones (1982) had used cue cards to develop fluency in performing the task, the cue cards were then removed, and students were asked to write summaries without these prompts. In the study by King (1990), in which students used half-completed sentences as references when generating questions, the teacher withdrew the supports after the guided practice, and students were left to generate questions on their own.

As students used cue cards during guided practice, they gradually internalized the prompts on the procedural prompt or the process that accompanied their use. Once the cue cards were removed, students were able to rely on the internalized structure of the prompt.

Increase the Complexity and Difficulty of the Material. Increasing the complexity of material was evident in the study by Palincsar (1987), in which students learning to generate questions began by working on a single sentence, then a paragraph, and finally, an entire passage. Schoenfeld (1985) sequenced the problems he presented to his students when teaching mathematical problem-solving. He first gave students problems they were incapable of solving on their own; this provided the motivation for learning the problem-solving strategy he planned to introduce. After presenting the strategy, he provided problems that were easily solved when the strategy was applied. As students became skilled at applying the strategy, a new strategy was introduced. Interspersed among these new problems were several problems requiring the application of previously taught problem-solving strategies. These problems forced students to apply the strategies learned to the type of problems encountered. As the course progressed, students were expected to combine strategies to solve complex problems.

Diminish the Support Provided to Students. In some studies, the support that students received from other students was also diminished as work progressed. For example, in the study by Nolte and Singer (1985), students first spent 3 days working in groups of five or six, and then 3 days working in pairs before working alone on the task.

In the Englert et al. (1991) study, in which students were taught cognitive strategies in writing, students first participated in a collaborative dialogue that centered on the application of the newly learned strategies to a whole-class writing project. Students were then allowed to choose their own topic, applying the same strategies used in the group writing. Students were encouraged to collaborate with a peer or peers by sharing ideas, discussing each other's writing, asking questions, getting feedback, reporting progress, or asking advice. The teacher provided additional support by finding examples of strategy use or problems found in the students' writing, displaying them on an overhead projector. The teacher initiated a class dialogue on the students' examples, focusing the discussion on the strategies used, the problems encountered, and possible solutions. After the students completed this piece of writing, the teacher asked them to independently write another paper for publication in a class book.

Provide for Consolidation Activities. When a series of steps have been taught and practiced separately, as in some summarizing and writing strategies, one of the final tasks during guided practice is having the students practice putting the component parts of the strategy together. A teacher can then (a) assess student implementation of the complete strategy, (b) correct errors, and (c) determine whether additional teaching or practice is necessary. Such assessment is important before students begin independent practice.

Check for Student Mastery. Before independent practice can begin, it is important to check students to see if the tasks have been learned, and to provide additional instruction and practice where necessary. Thus, after students are taught to generate questions, they need to be tested on their mastery of this task. To some extent, a teacher is receiving feedback from students as they practice the task, but there is also an advantage to obtaining more systematic feedback, such as when all students are given the same passage or paragraph and are asked to generate questions. In this systematic way, all students, even the quiet ones, can be checked, and additional instruction can be provided for those who need it.

Provide Independent Practice With New Examples

The goal of the independent practice is to develop "unitization" of the strategy, that is, the blending of elements of the strategy into a unified whole. The extensive practice, and practice with a variety of material—alone, in groups, or in pairs—also *decontextualizes* the learning. That is, the strategies become free of their original "bindings" and can now be applied easily and unconsciously to various situations (Collins, Brown, & Newman, 1989). More accurately, the variety of materials serves to link the strategy to a richer set of contexts, and all of these contexts now suggest the strategy.

Cognitive Strategy Instruction in Writing, the program implemented in the Englert et al. (1991) study, provided students with several opportunities to apply the strategies they had been taught—first in a whole-group setting, then individually with peer and teacher assistance, and then independently. As students worked in class on the second writing assignment, intermittent class discussions focused on examples of student work placed on the overhead projector. These examples illustrated the flexibility of the strategies when applied to a number of different topics and in a number of different ways. The students then independently applied the strategies to a third and final writing assignment on a topic of their choice.

SUMMARY AND DISCUSSION

This review has yielded a number of new instructional procedures that might be added to the teacher's armamentarium. These elements enlarge our technical vocabulary and repertoire of instructional practices useful in the teaching of both well-structured skills and cognitive strategies in the classroom.

Scaffolds. One advancement in this research is the introduction of the concept of scaffolds (Palincsar & Brown, 1984; Wood, Bruner, & Ross, 1976). The scaffolds, as well as procedures for instruction in the use of these scaffolds, provide us with suggestions for thinking about ways to help students learn a variety of cognitive strategies.

Procedural Prompts. Another new concept is that of providing students with procedural prompts. These prompts are a special type of scaffold, one that is specific to the cognitive strategy being taught, yet flexible enough to allow application to a variety of contexts. Examples include prompts that help students generate questions, prompts that suggest procedures for summarizing, and questions to consider when planning an essay.

In summary, because higher-level cognitive strategies cannot be taught as a series of explicit steps, there is a need for a great deal of student practice to help overcome this problem. This practice can take a variety of forms, yet all of them apply the procedures of scaffolding and fading. As guided practice begins, the majority of the task is completed by the teacher through modeling and thinking aloud. As practice progresses, students take on more responsibility in completing the task, and teacher support is gradually withdrawn. As guided practice nears completion, the students complete all of the task independently, with little or no support provided by the teacher. Previously withdrawn scaffolds can be temporarily reintroduced if students encounter difficulties.

Teaching Without Procedural Prompts. There are some tasks that are so difficult that procedural prompts have not been developed, and other tasks in which the procedural prompts can only serve to scaffold a part of the task. What does one do then? The tentative answer is that, in these cases, the teacher spends more time modeling and thinking aloud, more time discussing the models, and more time providing checklists and expert models for comparison.

New Instructional Procedures. It is also possible to identify 10 new instructional procedures that appear in these studies, but did not appear in previous reviews of research on teaching by Brophy and Good (1986) and Rosenshine and Stevens (1986):

1. Provide cognitive strategies.
2. Model use of the procedural prompt.
3. Think out loud.
4. Begin with simplified material.
5. Provide cue cards.

6. Begin with half-done material.
7. Anticipate errors and difficult areas.
8. Use reciprocal teaching.
9. Provide checklists.
10. Provide expert models for comparison.

However, if one studies these new concepts, there is no conflict. That is, all the new variables can also be applied to the teaching of well-structured skills. Thus, this assists the teaching of both well-structured skills and cognitive strategies.

The results of this research suggest that, instead of a dichotomy, there is a continuum from well-structured explicit skills to cognitive strategies. At all points in the continuum, some instructional elements, such as presenting information in small steps and providing guided practice, are important. Yet, as one moves from well-structured to cognitive strategies, there is an increased instructional value in providing students with scaffolds, (e.g., models, prompts, think alouds, simplified problems, suggestions, and hints) during the presentation and guided practice phases.

The variables uncovered in this review are at a middle-level of specificity. That is, they provide support for the student, but they do not specify each and every step to be taken. There is something appealing about this middle-level. It is neither the specificity of behavioral objectives that seemed overly demanding to some, nor is it the lack of instruction that many criticized in discovery learning settings. Perhaps it is the beginning of a synthesis.

ACKNOWLEDGMENTS

Our thanks to Mike Pressley, whose exquisite review of the literature on cognitive strategy instruction (Pressley et al., 1990) provided a scaffold for this work. Jim Raths provided valuable and useful comments on this chapter.

REFERENCES

Alvermann, D. (1991). Secondary school reading. In P. D. Pearson (Ed.), *Handbook of reading research* (Vol. 2, pp. 551–571). White Plains, NY: Longman.

Anderson, V. (1991, April). *Training teachers to foster active reading strategies in reading-disabled adolescents.* Paper presented at the annual meeting of the American Educational Research Association, Chicago.

Baumann, J. F. (1984). The effectiveness of a direct instruction paradigm for teaching main idea comprehension. *Reading Research Quarterly, 20,* 93–115.

Bereiter, C., & Bird, M. (1985). Use of thinking aloud in identification and teaching of reading comprehension strategies. *Cognition and Instruction, 2,* 131–156.

Bickhard, M. H. (1992). Scaffolding and self-scaffolding: Central aspects of development. In L. T. Winegar & J. Valsiner (Eds.), *Children's development within social context* (Vol. 2). Hillsdale, NJ: Lawrence Erlbaum Associates.

Billingsley, B. S., & Wildman, T. M. (1984). Question generation and reading comprehension. *Learning Disability Research, 4,* 36–44.

Blaha, B. A. (1979). *The effects of answering self-generated questions on reading.* Unpublished doctoral dissertation, Boston University School of Education.

Borko, H., & Livingston, C. (1989). Cognition and improvisation: Differences in mathematics instruction by expert and novice teachers. *American Educational Research Journal, 26,* 473–499.

Brady, P. L. (1990). *Improving the reading comprehension of middle school students through reciprocal teaching and semantic mapping strategies.* Unpublished doctoral dissertation, University of Oregon.

Brophy, J. E., & Good, T. L. (1986). Teacher behavior and student achievement. In M. C. Wittrock (Ed.), *Handbook of research on teaching* (3rd ed., pp. 328–376). New York: Macmillan.

Brown, A. L., & Campione, J. C. (1986). Psychological theory and the study of learning disabilities. *American Psychologist, 41,* 1059–1068.

Brown, A. L., & Palincsar, A. S. (1989). Guided, cooperative learning and individual knowledge acquisition. In L. B. Resnick (Ed.), *Knowing, learning, and instruction: Essays in honor of Robert Glaser* (pp. 393–451). Hillsdale, NJ: Lawrence Erlbaum Associates.

Collins, A., Brown, J. S., & Newman, S. E. (1989). Cognitive apprenticeship: Teaching the crafts of reading, writing, and mathematics. In L. B. Resnick (Ed.), *Knowing, learning, and instruction: Essays in honor of Robert Glaser* (pp. 393–451). Hillsdale, NJ: Lawrence Erlbaum Associates.

Davey, B., & McBride, S. (1986). Effects of question-generation on reading comprehension. *Journal of Educational Psychology, 78,* 256–262.

Dermody, M. M. (1988). *Effects of metacognitive strategy training on fourth graders' reading comprehension.* Unpublished doctoral dissertation, University of New Orleans.

Doyle, W. (1983). Academic work. *Review of Educational Research, 53,* 159–199.

Durkin, D. (1979). What classroom observations reveal about reading comprehension. *Reading Research Quarterly, 14,* 544–581.

Englert, C. S., Raphael, T. E., Anderson, L. M., Anthony, H. M., & Stevens, D. D. (1991). Making strategies and self-talk visible: Writing instruction in regular and special education classrooms. *American Educational Research Journal, 28,* 337–372.

King, A. (1990). Enhancing peer interaction and learning in the classroom through reciprocal peer questioning. *American Educational Research Journal, 27,* 664–687.

Lonberger, R. B. (1988). *The effects of training in a self-generated learning strategy on the prose processing abilities of fourth and sixth graders.* Unpublished doctoral dissertation, State University of New York at Buffalo.

Manning, B. H. (1988). Application of cognitive behavior modification: First and third graders' self-management of classroom behaviors. *American Educational Research Journal, 25,* 193–212.

Meichenbaum, D., & Goodman, J. (1971). Training impulsive children to talk to themselves: A means of developing self-control. *Journal of Abnormal Psychology, 77,* 115–126.

Nolte, R. Y., & Singer, H. (1985). Active comprehension: Teaching a process of reading comprehension and its effects on reading achievement. *The Reading Teacher, 39,* 24–31.

Palincsar, A. S. (1986). The role of dialogue in providing scaffolded instruction. *Educational Psychologist, 21,* 73–98.

Palincsar, A. S. (1987, April). *Collaborating for collaborative learning of text comprehension.* Paper presented at the annual conference of the American Educational Research Association, Washington, DC.

Palincsar, A. S., & Brown, A. L. (1984). Reciprocal teaching of comprehension-fostering and comprehension-monitoring activities. *Cognition and Instruction, 2*, 117–175.

Palincsar, A. S., David, Y., Winn, J., Snyder, B., & Stevens, D. (1989, November). The differential effects of three procedures for teaching strategic reading. Paper presented at the annual meeting of the National Reading Conference, Austin, TX.

Paris, S. G., Wixson, K. K., & Palincsar, A. S. (1986). Instructional approaches to reading comprehension. In E. Z. Rothkof (Ed.), *Review of research in education, 13*. Washington, DC: American Educational Research Association.

Perkins, D. N., Simmons, R., & Tishman, S. (1989, March). *Teaching cognitive and metacognitive strategies*. Paper presented at the annual meeting of the American Educational Research Association, San Francisco.

Pressley, M., Burkell, J., Cariglia-Bull, T., Lysynchuk, L., McGoldrick, J. A., Schneider, B., Symons, S., & Woloshyn, V. E. (1990). *Cognitive strategy instruction*. Cambridge, MA: Brookline Books.

Raphael, T. E., & Pearson, P. D. (1985). Increasing student awareness of sources of information for answering questions. *American Educational Research Journal, 22*, 217–237.

Rinehart, S. D., Stahl, S. A., & Erickson, L. G. (1986). Some effects of summarization training on reading and studying. *Reading Research Quarterly, 21*, 422–437.

Rosenshine, B., & Stevens, R. (1986). Teaching functions. In M. C. Wittrock (Ed.), *Handbook of research on teaching* (3rd ed. pp. 745–799). New York: Macmillan.

Scardamalia, M., & Bereiter, C., & Steinbach, R. (1984). Teachability of reflective processes in written composition. *Cognitive Science, 8*, 173–190.

Schoenfeld, A. H. (1985). *Mathematical problem solving*. New York: Academic Press.

Singer, H., & Donlan, D. (1982). Active comprehension: Problem-solving schema with question generation of complex short stories. *Reading Research Quarterly, 17*, 166–186.

Taylor, B. M. (1985). Improving middle-grade students' reading and writing of expository text. *Journal of Educational Research, 79*, 119–125.

Tobias, S. (1982). When do instructional methods make a difference? *Educational Researcher, 11*, 4–10.

Vygotsky, L. S. (1962). *Thought and language*. Cambridge, MA: The MIT. Press.

Vygotsky, L. S. (1978). *Mind in society: The development of higher psychological processes*. Cambridge, MA: Harvard University Press.

Wong, Y. L., & Jones, W. (1982). Increasing metacomprehension in learning disabled and normally achieving students through self-questioning training. *Learning Disability Quarterly, 5*, 228–239.

Wood, D. J., Bruner, J. S., & Ross, G. (1976). The role of tutoring in problem solving. *Journal of Child Psychology and Psychiatry, 17*, 89–100.

CHAPTER FIVE

Reading, Writing, and Language Arts in Success for All

Nancy A. Madden
Robert E. Slavin
Barbara A. Wasik
Lawrence J. Dolan
Center for Research on the Education of Students Placed at Risk
Johns Hopkins University, Baltimore, MD

Virtually every child has the potential to be a skillful, strategic, and joyful reader, yet few ever attain their full potential. Many fail to learn to decode quickly and smoothly enough to understand or enjoy what they read. Many decode adequately, but do not learn how to read for meaning. Many can decode and understand text, but never learn the pleasure and power of reading. In particular, many children fail to learn to read adequately in the primary grades, and are then retained, assigned to special education or long-term remediation, or put in the low reading group for many years. Whatever the factors that interfered with reading success in the early grades, the fact of failure and the consequent shame and frustration have long-term impacts on students' academic motivation and performance. Students who fail to read well early in their school careers rarely catch up, regardless of exposure to remedial or special education programs (see Slavin, Karweit, & Wasik, 1994).

Any rational analysis of reading failure must arrive at an emphasis on prevention and early intervention. Intervening after children have fallen far behind makes no sense. What was first an achievement problem has become a problem of low self-esteem, anxiety, poor motivation, and avoidance. The problem of early reading failure is endemic in all schools, but epidemic in schools serving many disadvantaged students. Students from impoverished homes arrive at school with few literacy experiences, and often with languages or dialects different from those of the school. When these children run into problems with reading, their parents are less likely to help them.

109

Compounding these problems, disadvantaged students usually attend underfunded urban or rural schools, which are less able than other schools to help children who are struggling.

SUCCESS FOR ALL

Success for All is a program designed to prevent reading failure in high-poverty schools. The idea behind Success for All is to realign resources and use research-based instructional programs to ensure that children do not fall behind in reading in the early grades, and that they continue to grow in reading, writing, and language arts throughout the elementary years (Slavin, Madden, Dolan, & Wasik, 1996).

Success for All is not only a reading program. It emphasizes: (a) effective prekindergarten and kindergarten approaches, (b) one-to-one tutoring for first graders who are at risk for reading failure, (c) an active family support program, and (d) other elements. Most schools implement writing/language arts programs adapted from our Cooperative Integrated Reading and Composition (CIRC) model. This chapter emphasizes the reading approaches used in Success for All. It is important to keep in mind that these reading approaches are used in the context of other interventions that also affect student success. These other elements of Success for All are described briefly following a detailed description of the reading model.

READING PROGRAMS IN SUCCESS FOR ALL

Although Success for All ultimately incorporates reform in most of the elementary school curriculum and instruction, the heart of the instructional program is reading. The reason for this is obvious; in the early grades, success in school is virtually synonymous with success in reading. Few, if any, students in Grades 1–3 are retained or assigned to special education solely on the basis of deficits in math performance. A child who *can* read is not guaranteed to be a success in elementary school, but a child who *cannot* read is guaranteed to be a failure.

The amount of reading failure in the early grades in schools serving disadvantaged students is shocking. In our studies of Success for All, we have consistently found that, at the end of first grade, about a quarter of students in our control schools cannot read and comprehend the following passage: "I have a little black dog. He has a pink nose. He has a little tail. He can jump and run" (Durrell & Catterson, 1980).

On the National Assessment of Educational Progress, only 39% of African-American 9-year-olds could read at the "basic" level, compared with

68% of Whites (Mullis & Jenkins, 1990). In many urban districts, retention rates for first graders have topped 20% in recent years. What these statistics mean is that, despite some improvements over the past 20 years, the reading performance of disadvantaged and minority children is still seriously lacking, and the deficits begin early. The consequences of early reading failure are severe. A child who is not reading adequately by the end of third grade is headed for serious trouble.

The philosophy that guides the development of the reading curriculum in Success for All emphasizes the need for reading instruction to work for *all* students. We recognize that different children learn to read in different ways, thus our approach emphasizes teaching reading many different ways at the same time. For example, in each beginning reading lesson, students read silently and aloud, sing, trace letters with their fingers, make discriminations, discuss stories, make predictions, use context clues, and engage in many other activities. Teaching the same concepts and skills in many different ways provides reinforcement and allows the curriculum to correspond to the learning strengths of every child.

Grouping

Homeroom classes in Success for All are fully heterogeneous. However, to have enough instructional time to teach reading in many different ways, students are regrouped for reading across grade lines according to reading level, so that all reading classes contain just one level. For example, a 2–1 reading class might contain first, second, and third graders all reading at the same level. During reading time (usually 90 minutes per day), additional teachers are available to teach reading (e.g., certified tutors and, in some schools, special education or ESL teachers). This means that reading classes are smaller than homeroom classes. Based on regular curriculum-based assessments given every 8 weeks, reading group assignments are constantly reexamined. Students capable of moving to a higher performing group are accelerated, whereas those who are not performing adequately are given tutoring, family support services, modifications in curriculum or instruction, or other services to help them keep up.

There are many reasons for cross-class and cross-grade grouping for reading in Success for All. First, having all students at one reading level avoids the use of reading groups *within* the class. The problem with reading groups is that when the teacher is working with one group, the other children are at their desks doing seatwork or other independent tasks of little instructional value. To have a full 90 minutes of direct, active instruction by the teacher, having only one reading group is essential. Research on cross-grade grouping for reading, often called the Joplin Plan, has shown that this method increases student achievement (Slavin, 1987).

In addition, use of cross-class and cross-grade grouping allows the use of tutors and other certified staff as reading teachers. This has many benefits. First, it reduces class size for reading, which has small but consistent benefits for achievement in the early grades (Slavin, 1994). Perhaps of equal importance, it gives tutors and other supplementary teachers experience in teaching the reading program, so that they know exactly what their students are experiencing. When a student is struggling with Lesson 37, the tutor knows what Lesson 37 is because he or she has taught it.

Eight-Week Assessments

A critical feature of reading instruction in Success for All at all grade levels is assessment of student progress every 8 weeks. These assessments are closely linked to the curriculum. In the early grades, they may include some written and some oral assessments; in the later grades, they often use "magazine tests" or other assessments provided with basal series (if the district uses basals). Eight-week assessments usually include assessments of skills above students' current level of performance to facilitate decisions to accelerate students to a higher reading group.

Eight-week assessments are used for three essential purposes: to change students' reading groupings (i.e., to identify students capable of being accelerated), to decide which students are in the greatest need for tutoring and which no longer need tutoring, and to check on the progress of every child. They can indicate to school staff that a given student is not making adequate progress, and lead them to try other strategies. The 8-week assessments are given and scored by reading teachers, but are collated and interpreted by the facilitator. The facilitator then uses them to review the progress of all children, and to suggest changes in grouping, tutoring assignments, or other approaches to the reading teachers.

READING APPROACHES

The Success for All reading approach is divided into two programs. Beginning Reading (Madden & Livermon, 1990) is introduced in the middle of kindergarten or the beginning of first grade, depending on the district's goals for kindergarten. Beginning Reading continues through what would usually be thought of as the primer level, and is usually completed in early spring of first grade. Starting at the first reader level, students go on to what we call Beyond the Basics, which continues through the fifth or sixth grade. Beginning Reading replaces the usual basals and workbooks with a completely different set of materials. Beyond the Basics (Madden, Slavin, Stevens, & Farnish, 1989) uses the district's usual basals, anthologies, and/or novels, but replaces workbooks and other supplementary materials. However, it uses these readings in a very different way than is typical of traditional reading instruction. Beginning Reading and Beyond the Basics are described in the following sections.

Beginning Reading

The Beginning Reading program used in Success for All is based on research that advocates: (a) students learning to read in meaningful contexts, and (b) a systematic presentation of word-attack skills (see Adams, 1990). Three basic components—reading of children's literature by the teacher, "shared story" lessons, and systematic language development—combine to address first graders' learning needs in a variety of ways. Teachers read children's literature to students every day to expose them to the joy and meaning of reading, as well as concepts of print.

The Beginning Reading's shared story curriculum emphasizes immediate application of skills to real reading. For example, by the fifth lesson (a lesson usually takes about two class periods), when students have learned only three letter sounds, they read an entire book. This book is part of a series of "shared stories," which contain some material written in small type to be read by the teacher and other material in large type to be read by students. The adult text adds background and richness to the story that would not be possible with the limited vocabulary of an early reader. In addition, pictures are used to represent certain words so that students can read interesting stories long before they even know the entire alphabet. An example of a shared story appears in the Appendix.

Although shared stories are designed to be meaningful and interesting, the students' portions use a phonetically regular vocabulary so that the skills students are learning will work in cracking the reading code. At Lesson 56, students begin to use the Walker Learn to Read Series, an engaging set of stories that uses some phonetically controlled vocabulary. Students learn many sight words along the way, but the intention of Beginning Reading is to empower students—by giving them decoding strategies that will work, and by giving them interesting, worthwhile material that they can successfully read using their new skills.

In addition to immediate application of skills in meaningful contexts, another major principle of Beginning Reading is that students need to learn comprehension strategies at their reading level as well as their receptive language level. This means that the teacher reads children's literature to students and engages students in discussions, retelling of the stories, and writing. The idea is to build reading-comprehension skill with material more difficult than that which students could read on their own. This process begins in preschool and kindergarten with the Story Telling and Retelling

(STaR) program, and continues through part of the first grade. At that point, students begin a Listening Comprehension program (Stevens & Shaw, 1990), in which teachers continue to read to children and teach them to: (a) identify characters, settings, problems, and problem solutions in narratives; (b) visualize descriptive elements of stories; (c) identify sequences of events; (d) predict story outcomes; (e) identify topics and main ideas in expository selections; and so on. Another key objective of Beginning Reading is to build students' vocabularies and receptive and expressive language skills. We use the Peabody Language Development kits for this purpose beginning in preschool and kindergarten, and continue with these materials through the end of Beginning Reading.

Beginning Reading makes extensive use of partner learning. Students take turns reading to each other and helping each other with difficult words, and they help each other with "share sheets" to reinforce skills the teacher has taught. The partner reading activity replaces the "round robin reading," or ordered reading turns, typical of traditional reading groups. While students are reading to each other, the teacher circulates among the students to listen in on them, and occasionally asks a student to read to him or her. This gives students substantial practice in oral reading and rereading without creating the situation typical of the traditional reading group—in which one student is reading aloud while eight or more students are supposedly listening. When a pair of students feels that both partners have mastered the story, they read it to the class in a "reading celebration," followed by comments and applause.

Beginning Reading lessons emphasize a rapid pace of instruction, a variety of activities, and many opportunities for students to participate. Each day following STaR or Listening Comprehension, the shared story lesson begins with a group or partner rereading a familiar shared story and a quick writing review of some of the words and sounds from that story. Then students sing an alphabet song to coax "Alphie" (a puppet) to come out of his box. Alphie brings the students the letter of the day, including a silly tongue twister. For example, Alphie might say: "A lot of words start with the sound /s/. Listen to this: 'Sam said he was sorry he put salt in Sally's sandwich.' " The teacher then works with the tongue twister to emphasize the /s/ sound. Alphie shows the students objects and pictures that do or do not start with the sound, and students use whole-class responding (e.g., choral responses, pointing, or signing) to discriminate between them. Students learn the shapes of letters by tracing them in the air and on each others' backs, and by learning a little couplet: "Curve left, curve right, around and stop. The sound for s is /s/."

The lesson goes on to help students (a) identify letter sounds within words, (b) come up with words of their own using the sound, (c) match the written letter with pictures, (d) use sound-blending skills to stretch and compress words, (e) spell words from their sounds, and so on. The idea here is to teach the same discriminations many ways, involve many sensory modalities, and maintain students' active engagement, enthusiasm, and interest. The words and sounds practiced are immediately used in a new shared story, which is read, discussed, and then reread for fluency.

Beyond the Basics

Beyond the Basics (Madden et al., 1989) is the reading approach used in Success for All from the first reader level (usually spring of first grade) to the end of elementary school. It is an adaptation of CIRC, a cooperative learning program that encompasses both reading and writing/language arts. Studies of CIRC have shown it to be effective in increasing students' reading, writing, and language achievement (Stevens, Madden, Slavin, & Farnish, 1987).

The curricular focus of Beyond the Basics is primarily on building comprehension and thinking skills, fluency, and pleasure in reading. Beyond the Basics assumes that students coming out of Beginning Reading have solid word-attack skills, but need to build on this foundation to understand and enjoy increasingly complex material.

As in Beginning Reading, students in Beyond the Basics are regrouped for reading across grade lines, so a 3–1 reading class could be composed of second, third, and fourth graders. In addition, students are assigned to four- or five-member learning teams that are heterogeneous in performance level, sex, and age. These teams choose team names and sit together at most times. The teams have a responsibility to see that all team members are learning the material being taught in class. Each week, students take a set of quizzes. These contribute to a team score, and the teams can earn certificates and other recognition based on the team's average quiz scores. Students also contribute points to their teams by completing book reports and writing assignments, and by returning completed parent forms indicating that they have been reading at home each evening. The main activities of Beyond the Basics are described in the following section (adapted from Slavin, Madden, & Stevens, 1989–1990).

Basal-Related Activities

Students use their regular basal readers, novels, anthologies, or whatever materials are available in the school. Stories are introduced and discussed by the teacher. During these lessons, teachers set a purpose for reading, introduce new vocabulary, review old vocabulary, discuss the stories after students have read them, and so on. Presentation methods for each segment of the lesson are structured. For example, teachers are taught to use a vocabulary presentation procedure that requires (a) a demonstration of understanding of word meaning by each individual, (b) a review of methods of word attack, (c) repetitive oral reading of vocabulary to achieve automaticity, and (d) use of the vocabulary words' meanings to help introduce the story's content. Story discussions are structured to emphasize such skills as making and supporting predictions about the story, and understanding major structural components of the story (e.g., problem and solution in a narrative).

After the stories are introduced, students are given a series of activities to do in their teams when they are not working with the teacher in a reading group. The sequence of activities is as follows:

1. *Partner Reading.* Students read the story silently first, and then take turns reading the story aloud with their partners, alternating readers after each paragraph. As the partner reads, the listener follows along and corrects any errors the reader makes.

2. *Story Structure and Story-Related Writing.* Students are given questions related to each narrative story emphasizing the story structure (e.g., characters, setting, problem, and problem solution). Halfway through the story, they are instructed to stop reading and identify the characters, the setting, and the problem in the story, and to predict how the problem will be resolved. At the end of the story, students respond to the story as a whole and write a few paragraphs on a topic related to the story (e.g., they might be asked to write a different ending to the story).

3. *Words Out Loud.* Students are given a list of new or difficult words used in the story, which they must be able to read correctly in any order without hesitating or stumbling. These words are presented by the teacher in the reading group, and then students practice their lists with their partners or other teammates until they can read them smoothly.

4. *Word Meaning.* Students are given a list of story words that are new in their speaking vocabularies, and are asked to write a sentence for each that shows the meaning of the word (i.e., "An *octopus* grabbed the swimmer with its eight long legs," not "I have an *octopus*"). At higher grade levels, students are asked to look up some of the words in the dictionary and paraphrase the definition.

5. *Story Retell.* After reading the story and discussing it in their reading groups, students summarize the main points of the story to their partners. The partners have a list of essential story elements that they use to check the completeness of the story summaries.

6. *Spelling.* Students pretest one another on a list of spelling words each week, and then work over the course of the week to help one another master the list. Students use a "disappearing list" strategy, in which they make new lists of missed words after each assessment until the list disappears; they can go back to the full list, repeating the process as many times as necessary.

Partner Checking. After students complete each of these activities, their partners initial a student assignment record form indicating that they have completed and/or achieved criterion on that task. Students are given daily expectations as to the number of activities to be completed, but they can go at their own rate and complete the activities earlier if they wish, creating additional time for independent reading.

Tests. At the end of three class periods, students are given a comprehension test on the story, asked to write meaningful sentences for certain vocabulary words, and asked to read the word list aloud to the teacher. Students are not permitted to help one another on these tests. The test scores and evaluations of the story-related writing are major components of students' weekly team scores.

Direct Instruction in Reading Comprehension

Students receive direct instruction from the teacher in reading-comprehension skills, such as identifying main ideas, drawing conclusions, and comparing and contrasting ideas. A special curriculum was designed for this purpose. After each lesson, students work on reading-comprehension work sheets and/or games as a whole team, first gaining consensus on one set of work sheet items, then practicing independently, assessing one another's work, and discussing any remaining problems on a second set of items.

Independent Reading

Every evening, students are asked to read a trade book of their choice for at least 20 minutes. In most schools, classroom libraries of paperback books are established for this purpose. Parents initial forms indicating that students have read for the required time, and students contribute points to their teams if they submit a completed form each week. In a twice-weekly "book club," students discuss the books they have been reading and present more formal book reports, trying to entice others to take home the same book. Independent reading and book reports replace all other homework in reading and language arts. If students complete their basal-related or other activities early, they may also read their independent reading books in class.

Listening Comprehension

Each day, the teacher presents a lesson focusing on comprehension of stories at students' interest level, but above their current reading level. This lesson uses stories from children's literature to teach such skills as visualization of story characters and settings, identification of and attempts to solve problems, story mapping, and sequence of events in narratives.

WRITING AND LANGUAGE ARTS

Writing and language arts are critical elements of the Success for All program, particularly because writing is the opposite side of the reading coin. Writing is an important part of the Success for All reading program from early on. However, a formal writing/language arts instructional program is not usually introduced until most teachers are comfortable with the reading program. In practice, this usually means that the writing/language arts program is introduced in the spring of the first implementation year or in the fall of the second year.

Writing/language arts instruction in Success for All is provided to students in their heterogeneous homerooms, not in their reading groups. The basic philosophy behind the writing/language arts program is that writing should be given the main emphasis, and that language arts, especially mechanics and usage, should be taught in the context of writing, not as a separate topic.

There are two levels in the Success for All writing/language arts approach. Both are based on the ideas of writing process (Calkins, 1983; Graves, 1983), which emphasizes writing for a real audience, writing for revision, and gradually building spelling and mechanics in the context of writing. Writing from the Heart, used in Grades 1–2, uses an informal version of writing process. CIRC Writing, used in Grades 3–6, uses a more formal writing process: regular four-member peer-response groups, and students working compositions through from plan to draft to revision to editing to publication. These programs are described next.

Writing from the Heart

A young child thinks of writing as an extension of oral communication. Given the undivided attention of an audience, most children will talk endlessly about their experiences. Young authors rarely have a problem of too little to say; their problem is overcoming the barriers they perceive to putting their ideas down on paper.

The goal of Writing from the Heart (Madden, Wasik, & Petza, 1989), the writing/language arts program used in Grades 1–2 in Success for All, is to tap students' innate desire, energy, and enthusiasm for communication, and to move them to the next step of sharing their ideas with others through writing. When writing is seen as mastery of spelling and mechanics, it is a formidable task. Students will ultimately need to master these skills, but first they need to develop pleasure and fluency in putting their thoughts on paper. Most important, students need to see writing as a personal expression, not an ordinary school task. They must put their hearts into their writing, not just their minds.

Writing from the Heart is a writing process model, which means that students write for a real audience and learn to revise their writing until it is ready for "publication." Students do not work in formal writing teams (that will come in third grade), but rather informally with partners while they are writing. The main elements of Writing from the Heart are as follows:

1. *Modeling and Motivating Writing.* At the beginning of each lesson, the teacher provides a model or motivator for writing. For example, the teacher may read a story that is like what students will be writing, or may ask students to describe experiences that relate to a particular kind of writing. The teacher may introduce formats to help students plan their writing. For example, in writing about "myself," students are given a set of questions to answer about themselves, which they then use to put into a story.

2. *Writing a "Sloppy Copy."* Students are encouraged to write a "sloppy copy"—a first draft of their composition. They are taught to use "sound spelling" (invented spelling) if they cannot spell a word. For example, *dinasr* is a way a student might write *dinosaur.*

3. *Partner Sharing.* At several points in the writing process, students share their writing with partners and receive feedback and ideas from them.

4. *Revision.* Beginning several weeks after the program's start, students learn to revise their compositions using feedback from partners and the teacher. Specific revision skills are taught and modeled in the lessons.

5. *Editing.* In preparation for publication, the teacher helps each child prepare a perfect draft of his or her composition, complete with pictures.

6. *Publication.* Final drafts of students' writings are "published" in a class book, read to the class, and recognized in a variety of ways.

7. *Sharing and Celebration.* At many points in the writing process, students have opportunities to share their writing with the class. The teacher sets up a special "author's chair" from which the "authors" present their latest works. Authors are taught to ask three questions of their audience:

- What did you hear? Can you tell me about my story?
- What did you like about my story?
- What else would you like to know about my story?

The teacher models use of the author's chair by presenting his or her own writing and models answers to the author's questions.

Writing from the Heart prepares students for the CIRC Writing program, starting in Grade 3, by convincing students that they are authors and have something to say; by teaching them that writing is a process of thinking, drafting, revising, and polishing ideas; and by letting them know that writing is fun. They are then ready to learn more about the craft of writing with more formal instruction in tricks of the trade, style, mechanics, and usage.

CIRC Writing/Language Arts

The CIRC Writing/Language Arts program used in the upper elementary grades is one developed earlier for Grades 3 and up (Madden, Stevens, Farnish, & Slavin, 1990). In this program, students are assigned to four- or five-member heterogeneous writing teams. The CIRC Writing/Language Acts program has two major instructional formats: 3 days each week are used for writing process activities, and 2 days are used for language arts instruction.

Writing Process Activities

Writing Concept Lessons.   Each writing process day begins with a brief lesson on a writing concept. For example, the first lesson is on "mind movies" (i.e., visualization of events in a narrative to see where additional detail or description is needed). Other lessons include organizing imaginative narratives; using observation to add life to descriptions; and writing personal narratives, mysteries, persuasive arguments, explanations, and so on. The writing concept lessons are meant to spark ideas and help students expand on their writing, and to evaluate their own and others' compositions.

Writing Process.   Most of the writing/language arts period is spent with students writing their own compositions while the teacher circulates among the teams and conferences with individual students. Students draft many compositions, and then choose a smaller number to carry through to publication. The steps are as follows:

1. *Prewriting.* Students discuss with their teammates a topic they would like to address and an audience for their writing. They then draft a plan, using a "skeleton planning form," an "idea net," or other forms to organize their thinking.
2. *Drafting.* After students prepare a plan in consultation with teammates, they write a first draft, focusing on getting ideas on paper, rather than spelling and mechanics (which come later).
3. *Revision.* Students read their drafts to their teammates. The teammates are taught to rephrase the main idea of the story in their own words, mention two things they liked about the story, and note two things they would like to hear more about. The teacher may also conference with students at the revision stage to applaud students' ideas and suggest additions and changes.
4. *Editing.* Once authors are satisfied with the content of the writing, they are ready to correct the mechanics, usage, and spelling. Students work with a partner to go through an editing checklist. The checklist starts with a small number of goals (e.g., correct capitalization and end punctuation), but then adds goals as students complete language arts lessons. For example,

after a lesson on subject–verb agreement or run-on sentences is completed, these goals may be added to the checklist. First the authors check the composition against the checklist, then a teammate does so, and finally the teacher checks it.

5. *Publication.* Publication involves the creation of the final draft and celebration of the author's writing. Students carefully rewrite their work, incorporating all final corrections made by the teacher. Then they present their compositions to the class from a fancy "author's chair," and may contribute their writing to a team book or a team section of a class book. These books are proudly displayed in the class or library. In addition, students may be asked to read their compositions to other classes, or to otherwise celebrate and disseminate their work.

Revision and Editing Skills Lessons

About 2 days each week, the teacher teaches structured lessons on language mechanics skills. These are presented as skills for revision and editing because their purpose is to directly support students' writing. The teacher determines the order of lessons according to problems students are experiencing and skills they need for upcoming writing. For example, the teacher may notice that many students are having problems with complete sentences, or may anticipate that, because students are about to write dialogue, they may need to learn how to use quotation marks.

Students work in their four-member writing teams to help one another master the skills taught by the teacher. The students work on examples, compare answers with each other, resolve discrepancies, explain ideas to each other, and so on. Ultimately, students are quizzed on the skill, and the teams can earn certificates or other recognition based on the average performance of all team members. As noted earlier, immediately after a revision and editing skills lesson, the new skill is added to the editing checklist so language arts skills are immediately put into practice in students' writing.

Other Program Elements

Reading Tutors. One of the most important elements of the Success for All model is the use of tutors to support students' success in reading. One-to-one tutoring is the most effective form of instruction known (see Wasik & Slavin, 1993). Tutors are certified teachers with experience teaching Chapter I, special education, and/or primary reading. Tutors work one on one with students who are having difficulties keeping up with their reading groups. Students are taken from their homeroom classes by the tutors for 20-minute sessions during times other than reading or math periods. In general, tutors support students' success in the regular reading curriculum, rather than teaching different objectives. For example, if the regular reading teacher is working on stories with long vowels or is teaching comprehension-monitoring strategies, so does the tutor. However, tutors identify learning deficits and use different strategies to teach the same skills.

During daily 90-minute reading periods, tutors serve as additional reading teachers to reduce class size for reading. Information on students' specific deficits and needs pass between reading teachers and tutors on brief forms, and reading teachers and tutors are given regular meeting times to coordinate their approaches with individual children.

Initial decisions about reading group placement and need for tutoring are made based on informal reading inventories given to each child by the tutors. After this, reading group placements and tutoring assignments are made based on 8-week assessments, which include teacher judgments as well as more formal assessments. First graders receive first priority for tutoring because the tutor's primary function is to help all students be successful in reading the first time—before they become remedial readers.

Preschool and Kindergarten. Most Success for All schools provide a half-day preschool and/or a full-day kindergarten for all eligible students. Preschool and kindergarten provide a balanced and developmentally appropriate learning experience for young children. The curriculum emphasizes the development and use of language. It provides a balance of academic readiness and nonacademic music, art, and movement activities. Readiness activities include use of integrated thematic units, Peabody Language Development Kits, and STaR, in which students retell stories read by the teachers.

Family Support Team. A Family Support Team, consisting of social workers, parent liaisons, counselors, and others who work in the school, provides parenting education and works to involve parents in support of their children's success in school. Also, family support staff are called on to provide assistance when there are indications that students are not working up to their full potential because of problems at home. For example, families of students who do not receive adequate sleep or nutrition, need glasses, do not attend school regularly, or exhibit serious behavior problems receive family support assistance. Links with appropriate community service agencies are made to provide as much focused service as possible for parents and children.

Program Facilitator. A program facilitator works at the school full time to oversee (with the principal) the operation of the Success for All model. The facilitator helps plan the Success for All program, helps the principal with scheduling, and visits classes and tutoring sessions frequently to help teachers and tutors with individual problems. The program facilitator may work with individual children having particular difficulties to find successful strategies for teaching them, and then return the children to the tutors or teachers. He or she helps teachers and tutors deal with any behavioral or other special problems, and coordinates the activities of the Family Support Team with the instructional staff.

Teachers and Teacher Training. The teachers and tutors are regular teachers. They receive detailed teachers' manuals, supplemented by 3 days of inservice at the beginning of the school year and several inservice sessions throughout the year on such topics as classroom management, instructional pace, and curriculum implementation.

Special Education. Every effort is made to deal with students' learning problems within the context of the regular classroom, as supplemented by tutors. Special education resource services are still provided for students assigned to special education in previous years, but no new assignments to resource services are made for reading problems, on the assumption that tutoring services available to all students will be more appropriate. Self-contained services for seriously handicapped students are maintained for those students whose needs cannot be met in the regular class.

RESEARCH ON SUCCESS FOR ALL

Formal evaluations of Success for All have been carried out in seven school districts: Baltimore, Philadelphia, Memphis, Montgomery (AL), Charleston (SC), Ft. Wayne (IN), and Caldwell (ID). The schools ranged in percents of students in poverty from 42% to 100%; 11 of the 15 exceeded 75%. Ten of the schools served entirely African-American populations, and five were integrated. In each district, schools implementing Success for All were compared with matched control schools, and in most cases children were then matched within the matched schools. The reading measures were Word Identification, Word Attack, and Passage Comprehension from the Woodcock Reading Mastery Test, and the Durrell Oral Reading Test, all of which were individually administered to students (for more details on the research designs and findings, see Madden, Slavin, Karweit, Dolan, & Wasik, 1993; Slavin, Madden, Dolan, Wasik, Ross, Smith, & Dianda, 1996; Slavin, Madden, Karweit, Dolan, & Wasik, 1992).

The results pooled across measures, schools, and years, for all children who were in the program since first grade, are summarized in Fig. 5.1. Effects were substantially positive at every grade level, 1–5. For students in general, effect sizes (proportion of a standard deviation by which experimental schools exceed controls) averaged about 50% of a standard deviation, which is considered a large impact. For students in the lowest 25% of their grades effect sizes ranged from +1.03 for first graders to +1.68 for fourth graders. In grade equivalent terms, Success for All students exceeded controls by about three months at the end of first grade, by more than a full year

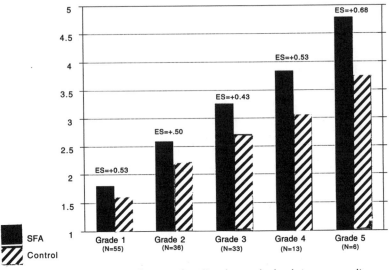

FIG. 5.1. Comparison of Success for All and control schools in mean reading grade equivalents and effect sizes (1988–1994). Adapted from Slavin, Madden, Dolan, Wasik, Ross, Smith, and Dianda (1996).

by the end of fifth grade. Follow up assessments have found that the fifth grade differences are maintained into sixth and seventh grades, after students have left the program.

In addition to strong and consistent effects on reading, Success for All studies have found substantial effects on reducing retentions and special education placements, and on increasing attendance (Slavin et al., 1992, 1996). The overall findings of Success for All research cannot address the effectiveness of the reading and writing/language arts elements per se because the program also incorporates tutoring, family support, and other elements. However, several studies have examined the reading and writing/language arts programs separately from the overall model. Madden, Slavin, Karweit, Dolan, and Wasik (1990) evaluated the Beginning Reading program by itself in three schools and found it to be more effective than a traditional control group. Three studies of CIRC (Stevens, Madden, Slavin, & Farnish, 1987; Stevens & Slavin, 1995) have shown the effectiveness of this approach used in Success for All for reading, writing, and language arts in the upper elementary grades.

CONCLUSION

Research on Success for All has shown unequivocally that reading failure can be substantially reduced in schools serving many disadvantaged children. Along with findings supporting other approaches to reading, discussed elsewhere in this volume, the research on Success for All shows that reading failure is unnecessary for the great majority of children. The policy consequences of these findings should be great. If we know that reading failure can be routinely eliminated, even in the most difficult schools, then we have a practical and moral responsibility to see that every child achieves skill and joy in reading.

ACKNOWLEDGMENTS

Portions of this chapter are adapted from Slavin, Madden, Karweit, Dolan, and Wasik (1992). This chapter was written under funding from the Office of Educational Research and Improvement, U.S. Department of Education (No. OERI-R-117-R90002). However, any opinions expressed are those of the authors and do not represent OERI positions or policies.

REFERENCES

Adams, M. J. (1990). *Beginning to read: Thinking and learning about print.* Cambridge, MA: MIT Press.

Calkins, L. M. (1983). *Lessons from a child: On the teaching and learning of writing.* Exeter, NH: Heinemann.

Durrell, D., & Catterson, J. (1980). *Durrell analysis of reading difficulty.* New York: The Psychological Corporation.

Graves, D. (1983). *Writing: Teachers and children at work.* Exeter, NH: Heinemann.

Madden, N. A., & Livermon, B. J. (1990). *Success for All beginning reading: A manual for teachers* (3rd ed.). Baltimore, MD: The Johns Hopkins University, Center for Research on Effective Schooling for Disadvantaged Students.

Madden, N. A., Slavin, R. E., Karweit, N. L., Dolan, L., & Wasik, B. A. (1990, April). *Success for All: Effects of variations in duration and resources of a schoolwide elementary restructuring program.* Paper presented at the annual convention of the American Educational Research Association, Boston.

Madden, N. A., Slavin, R. E., Karweit, N. L., Dolan, L. J., & Wasik, B. A. (1993). Success for All: Longitudinal effects of a restructuring program for inner-city elementary schools. *American Educational Research Journal, 30,* 123–148.

Madden, N. A., Slavin, R. E., Stevens, R. J., & Farnish, A. M. (1989). *Success for All: Beyond the basics in reading.* Baltimore, MD: Johns Hopkins University, Center for Research on Effective Schooling for Disadvantaged Students.

Madden, N. A., Stevens, R. J., Farnish, A. M., & Slavin, R. E. (1990). *Cooperative Integrated Reading and Composition-Writing: Teachers manual.* Baltimore, MD: Johns Hopkins University, Center for Research on Effective Schooling for Disadvantaged Students.

Madden, N. A., Wasik, B. A., & Petza, R. J. (1989). *Writing from the Heart: A writing process approach for first and second graders.* Baltimore, MD: Johns Hopkins University, Center for Research on Effective Schooling for Disadvantaged Students.

Mullis, I. V. S., & Jenkins, L. B. (1990). *The reading report card, 1971–88.* Washington, DC: U.S. Department of Education.

Slavin, R. E. (1987). Ability grouping and student achievement in elementary schools: A best-evidence synthesis. *Review of Educational Research, 57,* 347–350.

Slavin, R. E. (1994). School and classroom organization in beginning reading: Class size, aides, and instructional grouping. In R. E. Slavin, N. L. Karweit, & B. A. Wasik (Eds.), *Preventing early school failure: Research, policy, and practice* (pp. 122–142). Boston: Allyn & Bacon.

Slavin, R. E., Karweit, N. L., & Wasik, B. A. (Eds.). (1994). *Preventing early school failure: Research, policy, and practice.* Boston: Allyn & Bacon.

Slavin, R. E., Madden, N. A., Dolan, L. J., & Wasik, B. A. (1996). *Every child, every school: Success for All.* Thousand Oaks, CA: Corwin.

Slavin, R. E., Madden, N. A., Dolan, L. J., Wasik, B. A., Ross, S., Smith, L., & Dianda, M. (1996). Success for All: A summary of research. *Journal of Education for Students Placed at Risk, 1,* 41–76.

Slavin, R. E., Madden, N. A., Karweit, N. L., Dolan, L., & Wasik, B. A. (1992). *Success for All: A relentless approach to prevention and early intervention in elementary schools.* Arlington, VA: Educational Research Service.

Slavin, R. E., Madden, N. A., & Stevens, R. J. (1989–1990). Cooperative learning models for the 3 R's. *Educational Leadership, 47*(4), 22–28.

Stevens, R. J., Madden, N. A., Slavin, R. E., & Farnish, A. M. (1987). Cooperative Integrated Reading and Composition: Two field experiments. *Reading Research Quarterly, 22,* 433–454.

Stevens, R. J., & Shaw, A. H. (1990). *Listening comprehension.* Baltimore, MD: Johns Hopkins University, Center for Research on Effective Schooling for Disadvantaged Students.

Stevens, R. J., & Slavin, R. E. (1995). The effects of a cooperative learning approach in reading and writing on academically handicapped and nonhandicapped students' achievement, attitudes, and metacognition in reading and writing. *Elementary School Journal, 95*(3), 241–262.

Wasik, B. A., & Slavin, R. E. (1993). Preventing early reading failure with one-to-one tutoring: A review of five programs. *Reading Research Quarterly, 28,* 178–200.

APPENDIX

Shared Story 18
Story by Laura Burton Rice; Illustrations by Jennifer Clark. Copyright (1994) by
New American Schools Development Corporation. Reproduced by permission.

Scott and Tanya practice kicking her ball during recess. Lana joins them. What will happen to the ball?

Scott rolls the ball.

BAM!

Tanya kicks it.

She fast.

Lana says, "The ball is off the field!"

Scott and Tanya look for the ball in the bushes while Lana looks on the other side of the playground. Suddenly, Scott sees something. What is it?

"Look, Tanya!" gasps Scott.

Tanya looks.

She sees a big fat dog.

The dog fast.

It bumps into Tanya.

She sits in the mud.

Poor Tanya! How do you think she feels about being pushed into the mud?

"Ick!" says Tanya. "Mud is not fun.
Go, dog!"
The big dog sits.
He pants.

Paco starts to shake. He turns pale. What has Paco seen that has scared him?

Paco says, "See the dog's fangs!"
"FANGS!!" says Tanya.
The big dog says, "RUFF!"
The kids climb up the jungle gym.
"Can we fit?" asks Paco.

Lana runs fast.
"Fang!" Lana says.
She skids to a stop.
"Fang is not bad," says Lana.

Lana explains that Fang is her St. Bernard. He is gentle, even though he has big teeth. He follows her to school when he gets lonely. What will the other children do now?

Lana says, "Fang is a fun dog.
He likes kids."
The kids get off the jungle gym.

All of a sudden, Derrick has an idea. What do you think it is?

Derrick says, "Dogs can sniff.
Can Fang sniff the ball?"
Lana nods.
"Get the ball, Fang," says Lana.

Fang puts his nose to the ground. Do you think he can find the ball?

Fang .
He sniffs.
He digs fast in a stack of leaves.
The kids say, "Fang got the ball back!"

Fang is a hero. He has found the missing ball!

CHAPTER SIX

Creating Readers Who Read for Meaning and Love to Read: The Benchmark School Reading Program

Robert W. Gaskins
University of Kentucky, Lexington

Irene W. Gaskins
Benchmark School, Media, PA

The Benchmark staff believes that exemplary reading instruction provides students with three keys to successful learning: knowledge, strategies, and motivation. None is sufficient alone; yet together they provide students with the components necessary to become independent readers. For example, a broad foundation of knowledge presents the opportunity for students to interpret situations from various perspectives. Cognitive and metacognitive strategies supply the tools for flexibly applying that knowledge, while motivation is the force driving the use of strategies and the construction of knowledge. Thus, at Benchmark—a Grades 1–8 school for poor readers with average or better intelligence—the instructional program is designed to foster students who possess knowledge, strategies, and motivation, and who become self-regulated readers and learners. The Benchmark program is grounded in continuous analysis and application of cognitive research, and is refined through research and practice in Benchmark classrooms. In what follows, we describe the principles that form the foundation of the Benchmark perspective on learning to read and the instructional program that continues to evolve from that perspective.

THEORY

The theory of learning that provides the basis for the Benchmark instructional program is derived from current cognitive science. We define *learning* as follows:

Learning is the process through which an individual's mental representations of concepts change as a result of interacting with the environment. The product of this process is a more elaborated or usable understanding. This understanding is constructed by the learner, yet is also socially mediated, thus affected by the interpretations of others. The learner employs cognitive and metacognitive strategies to select, organize, synthesize, and monitor incoming information. Ideally, learning is not merely adding information to a static mental representation, but rather old understandings are transformed into new and deeper understandings. Key factors in determining what is learned include the learner's attitude toward learning and willingness to take risks, as well as the amount of time and strategic effort devoted to learning. Learning is most effective when learners are actively engaged in completing tasks that they view as real world and meaningful.

This learning theory is the basis for the Benchmark instructional program, as well as the foundation for two courses for Benchmark students about learning and thinking (Psych 101 and Learning and Thinking [LAT]). In these courses, students are engaged in experiments and discussions about how the mind works, factors that affect learning, and characteristics of people who demonstrate exceptional abilities. The goals of Psych 101 and LAT are for students to (a) develop an understanding of why metacognitive and cognitive strategies are important, and (b) demonstrate the motivation to use these strategies to control factors that affect learning. Another goal is to foster the development of learner characteristics usually found among individuals who have achieved success as thinkers and problem solvers.

Psych 101 is taught 15 minutes a day, four times a week to middle-school students; LAT is a 10-session course taught to lower school students. Students love being allowed to take part in what they consider to be a college-level course, and teachers regularly comment about how these courses complement their efforts. One of the many advantages of these courses is that they provide students and teachers with a common language to talk about how the mind works. In addition, the staff has discovered that motivation for learning strategies that foster construction of meaning from text increases when students have a basic understanding of how the mind works and why the strategies are helpful. Further details about these courses can be found in Gaskins and Elliot (1991). Some of the tenets of learning theory, on which the courses are based, are discussed in more detail later.

Learning Is Socially Mediated

People learn about the world through a variety of experiences, but the way they structure those experiences and make meaning of them is shaped by the communities in which they interact. These communities shape values, beliefs, attitudes, and thinking processes, and thus play a significant role in determining what is learned, the way people learn, their disposition toward learning (Resnick, 1987), and the way they view themselves as learners and members of the community (Johnson & Johnson, 1991).

For centuries, civilizations have viewed social interaction as the most efficient means of learning. More recently, research has confirmed that social interaction has a significant and positive impact on learning (Collins, Brown, & Newman, 1989; Johnson & Johnson, 1991; Slavin, 1990). Further, studies have shown that when students work cooperatively, as opposed to competitively or individually, student achievement is increased, attitudes toward learning are better, social bonds between students are more positive, and students' self-esteem is higher (Johnson & Johnson, 1991; Johnson, Johnson, & Holubec, 1990; Slavin, 1990). Simply having students work together, of course, does not automatically produce these positive results. Certain conditions must be present for these effects to be realized (see Johnson & Johnson, 1991). Even so, the essential points of this research are not disputed: One's environment impacts what is learned, and social interaction facilitates learning. These tenets are basic to developing learners, thinkers, and problem solvers.

Learning Requires Active Construction

Learning is not only a socially mediated process—it is also a process that requires active processing. Contrary to the way instruction may have been delivered in the past, present-day learning theorists have documented, time and again, that real learning that is applicable to other situations is not accomplished by students passively receiving knowledge as if they were empty vessels to be filled with ideas. The result of passively receiving knowledge is inert or unusable knowledge (Bereiter & Scardamalia, 1985; Nickerson, 1988; Resnick & Klopfer, 1989).

In a learning situation, students control what will be the focus of their attention, how they will interpret that situation, and whether they will be actively involved (Wittrock, 1986). This control is influenced by their current knowledge, which in turn shapes the meaning they construct and, to a large extent, determines what they will learn (Anderson & Pearson, 1984; Nickerson, 1988). Thus, although students' current understanding of the world is the starting point for learning, it is activity that makes learning happen. Students must actively employ cognitive and metacognitive strategies to manage the meaning-making process. Some of these strategic actions include constructing, elaborating, and modifying conceptual knowledge (Bruer, 1993).

Cognitive and metacognitive strategies are the means for tapping into and using conceptual knowledge. Cognitive strategies are courses of action or plans for thinking. They are specific ways to approach a learning task. Metacognitive strategies function in an executive role, and include procedures for analyzing and taking control of the task, the environment, personal characteristics, and strategies for dealing with a particular situation (Gaskins & Elliot, 1991). Thus, metacognitive strategies involve not only awareness of factors affecting the completion of a learning task, but the ability to take control of those factors by implementing and monitoring a plan for learning (Brown, 1985; Flavell, 1985). Therefore, it is clear that both cognitive and metacognitive strategies are essential for the active construction required in learning.

Learning Requires Motivation
and the Confidence to Take Risks

If students are to become independent learners, it is imperative that they have the cognitive tools necessary to address a variety of learning tasks. Even so, strategies alone do not create independent learners. As Paris, Lipson, and Wixson (1983) suggested, independent learners possess both skill (strategies) and will (motivation). With regard to motivation, students need to have a desire to learn and the confidence to take risks (Ames, 1992; Dweck, 1986; R. Gaskins, 1992; Schunk, 1991). Without these motivational components, students may be unwilling to apply their conceptual and strategic knowledge to the tasks before them.

Research suggests that motivation to learn and confidence to take risks are related to a number of issues: the students' goal orientations, the tasks they are asked to complete, the assessment procedures used in the classroom, and the management system in place. In short, motivation and confidence are fostered by an environment that promotes learning goal orientation, rather than performance goal orientation (Ames, 1992; Ames & Archer, 1988; Dweck, 1986). Learning goal orientation is created through student engagement in tasks they view as meaningful, challenging, and interesting, as well as tasks that involve a social component. In addition, it is important that students have a sense of control over the process or products of the tasks. Using assessment that is non-normative and implementing a management system that provides students with a sense of autonomy, while still including ample support, are also important (Ames, 1992). When these conditions are met, studies indicate that motivation to learn increases, as does confidence to take risks. Consequently, learning is facilitated.

Learning Is a Product of Time and Effort

Knowledge, strategies, and motivation are essential components of efficient and effective functioning, but these components cannot be developed and integrated to produce proficient performance without time and effort being devoted to practice. The amount of time and effort devoted to learning a concept, skill, or strategy is related to the level of expertise that a student will develop in that area (Glaser & Chi, 1988). In short, the more one practices, the more proficient one becomes.

In particular, practice helps students develop proficiency in applying specific skills and strategies, as well as motivation and confidence related to these situations. But not just any practice will lead to these results. For the practice to be productive, tasks must be kept at an optimal level of difficulty. In addition, these tasks must be deemed purposeful by the person practicing, and the tasks (or the goal of proficiency) must be sufficiently motivating to sustain the person's engagement (Ames, 1992; Brophy, 1987). If these conditions are met, time and effort spent practicing are likely to lead to increased proficiency in learning.

Learning Is Purposeful

Finally, it is important to remember that the ultimate goal of teaching is to help students function effectively in the real world. Most students desire instruction that moves them toward this goal. Thus, students often ask, "Why do we have to learn this?" and "When will I ever use this outside of school?" These are excellent questions; if we cannot answer them, we should reconsider what we are doing.

Research suggests that one of the key characteristics of tasks that foster student effort and active involvement is the meaningfulness of the task to the students (e.g., Ames, 1992; Brophy, 1987). For this reason, it is good practice to discover what students value and consider meaningful. This information can be used as a starting point in designing real-world instructional activities that students view as worth their effort. If students are to become proficient learners, thinkers, and problem solvers in the real world, they must be prepared to face the complexities and challenges of real-world tasks. As was mentioned earlier, having extensive conceptual and strategic knowledge alone is not sufficient for success. What is important is having the motivation, confidence, and ability to apply this knowledge in a creative and flexible manner. These characteristics are fostered by experiences with tasks that students view as purposeful and that require the integration of knowledge in a creative and flexible manner.

WHAT IS READING?

Reading Must Make Sense

If teachers are to successfully guide students to proficiency in reading, they need to be clear about what they mean by reading and what they think are the characteristics of proficient readers. This clarification is necessary because a teacher's definition of *reading* and the qualities the teacher believes exemplify proficient readers shape how and what students are taught. Thus, at Benchmark staff meetings, we regularly update our definition of *reading* and discuss the implications of our definition for classroom instruction. We also discuss what characteristics proficient readers demonstrate so that we can consciously help students develop those characteristics.

Our definition of *reading* is best exemplified by the first reading lesson introduced to a new-to-Benchmark student. The lesson is developed around this objective: reading must make sense. The need to begin with this objective often becomes obvious when a child is screened for admission to the school. To determine a tentative instructional placement for each child, a staff member conducts an informal reading lesson using a variety of texts, and asks the child to read a portion for a specific purpose. After the child has "read" a passage, the teacher probes for the child's reaction: "So, what did you think? Did any of that make sense to you?" To such probes it is not uncommon for a child to respond, "No, but when I read at school it doesn't make sense either." Another common response is, "I was just reading the words, I wasn't paying attention." Thus, our first hurdle is to convince students that reading is more than saying the words; reading has to make sense. As instruction progresses over the weeks and months, we regularly remind students that the purpose of reading is to construct meaning from print.

Prior to their Benchmark experience, poor readers have often been focused on "sounding out" or "reading words right." Thus, initially our instructional emphasis on readers being actively involved in constructing meaning feels strange to them. We assure these students that reading does involve deciphering alphabetic symbols and putting them together to make words and phrases; we share with students that automaticity in decoding is a high priority because it is necessary for reading fluency. Nevertheless, we want students to be aware that, although we explicitly teach them how to use words they do know to decode unknown words (Gaskins et al., 1988; Gaskins, Gaskins, & Gaskins, 1991), letter–sound knowledge and word recognition are only the means to constructing meaning. Our focus is on reading as communication and, as such, a vehicle for learning and enjoyment. The desired outcome of reading instruction is meaning. The message to students is: Where there is no meaning, no communication occurs, and meaning is what reading is all about.

In addition, as we discuss the meaning of reading with students, we emphasize that reading is an active process in which meaning is constructed based on readers' experience and the text, rather than meaning being present in the text. Teachers share personal experiences to make the point that reading is not a passive transmittal of information. As Rosenblatt (1978) suggested, reading requires a transaction between readers and the text. Teachers employ mental modeling (Duffy, Roehler, & Herrmann, 1988) to illustrate how strategies and prior knowledge are flexibly applied to create meaning through this transaction.

Teachers discuss how reading requires readers to make inferences. They convey the notion that, whereas the author provides guidelines for these inferences through social, linguistic, and literary conventions, it is readers who decide what inferences and conclusions are to be drawn and what meaning is ultimately to be created (Culler, 1975; Fish, 1980; Iser, 1978; Mailloux, 1982; Rosenblatt, 1983). As a result, the created meaning is often not identical to the author's intended meaning when the text was written. What teachers make clear is that these differences in meaning are inevitable and acceptable if they are text based.

Reading is an act of interpretation, not an act of lifting from the text a meaning that is present in the text (Iser, 1978; Mailloux, 1982). Readers may see more or less in a text than the author intended due to their existing knowledge structures and the particular schemata that have been activated to make meaning of the text—that is the nature of reading. Certainly there are language and meaning conventions that are widely accepted in a particular society or community, and therefore people from the same community often share similar perspectives on the meaning of texts. But even within a community, no two people have had exactly the same experiences, nor have they structured their knowledge in exactly the same way (e.g., Mailloux, 1982; Rosenblatt, 1983). Hence, it is inevitable that a particular text means something different to each person who reads it. Moreover, it should be understood that these differences in meaning should not be a cause for dismay, but a cause for celebration. These differences hold the potential to provide fresh perspectives and insights into texts, as well as each other and the human race in general.

Based on the premise that reading is an act of interpretation, Benchmark teachers encourage students to think beyond whether the meaning they construct from a text is right or wrong to whether it is logically based on the language the author has chosen to use. Benchmark teachers believe that each student's interpretation is valid to the extent it follows logically from the transaction between the text and the student's background of knowledge. Teachers do not impose interpretations or the reasons supporting them, but rather help students explore viable interpretations of the text. The teacher's intent is that students construct and accept as valid logically consistent interpretations of text, rather than try to guess the "right" interpretation.

Characteristics of Good Readers

The characteristics that Benchmark teachers believe exemplify proficient readers stem from their definition of *reading*. They believe that proficient readers are those who demonstrate awareness of the factors affecting the construction of meaning, and those who take control of those factors by employing strategies and assessing progress toward their reading goal. In large part, meaning is constructed based on each reader's conceptual knowledge and his or her control of cognitive and metacognitive strategies (plus, in many cases, input from social interaction with peers). Thus, it is not surprising that a broad base of both conceptual knowledge and skills/strategies, as well as the disposition, motivation, and understanding of how to integrate and flexibly apply this knowledge, are characteristics that Benchmark teachers seek to develop. At the same time, we realize that the diverse background of concepts and the depth of awareness students acquire at Benchmark about strategies will be useless unless students become engaged in reading and desire to apply their knowledge and strategies to constructing meaning on an ongoing basis.

Thus, another characteristic that Benchmark teachers strive to develop is a love of reading. Successful readers enjoy reading and look for opportunities to read. They can get lost in a book. Because motivation to read is crucial for poor readers to become successful readers, Benchmark teachers emphasize reading for enjoyment, as well as reading for practical purposes such as problem solving. We have discovered that students who find reading satisfying, read often—and the result is expertise in reading. Benchmark teachers witness daily the motivation exhibited by students who have experienced the pleasure and satisfaction that result from being able to read fluently, and have discovered the new experiences that await them between the covers of each book. These successes and discoveries provide the motivation for poor readers to become lifelong readers, learners, thinkers, and problem solvers, while conceptual knowledge and control over cognitive and metacognitive strategies provide the thinking tools.

PROFESSIONAL DEVELOPMENT

Because we believe that what a teacher knows plays an important role in determining students' academic success (Shulman, 1986), it follows that professional development is a high priority at Benchmark (Gaskins, 1988; Gaskins, Cunicelli, & Satlow, 1992). The staff's theoretical understanding of reading and thinking evolves daily as a result of new-teacher training, peer collaboration, classroom observations, teacher–supervisor interactive journals, weekly meetings with supervisors, inservice, professional reading, research seminar, retreats, professional writing, and participation in program development.

Clarity regarding the school's mission is Step 1 in our professional development plan. Benchmark provides a variety of opportunities for the staff to assess and define the school's mission, and to determine how to accomplish that mission. The school's mission statement encapsulates our core beliefs and desired outcomes, and becomes the touchstone for teachers in making moment-to-moment instructional decisions. Benchmark's mission is to help students develop the dispositions and competencies they need to become proficient, self-regulated, and lifelong readers who use reading to learn, think, and problem solve effectively. To accomplish these outcomes, students need knowledge, control, and motivation. We believe that accomplishing our mission provides the key to both enjoyment and opportunity.

Professional Development for Teachers Who Are New to Benchmark

Throughout the 26-year history of Benchmark, we have tried different approaches to training and supporting new teachers. What has proved most successful is for teachers to begin their careers as teaching assistants (TA) working with master teachers and the TA trainer, while also taking advantage of the many professional development opportunities at Benchmark. Training focuses on sharing with TAs the instructional approaches that Benchmark teachers have found successful in managing and teaching the poor readers who attend Benchmark. Prior to the beginning of school, TAs have the option of attending the 2-week training program provided for teachers. Then, during the first week of school, an afternoon of training is provided to orient TAs and to review with them the contents of the TA handbook.

TAs work closely with and learn from classroom teachers, as well as the TA trainer. The TA trainer is a veteran Benchmark teacher who regularly visits classrooms to model ways to elicit and guide student responses to independent reading, to conduct demonstration reading lessons, and to observe the TA and provide feedback. After each visit, the TA and trainer meet to discuss what transpired in the classroom and to plan future lessons, such as deciding how the process objective introduced by the TA trainer will continue to be taught and guided by the TA. The TA trainer also conducts monthly group-training sessions. These sessions usually focus on a particular aspect of the reading program, such as how to help students decode unknown words or how to teach specific strategies to foster active engagement in reading. Also, there is always time to ask questions and discuss why we teach the way we do at Benchmark.

Preparation for becoming a Benchmark teacher continues for many of the TAs when they assume responsibility for their own classrooms—during the 6-week summer language arts program. Teachers have found this an ideal way to ease into teaching at Benchmark because the summer program includes only reading and writing instruction. Thus, the new teacher is not inundated with preparations for the full-day curriculum of the school year. Prior to the beginning of summer school, teachers attend a week of inservice. Portions of that week are devoted to: teaching new teachers methods that have worked in previous summer sessions, meeting with one's supervisor to work out such details as selecting books or organizing homework folders, planning lessons, and setting up classrooms. Supervisors are present in the school to assist teachers with any questions or problems that arise. During summer school, new teachers have the benefit of having a supervisor work with them in the classroom every day. Summer school is geared so that the 300 students who attend have a successful learning experience, as does the staff.

Ongoing Professional Development

Professional development for veteran Benchmark teachers is ongoing and comes in many varieties: peer collaboration, classroom observations, interactive journals, meetings, professional reading, and program development. Peer collaboration may have more influence on how teachers teach at Benchmark than any other aspect of professional development. Collaboration occurs because time for it is built into the school day. Three opportunities for collaboration take place each week: lower and middle-school team meetings, where teachers discuss instruction and students; individual teacher–supervisor meetings to plan instruction and problem solve; and meetings among three or four teachers and the principal to discuss curriculum. Through all of these vehicles, teachers learn about other teachers' instruction; as a result, instruction in all classrooms is enhanced.

Supervisors and the principal observe in classrooms each day and share what they learn with other staff members, as well as give input to the teachers they observe. Teacher–supervisor interactive journals are one means of communication. Supervisors observe a lesson and write their impressions about how instruction is impacting students, perhaps making suggestions, often asking questions. The teachers then write reactions to the supervisor's input, sometimes requesting that the supervisor teach while the teacher observes, sometimes proposing an alternative plan of attack with the students.

Once a month, students are dismissed early to create extra time for professional development. This monthly inservice is provided by nationally known educators whose work interests the staff. Both the weekly research seminars, at which the staff discusses professional reading, and the day-long retreats for curriculum development serve as preparation for and follow-up to these inservice programs.

Professional development is further enhanced by the staff's involvement in the school's research and development projects, such as the 1988–1994 James S. McDonnell Foundation project to develop learners, thinkers, and problem solvers across the curriculum. The professional writing for publication that results from these projects is critiqued by the staff—another means of professional development. The elements of professional development described previously are further elaborated by Gaskins (1994).

PRINCIPLES FOR INSTRUCTION

The theory of learning and definition of reading discussed earlier set forth the major concepts that undergird Benchmark's instructional program. We now discuss how theory has been turned into practice as we describe the five principles guiding reading instruction in Benchmark classrooms: (a) focus on the desired outcomes of instruction, (b) create a safe environment for risk taking, (c) plan yet be dynamic and flexible, (d) teach actively and across the curriculum, and (e) encourage extensive reading and sharing. We describe how these principles come to life in Benchmark classrooms.

Focus on the Desired Outcomes of Instruction

Benchmark teachers share with students *what* the school's mission is and *how* this mission is translated into student outcomes. They also explain *why* the mission and desired outcomes are important. In discussing the rationale, teachers provide real-world examples to help students become aware that those who develop proficiency in reading will have more educational and career options than those who choose not to read or those who cannot read well. Examples are drawn from both school and the workplace to illustrate that reading provides the primary avenue by which people learn and expand their knowledge, thus becoming equipped for the effective thinking and problem solving that schools and the workplace require. In addition, teachers lead students to discover that reading introduces them to a vast array of people, places, and ideas that they might otherwise never experience. Teachers are convinced that, if students understand that reading affects both how intelligently they function and the quality of their lives, they will be more willing to expend the necessary effort to become better readers. For all these reasons, helping students become proficient readers who enjoy reading is a goal for Benchmark teachers.

Teach to a Few Valued Outcomes. One's destination determines the course in reaching it. Thus, staff members look at the school's exit outcomes to determine what role each can play in preparing students to achieve those outcomes. Examples of outcomes students should achieve before entering ninth grade in another school include:

1. Demonstrate the dispositions and competencies they need to be independent, proficient, self-regulated, and lifelong readers who love to read.
2. Value reading as a primary way to learn and expand their knowledge, thus becoming equipped for the effective thinking and problem solving that schools and the workplace require.

3. Make interpretations of what they read that are valid to the extent that they follow logically from a transaction between the text and students' background knowledge.

4. Demonstrate awareness of the factors affecting the construction of meaning, and take control of those factors by employing active-reader strategies, assessing progress toward their reading goal, and using fix-up strategies when necessary.

5. Realize that reading is an active process of constructing meaning from text, rather than a passive transmittal of information.

Once the school's outcomes are established, teachers analyze the outcomes into components that can become outcomes for the particular levels they teach. For example, teachers of beginning readers listed some of the following outcomes for their students this year:

1. Understand that what they read must make sense; when reading does not make sense, they should take remedial action to gain understanding.

2. Demonstrate affective involvement in reading; for example, by writing a free-response journal entry about feelings evoked by a story or book.

3. Demonstrate active/strategic involvement in reading by surveying, accessing background knowledge, predicting, reading for a purpose, changing a prediction based on information in the text, integrating new information with prior knowledge, implementing a decoding strategy to unlock an unknown word, and so on.

4. Select engaging and appropriate books for independent reading, and convey to others (by such activities as writing enthusiastic book reviews, presenting book commercials, and writing in the class response journal) that reading is a pleasurable activity.

5. Retell/summarize fiction succinctly by identifying major characters, setting, problem, and solution.

6. Draw inferences by integrating appropriate information from background knowledge and the text.

7. Demonstrate a belief in the value of using cognitive and metacognitive strategies to enhance decoding and comprehension by describing what, how, and why various strategies enhance the completion of a specific task.

8. Monitor understanding and take remedial action when necessary.

Create a Safe Environment for Risk Taking

Benchmark teachers believe that reading instruction should be presented in an environment that students view as safe. Thus, classrooms are characterized by genuine affection, routines, and standards. Collaboration and learning are the goals, rather than the completion of tasks. Similarly, Wittrock (1991) reported that students prefer teachers who are warm, friendly, supportive, and communicative, and who provide an environment that is orderly, motivational, and disciplined. Classroom environments with these characteristics are crucial for poor readers because developing expertise in the skills and strategies necessary for learning to read requires risks. Poor readers have a history of failure and public embarrassment, so tend to be reluctant to take risks (e.g., Johnston & Winograd, 1985). Only when students view their classroom as safe will they become risk takers.

Create Environments Characterized by Care, Routine, Standards, and Collaboration. Although the students soon become partners in developing and maintaining a nurturing environment, it is Benchmark teachers who play the central role in creating a safe environment. Not only are teachers responsible for selecting activities that occur in the classroom, but they also hold the key to the social, emotional, and intellectual climate of the classroom. Together these factors shape students' attitudes and behaviors toward learning (Ames, 1992). Although creating a nurturing environment certainly involves many factors, the most important may be that Benchmark teachers genuinely care about their students and are committed to helping them succeed. Although it is true that self-confidence and motivation cannot be instilled in a person, knowing that a trusted person will provide support and guidance when it is needed appears to make students more willing to take risks and to strive to reach their full potential (Bowlby, 1979; R. Gaskins, 1992; Mann, 1986). Further, the way teachers structure learning activities, such as the level of task difficulty (Brophy & Good, 1986), as well as the tone and means of teacher feedback, affects students' self-concepts and expectations about their future school performance (Wittrock, 1986).

One of the many potentially unsettling experiences for poor readers is entering a classroom where both the teacher and other students may be unknown. A teacher who does everything possible to foster group feelings as quickly as possible will have gone a long way in getting students off to a good start. To ease transition to a new class, Benchmark students and their parent(s) begin each school year by special appointment with the teacher. During the first week of school, each student meets with his or her new teacher for an individual, 1-hour meeting. While the child and teacher discuss their expectations for the year, the parent(s) complete a questionnaire sharing information they would like the teacher to know about their child. They comment on such things as characteristics that make the child fun to know, insights they may have about how their child learns, and chores the child does around the house. Then, near the end of the hour, the teacher invites the parent(s) to join the meeting with the student. During this short meeting, the child shares what he or she has learned about expectations for the class, and hears the parent(s) share the positive characteristics the child brings to the learning environment. The teacher shares his or her plans for teaching the child, including the use of portfolios instead of grades to monitor progress. By the end of the meeting, the student usually has a positive feeling about his or her chances of meeting with success in the classroom, and is well on the way to being convinced that the teacher cares about him or her.

Another way the Benchmark staff demonstrate that they care is by volunteering to be mentors for students who are at risk for experiencing difficulty, even in the nurturing environment found at Benchmark. Between 40 and 50 of the 175 Benchmark students are assigned volunteer mentors—staff members who meet with the students individually at least once a week and are available on an as-needed basis. The support that the mentors provide ranges from providing scaffolded instruction on how to apply cognitive and metacognitive strategies, to providing advice on how to handle social situations that have arisen, to being available to share students' excitement when something positive occurs that they want to talk about. The goal of the mentor program is to develop self-regulated learners who have the knowledge, strategies, and motivation necessary to succeed not only academically, but in every phase of their lives (R. Gaskins, 1992).

Care, trust, and commitment to helping every student succeed permeate all aspects of classroom life at Benchmark. This becomes manifest as teachers develop routines for accomplishing frequently occurring tasks, standards by which the students can evaluate themselves, and social interactions such as collaboration, which can enhance learning. Familiar routines are important because they "decrease the collective information-processing load" (Clark & Peterson, 1986, p. 293) and create a safe and predictable environment. Standards clearly spell out what teachers expect, providing a goal toward which students can strive and criteria against which they can assess their progress, thus negating the need for them to measure themselves against others. Standards are seen as developmental, and steady progress toward achieving the standards through strategic effort is the measure of success. Teachers are interested in each student's individual progress, and do not compare students to their peers. Moreover, they encourage students to do the same. Portfolios and regular portfolio conferences throughout the school year support this philosophy.

At Benchmark, meeting standards is a collaborative venture, in which students support one another by sharing conceptual knowledge as well as knowledge about how to complete tasks. Collaboration is encouraged as a means of constructing understanding of both the text and the skills and strategies that are taught. Because teachers model and reinforce interactions that are characterized by care, trust, and commitment, students tend to emulate these characteristics in their interactions with one another.

Promote Learning, Not Performance. Students' attitudes and behavior related to taking the risks necessary to learn to read are influenced by whether the classroom goal orientation is toward learning or performance (Ames, 1992; Ames & Archer, 1988; Elliot & Dweck, 1988). We have discovered that teachers who value strategic effort over ability and learning over performance increase the likelihood that poor readers will risk venturing an explanation of a text or decoding an unknown word. Thus, in Benchmark classrooms, where the orientation is toward learning, students are willing to take risks. They dare to value the processes of learning and understanding, and they begin to see success as depending on planful and strategic effort. In their former schools, these same students were oriented toward performance goals and were concerned about such things as being judged competent, showing evidence of ability by achieving good grades, or succeeding with the least possible effort. They placed value on ability and completing tasks. Their aim in former schools was to demonstrate their abilities by outperforming others and to avoid any display of incompetence (e.g., Ames, 1992; Dweck, 1986; Meece, Blumenfeld, & Hoyle, 1988).

Our goal is to create a safe classroom environment in which students feel comfortable enough to: (a) know when they do not understand something and ask for clarification; (b) measure their progress not as compared with others, but progress they have made as compared with themselves; and (c) place a high priority on strategic effort and learning goals, rather than on being the first to finish or on seeming unconcerned. We have discovered that what teachers value—effort or ability, learning or performance—influences students' goal orientation and profoundly affects their response to instruction. Dweck (1986) discussed the specific effect of goal orientations on risk taking: ". . . with a learning goal, children are willing to risk displays of ignorance in order to acquire skills and knowledge. Instead of calculating their exact ability level and how it will be judged (as with a performance goal), they can think more about the value of the skill to be developed or their interest in the task to be undertaken" (p. 1042).

As Dweck suggested and we have experienced, when learning is the goal, the anxiety related to risk taking is reduced or nullified. This is because the focus is on individual progress and the development of expertise as a result of effort. Conversely, with performance goals, the focus is on ability, and thus challenging tasks tend to be avoided for fear of failure (Dweck, 1986; Dweck & Leggett, 1988; Elliot & Dweck, 1988). Furthermore, when failure does occur, students with performance goal orientations are likely to see failure as evidence of a lack of competence (Jagacinski & Nicholls, 1987). For these students, learning remains an anxiety-producing endeavor. Thus, it is clear why Benchmark teachers strive to promote learning, thereby creating an environment that fosters risk taking, rather than failure avoidance.

Plan Yet Be Dynamic and Flexible

The ability to maximize student engagement in purposeful learning at an appropriate level is the product of a teacher's theoretical and pedagogical understandings (Shulman, 1986) and the teacher's organization of that understanding into a plan of instruction (Dole, Duffy, Roehler, & Pearson, 1991). The critical importance of teacher planning is underscored by research that consistently verifies the link between student achievement and the pacing and quality of instruction (Brophy & Good, 1986; Wittrock, 1986). Research and experience have also led Benchmark teachers to the understanding that the "amount learned is related to the opportunity to learn" (Brophy & Good, 1986, p. 360), and that the time poor readers spend engaged in reading at an appropriate level correlates with progress in reading. Because the way teachers use their time with students is a critical factor in determining the progress made by poor readers, it is imperative that activities for the instructional and independent portions of the school day be planned carefully by knowledgeable teachers. Lack of knowledgeable planning can result in lost opportunities for learning, such as instruction that is too difficult even with teacher assistance or instruction that students regard as serving no authentic purpose. Further, poor planning may result in instruction being cut short due to unnecessarily long transitions between activities.

Determine Students' Appropriate Levels. At Benchmark, teacher planning begins by determining the zone within which each student can be instructed successfully. Determination of this zone requires that a teacher be aware of a variety of student factors, such as interests, beliefs about learning and self as a learner, background of knowledge about specific concepts, and awareness and use of cognitive and metacognitive strategies. Beliefs about learning and self as a learner are particularly influential in determining the characteristic way in which each student approaches a learning task. Based on the teacher's understanding of these student factors, instruction is planned at a level where each student can perform comfortably and successfully with assistance. Vygotsky (1978) referred to this optimal level of instruction as the *zone of proximal development.*

The zone of proximal development begins at the intersection of the highest level at which a student can successfully construct meaning without assistance (a student's independent level) and the level at which he or she needs teacher assistance to be successful (instructional level). Vygotsky (1962) described the zone of proximal development as the place where instruction "marches ahead of development and leads it; it must be aimed not so much at the ripe as at the ripening function" (p. 104). In this statement, he suggested that the optimal level of instruction is not the level at which the teacher reviews what the student can successfully accomplish independently, but rather the level where help is needed to develop concepts, skills, and strategies for which the student is developmentally ready. It is the level at which instruction is neither too easy nor too difficult when assistance is provided.

Organize for Maximum Academic Engagement. Although the issue of identifying students' optimal level for instruction is an essential one for planning effective instruction, an issue that is equally fundamental is ensuring that students spend the maximum time possible engaged in purposeful activities. These must be activities that guide students to acquire the skills and strategies they need to accomplish the valued outcomes of the school—in our case, becoming self-regulated readers, learners, thinkers, and problem solvers. How teachers organize for instruction is a key to accomplishing these outcomes. At Benchmark, organization occurs at three points: before the school year, before the school day, and before the activity (R. Gaskins, 1988).

Prior to the beginning of the school year, Benchmark teachers reflect on classroom routines and expectations of previous school years, and determine those that might be a match for the incoming students. For example, teachers think through behavioral expectations and establish how transitions will occur. Knowing that students need to clearly understand what is expected of them and why those expectations and routines are necessary, teachers plan a rationale to share with students at the time expectations and routines are explained. In addition, teachers think through how they will consistently reinforce expectations and routines until they become an integral part of the classroom milieu.

Organization before each school day entails planning in detail specific instructional sequences, including the design of activities, selection of materials, and placement of materials and plans where they are easily accessible. Benchmark teachers usually write their lesson plans in some detail. These written plans might include an instructional sequence to begin with an every-pupil-response (EPR) activity that taps students' understanding about the previous day's concept, theme, objective, or strategy. For example, a teacher might plan an EPR that asks students to write a prediction about what will happen next, including supporting evidence from the text. Other possibilities for EPRs include writing: (a) the theme or major concept of a text, (b) the strategies each student used to process the text and why these were chosen, (c) background information related to the text, (d) perplexities about what was read, and (e) applications that might be made to real-life situations based on what was read. Occasionally students are asked to draw and label a diagram that illustrates their understanding of a concept. (See I. Gaskins, Satlow, Hyson, Ostertag, & Six, 1994, for further examples of how EPRs are employed to enhance classroom talk.)

The next activity to plan might be how to guide students in decoding in context any unfamiliar words that are present in the text to be read that day. Teachers select words they anticipate students may have difficulty decoding, and place these words in context on index cards or sentence strips. They teach students two processes that can be helpful in decoding unknown words: (a) use the sense of the story, their background knowledge, and the initial consonant of the unknown word to guess what a word is; or (b) when context does not help, analyze the unknown words to find known spelling patterns (a vowel and what comes after it, such as -*an*, -*ope*, -*ink*, etc.). Thus, students use what they know to figure out what they do not know (Gaskins, Gaskins, & Gaskins, 1991).

Next, teachers may plan how to introduce a strategy or skill that will facilitate meaning-making when students read the text. Teachers plan exactly what the strategy will be (e.g., identifying important information; recognizing genre based on a survey of the text, then using characteristics associated with the genre to guide predictions and understanding; integrating text information and background information to make inferences). In addition, they plan the rationale for why that strategy is appropriate and helpful, and the other occasions when the strategy might be put to use. Most important, they think through and often write a precise explanation for how to implement the strategy.

Organization done before the activity includes things a teacher does after he or she enters the classroom each day to organize materials, setting, schedule, and so on so that every minute of each student's day is profitably spent engaged in reading and instruction. Teachers may place the books and lesson plan for a reading lesson near where they will be used, or arrange chairs or desks for a reading discussion. The routine for the day is often written on the chalkboard, and guidelines for an activity or implementing a strategy may be posted.

Provide Instruction That Is Dynamic and Flexible. Although short- and long-term planning is essential to maximizing students' engaged time in purposeful reading activities, Benchmark teachers recognize that they must be willing to deviate from those plans when students' comments, questions, or general responses suggest that other concepts or strategies need attention before the stated objectives of their lesson can be addressed. This flexibility does not imply that teachers digress onto meaningless tangents. What it does suggest is that teachers make the most of situations that arise spontaneously to enhance opportunities for social, emotional, and intellectual growth. These situations may include an unexpected need for a strategy to be taught or reviewed, a lack of understanding that was not anticipated, a lack of background knowledge that was assumed, or an unforeseen emotional response.

It is not unusual for Benchmark teachers to plan reading instruction for the week ahead, only to discover that students do not have the prerequisite background of knowledge or skills necessary to proceed with the new strategy. Thus, the planned reading lesson has to be set aside until the prerequisite skills can be taught. For example, one Monday, a teacher was planning to teach students how to select information from text that was pertinent to a science problem about heat. However, after introducing the what, why, when, and how of the objective, she discovered that students were not able to find the passages of text to use for solving the problem because they were having trouble generating appropriate topics and sub-topics to use in the book's index. Thus, the teacher put aside her original plan for a few days while she taught students how to generate topics and use the index.

In summary, Benchmark teachers recognize and take advantage of teach-able moments, but, perhaps even more important, they understand that carefully planned instruction, based on students' present understandings, needs, and learner characteristics, creates the opportunity for many teachable moments in the first place.

Teach Actively and Across the Curriculum

Benchmark classrooms are rich with a variety of texts, trade books, literature anthologies, magazines, and other materials and experiences. Yet like Cazden (1991), we know of no research evidence that suggests that immersion in such an environment will be sufficient for improving reading, thus students are not left on their own to discover how to read. Benchmark teachers believe that learning to read is a socially mediated process, thus they actively engage students in instructional dialogues. We agree with Delpit (1986, 1988) that teaching must be deliberate. Further, we believe that active teaching of reading cannot take place solely during a class period designated for reading or language arts, but rather must take place across the curriculum.

Teach Reading Across the Curriculum. Benchmark teachers recognize that when students complete their schooling, regardless of their life situations or occupations, reading will play a role in their ability to function successfully. To read to complete real-life tasks effectively, students need to have had experiences completing similar tasks using similar text resources for similar purposes. In addition, if they are to be successful in completing such tasks, they need to develop an understanding of how to select appropriate resources to match their purposes.

Given this reality, Benchmark students are provided with opportunities to engage in a variety of text-based activities, as well as instruction and assistance about how to succeed. They receive instruction about what strategies are effective for reading and understanding various print resources, as well as instruction in how, why, and when to use various strategies and texts for specific purposes (e.g., see I. Gaskins, Guthrie, et al., 1994, in preparation). Benchmark teachers believe that the most appropriate time to provide such reading opportunities and instruction is when they are relevant to completing a task. Given that real-world activities cut across the curriculum, reading instruction must also cut across the curriculum. For example, in teaching science, a teacher found the need to teach students that the first step in searching for information to support their explanations of solutions was to generate key words. Thus, students were taught how to generate possible topics to consult in the index. This also led to teaching students how to choose appropriate pages to search, and how to select only information that satisfied their purpose—all real-world skills. A discussion about how to search for information might begin like this:

> T: Some of you seem to be having difficulty finding information to support your explanations of why the diameter of your inflated balloon decreased after a night in the refrigerator. Let's talk about the process for searching for specific information. The first thing we need to do is think of words we can find in the index that are related to our problem. I'll give you about one minute to jot down words related to the balloon problem. (Students list words as the teacher circulates among them supporting their efforts.)
>
> T: Now turn to your partner and decide between you which two or three words will probably be most helpful in finding an explanation for the balloon's decreased size. (Students spend about one minute talking to their partners.)
>
> T: The conversation you just had with your partner is one you can also have with yourself. When you need to search for information, you can talk to yourself about words related to the problem you are researching. Remember, all smart people talk to themselves. If you are still stuck after you have talked in your head, then brainstorm with a friend as we have just done. Finding the best words related to your problem is the key to a successful search—using the wrong words will cause you to waste a lot of time and you still may not be successful.
>
> T: Now let's share the several words you listed related to the balloon problem. (The students share their words and, as they do, the teacher asks each student why he or she thinks the word is related to the balloon problem; then asks the class to evaluate the word as to its helpfulness for locating information about the balloon problem. The class decides that *heat* and *molecules* are the best two words to find in the index and the search is begun.)

The reading instruction that occurs in all curriculum areas at Benchmark retains the same essential qualities found during the reading and language arts time block. The instruction is explicit, informed, interactive, responsive, and scaffolded (I. Gaskins, 1994; I. Gaskins & Elliot, 1991; I. Gaskins et al., 1993). In the remainder of this section, we discuss each of these qualities.

Provide Instruction That Is Explicit and Informed. For the past decade, two of the defining characteristics of instruction at Benchmark have been that instruction is explicit and informed. When concepts, skills, and strategies are introduced, whether as part of a strategy lesson on drawing inferences, as part of the supplemental word-identification program, or as part of any other instructional sequence, teachers explicitly explain *what* the concept, skill, or strategy is and *how* to use it, as well as inform students as to *why* the concept, skill, or strategy is important, and *when* they might use it. Research suggests that being "informed" about the why and when helps students transfer what has been learned to novel situations (Baumann & Schmitt, 1986). The use of explicit and informed instruction is particularly important for the Benchmark population because poor readers often do not discover concepts, skills, and strategies on their own, as good readers often do (Chan & Cole, 1986; Wong, 1985). Thus, at Benchmark, explicit and informed reading instruction, by necessity, is and is likely to remain firmly entrenched.

The dialogue for explicitly introducing a new strategy might sound something like the following, with the teacher filling in the specifics about the strategy being taught.

What: "Today we are going to learn . . ." "What this means is . . ."

Why: "This is an important strategy because . . ."

When: "You can use this strategy when . . ." "Tomorrow I want you to tell me a time during your reading when you applied the strategy we are learning today."

How: The teacher next tells the students exactly how to do the strategy, being very explicit about the self-talk (what students should say to themselves as they employ the strategy) and usually illustrating the use of the strategy with a personal experience.

This is how part of one teacher's explicit instruction sounded on the day she introduced summarizing as a way to self-monitor:

T: Today we are going to learn a strategy for self-monitoring. What this means is we are going to learn one way to figure out whether we understand what we are reading. Why do you think it is important to self-monitor as you read?
S: Because reading has got to make sense and, if it doesn't, you've got to fix it.
S: Because if you don't think about what you're reading, you won't know what you read when you get through.
S: Strategies keep you actively involved.
T: Those are all fine reasons. You seem to be saying that it is important that you take some kind of strategic mental action while you are reading to be

sure that you are making meaning. Self-monitoring is a strategy you can use whenever you read, at home or in school. Tomorrow I want you to tell me a time between now and our reading time when you used self-monitoring in your reading.

One way I self-monitor is to read a portion of text, then stop and try to say in my own words what the important points were that I just read. In reading social studies or science, however, I find when I just say the summary to myself, I sometimes kid myself into thinking I understand when I don't. Therefore, when the information is new to me and it is important that I understand what I am reading, I usually not only say the summary to myself, but, after I say it, I write the summary. When I can't write a summary of what I read in my own words, then it usually means I didn't understand it.

Some of you were having difficulty yesterday with the trade books you were reading to help you understand heat. I photocopied one of the chapters so we could work on it together. Follow along as I read the first page and think aloud about the main point in each paragraph, then I'll try to pull these main points together to check my understanding. I already tried this and discovered my understanding of heat is pretty fuzzy, so I know the strategy of summarizing works for monitoring or checking my understanding.

On the days following the introduction of a strategy, the teacher may lead a discussion that is initiated by some of these questions:

What: "What strategy have we been using to. . .?" "What do you say to yourself to guide yourself in using the strategy?"

Why: "Why is . . . an important strategy? How will it help you understand and remember what you read?"

When: "When did you use the strategy?"

How: "Can someone tell me how to do the strategy we are learning?"

One particularly important component of the explicit and informed instruction provided at Benchmark is mental modeling (Duffy, Roehler, & Herrmann, 1988). When teachers model a skill or strategy, they do more than simply model the product or desired outcome. For example, they would not model making predictions by simply telling the students what they predict will happen in a text. Instead, they model the process of how they made that prediction. They think aloud about what clues are being used to make the prediction, why they chose each clue, and how they put the clues together to make a prediction. In so doing, they allow students to view the otherwise hidden mental processes behind successful skill and strategy use. Benchmark teachers walk students through how to do what they need to do, rather than expecting that they already know how to do such things as predict, infer, or monitor.

Employ an Instructional Model That Is Interactive and Responsive.
Although the explicit and informed nature of instruction at Benchmark might suggest that the school's instruction follows a direct-instruction model, it does not. Benchmark teachers embed explicit and informed instruction in an interactive and responsive instructional model. Research suggests that the most common instructional interaction pattern found in classrooms is one in which the teacher *i*nitiates a topic through a question, a student *r*esponds, and the teacher *e*valuates that response (IRE interaction pattern; e.g., Cazden, 1988). This is an interaction pattern common to a direct-instruction model, but foreign to Benchmark classrooms. An IRE pattern focuses on whether students have the "right" answer, rather than on helping students understand the process of how one constructs meaning. It also requires students to create the same meaning that the teacher constructed, rather than create their own understanding of the text and explore possible meanings (e.g., Au, 1993). Because Benchmark teachers emphasize an understanding of the process of learning enroute to developing self-regulated thinkers, an IRE pattern is rare in Benchmark classrooms.

Instead, in Benchmark classrooms, the interactive patterns are truly interactive (as opposed to teacher-directed IREs). Teachers respond to students' needs to help them develop a deeper understanding of the conceptual and strategic information being discussed. In the responsive-interactive cycles, either the teacher or the student functions as the initiator and responder in the interaction, although the teacher guides the discussion by being responsive and encouraging student comments or questions. The key difference in the Benchmark approach is that teacher comments or questions are responsive to the students' remarks, rather than being primarily evaluative. This responsiveness can take the form of encouraging elaboration, seeking clarification, or adding information that supports students' ideas (I. Gaskins et al., 1993). The responsive quality of interactions at Benchmark is crucial to students' development toward becoming self-regulated readers and learners. As Duffy and Roehler (1987) suggested, responsiveness is "the heart of instructional effectiveness, because it is the teachers' sensitivity to students' restructuring and their responsiveness to these understandings which determine what students ultimately come to understand" (p. 417).

Scaffold Instruction. The final characteristic of Benchmark instruction is that instruction is scaffolded. As students develop toward independence and self-regulation, they need support and guidance. But the question that all teachers grapple with is, How much support should be provided? When constructing a building, scaffolding is a streamline, yet sturdy, material used to provide support as the building is constructed. In a similar fashion, scaffolded instruction suggests that students receive the support necessary for them to succeed, but no more than is necessary.

Typically, there is a pattern to the amount of support students need when learning a concept, skill, or strategy. Usually our students need the most support when what is being learned is first introduced, and they require progressively less support over time and in familiar situations. However, additional support is often needed when what was learned in one situation is to be applied in a novel situation. The process of the teacher reducing support and guidance is often referred to as a gradual release of responsibility from the teacher to the student (Pearson & Gallagher, 1983).

Although this pattern of gradually releasing support is generally the case, Benchmark teachers are prepared to exercise a range of support. For students who need a great deal of support, teachers may reteach or model a skill or strategy, or reintroduce a concept. For students ready to assume some of the responsibility for applying a concept or process, teachers may provide cues to use specific elements of the concept, skill, or strategy. If students are ready to assume even more responsibility, they may need only a general cue to be successful. If they are still more independent, they may require only a single cue to call to mind a concept or process that might be useful in this situation (Beed, Hawkins, & Roller, 1991). We have found that the exact level of support students need varies depending on their level of understanding of the concept, skill, or strategy, as well as factors related to the text, task, and their own learner characteristics. The general principle that Benchmark teachers use throughout is: provide students with the least amount of support necessary for them to be successful. This practice moves students toward independence and self-regulation.

Encourage Extensive Reading and Sharing

Provide Opportunities for Voluminous Reading. One of the cornerstones of instruction at Benchmark is the belief that progress in reading is correlated with the number of words read. Benchmark teachers recognize that, to develop expertise, practice at a comfortable level is necessary. Providing ample opportunity for practice allows students to refine skills and develop new ones within a safe environment. To enhance progress in the area of reading, children at Benchmark spend a great deal of time, in and out of school, reading independent-level trade books and instructional-level texts.

In the classroom, large blocks of time are devoted to silent reading. For example, during reading instruction, the majority of the time is devoted to actually reading text, while instruction and discussion about the text are brief and designed to support the reading. Likewise, when the teacher is instructing one group of students and the remaining students are completing work independently, those working independently spend the majority of their time reading, rather than completing workbook pages or completing written responses to what was read.

Students are also expected to read at least a half hour each evening at home. They have the opportunity to visit the library daily, and are expected to take home enough reading material for 30 minutes of reading in the evening. Combining this reading with that completed in school, it is not unusual during one school year for each primary-level student to read 20 literature basal anthologies and hundreds of trade books. About 10% of the students supplement their silent reading by also taking part in a taped-repeated reading program, which enables them to experience books at an appropriate conceptual level. Thus, it is clear that practice in the area of reading is a high priority at Benchmark.

Provide Opportunities for Sharing. Although teachers at Benchmark recognize the importance of practice to see improvement, they also recognize that refining skills and developing new ones need not and should not be a solitary endeavor. Benchmark teachers believe that sharing ideas with others fosters the construction of meaning. As students collaborate with others about what they read, they share their interpretations of the text, strategies that they found useful, interesting observations about the text, and their feelings about the characters, plot, and author's style. The result is that students gain new perspectives, as well as receive feedback on their own ideas. Thus, sharing thoughts about the what and how of reading expands students' conceptual and strategic knowledge, as well as increases their motivation to read. Students are enthusiastic about discussing what they have read when what they are reading is at a comfortable level, and they possess the skills and background knowledge to read with understanding.

Each day students at Benchmark are given many opportunities to share their ideas about books. Students may confer in pairs about the books (or chapters in books) that they read the previous evening. In these paired sharings, students take turns sharing perceptions and asking each other questions about the books they are reading. Sharing also takes place in small discussion groups, especially when two or three students have elected to read the same book. Although the teacher may be a participant in these groups, and often initiates the discussions, students tend to carry the discussions, raising questions and making comments in the flow of the interaction. Rather than direct these discussions, teachers simply listen and interject questions and ideas when necessary to keep the discussion progressing in a fruitful manner. Usually these discussions are characterized by lively exchanges of ideas, and function both to broaden students' understanding and generate enthusiasm for reading.

One teacher begins the day with book commercials. Students give 60-second commercials for a book they think other students will enjoy. There is always a run on books for which commercials have been given, and students regard the commercials as a reliable guide for selecting interesting books. For example, one 9-year-old kept her class enthralled for over a week with her daily commercials about the audacious deeds of Gilly Hopkins (Paterson, 1978). In summary, practice and sharing are important components of the Benchmark reading program. These two aspects of the program serve the crucial functions of developing knowledge, skills, and strategies, and building confidence, motivation, and enthusiasm for reading.

SUMMARY

The foundation for teaching reading at Benchmark is a theory of learning based on the research of cognitive scientists. This theory suggests that learning is a socially mediated, knowledge-based process that requires active construction of meaning. It also acknowledges other factors that affect learning: one's attitude toward learning and about oneself as a learner, the amount of time and effort devoted to learning, and the purposeful nature of activities. We believe that the goal of learning to read is for learners to construct meaning based on their experiences and the text. Based on our theory of learning and definition of reading, the Benchmark faculty has delineated five instructional principles that guide professional development and reading instruction: focus on the desired outcomes of instruction, create a safe environment for risk taking, plan yet be dynamic and flexible, teach actively across the curriculum, and encourage extensive reading and sharing.

The learning theory and instructional principles undergird the reading program, as well as all instruction at Benchmark. At Benchmark, an effort is made to present an integrated, total-school program that builds students' conceptual and strategic knowledge, and helps them see the relevance of this knowledge for a wide array of situations encountered outside of school. Innovative programs such as Psych 101 and LAT, which teach students about how the mind works, and the mentor program, which provides volunteer mentors for students who are having the most difficulty, also help convey to students the value of becoming self-regulated readers, learners, thinkers, and problem solvers.

Benchmark teachers are pleased with the instructional program that has evolved over time. However, they continue to strive to make the program better. In fact, this is one of the secrets to its success—the program is always evolving. Staff development programs, including the weekly research seminar and monthly inservice meetings with nationally recognized speakers, are always directed toward the goal of constant refinement and development. Areas of the curriculum that have not been a priority in the past, but in which students are weak, such as spelling, grammar, and vocabulary development, will be given close scrutiny in the year ahead. In addition, strategies for word identification, meaning construction, and writing will continue to be refined. The intended result of these efforts is to continue providing Benchmark students with the most effective program possible based on the most up-to-date research—a program that fosters a love of reading and a love of learning, and that provides students with the knowledge, skills, strategies, and motivation to become self-regulated readers and learners.

REFERENCES

Ames, C. (1992). Classrooms: Goals, structures, and student motivation. *Journal of Educational Psychology, 84*, 261–271.

Ames, C., & Archer, J. (1988). Achievement goals in the classroom: Students' learning strategies and motivation processes. *Journal of Educational Psychology, 80*, 260–267.

Anderson, R. C., & Pearson, P. D. (1984). A schema-theoretic view of basic processes in reading comprehension. In P. D. Pearson, R. Barr, M. L. Kamil, & P. Mosenthal (Eds.), *Handbook of reading research* (pp. 255–291). New York: Longman.

Au, K. H. (1993). *Literacy instruction in multicultural settings*. New York: Harcourt Brace.

Baumann, J. F., & Schmitt, M. C. (1986). The what, why, how, and when of comprehension instruction. *The Reading Teacher, 39*, 640–647.

Beed, P. L., Hawkins, E. M., & Roller, C. M. (1991). Moving learners toward independence: The power of scaffolded instruction. *The Reading Teacher, 44*, 648–655.

Bereiter, C., & Scardamalia, M. (1985). Cognitive coping strategies and the problem of "inert knowledge." In S. F. Chipman, J. W. Segal, & R. Glaser (Eds.), *Thinking and learning skills: Vol. 2. Research and open questions* (pp. 65–80). Hillsdale, NJ: Lawrence Erlbaum Associates.

Bowlby, J. (1979). *The making and breaking of affective bonds*. London, England: Tavistock.

Brophy, J. E. (1987). Synthesis of research on strategies for motivating students to learn. *Educational Leadership, 44*, 40–48.

Brophy, J. E., & Good, T. (1986). Teacher behavior and student achievement. In M. Wittrock (Ed.), *Handbook of research on teaching* (pp. 328–375). New York: Macmillan.

Brown, A. L. (1985). *Teaching students to think as they read: Implications for curriculum reform* (Reading Ed. Rep. No. 58). Urbana-Champaign, IL: University of Illinois, Center for the Study of Reading.

Bruer, J. T. (1993). *Schools for thought: A science of learning in the classroom*. Cambridge, MA: MIT Press.

Cazden, C. B. (1988). *Classroom discourse: The language of teaching and learning*. Portsmouth, NH: Heinemann.

Cazden, C. B. (1991). Contemporary issues and future directions: Active learners and active teachers. In J. Flood, J. M. Jensen, D. Lapp, & J. R. Squire (Eds.), *Handbook of research on teaching the language arts* (pp. 418–422). New York: Macmillan.

Chan, L. K. S., & Cole, P. G. (1986). The effects of comprehension monitoring training on the reading competence of learning disabled and regular class students. *Remedial and Special Education, 7*, 33–40.

Clark, C. M., & Peterson, P. L. (1986). Teachers' thought processes. In M. C. Wittrock (Ed.), *Handbook of research on teaching* (pp. 255–297). New York: Macmillan.

Collins, A., Brown, J. S., & Newman, S. E. (1989). Cognitive apprenticeship: Teaching the crafts of reading, writing, and mathematics. In L. B. Resnick (Ed.), *Knowing, learning, and instruction: Essays in honor of Robert Glaser* (pp. 453–494). Hillsdale, NJ: Lawrence Erlbaum Associates.

Culler, J. (1975). *Structuralist poetics: Stucturalism, linguistics, and the study of literature*. Ithaca, NY: Cornell University Press.

Delpit, L. D. (1986). Skills and other dilemmas of a progressive Black educator. *Harvard Educational Review, 56*, 379–385.

Delpit, L. D. (1988). The silenced dialogue: Power and pedagogy in educating other people's children. *Harvard Educational Review, 58*, 280–298.

Dole, J., Duffy, G. G., Roehler, L. R., & Pearson, P. D. (1991). Moving from the old to the new: Research on reading comprehension instruction. *Review of Educational Research, 61*, 239–264.

Duffy, G. G., & Roehler, L. R. (1987). Teaching reading skills as strategies. *The Reading Teacher, 40*, 414–418.

Duffy, G. G., Roehler, L. R., & Herrmann, B. A. (1988). Modeling mental processes helps poor readers become strategic readers. *The Reading Teacher, 41*, 762–767.

Dweck, C. S. (1986). Motivational processes affecting learning. *American Psychology, 41*, 1040–1048.

Dweck, C. S., & Leggett, E. L. (1988). A social-cognitive approach to motivation and personality. *Psychological Review, 95*, 256–273.

Elliott, E. S., & Dweck, C. S. (1988). Goals: An approach to motivation and achievement. *Journal of Personality and Social Psychology, 54*, 5–12.

Fish, S. (1980). *Is there a text in this class?: The authority of interpretive communities.* Cambridge, MA: Harvard University Press.

Flavell, J. H. (1985). *Cognitive development* (2nd ed.). Englewood Cliffs, NJ: Prentice-Hall.

Gaskins, I. W. (1988). Helping teachers adapt to the needs of students with learning problems. In S. J. Samuels & P. D. Pearson (Eds.), *Changing school reading programs* (pp. 143–159). Newark, DE: International Reading Association.

Gaskins, I. W. (1994). Classroom applications of cognitive science: Teaching poor readers how to learn, think, and problem-solve. In K. McGilly (Ed.), *Classroom lessons: Integrating cognitive theory and classroom practice* (pp. 129–154). Boston, MA: Bradford Books.

Gaskins, I. W., Anderson, R. C., Guthrie, J. T., Satlow, E., Boehnlein, F., Cunicelli, E., & Benedict, J. (in preparation). *Poor readers' patterns of growth during two years of strategy instruction.*

Gaskins, I. W., Anderson, R. C., Pressley, M., Cunicelli, E. A., & Satlow, E. (1993). Six teachers' dialogue during cognitive process instruction. *The Elementary School Journal, 93*, 277–304.

Gaskins, I. W., Cunicelli, E. A., & Satlow, E. (1992). Implementing an across-the-curriculum strategies program: Reactions to change. In M. Pressley, K. Harris, & J. Guthrie (Eds.), *Promoting academic competence and literacy: Cognitive research and instructional innovation* (pp. 409–426). Boston: Academic Press.

Gaskins, I. W., Downer, M., Anderson, R. C., Cunningham, P. M., Gaskins, R. W., Schommer, M., & the Teachers of Benchmark School. (1988). A metacognitive approach to phonics: Using what you know to decode what you don't know. *Remedial and Special Education, 9*, 36–41, 66.

Gaskins, I. W., & Elliot, T. T. (1991). *Implementing cognitive strategy instruction across school: The Benchmark manual for teachers.* Cambridge, MA: Brookline Books.

Gaskins, I. W., Guthrie, J. T., Satlow, E., Ostertag, J., Six, L., Byrne, J., & Connor, B. (1994). Integrating instruction of science, reading, and writing: Goals, teacher development, and assessment. *Journal of Research in Science Teaching, 31*, 1039–1056.

Gaskins, I. W., Satlow, E., Hyson, D., Ostertag, J., & Six, L. (1994). Classroom talk about text: Learning in science class. *Journal of Reading, 37*, 558–565.

Gaskins, R. W. (1988). The missing ingredients: Time on task, direct instruction, and writing. *The Reading Teacher, 41*, 750–755.

Gaskins, R. W. (1992). When good instruction is not enough: A mentor program. *The Reading Teacher, 45*, 568–572.

Gaskins, R. W., Gaskins, J. C., & Gaskins, I. W. (1991). A decoding program for poor readers—and the rest of the class, too! *Language Arts, 68*, 213–225.

Glaser, R., & Chi, M. T. H. (1988). Overview. In M. T. H. Chi, R. Glaser, & M. J. Farr (Eds.), *The nature of expertise* (pp. xv–xxviii). Hillsdale, NJ: Lawrence Erlbaum Associates.

Iser, W. (1978). *The act of reading: A theory of aesthetic response.* Baltimore, MD: Johns Hopkins University Press.

Jagacinski, C. M., & Nicholls, J. G. (1987). Competence and affect in task involvement and ego-involvement: The impact of social comparison information. *Journal of Educational Psychology, 79,* 107–114.

Johnson, D. W., & Johnson, R. T. (1991). *Learning together and alone: Cooperative, competitive, and individualistic learning* (3rd ed.). Englewood Cliffs, NJ: Prentice-Hall.

Johnson, E. W., Johnson, R. T., & Holubec, E. (1990). *Circles of learning: Cooperation in the classroom* (3rd ed.). Edina, MN: Interaction.

Johnston, P. H., & Winograd, P. N. (1985). Passive failure in reading. *Journal of Reading Behavior, 4,* 279–301.

Mailloux, S. (1982). *Interpretive conventions: The reader in the study of American fiction.* Ithaca, NY: Cornell University Press.

Mann, D. (1986). Can we help dropouts: Thinking about the undoable. *Teachers College Record, 87,* 307–323.

Meece, J. L., Blumenfeld, P. C., & Hoyle, R. H. (1988). Students' goal orientations and cognitive engagement in classroom activities. *Journal of Educational Psychology, 80,* 514–523.

Nickerson, R. S. (1988). On improving thinking through instruction. In E. Z. Rothkopf (Ed.), *Review of educational research* (Vol. 15, pp. 3–57). Washington, DC: American Educational Research Association.

Paris, S. G., Lipson, M. Y., & Wixson, K. K. (1983). Becoming a strategic reader. *Contemporary Educational Psychology, 8,* 293–316.

Paterson, K. (1978). *The Great Gilly Hopkins.* New York: Thomas Y. Crowell Co.

Pearson, P. D., & Gallagher, M. C. (1983). The instruction of reading comprehension. *Contemporary Educational Psychology, 8,* 317–344.

Resnick, L. B. (1987). *Education and learning to think.* Washington, DC: National Academy Press.

Resnick, L. B., & Klopfer, L. E. (1989). Toward the thinking curriculum: An overview. In L. B. Resnick & L. E. Klopfer (Eds.), *Toward the thinking curriculum: Current cognitive research* (pp. 1–18). Alexandria, VA: Association for Supervision and Curriculum Development.

Rosenblatt, L. M. (1978). *The reader, the text, the poem: The transactional theory of the literary work.* Carbondale, IL: Southern Illinois University Press.

Rosenblatt, L. M. (1983). *Literature as exploration* (4th ed.). New York: The Modern Language Association of America.

Schunk, D. H. (1991). Self-efficacy and academic motivation. *Educational Psychologist, 26,* 207–231.

Shulman, L. S. (1986). Paradigms and research programs in the study of teaching: A contemporary perspective. In M. C. Wittrock (Ed.), *Handbook of research on teaching* (3rd ed., pp. 3–36). New York: Macmillan.

Slavin, R. D. (1990). *Cooperative learning: Theory, research, and practice.* Englewood Cliffs, NJ: Prentice-Hall.

Vygotsky, L. S. (1962). *Thought and language.* Cambridge, MA: MIT Press.

Vygotsky, L. S. (1978). *Mind in society.* Cambridge, MA: Harvard University Press.

Wittrock, M. C. (1986). Students' thought processes. In M. C. Wittrock (Ed.), *Handbook on research on teaching* (pp. 297–314). New York: Macmillan.

Wittrock, M. C. (1991). Generative teaching of comprehension. *Elementary School Journal, 92,* 170–184.

Wong, B. Y. L. (1985). Self-questioning instruction research: A review. *Review of Educational Research, 55,* 227–268.

CHAPTER SEVEN

Teaching From Theory: Decision Making in Reading Recovery

Adria F. Klein
Patricia R. Kelly
California State University, San Bernardino

Gay Su Pinnell
The Ohio State University, Columbus

Good readers move rapidly through written texts using many sources of information to problem solve while keeping attention focused on meaning. Josie, a fluent reader at the end of first grade, demonstrated many of the behaviors that proficient readers use as she read aloud *You'll Soon Grow into Them, Titch* (Hutchins, 1983), a book that was easy for her, but still presented a few challenges. In a brief portion of the running record of reading behaviors taken by her teacher, it was evident that Josie self-corrected, reread as needed, and occasionally substituted a meaningful word for another word. For example, about two thirds of the way through the book, the text read, "They bought a brand-new pair of pants . . ." (Hutchins, 1983, p. 15). Josie read *brought* instead of *bought*, which fit the structure of the sentence, but not the intended meaning; she then quickly self-corrected. She also commented to her teacher on the difference between the two words, demonstrating her ability to attend to visual detail. A bit further in the text, after reading, "Titch *wrote* the new clothes," she self-corrected the word *wore* for *wrote*, and then repeated the phrase, thus demonstrating her ability to use meaning and knowledge of language syntax to disconfirm her initial prediction of *wrote*. At yet another point, she read the word *and* for *a* in the sentence, "They bought a brand new pair of pants, *a* brand-new sweater. . . ." In this text, this substitution is an example of a meaningful miscue that good readers often make and then ignore, which Josie did.

Josie enjoyed the story and evidenced independent, effective problem solving while reading it. Her behavior indicated that she could integrate

several sources of information (e.g., meaning, structure/syntax, visual information, and prior experience) while reading fluently for meaning. Although
she could not read when she began first grade, Josie quickly became a
reader. Presented with opportunities to write and read, she brought her
considerable background of experience to bear on the process of becoming
literate. When she acquired "items" of knowledge (e.g., letter shapes and
names of particular words), she seemed to learn them in orchestrated ways,
as Clay (1991) described. Josie not only accessed information, but figured
out how to use sources of information strategically while operating on extended texts. She knew stories as experiences to enjoy—that they might be
funny, surprising, or scary—and she was willing to sort out the details of
written language (a sometimes tedious process) as she pursued the meaning.
Her early successes with simple, but enjoyable, stories gave her confidence
and spurred her on to try harder texts. Constructing pieces of writing helped
her figure out how words work, and, concentrating on producing her own
messages, she noticed and used letters and words in meaningful ways.

Many first graders are like Josie, but some have a less than positive
experience as they try learning to read in the school setting. For these children,
first experiences are confusing and do not provide the motivation or support
to help them develop a working knowledge of the reading process. This
chapter examines the reading and writing of children who have difficulty
sorting out the complexities of written language—those for whom the likelihood is high that confusions will persist, making it almost impossible for them
to fully participate in the classroom's ongoing literacy activities.

In our experience, children who struggle with the literacy concepts that
many first graders take on easily need a special kind of support in the
acquisition stage. Although most children acquire the networks of strategies
they need for effective and efficient reading in the context of literate classrooms, some children need additional resources and "many more supportive
interactions with teachers" (Clay, 1991, p. 345) to develop self-extending
systems in reading and writing. Reading Recovery, a short-term intervention
provided at an early point in a child's learning to read and write, provides
the type of support that fosters literacy development among these children.
In this chapter, we describe the theoretical foundations and procedures of
Reading Recovery, and discuss how teachers develop a theoretical base for
making the kind of powerful instructional moves that assist struggling readers
to become, like Josie, independent readers.

LEARNING TO READ

Reading is a complex process in which meaning is central. It is both a
strategic and a constructive process. The beginning reader acquires a network
of strategies for operating on text, including strategies that maintain fluency,

those that detect and correct errors, and those for problem solving new words. This model of reading "assumes that in order to read with understanding we call up and use a repertoire of strategies acting upon stores of knowledge to extract messages from print" (Clay, 1991, p. 326). Learning to read involves actively constructing this network of strategies.

Readers apply different kinds of knowledge or schema, depending on the way the text is written and what the reader knows about the subject (Mason & Au, 1990; Rumelhart, 1981). The child comes to school with an impressive system for understanding and using oral language, as well as prior knowledge and past experiences, all of which are the foundations for learning to read. In attempting to extract meaning from print, readers use several sources of information. They use their understandings about language, including meaning and sentence structures. Knowledge about conventions of print, such as directional rules and punctuation, is also used, along with visual information and patterns of sounds in words.

Beginning readers need to learn to use all of these sources of information in constructing meaning from print. They learn to read by reading and writing. An environment that engages young children in a rich array of literacy activities supports children's taking on the behaviors of good readers and writers; as a result, they develop the required internal strategic processes. According to Clay (1993), ". . . the brain probably constructs circuits which link several quite different parts of the brain and that such circuits only become functional for those persons who learn to do those things. We create many of the necessary links in the brain as we learn to engage in literate activities" (p. 11).

Reading and writing are mutually enhancing processes and, as such, should be taught in an interrelated manner. Writing is an analytical activity that requires close attention to print. It is through writing that children learn about the conventions of print, visual features of print, and how the sounds of speech are coded in print (Clay, 1991, 1993). Finally, and most important, reading is a self-extending system—one that expands and improves the effectiveness of strategies the reader brings to the task with each new reading opportunity (Clay, 1991).

DECISION MAKING IN READING RECOVERY

Reading Recovery provides rich, individualized literacy opportunities for the lowest achieving 20% of the children in a first-grade class. Marie Clay, a New Zealand psychologist, did extensive research, then developed and field tested the program in the late 1970s. Clay's (1979, 1985) research and the research of others (Lyons, Pinnell, & DeFord, 1993) provide evidence that short-term intervention at an early point in a child's learning to read and write can substantially reduce the chances of failure and the need for re-mediation.

Children are recommended for Reading Recovery by their first-grade teachers. After administration of Clay's Observation Survey (1979, 1993), the results are discussed with the teacher, and the lowest achieving children from the classroom are selected. A Reading Recovery teacher usually works with four first graders for a half hour each day, for 12–20 weeks. For the first 10 days, the teacher and child explore reading and writing together in an informal way, although the teacher is observing closely to gain more information about the child's knowledge base. The emphasis during this time (called "roaming around the known") is on moving flexibly around the body of knowledge that the child has already developed. This small body of knowledge acts as a springboard for trying new things (Clay, 1979). Both the teacher and child get a better sense of what is known and, often, dis-coveries are made. Shared reading, collaborative writing of stories, reading aloud, and talking about books are all part of "roaming around the known." Clay (1979) stated that, "the most important reason for roaming around the known is that it requires the teacher to stop teaching from her preconceived ideas. She has to work from the child's responses. This will be her focus throughout the programme" (p. 55).

After 10 days, a more routine lesson structure is adopted. This frame-work of activities serves as a context for the teacher–child interactions, which are adjusted for the individual child's responses. Reading Recovery has been described by a group of British researchers as "both highly structured and closely differentiated, according to the needs of the individual child" (HMSO, 1993, p. 3). These researchers went on to describe the Reading Recovery lesson as "a highly organised, intensive and, it must be stressed, enjoyable occasion. Moreover, it is not confined to reading alone—writing and a good deal of speaking and listening also feature strongly" (HMSO, 1993, p. 5).

Lessons are tailored to fit all children in the program. The children read many little books and write their own stories/messages. The lessons are designed to actively engage the children daily in a variety of reading and writing opportunities that support further learning. Each lesson and each child's program vary according to the child's strengths; the teacher carefully considers interests and needs, and makes ongoing adjustments. Decision making is a key factor in the teacher's ability to follow children's intentions, and to respond and guide in ways that reveal critical processes for problem solving in reading. Careful observation of children reading and writing text is the basis for the Reading Recovery lesson. "The goal is to teach children to use their knowledge and to see the purpose for it" (DeFord, Lyons, & Pinnell, 1991, p. 13). These children, who are low achievers at the beginning of the program, make accelerated progress and catch up with their average peers. When that occurs (and is substantiated by objective assessment), the one-to-one instruction is discontinued, and the Reading Recovery teacher then begins with another child. By the end of a school year, the experienced teacher, working half days in Reading Recovery and the other half day in another assignment, can teach 10–12 children to read.

The Reading Recovery lessons vary from child to child, and from day to day, because they are dynamically designed to meet each child's individual needs and work from each child's strengths. The teacher and child sit side by side to read and write collaboratively. This individualized setting provides opportunities for the teacher to systematically observe the child's efforts, and to take advantage of what the child is doing while engaged in supported literacy activities. Each day, the lessons include (a) rereading familiar books; (b) taking a running record of text reading, (c) an opportunity to further the child's understanding of how words work, (d) writing a story, and (e) reading a new book. The teacher uses the child's growing awareness and responses in shaping the day's lessons, taking advantage of possibilities to give attention to good attempts and explicitly teach extensions of what the child already understands and uses. The focus is on orchestration of information sources—both what the child brings to print and what he or she discovers while engaged in literacy events. By the selection of appropriate texts and supportive interactions, the teacher makes it easy for the child, scaffolding what is known and using it to foster growth in reading and writing.

The professional development program for teachers in Reading Recovery is a year-long, active process of developing and extending their personal theory of the reading process. From the beginning, the work with children supports the development of their theoretical understandings. Each week, the teachers participate in a university graduate-level course and view typical lessons behind one-way glass. Discussion among peers encourages the development of teacher decision making "on the run," while focusing analytic attention on the individual child being taught.

RESEARCH ON THE EFFECTIVENESS
OF READING RECOVERY

As a basis for developing Reading Recovery, Clay (1985) used her original research on young readers. She described in detail the behaviors of children in the initial stages of learning to read. These observations were the basis for the development of an observational survey (Clay, 1985, 1993), which teachers in New Zealand began to use as a check after children had experienced 1 year of school. Clay and her research team, prompted by teachers' concerns, began to look closely at children who were having difficulty. They developed a repertoire of reading and writing tasks that would serve as a structure for individual lessons. "A large number of techniques were piloted, observed, discussed, argued over, related to theory, analysed, written up, modified and tried out in various ways, and, most important, many were discarded" (Clay, 1985, p. 84).

Reading Recovery was an intervention not in the child, but in the system of education—a short-term infusion of daily one-to-one attention involving a student in a rich set of reading and writing activities, during which there was always a skilled assistant close at hand to help untangle confusions and make the literacy process accessible. Materials for the lessons were simple: (a) hundreds of short books arranged in a gradient of difficulty, (b) blank books and writing tools for children's own stories, (c) a chalkboard to vary writing surfaces, and (d) a set of magnetic alphabet letters for word construction. The heart of the instructional approach centered on the conversations between the teacher and child while involved in reading or writing.

Testing and Institutionalizing the Program in New Zealand

Reading Recovery was initiated in New Zealand during the early 1980s. Program evaluation data supported its immediate positive effects (see Clay, 1985). For this research, Clay used nonequivalent control groups to test the program's effectiveness. At the beginning of the year, the lowest achieving children were selected for Reading Recovery. The rest of the 6-year-olds, those not needing extra help, were considered the control group, making a tough test for Reading Recovery. By the end of the year, Clay found no differences between Reading Recovery children and the control group, indicating that the initially low-achieving children had caught up with their peers. Her studies also provided evidence that children continued to make progress after individual tutoring ended.

The program has been implemented in New Zealand for 12 years. Government figures indicate that the program has increased so that now over 20% of New Zealand 6-year-olds are served by Reading Recovery, and less than 1% of the population needs further help in reading (Clay, 1990). Recently, a team of researchers from the United Kingdom analyzed the program, making these statements:

> The great majority of pupils who undergo the programme reach its objective of matching the average band of reading attainment in the classes from which they are drawn; and most maintain the gains they have made. Pupils whose reading improves as a consequence of the programme are reported often to make additional gains—in confidence, school attendance and in other subjects, including mathematics. (HMSO, 1993, p. 4)

In our view, the development of Reading Recovery grew out of teachers' and researchers' willingness to observe children closely and ask questions about their learning. They found that these young children, all of whom were having difficulty in reading, were different from each other in what they already knew and what they attended to during reading and writing tasks. A one-to-one tutorial, based on close observation, was required to help these children extend their learning and use their strengths. Both the researchers who developed Reading Recovery and the teachers who were to implement it had to set aside their assumptions, hold a tentative theory, and take a fresh look at the children with whom they were working.

Despite success in New Zealand, questions still remained as to Reading Recovery's effectiveness and transportability. The British team claimed that:

> the low and generally stable figures for the proportions of pupils referred on for longer term help prompt further thought. Most prominently perhaps, they suggest that the scheme may have told us something fundamental about the remediable nature of much of the incidence of early reading difficulty encountered not only in New Zealand but in similarly long-established education systems in other advanced industrial societies such as our own. . . . They show what can be achieved by the combination of decisive policy and professional will. (HMSO, 1993, p. 12)

They went on to discuss transferability to other systems, "though Reading Recovery could probably have arisen in the first instance only when it did and in New Zealand, there is no reason to suppose that it is not transferable to other education systems" (HMSO, 1993, p. 23).

Research on Reading Recovery in the United States

Reading Recovery was first implemented in Ohio, where researchers at The Ohio State University conducted several empirical studies to assess the impact of the program (see Lyons, Pinnell, & DeFord, 1993; Pinnell, 1989). A small pilot study in 1984 demonstrated the program's potential; another study conducted from 1986 to 1989 was a longitudinal investigation involving two randomly assigned groups of children in 12 urban schools. One group received Reading Recovery, and the other received an alternative treatment provided by a paraprofessional. The results show that the majority of the children receiving Reading Recovery (74%) made accelerated progress; 3 years later, they could perform in reading at a level appropriate for their grade placement.

After these studies, questions still remained regarding precisely what factors contributed to Reading Recovery's success. Researchers were interested in exploring whether other one-to-one treatments would provide the same results, and whether the year-long training could be reduced. They wanted to compare Reading Recovery with other individual approaches using experienced, certified teachers. They also wanted to explore the potential of

Reading Recovery teachers working with small groups of children. A larger study conducted in 1988–1990 involved 10 school districts and compared several treatments, including Reading Recovery; Reading Recovery provided by teachers trained in a shorter, alternative program; fully trained Reading Recovery teachers working with groups; and a one-to-one skills tutoring program (Pinnell, Lyons, DeFord, Bryk, & Seltzer, 1994). Within each of four schools per district, students were randomly assigned either to one of the four treatment groups or to a control group. Thus, each treatment could be compared across 10 districts with its own control group. Data were submitted to a hierarchical linear model for analysis. The results indicate large effects on four measures of reading achievement for the traditional Reading Recovery design, with one-to-one instruction by fully trained teachers. The results of that study support the effectiveness of the Reading Recovery lesson framework and procedures and individual tutoring; the Reading Recovery staff development design emerged as a powerful factor in learning, showing an impact not only on teachers' working one to one, but, to a lesser degree, on teachers' work with groups.

This study also provided important insights into the teaching process. Analysis of videotaped data suggest that, even in Reading Recovery when procedures are applied in a mechanical way, the chance for success is not as high. The data from secondary analyses of qualitative data have helped to fine tune the process of teaching, and reveal that powerful teacher decision making is a key factor in helping the lowest achieving students succeed (see Lyons, Pinnell, & DeFord, 1993).

Replications as Evidence

Replications of Reading Recovery in New Zealand, Central Victoria, Australia, the United States, and Canada have confirmed that cross-national replication is possible (Clay, 1987). The program's success is related to level of coverage, quality of implementation, and factors such as mobility and absenteeism. However, figures from the National Data Center at The Ohio State University indicate that at least two thirds of U.S. children who have had the opportunity for a full program can be accelerated to average levels of performance within their respective schools. In districts with good resources and high coverage, the percentage of success is considerably higher (an annual report is available from The Ohio State University).

A VIEW OF INSTRUCTION AS ASSISTED LEARNING

The internal strategies necessary to read must be constructed by the individual learner. In Reading Recovery, the teacher serves as expert support to assist the learning process. Support varies in level and quantity according to the learner's strengths at any given time, but it is a critical factor for children who are having difficulty taking on reading and writing. Research on language learning supports the idea that caregivers act as supporters for children as they construct the language system. Adults act as conversational partners; even before speaking words, children participate in social conventions (see Cazden, 1988). The *scaffold* metaphor is sometimes used to illustrate the shifting support for language learning (see Cazden, 1988). However, it is difficult for any such image to portray the complex interactions that support learning. In literacy learning, too, children construct their own understandings, but lean on the social context to weave meaning around their first interactions with written language.

Parents and teachers demonstrate processes to children through reading aloud to them, but ultimately children must participate in the process. Seemingly casual conversation helps to make visible the problem-solving processes involved in reading. When a teacher says something like, "Let's check the picture" or "What do you think is going to happen next?", he or she suggests to young readers that the text is a coherent whole, and that readers constantly search for meaning and use it to check their predictions. In the example at the beginning of this chapter, when Josie read *wrote* for *wore*, she predicted and then disconfirmed her prediction. When she reread with the word *wore* in the sentence, she was doing a confirming check on her prediction.

Teachers in Reading Recovery are especially conscious of the power of their instructional interactions with students. They engage students in reading new texts, rereading familiar texts, and composing and writing their own messages. Working closely with their teacher, these initially confused first graders quickly begin to behave like readers and writers, using what they know to search, check, and confirm even before they have a large body of item knowledge (such as individual sight words, or letters and sounds).

From the beginning, with the teacher's support, children use the few items they know strategically; from this interactive process, they take on new information in a meaningful way. From a Vygotskian perspective, instruction is a "unique form of cooperation between the child and the adult that is the central element of the educational process" (cited in Moll, 1990, p. 2). In Reading Recovery, the teacher and student share activities, with the more expert teacher taking on the harder parts of the task so that the child can perform everything of which he or she is capable. The learner is supported through conversation and accomplishes much more than he or she could alone. Gradually, the young learner takes over the harder parts of the task and constructs an internal generating system, which Clay called a "self-extending system." The teacher must make decisions moment to moment during the lessons; these teaching moves continually adjust to students' responses and the expanding repertoire that has been established.

Making these "on-the-run" decisions is the most difficult challenge for a Reading Recovery teacher.

Reading Recovery teaching has been described as conversation (Kelly, Klein, & Pinnell, 1995). "Natural conversation assumes that there is some telling, some demonstrating, some encouraging, some suggesting, some praising, and all other types of human interactions" (Lyons, Pinnell, & DeFord, 1993, p. 54). The child makes imperfect, approximate attempts; the expert adult responds by recognizing the attempt and suggesting or encouraging behaviors that put problem-solving processes into action. The result is an extension of the child's powers. This process happens all the time in everyday life, but in Reading Recovery teachers are explicitly aware of their interactions. They build a knowledge base that consists of information about how people learn to read, and the kinds of teacher support that have been shown to be effective. But the knowledge base also includes information about the particular child—what he or she has demonstrated and what he or she knows. That specific knowledge makes the difference in powerful teaching. This tentatively held, in-process theory guides interactions. The teacher is always problem solving and learning with regard to the particular child.

Running records are especially helpful in the process. These easy-to-use records of reading behaviors provide "evidence of how the child works on words in text, what success he has, and what strengths he brings to the task. A teacher can quickly decide what might be the next most profitable learning point for that child and can test this out during teaching" (Clay, 1993, p. 81).

DECISION MAKING FROM A THEORY

Beginning to Problem Solve During "Roaming Around the Known"

The following glimpse of a teacher–student interaction, which took place in their third session, illustrates how teachers think about children's reading and writing behavior and explore what is known in the children's repertoire. Derek, the student, paused while reading the book *When Itchy Witchy Sneezes* (Cowley, 1986), and said, "I know how to spell the word *cat*." (This comment probably was motivated by the picture of a cat on the page.) He then spelled the word saying, "*c–a–t–*," and located *cat* on the page.

Pam, the teacher, was delighted to note Derek's association with prior experience and a known word in print; she recorded this observation in her lesson notes. From her initial assessment of his strengths (the Observation Survey), she knew that he could write the word *cat*, along with eight other words. But now she also knew that he could recognize *cat* while reading text.

Later, she would find ways to help him use the known word to support his developing fluency and flexibility. The purpose is not to develop knowledge of any particular word or words, but to learn a strategy for using what one knows. Even further on in lessons, she might help him generate new words from this known word, or use it as a support for word analysis to solve unknown words. Many other books, interesting to Derek and with good stories, would contain the word *cat*. This young student had high letter knowledge, but knew only a few words. Having a good idea of his repertoire of words would help the teacher support his extension of knowledge. By the time Derek finished the 10 "roaming around the known" sessions, he had increased his independent writing vocabulary to 17 words. These words could begin to serve as anchors in reading (i.e., Derek could use his knowledge of a few words to check his predictions while reading simple texts). These known words could also be the foundation for generating new words in writing. Thus, a few items of knowledge could be used by this beginning reader in strategic ways.

Problem Solving During Familiar Reading

Jason, in his 20th lesson in Reading Recovery, was reading books at the preprimer level. Generally, in the first part of a Reading Recovery lesson, children reread several books that have been previously read. In *The Red Rose* (Cowley, 1983, p. 11), the text said, " 'Gone,' said the caterpillar. And it went back home."

> Jason read, " 'Gone,' said the caterpillar. And it went a–." He hesitated and returned to the beginning of the line, reading again, "and it went." He stopped.
>
> "Good for you," said his teacher, Kathy, acknowledging that the child had been monitoring his reading. "What did you want it to say?"
>
> "Away," said Jason.
>
> "It went away. Are you right?"
>
> Jason said, "Mmm-hmm," indicating an affirmative.
>
> "That makes sense, doesn't it?" said his teacher. "Does it look like *away?*"
>
> "Uh-uh," said the child, shaking his head. "It has a *b.*"
>
> "Mmm-hmm," the teacher said. "Go back and try it again. Think about what would make sense and how it begins."
>
> They read together from the beginning of the page, "Gone, said the caterpillar, and it went . . ."

". . . back home," Jason read alone.

"Are you right?" asked the teacher. "Is that what it did? It went back home?"

"Yes," said Jason, and he continued reading to the end of the story.

"Good for you!" said Kathy.

In the previous example, Jason was using his own sense of language syntax and meaning to make predictions as he moved through the text. His hesitation at the word *went* probably indicated some sense of a discrepancy between his own prediction and the visual information contained in the print. The teacher acknowledged Jason's good use of information to predict when she asked him to express what he wanted the text to say; but then she asked him to check himself using other sources of information. Jason was able to notice visual aspects of print and use them to cross-check his own good predictions. He was already monitoring his reading, indicated by his going back to repeat the phrase, and the teacher's conversational intervention helped him go further in problem solving. This example shows the teacher paying careful attention to what the child knows, recognizing his predictions, and supporting his strategic use of several different sources of information, as good readers do.

Reading Independently for a Running Record Assessment

Each day, the teacher takes a running record on the child's reading of yesterday's new book (see Fig. 7.1). In Jason's lesson, he read *The Biggest Cake in the World* (Cowley, 1983), which had been introduced to him the day before. After the running record, Kathy and Jason had a quick discussion about the story.

"Well, tell me what you think. Was that a good story?"

Jason nodded and agreed, "Mmm-hmm."

"Would you like to have a big cake like that? A delicious cake like that?"

"Mmm-hmm," nodding again.

"Really good. Okay, I want to tell you something that you worked on that was very good. Right there on that page. What did you think about? Where was the tricky part? Show me."

Jason pointed to the word *trailer.*

"What did you want it to be?"

"Cart."

"Cart, and that's a very good guess, isn't it, because it could be a cart. But you knew something was wrong."

Running Record of Reading Behavior

Page Text	Reading Behavior	Analysis E	SC
2 Mrs. Delicious got a trunk full of flour	✓ delicious/T ✓ ✓ ✓✓ of ✓ / with	m⑤v	
for the biggest cake in the world.	✓ ✓ ✓ ✓ ✓ ✓ ✓		
3 Mrs. Delicious got a tank full of milk	✓ ✓ ✓ ✓ ¹truck/tank ✓ ²with/of ✓	¹⑥⑤ⓥ ²m⑤v	
for the biggest cake in the world.	✓ ✓ ✓ ✓ ✓ ✓ ✓		
4 Mrs. Delicious got a trailer of sugar	✓ ✓ ✓ ¹cart/tr—/trailor /T ³ful ✓ ✓	¹m⑤v ²m⑤(v) ³omission – syntactically acceptable	
for the biggest cake in the world.	✓ ✓ ✓ ✓ ✓ ✓ ✓		
5 Mrs. Delicious got a thousand eggs	✓ ✓ ✓ ✓ ✓ ✓		
for the biggest cake in the world.	✓ ✓ ✓ ✓ ✓ ✓ ✓		
6 Mrs. Delicious mixed and mixed	✓ ✓ got/mixed /sc ✓ ✓	m⑤v	m⑤sv
the biggest cake in the world.	✓ ✓ ✓ ✓ ✓		
7 Mrs. Delicious cooked and cooked	✓ ✓ ✓ ✓ ✓		
the biggest cake in the world.	✓ ✓ ✓ ✓ ✓ ✓		
8 Mrs. Delicious got a tractor to pull	✓ ✓ ✓ ✓ ✓ ✓ ✓		
the biggest cake in the world.	✓ ✓ ✓ ✓ ✓ ✓		
9 Mrs. Delicious got a chain-saw to cut	✓ ✓ ✓ ✓ ✓ ✓ ✓ ✓		
the biggest cake in the world.	✓ ✓ ✓ ✓ ✓ ✓		
10 (Picture -- no text)			
11 And all the people had a slice of	[✓ ✓ ✓ ✓ ✓ ✓ ✓] Omitted – read accurately afterwards ✓		
the biggest cake in the world.	[✓ ✓ ✓ ✓ ✓]		

Key for coding:

Accurate reading ✓ ✓ ✓ ✓

Substitution child's word / text

Self-correction child's word / text /sc

Told text / T

Repetition ✓ ✓ ✓ ✓ ✓ R

Key for analysis:

E = error

SC = self correction

M = using meaning as a cue

S = using syntax as a cue

V = using visual information as a cue

FIG. 7.1. Running record of Jason's reading.

"And I went t–."

"What would you see at the beginning if it were *cart*?"

"*C*."

"And what did you see at the beginning?"

"*T*."

"*T*, now let's look at that for a minute."

Using the chalkboard, Kathy wrote the first two letters of the word *trailer*, drawing Jason's attention to them and asking him to read the sentence again, telling him this time to get his mouth ready for the word *trailer*. He successfully completed the page. Finally, they went through the book together, noticing the illustrations and remembering the events of the story. Jason discovered that he had skipped the last page.

Learning How Words Work

A brief, but frequently used, part of Reading Recovery lessons focus on helping children learn to analyze words. A child who has good letter knowledge and knows some words is ready to discover relationships among the parts of words. After the running record book, the teacher might select from the child's repertoire a word that lends itself to exploring generalizations about how words work. For example, right after Jason completed reading *The Biggest Cake in the World* (Cowley, 1983), Kathy selected the word *go*, which Jason already could write and read. Using magnetic letters at the chalkboard, she modeled constructing the word *go* and then adding *ing* to make *going*. Then she asked Jason to do the same task several times. He was able to make *going* easily and quickly. Then Jason made several other words using *ing*. Starting with the word *look*, in addition to adding *ing*, he also made *looks*, using the *s* ending, which he already knew. All of this work took place in about 3 minutes, but Jason was learning important concepts about how words work. In later lessons, he will not need special attention to this kind of activity, but will use these generative principles to analyze words while reading text.

Learning About Written Language Through Writing

Through writing, Reading Recovery children have many opportunities to discover characteristics of written language. In Jason's lesson, Kathy invited him to compose a story about Mrs. Delicious. He decided to write: "She made the biggest cake in the world" (see Fig. 7.2). Kathy knew that Jason already knew how to write the word *he*, and she reminded him that he had previously written *she* and noticed that it was like a word he knew. Jason remembered the word *he* and wrote it on the practice page. In Reading Recovery lessons, children use a writing book turned sideways. The blank piece of paper at the top provides a space to work out words and practice; the bottom part shows the completed story (see Fig. 7.2).

"What did you do to *he* to make it say *she*?" she asked.

Jason immediately added the *s* and put the word on the story page. Kathy made sure to praise him for his quick problem solving.

Jason read, "She. . . ."

For the next word, *made*, Kathy drew three boxes representing the three sounds of the word (Clay, 1985). Jason pushed counters into the boxes,

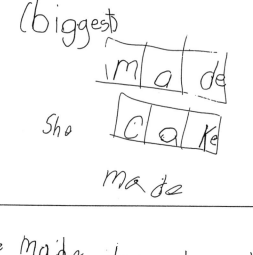

FIG. 7.2. The practice page and completed message page from Jason's writing book.

slowly saying, "Made." First he wrote the *m*, then pushed the counters again, writing the *a*, and finally he provided the *d*. Kathy added the *e* to make the word look right.

"I don't hear that," said Jason, pointing to the *e*.

"No you don't," said Kathy, "but you heard the *a*."

After that, Jason wrote the word *made* in his sentence and again on the practice page to help develop fluency. *Made* is a word that will be useful to him in many future stories, and it will be efficient for him to write it quickly.

He initially wrote the next word, *the*, with a capital letter. Then he stopped and asked for white correction tape to change it to a lower case—another example of self-monitoring. He knew how to write *big*, and the teacher added letters to make *biggest*. After writing each word, he went back to the beginning of his sentence to reread—to help himself recall the next word he wanted to write. On the word *cake*, he wrote the *c* and the *a*, and then suggested a *c* for the next letter. Quickly he changed his mind, saying, "*k*."

"How did you know it was a *k*?" Kathy asked.

Child provides info

"Because I recognized it," Jason said, and they briefly discussed another book that had the word *cake*.

"It wouldn't look right with a *c*," Kathy said.

They continued to the end of the message. During this writing time, Jason demonstrated that he could (a) hear and represent sounds with letters, (b) analyze words left to right, (c) write some known words, (d) use visual memory to decide which letter would be appropriate, (e) supply letters that do not have corresponding sounds, and (f) monitor his writing for appropriate conventions of print, such as spacing and use of capital letters. After he completed the message, the whole sentence was written quickly by the teacher on a strip of paper and cut apart for Jason to reassemble, which he did without difficulty.

Encountering New Texts

Each day, the students are introduced to a new book, which provides opportunities to solve problems on new texts with the teacher's support. Following Jason's writing, Kathy introduced *The Lion's Tail* (Scott, Foresman, 1976), a story about a lion who could not find his tail because he was sitting on it. The teacher established the concept of the story in the introduction before Jason began to read; both looked at the pictures and laughed about the lion's dilemma. As he began to read the story, Jason consistently predicted words from his sense of the meaning and from language structure, and he checked them—either discounting or confirming—with visual information. He had opportunities to engage in problem solving on words like *behind* and *along*. He repeated lines to capture a feeling for the language syntax and to confirm his initial attempts. Throughout this lesson, Kathy supported Jason's use of multiple sources of information in a flexible way while reading for meaning.

TEACHERS' LEARNING OVER TIME

We have described the Reading Recovery professional development program as ongoing. The initial training involves a year of weekly class sessions, during which teachers participate in behind-the-glass observation and discussion. They are guided by a teacher leader who has experienced a year of preparation in a full-time residential graduate program (for more information, see DeFord, Lyons, & Pinnell, 1991). After the first year, Reading Recovery teachers are expected to continue their learning—a process they sometimes refer to as "sifting and sorting." The assumption is that these teachers hold their theory tentatively, refining it based on their observations of and interactions with the children whom they teach. Over time, they learn through hundreds of case examples, which they interpret using theoretical tools. It is difficult to describe this process in all its complexity as teachers learn to become expert observers who are responsive to children's behavior. But we believe this is the key to successful outcomes in children's progress. The program cannot be efficiently and effectively adapted to individual children unless the teachers are working toward constructing their own decision-making systems.

Key part

Collaboration and colleague support are key elements of ongoing professional development in Reading Recovery. We briefly explore several principles that are inherent in the collegial learning context created by the program (see Lyons, Pinnell, & DeFord, 1993), and briefly discuss principles related to these strengths.

Observation

Observation contributes to teachers' learning in every phase of their work in Reading Recovery: (a) in their daily work with children, (b) in weekly course sessions, (c) in consultations with colleagues, and (d) in self-reflection through video- and audiotaping, and analysis of lesson records. The professional development program begins with observation; teachers learn to use careful and systematic observation techniques in the process of selecting students for Reading Recovery (see Clay, 1993). Using their observations of children's behavior in both structured and informal literacy tasks, they are able to collect and analyze a body of information related to each child's strengths. Following the initial assessment, teachers' decisions are based on their daily observations of children's writing and reading, and on their accumulated knowledge. The teachers keep precise records of their observations, and these inform their teaching decisions.

Observation is a key component of the weekly staff development sessions. Here, teachers have a common experience as they watch one or two of their peers teaching lessons behind the one-way glass. Through this process, they are able to sharpen their observational powers and relate them to decision making. Teachers begin to participate in colleague visits during the first year, and these become the basis of support for ongoing professional development in subsequent years of involvement in the program.

Assisted Learning

In a variety of ways, the teacher leader supports teachers in extending their understandings of how children learn to read and write. The leader models and demonstrates the Reading Recovery lesson's framework and procedures so that new teachers can begin to use them. Reading Recovery teachers immediately apply their learning with children, and they continue to learn through participation with the assistance of this more experienced and knowledgeable colleague. In behind-the-glass sessions, the teacher leader guides participants' observations, drawing their attention to significant behaviors that indicate shifts in understanding. The leader helps teachers explore new ideas, question, and challenge their own and each other's assumptions about the learning and teaching they are observing.

Language as a Foundation for Learning

Language surrounds the events within Reading Recovery; language mediates performances and creates systems of change. For teachers, cognitive activities are "awakened" through their social interactions with mentors and colleagues. Reading Recovery teachers learn a common language, which they use to communicate with each other in ways that stretch their thinking. In the behind-the-glass sessions, they are encouraged to put their tentative hypotheses into words, and then to refine their ideas through negotiation of meaning with their peers. This language process helps them build the internal knowledge systems they need as a basis for instructional decisions.

SUMMARY

In this chapter, we described Reading Recovery, a promising approach for helping young children who are having difficulty in initial literacy acquisition. We also have delineated the components of the Reading Recovery program and its systemic structure. We have emphasized the powerful instructional decision making that teachers develop through observation, training, and colleague support. No one aspect of Reading Recovery contains the elements of the program's success or accounts for the strong results documented in numerous studies. Mirroring the complexity of the literacy learning process, Reading Recovery is designed to help teachers engage children in reading and writing processes so that the children develop an internal sense of how written language works. The interrelated components of Reading Recovery are necessary to establish a system of intervention to ensure every child's early acquisition of literacy, along with the accompanying benefits.

REFERENCES

Cazden, C. B. (1988). *Classroom discourse: The language of teaching and learning*. Portsmouth, NH: Heinemann.

Clay, M. M. (1979). *Reading: The patterning of complex behavior* (2nd ed.). Portsmouth, NH: Heinemann.

Clay, M. M. (1985). *The early detection of reading difficulties* (3rd ed.). Portsmouth, NH: Heinemann.

Clay, M. M. (1987). Implementing Reading Recovery: Systemic adaptations to an educational innovation. *New Zealand Journal of Educational Studies, 22*, 35–58.

Clay, M. M. (1990). The Reading Recovery Programme, 1984–88: Coverage, outcomes and education board district figures. *New Zealand Journal of Educational Studies, 25*, 61–70.

Clay, M. M. (1991). *Becoming literate: The construction of inner control*. Portsmouth, NH: Heinemann.

Clay, M. M. (1993). *An observation survey of early literacy achievement*. Portsmouth, NH: Heinemann.

Cowley, J. (1983). *The red rose*. Bothell, WA: The Wright Group.

Cowley, J. (1983). *The biggest cake in the world*. Wellington, New Zealand: Ministry of Education.

Cowley, J. (1986). *When Itchy Witchy sneezes*. Bothell, WA: The Wright Group.

DeFord, D. E., Lyons, C. A., & Pinnell, G. S. (1991). *Bridges to literacy: Learning from Reading Recovery*. Portsmouth, NH: Heinemann.

HMSO. (1993). *Reading Recovery in New Zealand: A report from the Office of Her Majesty's Chief Inspector of Schools*. London: Author.

Hutchins, P. (1983). *You'll soon grow into them, Titch*. New York: Greenwillow Books.

Kelly, P., Klein, A., & Pinnell, G. S. (1995). Reading Recovery: Teaching through conversation. In D. Lancy (Ed.), *Children's emergent literacy: Social and cognitive processes*. Westport, CT: Praeger.

Lyons, C. A., Pinnell, G. S., & DeFord, D. E. (1993). *Partners in learning: Teachers and children in Reading Recovery*. New York: Teachers College Press.

Mason, J. M., & Au, K. H. (1990). *Reading instruction for today*. Glenview, IL: Scott, Foresman.

Moll, L. C. (1990). Introduction. In L. C. Moll (Ed.), *Vygotsky and education: Instructional implications and applications of sociohistorical psychology* (pp. 1–27). New York: Cambridge University Press.

Pinnell, G. S. (1989). Reading Recovery: Helping at-risk children learn to read. *The Elementary School Journal, 90*(2), 159–181.

Pinnell, G. S., Lyons, C. A., DeFord, D. E., Bryk, A., & Seltzer, M. (1994). Comparing instructional and theoretical models for the literacy education of high risk first graders. *Reading Research Quarterly*.

Rumelhart, D. E. (1981). Schemata: The building blocks of cognition. In J. T. Guthrie (Ed.), *Comprehension and teaching: Research reviews*. Newark, DE: International Reading Association.

Scott, Foresman. (1976). *The lion's tail*. Glenview, IL: Author.

CHAPTER EIGHT

A Sociocultural Model of Reading Instruction: The Kamehameha Elementary Education Program

Kathryn H. Au
University of Hawaii

From the point of view of a socio-historical school, research on reading must start with an understanding of how this historical backdrop, how contemporary social-historical contexts, shape the nature of instruction and the production of school failure. Educational failure is done in the classroom, it is done at home, it is done on the way from the classroom to home, it is done in the workplace, it is done everywhere. It is systemic. *If you're going to make a difference, you're going to have to be able to do it at many different levels of the system.*

(Cole & Griffin, 1983, p. 71)

Sociocultural theories, in particular that of Vygotsky, have exerted a significant influence on educators (Moll, 1990), including those concerned with literacy instruction (Hiebert, 1991). Interest in sociocultural theory has increased as the emphasis in psychology and sociology has shifted from earlier forms of constructivism to social constructivism (Mehan, 1981). One of the chief differences between the two forms is whether the constructive process is seen as largely internal and personal or social and interpersonal. The work of Piaget assumes the former; the work of Vygotsky, the latter. The first half of this chapter presents a discussion of sociocultural theory and literacy learning (for other accounts, refer to Gavelek, 1986; Goodman & Goodman, 1990; McCarthey & Raphael, 1989). The second half describes research conducted at the Kamehameha Elementary Education Program (KEEP), an example of an elementary reading/language arts program influenced by the sociocultural perspective (Tharp & Gallimore, 1988).

SOCIOCULTURAL THEORY
AND LITERACY INSTRUCTION

The term *sociohistorical* is often used in place of *sociocultural* to describe
the theoretical stance of Vygotsky, Luria, Leontiev, and their American interpreters, including Cole, Moll, and Wertsch. Both terms seem equally appropriate because social, cultural, and historical factors all play a part in this
school of thought.

One of the basic tenets of the sociocultural perspective is that human
experience is mediated by culture (Cole, 1990). Current thinking about the
concept of culture acknowledges a tension between two different views
(Wax, 1993). In one view, culture is seen as a relatively stable, integrated
whole encompassing a people's knowledge, beliefs, and ways of life. In the
other view, culture is seen as an active process of change, growth, and
development. Many proponents of sociocultural theory recognize the value
of seeing culture both as an outcome shaped by a people's history, experiences, and efforts, and as a dynamic process of change (Trueba, 1991).

People live in an environment that has been transformed by cultural
artifacts, the work of past and present generations. These artifacts have
developed over time, with the purpose of coordinating people's interactions
with the physical world and with one another (Cole, 1990). Cultural artifacts
have ideal or conceptual characteristics, as well as material or physical form.
Language and literacy are considered to be cultural artifacts, and, like other
cultural artifacts, serve to mediate people's interactions with the world.

From a sociocultural perspective, higher mental functions are recognized
to be historical as well as cultural phenomena (Cole, 1990). A higher mental
function, such as literacy, is an aspect of human behavior, present in some
form from man's beginnings, that has changed over time as a result of
cumulative historical experiences (Cole & Griffin, 1983). Sociocultural research on school literacy learning attempts to explore the links among historical conditions, current social and institutional contexts, interpsychological
functioning (that which takes place between people), and intrapsychological
functioning (that which takes place within the individual).

In research conducted in the 1930s, Vygotsky and his student, Luria,
treated literacy as a uniform ability that had a general effect on all aspects
of higher mental functioning (Luria, 1976; Wertsch, 1985). Recent advocates
of sociocultural theory criticize this position for at least two reasons. First,
literacy is not a single phenomenon, but differs from culture to culture,
making it necessary to acknowledge the existence of multiple literacies
(Cole, 1990; Heath, 1983). Second, the effects of literacy on higher mental
functioning are not general, but specific and context-bound, as shown in
the well-known study conducted by Scribner and Cole (1981) of the West
African Vai.

Vygotsky took a holistic approach to learning and insisted on the study of higher mental functions in all their complexity (Moll, 1990; Wertsch, 1985). He rejected reductionist approaches (i.e., that higher mental functions result from the accumulation of primitive psychological mechanisms; Moll, 1990). Research on school literacy learning conducted from a sociocultural perspective proceeds on the assumption that students need to engage in authentic literacy activities, not activities contrived for practice. School literacy activities should involve the full processes of reading and writing, not the practice of skills in isolation.

A basic premise of sociocultural theory is that human activity, including literacy learning, can only be understood through the study of its social origins. In the words of Leontiev (1981):

> Human psychology is concerned with the activity of concrete individuals, which takes place either in a collective—that is, jointly with other people—or in a situation in which the subject deals directly with the surrounding world of objects—for example, at the potter's wheel or the writer's desk. However, if we removed human activity from the system of social relationships and social life, it would have no structure. With all its varied forms, the human individual's activity is a system in the system of social relations. It does not exist without these relations. (p. 47; cited in Wertsch, 1985)

One of the major themes in Vygotsky's work is that individuals' higher mental functions originate in social life (Wertsch, 1990). Vygotsky believed that the internalization of higher mental functions involved a transfer from the interpsychological to the intrapsychological (i.e., from socially supported to individually controlled performance). The implication of this position is that literacy learning, like the learning of other higher mental functions, involves a movement from the interpsychological to the intrapsychological.

Vygotsky's theory calls into question the stimulus–response model, or the idea that human behavior is largely reactive, as reflected in the use of transmission approaches or conventional classroom recitation (Moll, 1990). His theory also casts doubt on innate ability (i.e., that the social world simply draws out already existing capacities, as reflected in the use of fixed ability groups for reading instruction).

The concept of the *zone of proximal development* is central to Vygotsky's thinking about the social origin of higher mental functions. He stated that the zone is the "difference between the child's actual level of development and the level of performance that he achieves in collaboration with the adult" (Vygotsky, 1987, p. 209). According to his theory, learning is mediated by the interactions between children and adults, or between children and knowledgeable peers. In a more general sense, the zone of proximal development may be seen as "the structure of joint activity in any context where there are participants who exercise differential responsibility by virtue of differential expertise" (Cole, 1985, p. 155). Sociocultural research on school literacy learning explores the teacher's role as a mediator, the use of instructional scaffolding, and the social systems within which children learn (Applebee, 1991; Moll, 1990).

Vygotsky (1987) differentiated between what he termed *everyday* and *scientific* concepts. Everyday or spontaneous concepts are the understandings gained by a child through daily experience, whereas scientific concepts are those acquired through formal instruction and schooling. The two types of concepts follow different courses of development. With everyday concepts, the child has more conscious awareness of the object than of the concept itself; with scientific concepts, the child has more conscious awareness of the concept than of the object. The two types of concepts are necessarily connected during the process of development. Everyday concepts mediate the downward growth of scientific concepts, providing the structures required for the emergence of their simpler, more elementary characteristics. Similarly, scientific concepts mediate the upward growth of everyday concepts, providing the structures required for the mastery of their more complex or higher characteristics. Research conducted from a sociocultural perspective assumes that school literacy learning activities should be designed to allow the productive interweaving of schooled knowledge (scientific concepts) and personal experience (everyday concepts).

In short, a sociocultural perspective begins with the assumption that reading, like other higher mental functions, is essentially social in nature. Even reading a book alone can be considered a social activity, because the reader is engaged with the author, the book is written in a language developed through long periods of use by other people, and the reader's concepts and schemata for responding to the book borrow from the thinking of others and result from previous social interactions.

School literacy learning is seen as a social process, affected not only by present but historical circumstances. Learning to read cannot logically be separated from the particular milieu in which it takes place. When children learn to read, or fail to learn to read, they do so in a particular social, cultural, and historical environment. Their success or failure in reading cannot be understood apart from that environment.

EXAMPLES OF SOCIOCULTURAL STUDIES OF READING

According to Wertsch (1991), sociocultural research tends to be comparative—for example, contrasting psychological activity in historical eras (Luria, 1976) or cultural contexts (Scribner & Cole, 1981). Yet Wertsch stated that sociocultural studies need not involve direct comparisons:

> . . . the main criterion is that the analysis be linked in some way with specific cultural, historical, or institutional factors. And even in the case of sociocultural

studies that involve no explicit comparison, the comparative method lurks just beneath the surface, since the notion of *situatedness* implies a contrast with other possibilities. (p. 18)

A study by McDermott and Gospodinoff (1981) involved the explicit comparison of lessons given in a first-grade classroom, in which the children were divided into three groups for reading instruction. They discovered striking differences between lessons given to the top group versus the bottom group. In the top group, the attention of the teacher and children was sustained in a posture or positioning called "looking at the book." In the bottom group, the attention of the teacher and children often wandered, with much time being spent in the positionings called "getting a turn to read" and "waiting for the teacher." The latter positioning occurred because the teacher often stopped the lesson to deal with problems experienced by children outside the group. McDermott and Gospodinoff demonstrated that the children in the class were attuned to changes in the positioning of the reading group, and knew that they could get the teacher's attention by interrupting during the lessons of the bottom group but not the top group. As a result, the bottom group consistently received less reading instruction than the top group. McDermott and Gospodinoff characterized the situation in this classroom as one of the rich getting richer and the poor getting poorer: Children in the top group had already learned to read before coming to school, whereas those in the bottom group had not.

McDermott and Gospodinoff linked their findings to conditions in society. The children in the top group were of middle-class, mainstream backgrounds, whereas all but two in the bottom group were of diverse cultural backgrounds. They rejected the notion that the bottom group children's failure in learning to read was entirely due to differences in communicative code, or the fact that the teacher did not understand or appreciate these children because they communicated in codes unfamiliar to her. Although the researchers acknowledged that miscommunication and differences in communicative codes exist, they questioned why these communicative differences persisted without remedy. They concluded that miscommunication was not repaired because both the teacher and the students had a political stake in perpetuating it and preserving the ethnic borders in the classroom.

> Our communicative codes, persuasive and entrapping as they are, do not turn us into communicative robots incapable of coming to grips with other people simply because they communicate differently. The social world is subject to negotiation. If codes exist, it is because we all help create them in the very process of communicating. If codes are keeping us apart, it is because it is adaptive for us to do so, given the constraints imposed on our behavior in the social order constituted by the codes. (p. 215)

McDermott and Gospodinoff pointed out that poor reading achievement, and the academic failure associated with it, can prevent low-income children of diverse backgrounds from advancing in society. In this study, interactions negotiated by the children and the teacher during reading lessons at the classroom level were a reflection of the school's function as a sorting mechanism, dividing each generation into the advantaged and disadvantaged. The children and teacher unknowingly collaborated in this process.

How might reading instruction be reorganized so that these systems of failure do not persist? From a sociocultural perspective, the starting point is to change the reading curriculum to focus on meaning and the process of interpreting the world, rather than on decoding and reading aloud. Cole and Griffin (1983) wrote:

> What a socio-historical point of view shows us is that we should be trying to instantiate a basic *activity* when teaching reading and not get blinded by the basic *skills*. Skills are always part of activities and settings, but they take on meaning in terms of how they are organized. So, instead of basic skills, a socio-historical approach talks about *basic activities* and instantiates those that are necessary and sufficient to carry out the whole process of reading in the general conditions of learning. (p. 73)

Moll and Diaz (1985, 1987) demonstrated dramatic changes in children's reading performance as a result of reorganizing instruction in the manner described by Cole and Griffin. They conducted their research with a group of Spanish-dominant fourth-grade students. The students received English reading instruction from their classroom teacher, and also participated in a program for Spanish reading instruction conducted by another teacher. Moll and Diaz observed that most of the students' English reading instruction consisted of round-robin reading, with attention to accurate word calling, pronunciation, and the definitions of individual words. Through interviews, Moll and Diaz discovered that some children had a good understanding of the texts, which they could express in Spanish but not English. Also, in the Spanish class, the children were reading texts considerably more difficult than those they were reading in English.

Moll and Diaz decided to reorganize instruction to see if the children could learn to read, comprehend, and discuss English texts at the fourth-grade level, instead of the below-grade-level texts being used in the classroom. They changed the focus from reading aloud to comprehension, reading the English story aloud to the students, reviewing the plot of the story in English, and conducting an initial discussion of the story, also in English. As expected, they found that they needed to provide considerable scaffolding for students during the discussion. After a discussion of unfamiliar vocabulary, they asked students to reread the story as homework and to make note of any other vocabulary they wanted to learn.

The next day, Moll and Diaz gave the students the chance to function as fourth graders in reading the text. They centered the discussion on comprehension questions taken from the teachers' guide for the story. The questions were challenging ones that English-speaking fourth graders in the school had experienced difficulty answering. The students were able to answer the questions, using Spanish to state their answers when they had trouble expressing themselves in English. Under these circumstances, with reorganized instruction, the students showed that they could function in reading at about the same level as their English-speaking peers. The key changes in this case were the emphasis on meaning-making and the mobilization of the students' Spanish language ability.

Moll and Diaz attributed their findings to schools devaluing home languages other than English. This devaluing is a reflection of power relations in this society: English, not Spanish, is the language of power in the United States. When meaning-making through reading is brought to the fore, and students are allowed to use the full range of language available to them, including the home language, higher levels of reading achievement become possible. In short, this study illustrates how success in learning to read can be created through the reorganization of institutional practices, just as failure in learning to read is sustained through the continuation of institutional practices.

As these studies show, research conducted from a sociocultural perspective suggests that achievement is largely a function of the opportunities and support that students receive for learning, rather than a function of their inherent ability. Both high and low levels of achievement are considered to be produced collaboratively through interactions among students, teachers, and others in the learning environment.

SOCIOCULTURAL LITERACY RESEARCH AT KEEP

Historical Background

KEEP's target students are children of Native Hawaiian ancestry enrolled in public elementary schools in low-income communities throughout Hawaii. The purpose of KEEP is to help these students achieve high levels of literacy in school.

In 1778, at the time of the arrival of the English explorer James Cook, the islands were inhabited by perhaps 400,000 Native Hawaiians. A century later, with the coming of whalers, traders, missionaries, and others, the native population was reduced to about 40,000, in large part due to Western diseases.

The physical devastation of the Hawaiian people was accompanied by a process of tremendous social, psychological, and economic dislocation, including the overturning of Native Hawaiian systems of religion and land tenure. The undermining of traditional values and institutions disrupted relationships among the chiefs, the common people, and the land, and it threatened Hawaiian ways of life (Kame'eleihiwa, 1992). In 1893, the fall of the Kingdom of Hawaii ended Native Hawaiians' control of their own nation, and led to the eventual annexation of the islands by the United States. Throughout the 20th century, Native Hawaiians continued to face severe social, economic, medical, and educational problems (Hammond, 1992).

The Hawaiian language was no less affected. Native Hawaiians had a rich oral tradition, including legends, proverbs and poetical sayings, and lengthy chants memorized to preserve family history and genealogy. They delighted in the subtleties of a language celebrated for its double and hidden meanings. Like other Polynesian languages, Hawaiian was not a written language. It became one in 1822, when American missionaries began translating the Bible into the Hawaiian language (Wilson, 1991).

In 1840, during the reign of Kamehameha III, the Kingdom of Hawaii established a public school system, with teaching to take place in Hawaiian. The community schools, staffed primarily by Native Hawaiians, taught reading and writing to tens of thousands of children and adults. Literacy spread rapidly through the population. By the late 1800s, the literacy rate was said to rival that of any country in the world (Wilson, 1991). Over 100 different Hawaiian-language newspapers were published during the 19th century.

English literacy was far less common among Native Hawaiians. In general, only a few Hawaiians, primarily those of chiefly or prosperous families in the islands' three largest towns, learned to speak, read, and write in English before the late 1800s (Reinecke, 1969). Because at that time Hawaiians made up the vast majority of the population, there was little reason for them to become literate in a language other than their own.

The fall of the monarchy presaged the rapid decline of the Hawaiian language. In 1896, the Republic of Hawaii passed a law making English the language of instruction in the public schools and forbidding the use of Hawaiian by teachers and students. The spread of English was hastened by the increasing influence of the United States and by successive waves of immigration to the islands. As the 20th century progressed, Hawaiian was spoken less and less, even among Native Hawaiians. By the late 1980s, the 30 or so children being raised on the remote island of Niihau were almost the only youngsters who spoke Hawaiian as their first language (Wilson, 1991).

Today the vast majority of Native Hawaiian children do not speak Hawaiian. Instead, their first language is Hawaii Creole English (HCE), a nonmainstream variety of English that developed in the period after 1890, under the influence of large groups of immigrants from China, Portugal, and Japan (Sato, 1985). HCE is also the first language of many non-Hawaiian children born in Hawaii, although standard American English is the language of power in the state. Because of its lower status, HCE tends to be viewed by educators and the general public as a form of broken English, rather than as a language in its own right (Sato, 1985).

Today, Native Hawaiians make up approximately 18% of Hawaii's population. There are over 38,000 students of Native Hawaiian ancestry enrolled in Hawaii's public schools. The vast majority of these students are taught to read and write in English, although a few receive instruction through the Hawaiian language-immersion program established in 1987. Standardized test results indicate that the English literacy proficiency of Native Hawaiian students is lower than that of students from other ethnic groups in the state (Brough, 1983). Schools with a high proportion of Native Hawaiian students tend to rank in the bottom quartile according to group norms. Native Hawaiians may have ambivalent attitudes about schooling and literacy, and parents who use effective strategies to teach their children other skills may not apply these same strategies to promote literacy (Levin, 1990). Although data are sketchy, some suggest that English literacy among Native Hawaiians at present is lower than the levels of literacy they attained in the Hawaiian language during the 19th century (Wilson, 1991).

In general terms, the situation of Native Hawaiians mirrors that of other diverse cultural groups within the United States, who have the status of subordinate groups with respect to the dominant, mainstream American culture (cf. Ogbu, 1981). From this perspective, it is not surprising that Hawaiian students from low-income families have not reached high levels of literacy through participation in typical school programs. Successful participation in school is often difficult for Native Hawaiian students from low-income families because the school reflects the values and ways of the dominant culture, rather than those of the students' own families and culture (Gallimore, Boggs, & Jordan, 1974). Native Hawaiian students from low-income families, like the African-American students studied by Fordham (1991), may feel they must make a choice between academic success in school or acceptance by peers and maintenance of their cultural identity.

In its efforts to address this challenging situation, KEEP has attempted to develop approaches based on the premise that schools and teachers need to help students develop ownership of literacy, as well as acquire the meaning-making strategies and skills of literacy. Another premise is that higher levels of literacy learning will result if literacy instruction is organized in a manner responsive to and accepting of students' home culture and language.

The KEEP Whole-Literacy Curriculum

Since 1989, KEEP has used a whole-literacy curriculum based on sociocultural assumptions (Au, Scheu, Kawakami, & Herman, 1990). Included in the assumptions underlying the curriculum is the idea that literacy has affective as well as cognitive dimensions, and that both should be represented in the framework. As shown in Fig. 8.1, the whole-literacy curriculum incorporates six aspects of literacy. Students' growth in each aspect of literacy is evaluated

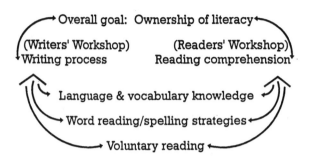

FIG. 8.1. The six aspects of literacy in the KEEP curriculum.

through portfolio assessment (for further information about this system, refer to Au, 1994).

Students' ownership of literacy is the overarching goal of the curriculum. Ownership means students value literacy and are willing to make literacy a part of their everyday lives (Au, Scheu, & Kawakami, 1990). Ownership may be an especially important consideration in classrooms like those with KEEP students, in which many students are of diverse cultural and linguistic backgrounds (Au & Kawakami, 1991). Students who experience ownership of literacy in school encounter the immediate rewards of schooling. The immediate, as opposed to delayed, rewards of schooling need to be highlighted for students of nonmainstream backgrounds, whose family experiences may not illustrate long-term connections among schooling, jobs, and other life opportunities (D'Amato, 1988; Ogbu, 1981). The priority given to ownership in the KEEP curriculum is consistent with a sociocultural perspective in recognizing the link between motivation for schooling and family and community history.

The writing process and reading comprehension, shown below ownership in the curriculum framework, are of equal importance. The *writing process* is seen as dynamic and nonlinear, involving activities such as planning, drafting, revising, editing, and publishing. *Reading comprehension* involves the ability to interpret text, respond to literature, and make connections between the text and one's own life. *Language* and *vocabulary knowledge* refers to the ability to understand and use appropriate terms and structures in both written and spoken English. *Word-reading strategies* include the use of meaning, visual/graphophonic, and structural cues to identify words (Clay, 1985). Finally, *voluntary reading* has to do with students' willingness to read books on their own.

KEEP teachers teach writing in ways described by Graves (1983), Calkins (1986, 1991), and other advocates of the process approach to writing. Writing is taught during an instructional period known as the "writers' workshop." Students select their own topics and engage in the full process of writing. Teachers provide students with minilessons covering all aspects of the writing process, from selecting a topic, to writing an interesting lead, to using correct punctuation. Skills of grammar and spelling are taught in the context of editing a piece in preparation for publishing. Students receive additional assistance through writing conferences conducted by the teacher or another student. Children share their writing through conferences and the "author's chair" (Graves & Hansen, 1983). Through sharing and mutual assistance, the teacher and students come together as a community of learners. The development of writing ability through participation in a community of learners is consistent with Vygotsky's notion that higher mental functions originate in and evolve through social interactions.

In parallel fashion, reading is taught during an instructional period known as the "readers' workshop." The emphasis in reading instruction is on response to literature. Response is considered to include both the aesthetic and efferent stances (Rosenblatt, 1978)—that is, both reading for enjoyment and reading to carry away information from the text.

KEEP's interpretation of the readers' workshop places considerable emphasis on the teacher's role in providing instruction and assuming responsibility for guiding students in how to read. KEEP teachers are familiar with Pearson's (1985) notion of the gradual release of responsibility, which draws on Vygotsky's idea of the movement from assisted to independent performance. At the heart of the readers' workshop are small-group, teacher-led discussions of literature. In addition, older students may participate in student-guided literature discussions.

Small-group, teacher-led literature discussions are usually conducted following the experience-text-relationship (ETR) approach (Au, 1979). In planning ETR lessons, the teacher considers how a particular book or story might be made interesting and meaningful. This involves thinking of a theme to be developed through discussion. Following Lukens (1990), a *theme* is defined as an overarching idea that gives meaning to the work as a whole. For example, third-grade teacher Joyce Ahuna-Ka'ai'ai based a series of ETR lessons on the theme of learning from grandparents (Au, 1992; Center for the Study of Reading, 1990). She chose this theme because she knew many of her students were close to their grandparents. The story, "Magic in a Glass Jar" (Bacmeister, 1964), was about a pair of children who were able to see a caterpillar turn into a moth because of their grandmother's knowledge of how silkworms were raised.

During the first phase of discussion, the experience or E phase, the teacher had the students discuss their background experiences related to the theme and content of the text about to be read. Specifically, she had the students talk about what they had learned from their grandparents, as well as what they knew about the lifecycle of moths and butterflies. The students also discussed how the brother and sister in the story were Japanese Americans with two names, one English and one Japanese, just as most of them had two names, English and Hawaiian.

The teacher then moved to the text or T phase, in which she had students read and discuss parts of the text. She had the students trace the events in the story, and they speculated about the story's title. One student thought the jar might be magic, while another pointed out that watching a caterpillar change into a moth might seem like magic to someone unaware of the lifecycle of these insects.

Finally, in the relationship or R phase, the teacher helped students draw relationships between the text and their background experiences. In Vygotskian terms, the R phase of ETR lessons allows for the interweaving of scientific and everyday concepts. The way this interweaving takes place is highly influenced by the students, as well as the teacher, because students are encouraged to contribute ideas and elaborate on one another's statements (for further information about cooperative forms of discussion, refer to the later section on the teacher's role).

Occasionally, the teacher begins by developing a particular theme for the story, only to discover that there is an alternate theme the students find more meaningful. Such an alternate theme began to emerge from the students during the discussion of "Magic in a Glass Jar." Although the teacher was guiding the discussion toward the theme of learning from grandparents, the students began developing a theme of their own—that of freedom, or the importance of letting the moth go free. When the teacher realized what was happening, she collaborated in helping the children articulate their theme. Although it was clear that the children understood the teacher's theme as well, their own theme of freedom was the one that made the story meaningful to them.

In addition to discussions, teachers have students write in response to literature, usually in an open-ended way with an element of student choice. For example, in a second-grade class, the teacher introduced children to different possibilities, including writing about one's favorite part of the story or writing a letter from one character to another. Eventually, students chose from a menu of six different options. In a fifth-grade class, students organized their responses in webs, including interesting words they had noticed, questions about characters, and connections to other books (an approach based on work by Pardo, 1992). Even in kindergarten and first-grade KEEP classes, children respond to literature with some kind of representation—often a combination of writing and drawing, and sometimes just drawing. Teachers usually have students complete their written responses to literature prior to the meeting of their small reading group. Often students share their written responses at the start of the lesson, and teachers then shape the discussion according to the points and questions students have raised.

Grouping practices in KEEP classrooms reflect the sociocultural perspective in recognizing that both success and failure in learning to read are socially constructed (Allington, 1983; McDermott & Gospodinoff, 1981; Moll

& Diaz, 1985). In particular, KEEP teachers avoid the use of fixed-ability groups by grouping students heterogeneously for reading instruction at least part of the time. For example, groups in a fifth-grade class were formed on the basis of students' interest in reading a particular novel. In a first-grade class, students were grouped according to their interest in doing research on a certain animal.

Heterogeneous grouping is more difficult to sustain in the primary grades (K–3) than in the upper elementary grades (4–6). KEEP teachers in primary classrooms frequently find it effective to group children on the basis of ability; this allows them to tailor instruction in word-reading strategies to the needs of particular subgroups within the classroom (cf. Slavin, 1987). For example, a first-grade teacher used ability grouping for the first and third quarters of the school year and heterogeneous grouping for the second and fourth quarters.

Listed below the writing process and reading comprehension in the curriculum framework are two skill areas: language and vocabulary development, and word-reading and spelling strategies. These are not taught separately, but are addressed through instruction embedded in the writers' and readers' workshops. The area of language and vocabulary development deals with students' ability to use language structures and new vocabulary to express ideas in oral and written forms. It also entails teaching students the strategies for deriving the meaning of new words from context (Herman & Weaver, 1988). In the writers' workshop, teachers introduce students to the use of descriptive language and encourage them to use specific terms and details in their writing. In the readers' workshop, teachers teach students to identify new and interesting words in the literature, and to make use of these words in oral discussions and written summaries.

Word-reading and spelling strategies are grouped together in recognition of the relationship between decoding and encoding in learning to read and write (Ehri, 1987). In the writers' workshop, KEEP teachers in the primary grades support the application of letter–sound relationships by encouraging children to use invented spelling when drafting. Teachers find that the use of invented spelling during writing significantly increases children's knowledge of letter–sound relationships and reduces the need for instruction in phonics during the readers' workshop. Students attend to conventional spelling when they correct their drafts during the editing phase. Teachers promote independence by teaching children to look for the conventional spellings of words on charts posted around the room, and in personal dictionaries, word lists, and books.

In the readers' workshop, KEEP teachers follow Clay's (1985) approach in teaching students to make simultaneous use of the information provided by meaning, structure, and visual cues. In kindergarten, first-, and second-grade classrooms, these lessons often occur following the shared reading of Big

Books (Holdaway, 1979). Teachers use masks, sentence strips, word cards, and pocket charts to call children's attention to the letter–sound relationships and other features of print encountered during the reading of Big Books.

Like ownership, voluntary reading has to do with the affective dimension of literacy. Voluntary reading involves students' willingness to select their own reading materials and to read on their own. All KEEP classrooms have a daily time when students read books of their own choosing. In kindergarten and first-grade classes, students may read with a partner or alone. In classes at the second-grade level and above, students engage in daily sustained silent reading (SSR). Most KEEP teachers assign their students to read from a book of their own choice every weeknight, for a time ranging from 10 to 30 minutes, depending on grade level.

Habits of voluntary reading do not develop automatically among most KEEP students, but must be promoted through teachers' guidance. Teachers make books accessible to students by setting up a classroom library and encouraging students to borrow books to read at home. For many students, the classroom is the only ready source of reading material. In some schools, students face restrictions on the number of books they may borrow from the school library, and many live in communities without a nearby public library. Perhaps one third of the students come from homes in which there are no children's books, magazines, or other written materials.

Even when books are accessible, students may not know how to select books they will enjoy (Au, Kunitake, & Blake, 1992). Teachers help by giving book talks and by inviting students to tell classmates about their favorite books. A KEEP teacher in a fourth-grade classroom used 14 different approaches to promote voluntary reading and a love of books. Among other things, she had her students read books aloud to first graders and organized a book club that met at recess time.

According to a sociocultural perspective, school literacy learning grows from social interactions with knowledgeable others within the classroom community of learners. Through the whole-literacy curriculum, KEEP seeks to structure these interactions around authentic, motivating literacy tasks involving the full processes of reading and writing. Specific skills and strategies are then taught in the context of these activities.

Instruction Responsive to Students' Culture

A sociocultural perspective suggests that teachers need to understand how to interact effectively with students so that they can serve in the role of knowledgeable other and guide students' literacy learning. Students' home cultures shape their perceptions of and interactions with teachers and classmates. Similarly, the mainstream culture and the school culture influence teachers' perceptions of and interactions with students.

The challenge in KEEP's work has been to identify difficulties, as well as to suggest how school practices might be changed to be responsive to the home culture (Jordan, 1985). No attempt is made to duplicate the home culture or the kinds of learning likely to occur at home. Instead, the purpose of culturally responsive instruction in the KEEP program is to promote academic achievement, particularly in literacy, as well as to give students a positive attitude toward learning and school. When instruction is culturally responsive, students are not asked to reject the values of their home culture to experience academic success. Instead, teachers seek to adjust instruction to create learning situations that students will find comfortable (Au, 1993). In this context, mainstream patterns of interaction and instruction can be gradually introduced.

From a sociocultural perspective, teachers' interactions with students, and students' interactions with one another, provide the ground for literacy learning in school. Research at KEEP suggests how these interactions can be shaped to be responsive to the students' home culture and effective in promoting school literacy learning.

Role of the Teacher. In the KEEP whole-literacy curriculum, interactions with the teacher are of primary importance in the students' school literacy development. Learning to be an effective KEEP teacher presents a special challenge. Teachers learn that they cannot expect the children's respect and obedience simply because they are in the authority role. Many Hawaiian children, raised in households with sibling caregiving, do not automatically turn to teachers when in need of help. Teachers must win the children over with praise and warmth, while showing that they are in charge and can command respect (Jordan, 1985). Teachers must speak to students in a clear and direct way, rather than giving indirect hints (cf. Delpit, 1988). The children look for a combination of "toughness" and "niceness" in their teachers, just as they look for these qualities in their friends (D'Amato, 1986). D'Amato suggested that the metaphor for the image teachers must project is that of a *smile with teeth.*

In addition to showing that they can command respect, teachers must be able to orchestrate discussions about literature in a culturally responsive manner. These discussions are conducted following participation structures different from those in typical mainstream classroom recitations. Teachers in mainstream classrooms often conduct lessons following the initiation-response-evaluation (IRE) participation structure (Mehan, 1979). One of the rules in this way of structuring interaction is that the teacher initiates the topic, usually by asking a question. Another rule is that the students cannot call out the answer, but must raise their hands and wait to be chosen. After the chosen student has responded to the question, the teacher evaluates his or her response. Then the cycle begins again with another teacher question.

Teachers who work in classrooms with young Hawaiian children often experience difficulty when they attempt to use the IRE participation structure. After the question has been asked, several children may eagerly shout out the answer, while the child who has been chosen to respond appears tongue-tied (Boggs, 1972). The discussion does not flow smoothly because the teacher must stop to quiet the group while urging the chosen child to speak up.

In contrast, teachers who center lessons on the use of talk storylike participation structures experience much more success in conducting discussions (Au, 1980). In this instance, the teacher still begins by asking a question, but does not insist that only one child respond at a time. Rather, the children are free to collaborate in producing an answer. One child may begin speaking, another child may elaborate on what the first child has said, and a third child may extend the answer further. Turn taking is managed by the children rather than the teacher, and there is usually a great deal of overlapping speech.

The following example is taken from a lesson given by an experienced KEEP teacher to a group of second-grade students. The illustration for the story, entitled "A Surprise for Pat," showed an ear of corn placed in the branches of a tree. The teacher asked the children to speculate about how the corn got there. (T is the teacher, A is Annabelle, E is Eloise, L is Leroy, M is Mary Anne, To is Tony, X is an unidentified child.)

T: Did they eat the corn?
    (T holds her book up, points.)
    ⌈Look, here it is.
M: ⌊Put it on the treeee.
A: ⌈(inaudible)
E: ⌊Yeah, I know (inaudible).
A: ⌈(inaudible)
E: |Yeah,
T: ⌊Maybe
    (T lifts books, points to something, puts book back on the table.)
    the squirrels put it on the tree.
    Maybe.
    (T leans forward, hands on chin.)
To: ⌈And the squirrels gonna eat it.
X: ⌊(inaudible)
T: You think a
    ⌈squirrel is gonna eat it.
L: ⌊It's too heavy
    ⌈for a squirrel.
E: ⌊Yeah, it is.
To: ⌈It's (inaudible)
T: ⌊It's too heavy, what does that mean?
    (T frowns, looks at Leroy.)

Notice how the teacher paraphrases children's responses to keep the discussion on track, while inviting children to continue the conversation. Talk storylike lessons show a feature known as the *balance of rights* (Au & Mason, 1981). The teacher controls the topic of discussion, but the students decide who will speak and when. Frequently, as in this example, the use of talk storylike participation structures leads to so much overlapping speech that observers unfamiliar with this type of interaction mistakenly assume that the teacher has lost control of the lesson.

Lessons conducted with talk storylike participation structures follow rules similar to those in a Hawaiian community speech event known as *talk story* (Watson, 1975). In talk story, the participants engage in co-narration (i.e., they speak in rhythmic alternation to present a narrative to the group). In this setting, the skilled speaker is one who knows how to involve others in the conversation, not one who holds the floor alone.

In many Hawaiian families, children are taught the value of working in cooperation with others for the well-being of their *'ohana*, or extended family. Competition and individual achievement are less highly prized than group contributions that benefit the family. Lessons with talk storylike participation structures appear to be effective, in part, because they reflect the value of cooperation, which students have learned in the family. In talk storylike lessons, students can work together to produce answers to teachers' questions and to interpret the text. In contrast, the IRE structure reflects typical Western values of competition: In this structure, students must perform as individuals.

The use of talk storylike participation structures appears to be related to improvements in students' engagement with academic content. In talk storylike lessons, compared with lessons conducted following the IRE pattern, Hawaiian students make more statements related to the text they are reading, cover more text information, and make more logical inferences (Au & Mason, 1981).

Peer-Group Dynamics. In addition to learning in teacher-guided lessons, students can improve their literacy through interactions with peers. Teaching and learning from peers is comfortable and familiar for many Hawaiian children, who often are raised in a system of sibling caretaking, in which they are cared for by older sisters and brothers as well as their parents (Gallimore et al., 1974). In households with sibling caretaking, children learn to turn to their brothers and sisters, as well as to adults, when in need of help. By the same token, children learn to assist other children. Sibling caretaking prepares Hawaiian children to participate in teaching and learning interactions with peers. Teaching–learning interactions with adults occur less often in Hawaiian households with sibling caretaking than they do in mainstream households (Gallimore et al., 1974), where adults may provide children with almost constant companionship (Heath, 1983).

In the classroom, then, young Hawaiian children who have been raised in households with sibling caretaking are more likely to turn to their peers than to the teacher when in need of help. Teachers can capitalize on the children's background with peer teaching–learning interactions by providing them with plenty of opportunity to work in pairs and small groups, and by allowing children to help one another with assignments (Jordan, 1985). Of course, teachers also need to teach children the difference between helping and doing another child's work.

In many KEEP classrooms, teachers have students pair up for reading—a practice variously labeled *paired reading, partner reading,* or *buddy reading.* Usually students take turns reading aloud to one another, a page or paragraph at a time. Students consult one another about the writing they do in response to literature. Sometimes small groups of students work together on projects designed to share their literary experiences with their classmates. For example, in one classroom, first graders made a movie roll of a picture book; in another, third graders worked together on posters advertising the novel they had read.

Interactions with friends, as well as with siblings, play an important part in the lives of most Hawaiian children. Many participate in friendship groups with the status of either leader or follower. Within and between these groups, children engage in rivalry to show that they are just as good as others (D'Amato, 1988). Rivalry differs from competition, which involves showing that one is better than others.

The influence of the peer group on many Hawaiian children is strong even in kindergarten and first grade. The organization of peer groups is complex, and teachers may not be aware of the roles that children have within the peer group and of the relationships among subgroups of peers. However, teachers need to have some knowledge of these roles and dynamics to prevent classroom management problems. Teachers must strive to be as fair as possible with the children, who are extremely sensitive to signs of teachers favoring some individuals or groups over others.

When setting up peer work groups in the classroom, KEEP teachers usually find that these groups function better when the children themselves are allowed to decide upon the roles they will assume (for example, who will be the notetaker, spokesperson, etc.). Teachers' assigning of roles, as opposed to permitting participants to work roles out among themselves, may put children in conflict with one another, for example, if a follower is put in charge over a leader (D'Amato, 1988).

Many Hawaiian children respond well in situations in which they can work cooperatively to achieve a goal as part of a group. When participating as members of a small group, children have many chances to contribute and to maintain their standing, and rivalry can be channeled in a positive direction (D'Amato, 1988). The children then receive recognition for the work they have accomplished as a group. In contrast, Hawaiian children may tend to feel uncomfortable in situations in which they must work individually in competition against other children. By the time they are in the upper grades, many children do not want to be singled out in front of their peers, even to be praised (Gallimore et al., 1974).

In short, Hawaiian children have the best chance for developing high levels of literacy in classrooms in which interactions with teachers and peers are responsive to students' home culture. Teachers can be more effective if they learn to structure their role as teachers and their interactions with students in a culturally responsive manner. Teachers can take advantage of students' ability to teach and learn from one another by giving students ample opportunity to work cooperatively in pairs and in small groups, giving them some latitude to work out their roles within these situations. In KEEP classrooms, the instructional environment is dynamically shaped through the collaboration of teachers and students, avoiding the kind of stand-off described by McDermott and Gospodinoff (1981). Instruction can then be reorganized to produce academic success in ways similar to those described by Moll and Diaz (1985).

CONCLUSION

Sociocultural theory, including the work of Vygotsky, appears to provide a promising framework for improving literacy instruction. The sociocultural perspective suggests that students learn to read and write through involvement in authentic tasks that do not separate literate activity from systems of social relationships. One of the key assumptions of sociocultural theory is that literacy learning is primarily a function of the social support systems available to students. Both success and failure in learning to read depend on students' interactions with their teachers and with one another. Students' expectations for these interactions are influenced by their home cultures, and teachers can be more effective in developing students' literacy if they understand how to structure interactions in a culturally responsive manner. In a culturally responsive classroom environment, such as that advocated by KEEP for Native Hawaiian children, teachers and students can work collaboratively toward shared academic goals. KEEP's example suggests that programs with a sociocultural perspective may provide an avenue for helping students of diverse cultural backgrounds achieve high levels of literacy in school.

REFERENCES

Allington, R. L. (1983). The reading instruction provided readers of differing abilities. *Elementary School Journal, 83*(5), 548–559.

Applebee, A. (1991). Literature: Whose heritage? In E. H. Hiebert (Ed.), *Literacy for a diverse society: Perspectives, practices, and policies* (pp. 228–236). New York: Teachers College Press.

Au, K. H. (1979). Using the experience-text-relationship *method* with minority children. *Reading Teacher, 32*(6), 677–679.

Au, K. H. (1980). Participation structures in a reading lesson with Hawaiian children: Analysis of a culturally appropriate instructional event. *Anthropology and Education Quarterly, 11*(2), 91–115.

Au, K. H. (1992). Constructing the theme of a story. *Language Arts, 69*(2), 106–111.

Au, K. H. (1993). *Literacy instruction in multicultural settings.* Fort Worth, TX: Harcourt Brace.

Au, K. H. (1994). Portfolio assessment: Experiences at the Kamehameha Elementary Education Program. In S. W. Valencia, E. H. Hiebert, & P. P. Afflerbach (Eds.), *Authentic reading assessment: Practices and possibilities* (pp. 103–126). Newark, DE: International Reading Association.

Au, K. H., & Kawakami, A. J. (1991). Culture and ownership: Schooling of minority students. *Childhood Education, 67*(5), 280–284.

Au, K. H., Kunitake, M. M., & Blake, K. M. (1992, December). *Students' perceptions of how they became interested in reading.* Paper presented at the annual meeting of the National Reading Conference, San Antonio, TX.

Au, K. H., & Mason, J. M. (1981). Social organizational factors in learning to read: The balance of rights hypothesis. *Reading Research Quarterly, 17*(1), 115–152.

Au, K. H., Scheu, J. A., & Kawakami, A. J. (1990). Assessment of students' ownership of literacy. *The Reading Teacher, 44*(2), 154–156.

Au, K. H., Scheu, J. A., Kawakami, A. J., & Herman, P. A. (1990). Assessment and accountability in a whole literacy curriculum. *The Reading Teacher, 43*(8), 574–578.

Bacmeister, R. (1964). Magic in a glass jar. In W. K. Durr, J. M. LePere, & R. H. Brown (Eds.), *Windchimes* (pp. 68–77). Boston: Houghton Mifflin.

Boggs, S. T. (1972). The meaning of questions and narratives to Hawaiian children. In C. Cazden, V. John, & D. Hymes (Eds.), *Functions of language in the classroom* (pp. 299–327). New York: Teachers College Press.

Brough, J. R., and the Staff of the Kamehameha Schools/Bishop Estate Program Evaluation and Planning Department. (1983). *Native Hawaiian Educational Assessment Final Report.* Honolulu: Kamehameha Schools.

Calkins, L. M. (1986). *The art of teaching writing.* Portsmouth, NH: Heinemann.

Calkins, L. M. (1991). *Living between the lines.* Portsmouth, NH: Heinemann.

Center for the Study of Reading. (1990). *Teaching reading: Strategies from successful classrooms* (Six-part videotape series). Urbana-Champaign: University of Illinois.

Clay, M. M. (1985). *The early detection of reading difficulties* (3rd ed.). Auckland: Heinemann.

Cole, M. (1985). The zone of proximal development: Where culture and cognition create each other. In J. V. Wertsch (Ed.), *Culture, communication, and cognition: Vygotskian perspectives* (pp. 146–161). Cambridge, England: Cambridge University Press.

Cole, M. (1990). Cognitive development and schooling. In L. C. Moll (Ed.), *Vygotsky and education: Instructional implications and applications of sociohistorical psychology* (pp. 89–110). Cambridge, England: Cambridge University Press.

Cole, M., & Griffin, P. (1983). A socio-historical approach to re-mediation. *The Quarterly Newsletter of the Laboratory of Comparative Human Cognition, 5*(4), 69–74.

D'Amato, J. (1986). *"We cool, tha's why": A study of personhood and place in a class of Hawaiian second graders.* Unpublished doctoral dissertation, University of Hawaii, Honolulu.

D'Amato, J. (1988). "Acting": Hawaiian children's resistance to teachers. *Elementary School Journal, 88*(5), 529–544.

Delpit, L. D. (1988). The silenced dialogue: Power and pedagogy in educating other people's children. *Harvard Educational Review, 58,* 280–298.

Ehri, L. C. (1987). Learning to read and spell words. *Journal of Reading Behavior, 19*(1), 5–31.

Fordham, S. (1991). Peer-proofing academic competition among Black adolescents: "Acting white" Black American style. In C. E. Sleeter (Ed.), *Empowerment through multicultural education* (pp. 69–93). Albany: State University of New York Press.

Gavelek, J. R. (1986). The social contexts of literacy and schooling: A developmental perspective. In T. E. Raphael (Ed.), *The contexts of school-based literacy* (pp. 3–26). New York: Random House.

Gallimore, R., Boggs, J. W., & Jordan, C. (1974). *Culture, behavior and education: A study of Hawaiian-Americans.* Beverly Hills: Sage.

Goodman, Y. M., & Goodman, K. S. (1990). Vygotsky in a whole-language perspective. In L. C. Moll (Ed.), *Vygotsky and education: Instructional implications and applications of sociohistorical psychology* (pp. 233–250). Cambridge, England: Cambridge University Press.

Graves, D. (1983). *Writing: Teachers and children at work.* Portsmouth, NH: Heinemann.

Graves, D., & Hansen, J. (1983). The author's chair. *Language Arts, 60*(2), 176–183.

Hammond, O. (1992). Needs assessment and Native Hawaiian education. *Pacific Proceedings, 1,* 25–34.

Heath, S. B. (1983). *Ways with words: Language, life, and work in communities and classrooms.* Cambridge, England: Cambridge University Press.

Herman, P. A., & Weaver, C. R. (1988, December). *Contextual strategies for learning word meanings: Middle grade students look in and look around.* Paper presented at the annual meeting of the National Reading Conference, Tucson, AZ.

Hiebert, E. H. (Ed.). (1991). *Literacy for a diverse society: Perspectives, practices, and policies.* New York: Teachers College Press.

Holdaway, D. (1979). *The foundations of literacy.* Sydney, Australia: Ashton Scholastic (distributed in the United States by Heinemann).

Jordan, C. (1985). Translating culture: From ethnographic information to educational program. *Anthropology and Education Quarterly, 16,* 105–123.

Kame'eleihiwa, L. (1992). *Native land and foreign desires.* Honolulu: Bishop Museum Press.

Leontiev, A. N. (1981). *Problems in the development of mind.* Moscow: Progress.

Levin, P. F. (1990). Culturally contextualized apprenticeship: Teaching and learning through helping in Hawaiian families. *Quarterly Newsletter of the Laboratory of Comparative Human Cognition, 12*(3), 80–86.

Lukens, R. J. (1990). *A critical handbook of children's literature* (4th ed.). Glenview, IL: Scott, Foresman.

Luria, A. R. (1976). *Cognitive development: Its cultural and social foundations.* Cambridge, MA: Harvard University Press.

McCarthey, S. J., & Raphael, T. E. (1989). *Alternative perspectives of reading/writing connections* (Occasional paper no. 130). East Lansing, MI: Institute for Research on Teaching, College of Education, Michigan State University.

McDermott, R. P., & Gospodinoff, K. (1981). Social contexts for ethnic borders and school failure. In H. T. Trueba, G. P. Guthrie, & K. H. Au (Eds.), *Culture and the bilingual classroom: Studies in classroom ethnography* (pp. 212–230). Rowley, MA: Newbury House.

Mehan, H. (1979). *Learning lessons.* Cambridge, MA: Harvard University Press.

Mehan, H. (1981). Social constructivism in psychology and sociology. *The Quarterly Newsletter of the Laboratory of Comparative Human Cognition, 3*(4), 71–77.

Moll, L. C. (1990). Introduction. In L. C. Moll (Ed.), *Vygotsky and education: Instructional implications and applications of sociohistorical psychology* (pp. 1–27). Cambridge, England: Cambridge University Press.

Moll, L. C., & Diaz, S. (1985). Ethnographic pedagogy: Promoting effective bilingual instruction. In E. Garcia & R. V. Padilla (Eds.), *Advances in bilingual education research* (pp. 127–149). Tucson: University of Arizona Press.

Moll, L. C., & Diaz, S. (1987). Change as the goal of educational research. *Anthropology and Education Quarterly, 18*(4), 300–311.

Ogbu, J. U. (1981). School ethnography: A multilevel approach. *Anthropology & Education Quarterly, 12*(1), 3–29.

Pardo, L. S. (1992, December). *Accommodating diversity in the elementary classroom: A look at literature-based instruction in an inner city school.* Paper presented at the annual meeting of the National Reading Conference, San Antonio, TX.

Pearson, P. D. (1985). Changing the face of reading comprehension instruction. *The Reading Teacher, 38*(8), 724–738.

Reinecke, J. (1969). *Language and dialect in Hawaii.* Honolulu: University of Hawaii Press.

Rosenblatt, L. (1978). *The reader, the text, the poem: The transactional theory of the literary work.* Carbondale, IL: Southern Illinois University Press.

Sato, C. J. (1985). Linguistic inequality in Hawaii: The post-creole dilemma. In N. Wolfson & J. Manes (Eds.), *Language of inequality* (pp. 255–272). Berlin: Mouton.

Scribner, S., & Cole, M. (1981). *The psychology of literacy.* Cambridge, MA: Harvard University Press.

Slavin, R. E. (1987). Ability grouping and student achievement in elementary schools: A best-evidence synthesis. *Review of Educational Research, 57*(3), 293–336.

Tharp, R., & Gallimore, R. (1988). *Rousing minds to life: Teaching, learning and schooling in social context.* Cambridge, England: Cambridge University Press.

Trueba, H. T. (1991). Comments on Foley's "Reconsidering anthropological explanations." *Anthropology & Education Quarterly, 22*(1), 87–94.

Vygotsky, L. S. (1987). Thinking and speech. In R. W. Rieber & A. S. Carton (Eds.), *The collected works of L. S. Vygotsky: Volume 1. Problems of general psychology* (pp. 37–285). New York: Plenum.

Watson, K. A. (1975). Transferable communication routines: Strategies and group identity in two speech events. *Language in Society, 4,* 53–72.

Wax, L. (1993). How culture misdirects multiculturalism. *Anthropology & Education Quarterly, 24*(2), 99–115.

Wertsch, J. V. (1985). *Vygotsky and the social formation of mind.* Cambridge, MA: Harvard University Press.

Wertsch, J. V. (1990). The voice of rationality in a sociocultural approach to mind. In L. C. Moll (Ed.), *Vygotsky and education: Instructional implications and applications of sociohistorical psychology* (pp. 111–126). Cambridge: Cambridge University Press.

Wertsch, J. V. (1991). *Voices of the mind: A sociocultural approach to mediated action.* Cambridge, MA: Harvard University Press.

Wilson, W. H. (1991). Hawaiian language in DOE unique. *Ke Kuamo'o, 1*(4), 4–6.

CHAPTER NINE

Fostering Literate Communities in School: A Case for Sociocultural Approaches to Reading Instruction

John F. O'Flahavan
National Reading Research Center
University of Maryland, College Park

Barbara L. Seidl
University of Wisconsin–Milwaukee

Numerous studies from a range of disciplines portray literate practices as embedded in the culture of the family and community (e.g., Heath, 1983; Scribner & Cole, 1981; Taylor, 1983). These studies demonstrate that learning to read is an apprenticeship in the use of specific intellectual strategies to serve particular purposes in culturally valued situations (Rogoff, 1990). Individuals appropriate these literate behaviors (Heath, 1991) across the life span by participating in activities that compel literate behavior, such as listening to a story, talking about a book with a friend, writing to express an opinion, searching a reference manual, and perusing a bus schedule.

The fundamental purpose of school-based literacy instruction should be to diversify students' abilities to use the many and varied forms of literacy in the pursuit of a broad range of personal and social interests. To this end, any approach to teaching reading must embrace reading as both a social and cognitive act (e.g., Bloome, 1983). It must also begin with the notion that a classroom is a culture in its own right, a system of socially constituted values, beliefs, and standards that evolve and guide people's thoughts, feelings, and behavior.

This chapter makes the case that the instructional models discussed in this volume are not comprehensive programs of instruction; rather, they represent facets of a broader approach to literacy instruction. Our perspective is grounded in the work of theorists such as Vygotsky, Wertsch, Leont'ev, and Rogoff; it depicts individual development as intersecting with the cultural, historical, and institutional characteristics of a given culture. At the

203

heart of our proposal is a curricular focus on the social and cognitive processes involved in sociocultural activity, the molar unit of life that orients the individual to the world (Leont'ev, 1981), not solely on the properties of a literate individual. A sociocultural perspective on how emergent members of literate cultures develop into knowledgeable, socially interactive, strategic, and motivated readers (Alvermann & Guthrie, 1993) views learning to read as situated apprenticeships in thinking and participation (cf. Rogoff, 1990). Development consists of broadening literacy-related contexts, through which an individual can navigate effectively (White & Siegel, 1984). In effect, learning to be literate requires readers to interlace their own developing understandings of the functions and forms of literacy with recent and long-standing achievements of the literate cultures in which they participate.

This chapter opens with a discussion of the assumptions underlying a sociocultural perspective on reading instruction. It then illustrates how the philosophical orientations and instructional methods underlying direct instruction, explicit instruction, response-centered instruction, and whole language can be viewed as part of a broader, sociocultural perspective. It closes with several guidelines for instruction.

ASSUMPTIONS UNDERLYING A SOCIOCULTURAL PERSPECTIVE ON LITERACY DEVELOPMENT

Socioculturalism offers a "unique seamlessness" of the individual, social, historical, and institutional factors that contribute to individual and cultural development (Rogoff, 1990). Learning to participate in cultural activity that depends on literate behavior, such as jotting down a list of groceries or writing a book review, requires literate members of a particular culture to apprentice the younger members into the valued practices of that culture. Thus, a sociocultural perspective on literacy development begins with the assumption that a literate action is mediated and cannot be separated from the milieu in which it is carried out.

The notion of *apprenticeship* as a model for children's cognitive development is appealing because it highlights the central role of active learners in a community of people who support, challenge, and guide novices in their development. Apprentices learn to "think, argue, act, and interact in increasingly knowledgeable ways with people who do something well, by doing it with them as legitimate, peripheral participants" (Lave, 1988, p. 2). Consequently, apprenticeship models focus our attention on "the active role of children in organizing development, the active support and use of other people in social interaction and arrangements of tasks and activities, and the socioculturally ordered nature of the institutional contexts, technologies, and goals of cognitive activities" (Rogoff, 1990, p. 39).

We have organized our discussion along the following themes: (a) social conventions shape literacy practice, (b) social processes within these practices influence individual literacy development, and (c) classrooms represent the intersection of mind and society.

Social Conventions Shape Literate Practice

Literate behavior is inextricably woven into the cultural activities of individuals in social networks and, as such, follows socially constructed conventions. Mainstream views of what it means to be literate have changed dramatically throughout history. What it means to exhibit literate behavior in 1990 is different from what it meant in 1700 and what it will mean in 2050. As cultural practices evolve inter- and intragenerationally, so, too, do the literate acts that support those practices.

In the Middle Ages, literacy was reserved for scribes and clerics for the purposes of religion and government. A person who could read, write, and speak Latin was considered literate. However, the spread of vernacular languages, the development of market economies (Thomas, 1986), social changes occurring during the Reformation (Haile, 1976), and a commitment to public schooling (Spufford, 1981) broke the church monopoly on literacy. Since then, literacy has evolved as a tool for the masses to be used in almost every aspect of daily life.

This "downward and outward" expansion of literate practice, as Venezky (1991) put it, paralleled dramatic changes in the functions, forms, and practices surrounding literate behavior:

> As the manuscript page, with its often perceptually complex graphical style, its unspaced arrangement of words, and its irregular orthography was replaced over time by the printed page, with its increasing legibility of print and regularity of spelling, and as exposure to literacy practices began at earlier ages and received more regular and intensive practice through a lifetime, reading for the average literate changed from a slow, oral production to a more rapid, silent practice. (Venezky, 1991, p. 46)

Where literacy was once practiced by an elite few for the purposes of recording, preserving, and memorizing sanctified texts, it now plays a role in a variety of social contexts, such as the home, community, school, and workplace (Guthrie & Greaney, 1991; Kaestle, 1985). The situations in each of these settings that compel literacy practice have evolved as well, as demands for literacy increased, purposes expanded, and processes evolved (Mikulecky, 1990).

The net result is the diversification of literate practices across a variety of social networks (Heath, 1991), a proliferation of literate forms to serve an array of purposes (Kaestle, 1991), and a view of cognitive processing that is determined by features of the situation (Guthrie & Greaney, 1991). It is into these socially constructed and evolving cultural functions, literate forms, social practices, cognitive strategies, and cultural conventions that individuals are born and must learn to navigate.

Individual Literacy Development and Sociocultural Activity

Individuals do not learn to navigate literate terrain alone. Knowledge of the relationships among function, form, strategies, and convention is learned in social context. The socialization practices and material arrangements of the home, school, community, and workplace consistently shape the ways individuals construe and organize literacy-related activity. However, before an individual can carry out or organize a particular culturally valued activity independently, he or she must negotiate that activity in interdependent situations:

> Cognitive development occurs in socioculturally organized activities in which children are active in learning and in managing their social partners, and their partners are active in structuring situations that provide children with access to observe and participate in culturally valued skills and perspectives. Collective activity, in turn, constitutes and transforms cultural practices with each successive generation. (Rogoff, 1990, p. 37)

Advances in the ability to function with increasing degrees of sophistication are mediated by the use of tools and sign systems that serve specific functions in activities. When human activity includes such tools, they "alter the entire flow and structure of mental functions" (Vygotsky, 1981, p. 137). These tools and sign systems can be construed as "technical tools" and "psychological tools," respectively (Wertsch, 1991). Contemporary examples of a technical tool are a computer-assisted drafting system used by an architect for design purposes and a time-based video editor used by a film producer to compile raw footage into a finished product. Psychological tools include sign systems such as language, diagrams, and alphabetic/arithmetic notation.

Socioculturalists posit that an individual's developing ability to appropriate the tools and signs of culture appears twice. First it appears on the social plane in the context of holistic, interpersonal activity. Vygotsky (1978) referred to this as the *interpsychological plane*. It is here that an individual comes in contact with the valued tools and signs of his or her culture, and where he or she receives his or her first lessons in how these tools and signs are embedded within specific activities. An individual's developing ability then appears on the intrapsychological plane. Continued social engagement in cultural activities, coupled with the learner's selective appropriation of these tools, transforms the learner's personal functioning.

Guided participation fosters an individual's appropriation of these tools and signs. Features of guided participation include frequent engagement in routine activities, tacit as well as explicit communication, organized support for novice's efforts, and gradual and inevitable transfer of responsibility for organizing and managing tasks to novices. More able participants build bridges between the known and the unfamiliar, and increase less able participants' contributions in the activity:

> Guided participation involves adults or children challenging, constraining, and supporting children in the process of posing and solving problems—through material arrangements of children's activities and responsibilities as well as through interpersonal communication, with children observing and participating at a comfortable but slightly challenging level. The processes of communication and shared participation in activities inherently engage children and their caregivers and companions in stretching children's understanding and skill to apply to new problems. Practical considerations of culturally organized activities . . . along with young children's eagerness to be involved, lead to the structuring of children's participation so that they can handle manageable but comfortably challenging subgoals of the activity that increase in complexity with children's developing skill and understanding. (Rogoff, 1990, p. 19)

Underlying the notion of guided participation is a mutual effort after intersubjectivity, "a sharing of focus and purpose between children and their more skilled partners and their challenging and exploring peers" (Rogoff, 1990, p. 8). More able participants are compelled to establish intersubjectivity with less able participants for the purpose of adapting activities to suit the less able participants' ability to contribute productively to the purpose and completion of the activity.

These adjustments for supporting the less able participant are made within the individual's zone of proximal development (ZPD)—the "distance between the actual developmental level as determined by independent problem solving and the level of potential development as determined through problem solving under adult guidance or in collaboration with more capable peers" (Vygotsky, 1978, p. 86). In any learning situation, there are certain aspects that the less able participant can accomplish autonomously, while completion of the remaining aspects requires guidance from a more able peer or adult. In those situations where the learner is not yet able to accomplish any aspect of the task, instruction is thought to be outside of the learner's ZPD. Thus, the ZPD defines the level of participation for the student in which instruction can be of greatest benefit to the student (Vygotsky, 1978).

In an apprenticeship model, both novice and expert focus on productive and culturally valued activity. Embedded within a community of people engaged in furthering these activities and developing their breath and depth of skill, a novice's participation is guided within his or her ZPD, while the more able partner is inherently interested in moving the learner from assisted to autonomous performance.

Therefore, the learner's ZPD shifts with transformations in the individual's ability to organize and manage dimensions of the activity. Assisted performance provided within the ZPD is temporary and adaptive (e.g., Tharp & Gallimore, 1988). The more able partner provides just the right amount of assistance that the learner needs to participate to his or her full potential, but no more. Hence, the learner assumes as much responsibility for the task as is practical and developmentally appropriate.

Classrooms at the Intersection of Mind and Society

Classroom activity represents the intersection between the sociocultural experiences of the child and the institutional agenda(s) of the broader society. With respect to literacy learning in school, reading curricula and the philosophies and methods associated with them tend to reflect the literate aspirations of the mainstream, or dominant, culture (Graff, 1979). As mainstream aspirations change, classroom pedagogy evolves. For example, reading in the 19th century was viewed as a facilitator and caretaker of memory. As a result, reading was taught through memorization and drill, with a focus on orthography and pronunciation (Smith, 1965). By the turn of the century, reading was widely believed to fulfill expressive and receptive functions, with an emphasis on silent reading. Educators of the day recognized the importance of silent reading, the reader's life experiences, and thinking during the reading process (Robinson, Faraone, Hittelman, & Unruh, 1990). Today, readers are believed to construct meaning through the integration of existing and new knowledge, and the flexible use of strategies to foster, monitor, regulate, and maintain comprehension (Dole, Duffy, Roehler, & Pearson, 1991)

Generally speaking, these shifts in the definition of what it meant to be literate paralleled shifts in psychology from behavioral to cognitive theories on reading (e.g., Anderson & Pearson, 1984). Consequently, the impetus of literacy instruction in schools changed: (a) from a focus on obtaining meaning during oral reading to active and constructive comprehension processes while reading silently; (b) from an emphasis on external control over students' comprehension processes (e.g., worksheets, drills, study guides) to individual metacognitive control; (c) from the *what* of comprehension (e.g., worksheets for distinguishing fact from fiction) to the *how* and *why* of comprehension; (d) from a discrete-skills approach to a holistic approach; and (e) from infrequent direct teaching of comprehension to specific and direct teaching accompanied by supervised and independent practice (Robinson et al., 1990).

However, students from all walks of life come to school with the knowledge and skills needed to participate in the sociocultural activities commonplace to their homes. Yet, students' households never function in isolation; they are connected to other households and institutions through diverse social networks (Moll & Greenberg, 1990). The essential function of these networks is to share and exchange funds of knowledge, the "essential cultural practices and bodies of knowledge and information that households use to survive, get ahead, and thrive" (Moll, 1992, p. 21).

For example, Moll and his colleagues (e.g., Moll, Amanti, Neff, & Gonzalez, 1992) surveyed the household funds of knowledge represented in one classroom of 30 children from low-income households. A composite portrait revealed remarkable diversity:

> We have visited families that know about different soils, cultivation of plants, seeding, and water distribution and management. Others know animal husbandry, veterinary medicine, ranch economy, and mechanics. Many families know about carpentry, masonry, electrical wiring, fencing, and building codes. Some families employ folk remedies, herbal cures, midwifery, and intricate first aid procedures. And family members with more schooling have knowledge about (and have worked in) archaeology, biology, and mathematics. (Moll, 1992, p. 22)

Although the Moll et al. *funds of knowledge* concept is focused mainly on the domain-specific knowledge that students appropriate from their experiences in and around the home, the concept can be extended to include students' literate funds of knowledge. Just as acquiring knowledge and information about everything from astronomy to zoology is contingent on the social networks in which one participates, the appropriation of literacy-related knowledge is dependent on the forms and functions of literacy in those same social networks (e.g., Taylor, 1983; Teale, 1986).

In most cases, the literacy experiences of the home prepare students for effective participation in the valued activity structures of the classroom, resulting in cultural congruence between home and school. Children who share a reading with an older sibling or parent on a daily basis in the 3 years preceding formal literacy instruction are poised to achieve in school-based literacy-related activity (Adams, 1990). This is especially true when the interpretive processes into which the child is socialized are grounded in similar interpretive processes in school reading lessons, such as recounting narratives and personal experiences related to texts, answering known-answer questions, and labeling pictures.

In an increasing number of cases, however, home and school experiences bear little resemblance, resulting in cultural disparity and diminished student achievement (e.g., Erickson, 1987). For example, Heath (1983) contrasted the diverse literacy practices and traditions of two working-class communities (Trackton and Roadville) in the same city located within the Piedmont region of the United States. Trackton homes tended to contain literate forms, such as the newspaper, advertisements, school homework, church materials, and school notices. Roadville homes contained an abundance of materials, including magazines, advertisements, newspapers, children's books, and church circulars. Social and individual practices surrounding these forms differed as well. Interpretive patterns, frequency of literate transactions between children and adults, and the degree to which a child was prepared for the work of school distinguished these two communities.

Cultural discontinuities exist on many fronts, and it is for this reason that some theorists argue that school oppresses already oppressed groups (e.g., Giroux, 1987, 1988). For example, texts read in school do not always reflect the many and varied cultural heritages in classrooms (Applebee, 1991), although huge benefits may accrue from the use of multicultural literature (Harris, 1994). In addition, teacher questioning practices (e.g., Heath, 1982) and the norms for participation in reading lessons (e.g., Au & Kawakami, 1985; Erickson & Mohatt, 1982; Phillips, 1972) often fail to incorporate features of home-based literacy transactions for minority students.

To be successful in school, students must demonstrate the literate behaviors valued in school. Unfortunately, schools have done a poor job of supporting the literacy development of those students who fail (Allington, 1991; Barr, 1989). A sociocultural perspective shifts the focus from the low-achieving student's personal qualities to the degree to which schools succeed or fail in intersecting the home and school cultures. Therefore, one of the primary aims of sociocultural approaches to literacy instruction is to design culturally responsive instruction (Au, 1993), instruction that reduces the disparity between school and out-of-school literacy experiences and diversifies students' abilities to participate more fully in a variety of literate communities. This requires a departure from familiar patterns of instruction grounded in transmission models of instruction to more adaptive, interactive, and reciprocal models (cf. Au, 1993; Dole et al., 1991). Teachers who adopt a sociocultural approach will be compelled to ascertain the breadth of the conceptual and literate funds of knowledge that students bring to the classroom community, and to identify where that knowledge is situated. This sets up a dialectic between the valued knowledge and sociocultural activity of students' lives outside of school and the valued outcomes implicit in the prescribed school curricula.

CONTEMPORARY MODELS OF READING INSTRUCTION IN SOCIOCULTURAL PERSPECTIVE

When viewed from a sociocultural perspective, the models examined in this volume—direct instruction, explicit instruction, response-centered instruction, and whole language—differ substantively from apprenticeship models in the ways that they address the social and personal functions of literacy

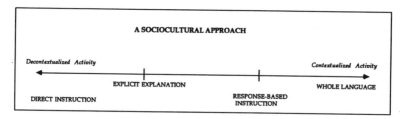

FIG. 9.1. A continuum of instructional models in reading.

and the role of literate behavior in sociocultural activity. The poles of the continuum in Fig. 9.1 represent the degree to which the instructional stance implicit in each model emanates from the purposeful flow of daily activity. Thus, direct instruction—grounded in its reliance on teacher-initiated activity and structured lessons that focus on one or two cognitive strategies at a time—represents a relatively decontextualized approach to literacy instruction. Conversely, whole language—grounded in its disposition to follow the lead of the learner in the context of authentic activity (Weaver, 1990)—represents a more contextualized view of instruction. We argue that sociocultural approaches to literacy instruction are the most contextualized because they wed individual, social, and cultural processes. We contend that a shift to sociocultural approaches increases the validity of these models because they represent the range of teaching stances required to apprentice students into valued literacy activities.

Direct Instruction and Explicit Explanation

The direct instruction and explicit explanation models share some of the same characteristics and, from a sociocultural perspective, some of the same shortcomings that a comprehensive approach to reading instruction must overcome. First, a sociocultural perspective emphasizes the role of literate behavior embedded within cultural activity, whereas direct instruction and explicit explanation focus on cognitive aspects of individual literate behavior and practice, with little regard for the cultural contexts of literate practice. The content of direct instruction and explicit explanation is based on a research base of how expert readers use strategies independently and automatically (Pressley & Brainerd, 1985; Segal, Chipman, & Glaser, 1985). Researchers hypothesize that low-achieving students, when given direct instruction or explicit explanation on what strategies are (declarative knowledge), how to use them (procedural knowledge), and when to use them (conditional knowledge), will develop higher levels of metacognitive awareness regarding the use of strategies in repairing breakdowns and monitoring their own learning (Duffy & Roehler, 1989). The outcome of this instruction is to promote the fluid coordination of these skills within each individual.

Less emphasis is placed on the kinds of classroom activities in which students participate.

Second, sociocultural approaches are grounded in social constructivism, an instructional orientation characterized by interactive and reciprocal flows of information and knowledge between students and teachers, whereas the literacy lessons in direct instruction and explicit explanation models reflect a transmission approach to instruction. Advocates of direct instruction models (e.g., Baumann, 1988; Rosenshine, 1986) stress academically focused, teacher-directed instruction that relies on sequenced and structured materials, and utilizes careful monitoring of student performance and immediate corrective feedback by the teacher. Direct instruction lessons consist of: a statement of goals, review of prior learning, presentation of material in small steps, clear and detailed instructions and explanations, involvement of the students in active practice, questions and other checks for understandings, guided practice, systematic feedback, and correction and independent practice (Rosenshine, 1986). With the more recent focus on comprehension strategy instruction, direct instruction in reading lessons may also include direct explanation, accompanied by teacher modeling of the strategy being used, a development of structures that provide for gradual transfer for responsibility of the strategy use from teacher to student, and information about the different conditions under which the strategy should be employed (Baumann, 1988).

The typical explicit explanation lesson also places the teacher at the center of knowledge construction. Teachers engage in "think alouds," model flexible use of strategies, and explain when and why particular strategies should be used (Baumann, Seifert-Kessell, & Jones, 1992; Pressley et al., 1992). Teachers also attempt to provide students with opportunities to use strategies in varying situations, and provide cues to help students recognize when transfer is possible (Pressley et al., 1992). Students are encouraged to be reflective in their use of strategies, and are provided individualized feedback during rehearsal and application of strategies.

More recent descriptions of direct instruction and explicit explanation approaches embrace a constructivist philosophy of learning. However, these approaches are driven by a preconceived curriculum (e.g., what all expert readers should know and do), and create the conditions in which knowledge tends to flow from teachers to students, sustaining the transmission mode of instruction. For the most part, transmission models of instruction are not suited to contemporary definitions of reading (e.g., Dole et al., 1991), nor are they particularly responsive to cultural differences (Au, 1993; Poplin, 1988).

Third, both models emphasize strategy training apart from the personal and social functions served by literacy practice. In fact, unlike sociocultural approaches, the role of cultural activity in and out of school in literacy learning is a secondary concern. In our view, subordinating the role of cultural activity to the acquisition of literacy strategies is a serious drawback. Talk about strategy (e.g., "What should you do now that your comprehension has failed?") can override talk about meaning and purpose ("I think this part of the chapter really lost my interest"), which are the more engaging features of literate discourse. Further, when a sense of an evolving, classroom-based learning community is lost, so, too, are the potential benefits, such as a chance to promote intellectual and literate diversity through the organization of new instructional patterns, the use of peer and expert modeling, and the inclusion of human and material resources from available learning communities (inside and outside of school).

Despite these shortcomings, direct instruction and explicit explanation have a place in a comprehensive approach to reading instruction. There are times when a teacher or more capable peer needs to reduce the complexity of a task for a learner, so that the learner can analyze or practice parts of the activity. However, the principles and practices underlying direct instruction and explicit explanation are most valid when subordinated within an approach that is sensitive to the sociocultural facets of literate practice. For example, direct instruction and explicit explanation make the most sense within an instructional regimen when a student (or group of students) requests specific information or guidance from the teacher, or when the teacher observes that a student (or group of students) requires specific literacy demonstrations that would further the student's ability to organize and manage the activity autonomously. If a teacher seeks to establish intersubjectivity with students, to focus instruction within learners' zones of proximal development, and to assist rather than direct performance, there will still be a need for teaching instances that require instructional styles characteristic of direct instruction (e.g., breaking a complex activity into subroutines) and explicit explanation (e.g., a more capable peer thinking aloud while reading a difficult passage). However, these instances will no longer frame daily literacy interactions.

Response-Centered and Whole Language Instruction

Response-centered and whole language instruction emanate from a constructivist philosophy on language and literacy learning (Watson, 1989; Weaver, 1990), an orientation that is diametrically opposed to a transmission model of teaching (see Fig. 9.1). Proponents of response-centered and whole language instruction view literacy acquisition as a natural process arising from its use in authentic cultural activity.

Proponents of response-centered instruction emphasize the meaning-making enterprise between the reader and the text (cf. Rosenblatt, 1978). Readers have a characteristic response manner that is linked to their personalities and is consistent across texts (Holland, 1975). In constructing their own reality from texts, readers' cognitive development greatly influences the manner in which they approach the story. Although diverse readers usually come to some shared agreement on the literal meaning of the text, all readers respond in various ways to different structures within the text. These responses take place within an interpretive community (DeGroff & Galda, 1992; Galda, 1988); to some degree, readers' participation in their community shapes their meaning-making processes (Fish, 1980).

The reading curriculum is centered around response activities that foster a sense of community, such as independent and collaborative reading and writing periods (e.g., Morrow, Sharkey, & Firestone, 1993) and peer discussion contexts (e.g., Short & Mitchell-Pierce, 1990). Instruction supports individual response, and attempts to deepen and widen children's appreciation and understanding of literature in a variety of forums (e.g., small group, partner work) and through different media, such as art, music, writing, and drama (Galda, 1988).

Whole language emerged as a theoretical framework from research that portrayed language learning as a synchronous social, conceptual, and linguistic process (Goodman, 1986; Harste, Woodward, & Burke 1984). Because whole language is described as a philosophy, rather than a set of practices or curricular ideals (Edelsky, Altweger, & Flores, 1991), definitions of *whole language* vary substantially. However, based on an analysis of 64 articles pertaining to whole language instruction, Bergeron (1990) synthesized the following definition:

> Whole language is a concept that embodies both a philosophy of language development as well as the instructional approaches embedded within, and supportive of, that philosophy. This concept includes the use of real literature and writing in the context of meaningful, functional, and cooperative experiences in order to develop in students motivation and interest in the process of learning. (p. 319)

Whole language proponents agree that becoming literate is not the mastery of a set of skills, but the development of a "super system" (Edelsky et al., 1991) whose subsystems are inextricably bound and cannot be divided into isolated pieces.

Bergeron (1990) also found that descriptions of whole language classrooms varied considerably. Notwithstanding this variation in practice, many teachers attempt to retain the holistic qualities of literacy learning by (a) organizing learning in themes; (b) contextualizing skill instruction; (c) integrating reading, writing, and talk opportunities; (d) inviting successive approximations of conventional literate behavior (e.g., conventional spelling); (e) moving from the whole to part; and so on. Few whole language teachers depend on direct instruction, standardized assessments, isolated skill instruction, ability grouping, worksheets, and segmented texts.

From a sociocultural perspective, response-centered and whole language approaches share similar shortcomings as comprehensive instructional approaches. First, although there is some evidence that many students progress well in whole language classrooms (Stephens, 1991), the research base supporting whole language is fraught with methodological problems and inconsistencies in the substantive findings (McKenna, Robinson, & Miller, 1990; Stahl & Miller, 1989).

Second, the outcomes of whole language instruction are not as clear with non-native English speakers or students who come to school having had nonmainstream experiences. A number of theorists have recognized that what appears to be an "authentic" literate practice or text from one cultural perspective may be "inauthentic" when viewed from a different perspective. Students who do not share the language and/or cultural experiences of the mainstream culture may lack the discourse forms and styles and background knowledge needed to achieve in more student-centered, process-oriented classrooms (Delpit, 1986, 1988). This is further exacerbated when a teacher takes a less interventionist stance, which is typical of many response-centered and whole language classrooms (Pearson, 1989).

Any one of the models discussed in this book is a partial response to the challenges stemming from an increasingly diverse society (Allington, 1995). None of these models provides the theoretical underpinnings that compel educators to either place curriculum in sociohistorical perspective, or align the literacy practices valued in school with those practiced in the homes of its students. Furthermore, none moves from a focus on the cognitive characteristics of the individual to individual or collective performance in valued activities.

TOWARD A SOCIOCULTURAL APPROACH TO LITERACY INSTRUCTION

All models of literacy instruction are grounded in their own conceptualizations of what it means to be literate. Direct instruction and explicit explanation models focus on specific cognitive dimensions of independent reading. As a result, teaching content is driven by a preconceived curriculum, instruction moves part to whole, literacy-related knowledge flows from teachers to students, and students practice being literate in individualistic situations. Response-centered and whole language models emphasize individual and communal development over time. As a result, teachers seek to adapt the content of instruction to suit the needs and interests of students, instruction moves from whole to part, literacy-related knowledge flows reciprocally between teachers and students, and students demonstrate literate behavior in individualistic and communal situations.

A sociocultural approach to literacy instruction defines *literacy* as a cultural act constrained by cognitive, social, and motivational dimensions. For example, Au (1993) defined *reading* as "the ability and the willingness to use reading and writing to construct meaning from printed text, in ways which meet the requirements of a particular social context" (p. 20). To this end, schools need to take an "additive" rather than a "subtractive" stance on broadening students' abilities to function effectively in mainstream as well as more familiar social contexts (Cummins, 1986). Just as speaking more than one language affords greater access to more than one culture, so, too, will a diverse literacy repertoire provide access to multiple literacy communities. In short, instructional strategies that embrace diversity are crucial.

Creating instruction that is responsive to the demands of a variety of social contexts requires teachers and students to take a social constructivist stance toward curriculum and learning. It also requires teachers to alter instructional patterns in school. Meeting this challenge requires attention to three principles. First, sociocultural approaches to literacy instruction begin with the creation of a classroom community that unites diverse purposes and practices. Such a community recognizes the disparity in norms, values, and expectations concerning literate practices that children bring with them, and provides opportunity to diversify these practices.

Second, sociocultural approaches to literacy instruction use students' familiar literacy experiences rather than a set of prescribed, curricular goals as a point-of-departure for learning activities. Consequently, teachers and students shape the curriculum at the intersection of the students' funds of knowledge and the school's curricular goals.

Third, sociocultural approaches to literacy instruction recognize that activity settings include the personnel, occasion, motivations, goals, place, and timeframe to invite cultural participation (Gallimore & Tharp, 1990). Activity, concept, and culture are interdependent (Brown, Collins, & Duguid, 1989, p. 33). Goals in authentic activity are embedded within the social conditions that provide a motive and context for aquiring new knowledge or skills, sustain interest in learning, and provide the standards and opportunity for self-assessment (Brown et al., 1989; Moll & Greenberg, 1990). Knowledge is often distributed across participants engaged in the activity. While each participant may not master every aspect of the task at the same time, there is opportunity to observe and reflect on the aspects not yet mastered. In this way, expertise is distributed among participants and gradually appropriated by individuals through repeated exposure and guided participation.

CONCLUSION

Children learn most readily in an environment in which the activity is valued, has a specific purpose, and is designed to adapt to their abilities to participate in the activity (Rogoff, 1990). More knowledgeable others assist in this endeavor by supplying demonstrations and explanations of the manner in which the task is best accomplished, and, when necessary, by scaffolding students' participation in components of the task. Each of the previously discussed instructional models has its place in this scheme. However, each achieves its ends best when contextualized in a more comprehensive, sociocultural approach.

When divorced from meaningful and engaging activity, any teaching approach can obstruct the desired end of literacy instruction—the increasingly complex coordination of the forms and functions of literacy as tools in the pursuit of personal and social goals (Shannon, 1989). However, one cannot assume that all children will acquire literacy naturally as a result of being immersed within a literate school community (Delpit, 1986). Natural and effortless appropriation of mainstream literate behavior may not be achieved easily for those children whose literacy experiences do not reflect the school culture's literate forms and functions.

From our perspective, the key instructional decisions do not hinge on which of the available instructional approaches is "best." The important concern relates to the relevancy of a particular approach given the instructional situation. For example, when a leaner requests specific help (e.g., "What's a good thing to do when I get to a word I don't know?") or when a small group of students could benefit from a more capable model (e.g., the teacher or a more able peer), a direct and explicit style of teaching is probably best.

A complete literacy program embraces the previously discussed instructional methodologies, and embeds them within a cogent whole that is sensitive to the sociocultural conditions that shape literate activity and give it value.

REFERENCES

Adams, M. J. (1990). *Beginning to read: Thinking and learning about print.* Cambridge, MA: MIT Press.

Allington, R. L., & Walmsley, S. A. (1995). *No quick fix: Rethinking literacy programs in America's elementary schools.* New York: Teachers College Press.

Allington, R. L. (1991). Children who find learning to read difficult: School responses to diversity. In E. H. Hiebert (Ed.), *Literacy for a diverse society: Perspectives, practices, and policies* (pp. 237–252). New York: Teachers College Press.

Alvermann, D. E., & Guthrie, J. T. (1993). *Themes and directions of the National Reading Research Center.* Perspectives in Reading Research (No. 1). Athens, GA: University of Georgia, National Reading Research Center.

Anderson, R. C., & Pearson, P. D. (1984). A schema-theoretic view of basic processes in reading comprehension. In P. D. Pearson, R. Barr, M. L. Kamil, & P. Mosenthal (Eds.), *Handbook of reading research* (pp. 255–292). New York: Longman.

Applebee, A. N. (1991). Literacy: Whose heritage? In E. H. Hiebert (Ed.), *Literacy for a diverse society: Perspectives, practices, and policies.* New York: Teachers College Press.

Au, K. H. (1993). *Literacy instruction in multicultural settings.* Fort Worth, TX: Harcourt Brace Jovanovich.

Au, K. H., & Kawakami, A. J. (1985). Influence of the social organization of instruction on children's text comprehension ability: A Vygotskyan perspective. In T. E. Raphael & R. E. Reynolds (Eds.), *The contexts of school-based literacy* (pp. 63–77). New York: Random House.

Barr, R. (1989). The social organization of literacy instruction. In S. McCormick & J. Zutell (Eds.), *Cognitive and social perspectives for literacy research and instruction: Thirty-eighth yearbook of the National Reading Conference* (pp. 19–33). Chicago, IL: National Reading Conference.

Baumann, J. F., Seifert-Kessell, N., & Jones, L. A. (1992). Effect of think-aloud instruction on elementary students' comeprehension monitoring abilities. *Journal of Reading Behavior, 24*(2), 143–172.

Baumann, J. F. (1988). Direct instruction reconsidered. *Journal of Reading Behavior, 31*(8), 712–718.

Bergeron, B. S. (1990). What does the term whole language mean? Consructing a definition from the literature. *Journal of Reading Behavior, 22*(4), 301–329.

Bloome, D. (1983). Reading as a social process. *Advances in Reading/Language Research, 2,* 165–195.

Brown, J. S., Collins, A., & Duguid, P. (1989, January). Situated cognition and the culture of learning. *Educational Researcher,* 32–42.

Cummins, J. (1986). Empowering minority students: A framework for intervention. *Harvard Educational Review, 56,* 18–35.

DeGroff, L., & Galda, L. (1992). Responding to literature: Activities for exploring books. In B. E. Cullinan (Ed.), *Invitation to read: More children's literature in the reading program* (pp. 122–137). Newark, DE: International Reading Association.

Delpit, L. D. (1986). Skills and other dilemmas of a progressive black educator. *Harvard Educational Review, 56,* 379–385.

Delpit, L. D. (1988). The silenced dialogue: Power and pedagogy in educating other people's children. *Harvard Educational Review, 58,* 280–298.

Dole, J. A., Duffy, G. G., Roehler, L. A., & Pearson, P. D. (1991). Moving from the old to the new: Research on reading comprehension instruction. *Review of Educational Research, 61*(2), 239–264.

Duffy, G. G., & Roehler, L. R. (1989). Improving reading instruction through the use of responsive elaboration. *Reading Teacher, 40,* 514–521.

Edelsky, C., Altwerger, B., & Flores, B. (1991). *Whole language: What's the difference.* Portsmouth, NH: Heinemann.

Erickson, F. (1987). Transformation and school success: The politics and culture of educational attainment. *Anthropology and Education Quarterly, 18*(4), 335–355.

Erickson, F., & Mohatt, G. (1982). Cultural organization of participant structures in two classrooms of Indian students. In G. D. Spindler (Ed.), *Doing the ethnography of schooling: Educational anthropology in action* (pp. 132–174). New York: Holt, Rinehart & Winston.

Fish, S. (1980). *Is there a text in this class? The authority of interpretive communities.* Cambridge, MA: Harvard University Press.

Galda, L. (1988). Readers, texts and contexts: A response-based view of literature in the classroom. *The New Advocate, 1,* 2, 92–102.

Giroux, H. A. (1987). Critical literacy and student experience: Donald Graves' approach to literacy. *Language Arts, 64*(2), 175–181.

Giroux, H. A. (1988). Literacy and the pedagogy of voice and political empowerment. *Educational Theory, 38,* 61–75.

Goodman, K. (1986). *What's whole in whole language?* Richmond Hill, Ontario: Scholastic-TAB.

Graff, H. (1979). *The literacy myth: Literacy and social structure in the nineteenth century city.* New York: Acadmic Press.

Guthrie, J. T., & Greaney, V. (1991). Literacy acts. In R. Barr, M. L. Kamil, P. Mosenthal, & P. D. Pearson (Eds.), *Handbook of reading research* (Vol. II, pp. 68–96). New York: Longman.

Haile, H. G. (1976). Luther and literacy. *Publications of the Modern Language Association, 91,* 816–828.

Harris, V. (1994). Multiculturalism and children's literature. In F. Lehr & J. Osborn (Eds.), *Reading, language, and literacy: Instruction for the twenty-first century.* Hillsdale, NJ: Lawrence Erlbaum Associates.

Harste, J. C., Woodward, V. A., & Burke, C. L. (1984). *Language stories and literacy lessons.* Portsmouth, NH: Heinemann.

Heath, S. B. (1982). Questioning at home and at school: A comparative study. In G. Spindler (Ed.), *Doing the ethnography of schooling: Educational anthropology in action* (pp. 102–131). New York: Holt, Rinehart & Winston.

Heath, S. B. (1983). *Ways with words.* New York: Cambridge University Press.

Heath, S. B. (1991). The sense of being literate: Historical and cross-cultural features. In R. Barr, M. L. Kamil, P. Mosenthal, & P. D. Pearson (Eds.), *Handbook of reading research* (Vol. II, pp. 3–25). New York: Longman.

Holland, N. (1975). *Five readers reading.* New Haven, CT: Yale University Press.

Kaestle, C. F. (1985). The history of literacy and the history of readers. *Review of research in education* (Vol. 12). Washington, DC: American Educational Research Association.

Kaestle, C. F. (1991). Standardization and diversity in American print culture, 1880 to the present. In C. F. Kaestle, H. Damon-Moore, L. C. Stedman, K. Tinsley, & W. V. Trollinger (Eds.), *Literacy in the United States: Readers and reading since 1880.* New Haven, CT: Yale University Press.

Lave, J. (1988, May). *The culture of acquisition and the practice of understanding* (Report No. IRL 88–0007). Palo Alto, CA: Institute for Research on Learning.

Leont'ev, A. N. (1981). The problem of activity in psychology. In J. V. Wertsch (Ed.), *The concept of activity in Soviet psychology.* Armonk, NY: Sharpe.

McKenna, M. C., Robinson, R. D., & Miller, J. W. (1990). Whole language: A research agenda for the nineties. *Educational Researcher, 19*(8) 3–6.

Mikulecky, L. (1990). Literacy for what purpose? In R. L. Venezky, D. A. Wagner, & B. S. Ciliberti (Eds.), *Toward defining literacy.* Newark, DE: International Reading Association.

Moll, L. C., & Greenberg, J. B. (1990). Creating zones of possibilities: Combining social contexts for instruction. In L. Moll (Ed.), *Vygotsky and education: Instructional implications and applications of sociohistorical psychology* (pp. 319–348). New York: Cambridge University Press.

Moll, L. C. (1992). Bilingual classroom studies and community analysis: Some recent trends. *Educational Researcher, 22*(2), 20–24.

Moll, L. C., Amanti, C., Neff, D., & Gonzalez, N. (1992). Funds of knowledge for teaching: Using a qualitative approach to connect homes and classrooms. *Theory Into Practice, 31*(2), 132–141.

Morrow, L. M., Sharkey, E., & Firestone, W. A. (1993). *Promoting independent reading and writing through self-directed literacy activities in a collaborative setting* (Reading Res. Rep. No. 2). Athens, GA: National Reading Research Center, Universities of Georgia and Maryland.

Pearson, P. (1989). Reading the whole-language movement. *Elementary School Journal, 90*(2), 231–241.

Phillips, S. U. (1972). Participant structures and communicative competence: Warm Springs children in community and classroom. In C. B. Cazden, V. P. John, & D. Hymes (Eds.), *Functions of language in the classroom* (pp. 370–394). New York: Teachers College Press.

Poplin, M. S. (1988). The reductionistic fallacy in learning disabilities: Replicating the past by reducing the present. *Journal of Learning Disabilities, 21,* 389–400.

Pressley, M., & Brainerd, C. (Eds). (1985). *Cognitive learning and memory in children.* New York: Springer-Verlag.

Pressley, M., El-Dinary, P. B., Gaskins, I., Schuder, T., Bergman, J. L., Almasi, J., & Brown, R. (1992). Beyond direct explanation: Transactional instruction of reading comprehension strategies. *The Elementary School Journal, 92,* 5, 513–555.

Robinson, H. A., Faraone, V., Hittelman, D. R., & Unruh, E. (1990). *Reading comprehension instruction, 1783–1987.* Newark, DE: International Reading Association.

Rogoff, B. (1990). *Apprenticeship in thinking: Cognitive development in social context.* New York: Oxford University Press.

Rosenblatt, L. (1978). *The reader, the text, the poem.* Carbondale, IL: Southern Illinois University Press.

Rosenshine, B. V. (1986, April). Synthesis of research on explicit teaching. *Educational Leadership,* 60–69.

Scribner, S. S., & Cole, M. (1981). *The psychology of literacy.* Cambridge, MA: Harvard University Press.

Segal, J., Chipman, S., & Glaser, R. (Eds.). (1985). *Thinking and learning skills: Vol. 2. Research and open questions.* Hillsdale, NJ: Lawrence Erlbaum Associates.

Shannon, P. (1989). The struggle for control of literacy lessons. *Language Arts, 66*(6), 625–634.

Short, K. G., & Mitchell-Pierce, K. (1990). *Talking about books: Creating literate communities.* Portsmouth, NH: Heinemann.

Smith, N. B. (1965). *American reading instruction.* Newark, DE: International Reading Association.

Spufford, M. (1981). *Small books and pleasant histories.* London: Methuen.

Stahl, S., & Miller, P. (1989). Whole language and language experience approaches for beginning reading: A quantitative research synthesis. *Review of Educational Research, 59,* 87–116.

Stephens, D. (1991). *Whole language: A research perspective.* New York: Richard C. Owen.

Taylor, D. (1983). *Family literacy.* Portsmouth, NH: Heinemann.

Teale, W. H. (1986). Home background and young children's literacy development. In W. H. Teale & E. Sulzby (Eds.), *Emergent literacy: Writing and reading* (pp. 173–206). Norwood, NJ: Ablex.

Tharp, R., & Gallimore, R. (1988). *Rousing minds to life: Teaching, learning, and schooling in social context.* New York: Cambridge University Press.

Thomas, K. (1986). The meaning of literacy in early modern England. In G. Baumann (Ed.), *The written work: Literacy in transition* (pp. 97–131). Oxford: Clarendon.

Venezky, R. L. (1991). The development of literacy in the industrialized nations of the West. In R. Barr, M. L. Kamil, P. Mosenthal, & P. D. Pearson (Eds.), *Handbook of reading research* (Vol. II, pp. 46–67). New York: Longman.

Vygotsky, L. S. (1978). *Mind in society: The development of higher psychological processes.* Cambridge, MA: Harvard University Press.

Vygotsky, L. S. (1981). The genesis of higher mental functions. In J. Wertsch (Ed.), *The concept of activity in Soviet psychology.* Armonk, NY: Sharpe.

Watson, D. (1989). Defining and decribing whole language. *The Elementary School Journal, 90,* 129–141.

Weaver, C. (1990). *Understanding whole language: Principles and practices.* Portsmouth, NH: Heinemann.

Wertsch, J. V. (1991). *Voices of the mind.* Cambridge, MA: Harvard University Press.

White, S. H., & Siegel, A. W. (1984). Cognitive development in time and space. In B. Rogoff & J. Lave (Eds.), *Everday cognition: Its development in social context* (pp. 238–278). Cambridge, MA: Harvard University Press.

CHAPTER TEN

Whole-Language Approaches to Reading and Writing

Lee Gunderson
University of British Columbia, Canada

Whole language has become a major movement in literacy education, generating enthusiasm by its proponents and condemnation by its critics. This chapter discusses this issue in detail. First, it argues that traditional researchers have been frustrated in their attempts to define *whole language* because it is not definable in a conventional sense. Second, it proposes that whole-language programs vary from practitioner to practitioner relative to different construals of intertexts, and that, although its proponents argue that it is, whole language is not a philosophy in the traditional sense. Third, it suggests that whole language is supported by research, but not the comparative research expected by traditional educational researchers, who appear to confuse whole language with related approaches, such as language-experience and meaning-centered instruction. Fourth, it suggests that research involving such approaches as case studies is more appropriate to whole language. Fifth, it proposes that a pragmatic view of research focusing on the results of a program is more relevant to individual teachers than is a fundamentalist view.

DEFINING WHOLE LANGUAGE

Many are concerned about defining the term *whole language* for purposes of conducting research (Bergeron, 1990; Moorman, Blanton, & McLaughlin, 1992; Palmer, Gambrell, & Almasi 1991; Stahl & Miller, 1989). Bergeron (1990) surveyed 64 journal articles published between 1979 and 1989, which: ". . . defined whole language, provided research on whole language programs, or described elementary research or instructional procedures related to this term" (p. 307). Bergeron found that about 58% of the articles described whole language as a philosophy or approach. She found that *whole language* had been described as a method, philosophy, orientation, theory, theoretical orientation, program, curriculum, perspective on education, and attitude, and that individual authors had varied over time in their definition of the term. I selected a sample of writing about whole language written in journals[1] and books[2] over the last 10 years, and applied Bergeron's Analysis Checklist. I found that, in about 70% of the cases, journal articles described whole language as a philosophy or approach; in about 80% of the cases, books described whole language as a philosophy or approach. The view that whole language is a philosophy appears to be increasing. Bergeron developed a definition based on her analyses:

> Whole language is a concept that embodies both a philosophy of language-development and the instructional approaches embedded within, and supportive of, that philosophy. This concept includes the use of real literature and writing in the context of meaningful, functional, and cooperative experiences in order to develop in students motivation and interest in the process of learning. (p. 319)

Bergeron's definition operationalizes *whole language* as both a philosophy and approach, with an instructional outcome of "motivation and interest

---

[1]Allen, Michalove, Shockley, & West, 1991; Altwerger, Edelsky, & Flores, 1987; Brazee & Kristo, 1986; Cairney, 1985a, 1985b; Cambourne & Turbill, 1990; Chaney, 1990; Cooter & Flynt, 1989; Cullinan, 1992; Dudley-Marling & Dippo, 1991; Edelsky & Smith, 1984; Farris, 1989; Farris & Andersen, 1990; Ferguson, 1988; Fountas & Hannigan, 1989; Fox, 1986; French et al., 1990; K. Goodman, 1984, 1984–1985, 1986a, 1989, 1992a, 1992b; K. Goodman & Y. Goodman, 1979, 1983; Y. Goodman, 1985, 1989; Gunderson, 1994; Haese, 1991; Hahn, 1989; Harman & Edelsky, 1989; Harp, 1988; Harste, 1989, 1993; Heymsfeld, 1989; Hoffman, 1992; Hudelson, 1984; Kasten, 1992; King & Goodman, 1990; Lamme, 1989; Lamme & Lee, 1990; Lerner, Cousin, & Richeck, 1992; Lim & Watson, 1993; McCaslin, 1989; Maguire, 1989; Mather, 1992; Monson & Pahl, 1991; Newman, 1987, 1991; Newman & Church, 1990; Norris & Damico, 1990; Oldfather, 1993; Pace, 1992; Pahl & Monson, 1992; Pearson, 1989; Peetoom, 1991; Reutzel & Hollingsworth, 1988; Rich, 1985a, 1985b; Ridley, 1990; Ruddell, 1992; Shapiro, 1992; Slaughter, 1988; Spiegel, 1989, 1992; Staab, 1990; Stanek, 1991; Stice & Bertrand, 1992; Sumara & Walker, 1991; Tchudi, 1992; Thompson, 1992; Waldon, 1988; Watson, 1989; Zucker, 1993.

[2]Anderson, 1984; Baskwill & Whitman, 1986, 1988; Bloom, 1989; Butler & Turbill, 1984; Cairney, 1983; Calkins, 1991; Cambourne, 1988; Cambourne & Turbill, 1989; Edelsky, Altwerger, & Flores, 1991; Freeman & Freeman, 1992; Froese, 1994; K. Goodman, 1986; K. Goodman, Smith, Meredith, & Goodman, 1987; K. Goodman, Shannon, Freeman, & Murphy, 1988; K. Goodman, Goodman, & Hood, 1989; K. Goodman, Bird, & Goodman, 1990; Graves, 1983; Gunderson, 1989; Hancock & Hill, 1987; Hansen, 1982; Harste, Pierce, & Cairney, 1985; Harste & Short, 1986; Harste, Short, & Burke, 1988; Harste, Woodward, & Burke, 1984; Heald-Taylor, 1986, 1989; Lamme, 1984; Newman, 1985, 1990, 1992; Rhodes & Dudley-Marling, 1988; Rigg & Allen, 1989; Ringler & Weber, 1984; Routman, 1988; Smith, 1985, 1988; Stephens, 1991; Strickland & Morrow, 1989; Tovey & Kerber, 1986; Turbill, 1982, 1983; Watson, Burke, & Harste, 1989; Weaver, 1988, 1990; Willinsky, 1990; Yatvin, 1991.

in the process of learning." In contrast, Newman (1985) believed that, "Whole language isn't an instructional approach in the usual sense, but a philosophical stance" (p. 1). Dudley-Marling and Dippo (1991) noted, "The ways whole language advocates talk and write about whole language theory and practice are sometimes contradictory" (p. 648). The issues become even more complex because whole language is evolving. Harste (1989) observed that, "Whole language theory is changing. More and more whole-language theorists are talking about reading and writing as tools for learning rather than using such terms as 'learning to mean,' 'reading to mean,' and the like" (p. 244). Moorman et al. (1994) agreed that whole-language is evolving. However, they found in their analyses of 18 articles "three consistently recurring theoretical themes: general definitions, learning and teaching, and the reading process and reading instruction" (p. 311). Harste (1993) also suggested that research is changing—that the truth about teaching and learning does not exist independently, and that the researcher's task is not simply to discover the truth, but, ". . . to uncover the theory of meaning that was operating in the group" (p. 17). Harste predicted that whole-language programs ". . . will anchor themselves on such processes as transmediation or, said differently, on universal processes which undergird literacy across sign systems and disciplines" (p. 12). A key term used by many in reference to whole language is *philosophy*, but is it a philosophy?

PHILOSOPHY

Systematic formulations of how human beings come to believe are organized around considerations of metaphysics, epistemology, and axiology formulated broadly to investigate: What is real? What is true? What is good? Theory represents a set of beliefs, some of which are supported by evidence. "In education there is a claim to theory, to the possibility of setting down general ideas that will explain and rationalize the various phenomena occurring in the educational enterprise" (Morris & Pai, 1976, p. 6). In essence, philosophy is a theory of theories or a metatheory, "the single formula by which all human learning can be understood and managed" (Morris & Pai, 1976, p. 7)—a traditional philosophical view currently receiving considerable criticism. As a philosophy, whole language should address issues related to knowledge, truth, and belief.

WHOLE LANGUAGE AND PHILOSOPHY

Those who define *whole language* often refer to it as a philosophy. However, Watson (1989) believed that whole language is difficult to define because (a) most whole-language advocates reject definitions, (b) those who demand definitions usually disapprove of whole language, and (c) teachers (i.e., the

experts who have developed their own "personalized" whole-language programs) are not asked and thus remain silent. Harste (1989) concluded that,
"Whole language is essentially a theory of voice that operates in the premise
that all students must be heard" (p. 245), and that students should be asked,
"How are you different now that you have finished reading this text than
you were when you began?" (p. 244). He also proposed that, ". . . it is our
theory and we must take responsibility for it" (p. 247).

Although Harste (1993) proposed that whole-language advocates should
search for the universals in literacy learning, whole language is not a
philosophy in the traditional sense: It does not seek to formulate metanarratives (Gunderson, 1989), and it does not systematically address: What is real?
What is true? What is good? However, it does appear to be a complex and
changing chronicle representing the communication of multiple voices; it is a
text in the postmodern sense of the term—one containing philosophical
elements.

WHOLE LANGUAGE IS INTERTEXT, NOT PHILOSOPHY

Brown and Yule (1983) defined *text* as "evidence of an attempt by a producer
(speaker/writer) to communicate his (sic) message to a recipient (lis-
tener/reader)" (p. 24). The essential characteristic of a text is that it is "a
communicative occurrence" (Beaugrande & Dressler, 1981, p. 3). Any instance of discourse represents text if its function is to communicate. Discourses concern what can be said and thought, and who can speak (Foucault,
1974). Discussions and definitions of whole language are texts, some oral
and some written, and they exist not separately, but in reference to other
texts because texts cannot exist independently. De Beaugrande (1980),
Kristeva (1980), and Orr (1986) argued that the interpretation of one text
through reference to another is called *intertextuality*. Orr contended that
no text is written in a vacuum. Kristeva viewed intertextuality as dialogue—
one that can occur through writing, reading, speaking listening, and watching, with all those texts that exist in an individual's experience. Bloome and
Egan-Robertson (1993) defined *text* as "the product of *textualizing* which
can be a set of words, signs, representations, etc." (p. 311; italics original).
The environment within which a particular text exists is filled with multiple
references to other texts. Foucault (1972) noted that all texts are related to
other texts in ". . . a system of references to other books, other texts, other
sentences" (p. 165). All texts are related to other texts, which Derrida (1977)
suggested produces "an infinity of new contexts in a manner which is ab-
solutely illimitable" (p. 185). Any individual text can be analyzed by framing
it—by "an interpretive imposition that restricts an object by establishing
boundaries" (Culler, 1983, p. 196). Derrida (1979) suggested that framed

texts become invaginated because the boundary, or the frame, becomes part of the text and the intertext is subsumed with the text. It is proposed that: Whole language is not a philosophy in the traditional sense; rather, each construal is a framed composite propositional intertext.

Foucault (1974) suggested that meaning does not arise so much from discourse, but from those who use the discourse—those who have the power. Discourses are about what can be said and thought, as well as who can speak and with what authority. But why define *whole language* as an intertext when it would be simpler to define it in a manner similar to a dictionary?

THE ADVANTAGES AND DISADVANTAGES
OF WHOLE LANGUAGE AS INTERTEXT

A propositional intertext contains philosophical, educational, sociological, perceptual, and literacy propositions generated by an individual teacher in response to the multiple sources that inform him or her. In this respect, a propositional intertext is an individual view of teaching and learning—one that varies from teacher to teacher, from school to school, and from region to region. In this sense, it does not represent universals, but represents local belief, or the interpretive voice of the teacher. This is an advantage in that intertexts evolve over time as new propositions are added or existing ones are altered or eliminated. Individual teachers develop their literacy programs on the basis of a propositional intertext that is complex and evolving. For instance, Reutzel and Hollingsworth (1988) developed an intertext with the following propositions: "(h)umanism is the philosophical base, (c)hildren already know how to learn, (p)rocess is most important, and (l)anguage is indivisible" (p. 412). Their educational inferences were that: "(w)hole to parts learning is emphasized, (l)earning begins with the concrete and moves to the abstract, (i)nstruction is based on transactional/transformational theories in reading, and (i)nstruction is associated with theories of gestalt psychology" (p. 412).

However, a definition imposes limits on a concept, and frames it in ways that render it essentially immutable. Basal instruction, in which reading is well defined, represents a static view of reading and learning to read (and all of its attendant educational prescriptions). It is imposed on teachers and students (Shannon, 1989), and has been fairly consistent and rigid in form over the last half century.

A propositional intertext represents the voices of those who view literacy as a basic, perhaps natural, human activity framed by the teacher, whose view is often, but not necessarily, similar to that of the students. Whole-language proponents propose a view of learning that is literacy-centered, in which reading and writing are integral activities of thinking human beings, and are designed to produce independent critical learners. These are fairly well-engrained North American views not necessarily shared by individuals from other cultures (Early & Gunderson, 1993).

There are disadvantages to the view that whole language is an intertext; a major one involves validity. There are an infinite number of possible intertexts, as well as instructional applications inferred from them. How does one judge whether a particular intertext constitutes a whole-language intertext? Who is to judge that any particular intertext is whole language? What are the criteria by which the judgment is made? How does one go about recognizing that a particular intertext is a whole-language intertext? Should every text framed by an individual as whole language constitute a whole-language intertext? No, some putative whole-language texts are not whole language; that someone says a whole-language text is a whole-language text does not make it necessarily so. Good reasons must be provided. Substantiation of the speaker or writer's reasons for believing that a particular text is whole language involves appropriate justification determined relative to time and adequacy of standards. For purposes of discussion and debate, it is proposed here that the minimal set of propositions includes:

- that meaningful language is intact language;
- that active learning is meaningful learning;
- that speaking, listening, reading, writing, and watching are integrated, mutually reinforcing language activities;
- that the aesthetics of language are fundamental;
- that language is functional;
- that the learning of content and the learning of language are inseparable; and
- that literacy learning should involve the learning of process.

The disadvantage is that it establishes an authority.

The teacher's whole-language intertext provides a complex view of teaching and learning: It represents a blueprint of the causal links made among propositions, conclusions, and outcomes. Teachers are the best individuals to conduct research in the classroom because the intertext is their own individual construal of whole language, and the program is imbued with its features. The following section looks at two different programs and the intertexts that guided their development.

A Primary Classroom

Mrs. R. was a primary-school teacher in British Columbia, Canada. In 1987, she was 60 years old, a teaching veteran of 26 years, and had been a developing whole-language teacher for 5 years. The following is an outline of the propositions in Mrs. R.'s intertext: (a) whole stories are more mean-ingful than words or sentences; (b) phonics and word-recognition skills are important; (c) learning skills in meaningful contexts is superior to learning in isolation; (d) material containing real language is more meaningful than material containing contrived language; (e) writing and reading are interre-lated activities; (f) communication should be for a purpose; (g) the love of reading and writing is significant; (h) adult modeling is vital; (i) good chil-dren's literature motivates students to read; (j) meaningful learning is explo-ration; (k) independent learning is important; (l) taking risks in learning is essential to develop independent learning; (m) literacy independence is a primary goal; and (n) process is more important than product.

Her class consisted of 27 students, including 10 English as Second Lan-guage (ESL) students, 1 mentally challenged student, and 1 physically chal-lenged student. Her class was a "typical" primary whole-language class, with walls covered with various forms of printed language including: children's writing, posters of Hong Kong, a "group corner" where students were in-volved in whole-class activities such as the reading of Big Books and sharing time, a library center with a collection of children's books and books written and published by the students, a math center, a science center, a quiet reading center, a log book for each student's independent writing, home reading records to keep track of the books students take home to read with parents, group reading in which the teacher reads aloud and students "chime in," group language-experience activities, individual and small-group activi-ties organized, individual student–teacher conferences, teacher's clipboard recordings of observations about students' work, anecdotal notes about in-dividual students' progress, a parent volunteer who works at the publishing center using a computer word processing program, individual inductive phonics lessons, Uninterrupted Sustained Silent Writing (USSW), teaching and learning around themes, Uninterrupted Sustained Silent Reading (USSR), and the publication of a class newspaper.

An Intermediate Classroom

Mr. R. is an intermediate-level teacher in British Columbia, Canada. He was 48 years old, a veteran of 22 years, and an initially reluctant whole-language teacher who had been "working on his program" for 3 years. His seventh-grade class of 32 students has 27 ESL students, 6 behavioral problems, and 16 students from single-parent families. The following is an outline of Mr. R.'s whole-language intertext: (a) writing and reading are interrelated; (b) academic content, especially science and math, is the foundation of knowl-edge; (c) knowing how to find information is central; (d) the love of reading and writing has lifelong significance; (e) adult modeling of the pleasures and rewards of learning is important; (f) good literature motivates students to read; (g) meaningful learning is exploration; (h) independent learning is essential for independence; (i) cooperative and independent learning are interrelated; and (j) survival literacy skills often determine a student's chances of success in society.

Mr. R. was convinced that his students could not become independent learners without guidance. Hence, he implemented a highly controlled cooperative learning program, in which he carefully trained students in cooperative processes and procedures (Johnson, Johnson, & Holubec, 1988; Slavin et al., 1985). His goals were to: positively manage students' behavior, provide transitional scaffolding leading to independent learning, help maintain and keep records, and involve students in planning and managing their own learning. Mr. R. felt responsible for content, but he also knew that motivation was a key to learning. Mr. R. attempted to ensure that: his classroom contains a collection of books that accounts for students' varied interests; there are Portfolios containing varied materials, such as written compositions and audio- or videotapes; he has at least four centers with clearly identified learning activities; there is a book log for each student; there is a writing log for each student; there are student–teacher reaction logs; he maintains a conference log; the classroom library features students' published work; there are collections of high-interest materials; there is an individual learning development checklist; a teacher's management clipboard is maintained; and there is a first language library borrowed from his ESL parents. Students help search for materials, develop learning centers, and manage their own learning.

THE WHOLE-LANGUAGE INTERTEXTS

The criterion by which a particular whole-language intertext is measured is the "good reason" provided. These teachers made informed decisions and created learning environments that provided functional opportunities for students to use language. Mrs. R.'s program focused on printed text and activities that developed awareness of the language of books, whereas Mr. R.'s program focused on the learning of content and survival literacy skills.

Mrs. R. was convinced that learning phonics was important, and that the overwhelming majority of students learns phonics skills through meaningful reading and writing activities. When certain students consistently produced the same invented spelling, she used an inductive approach to help them learn the standard spelling. Such instruction was neither regularly scheduled nor considered an integral part of her program. Mr. R. focused on independent learning and academic content. Mrs. R.'s class was a primary whole-language classroom. It contained all the classic features of such a program, which had been developed over time and was a result of her interpretation of her intertext. The educational implications she drew from her propositional intertext produced a program that was unique. Mr. R.'s program was a result of his interpretation of his own unique intertext. Their educational decisions were, to a large degree, informed by research. They were able to cite research and individual researchers such as Ken Goodman, Yetta Goodman, Jerome Harste, and Jean Piaget. In addition, Mr. R. was well versed in the cooperative learning literature.

Bergeron's (1990) definition of whole language is a composite propositional intertext framed by "an interpretive imposition" related to a traditional educational research paradigm. It requires measurable outcomes and a search for metanarratives and a logical-positivist subtext—a "clearly stated unsaid or more precisely of the inter-said" (Dranch, 1983, p. 177). Bergeron's subtext is that a metanarrative, one concerning the truth about the learning of language in school, can be discovered by applying traditional research methodologies to a number of classrooms that evidence features of instruction imputed from the composite propositions in the intertext. The need for empirical research is a clear subtext in Bergeron's intertext, but research itself can be considered a kind of text: "If we get rid of traditional notions of 'objectivity' and 'scientific method' we shall be able to see the social sciences as continuous with literature—as interpreting other people to us, and thus enlarging and deepening our sense of community" (Rorty, 1980, p. 203).

Published research is complex, yet formulaic text. The typical research journal article involves complex research designs, various statistical analyses, and a variety of measurement procedures. In some cases, research is story; in other cases, it is description. In still other cases, it is text that infers the causal relationships among variables. Cherryholmes (1993) noted that, "The continuity with literature argument does not allege that social scientific research findings are another form of poetry or that they are structured like short stories or novels" (p. 2). The Western notions of *logical positivism* and *empiricism* have provided guidelines for reading research. Empirical researchers often appear to be searching for a "truth"—to discover an absolute meaning that is generalizable to every situation and every individual, even though there is fairly good consensus that the truth and grounded meaning in any final or transcendental sense are not within grasp. This view of research as interpretable text is bothersome to some. Stanovich (1988) noted, "It is science and the idea of depersonalized knowledge that frees individuals from slavish dependence on authority; and it is subjective, personalized views of knowledge that degrade the human intellect by creating conditions in which it is inevitably subjugated to an elect few whose personal knowledge is not accessible to all" (p. 210). However, Peirce (cited in Thayer, 1984) suggested that pragmatic reading, a process in which we look for the consequences of research findings, is more appropriate than fundamentalist reading. Moorman et al. (1994) concluded that "Any text can be interpreted in many different ways" (p. 311). The basic question is this: If a research finding is true, what consequences does it have? Consequences can only have meaning within one's purposes. In this respect, the reading of a study can have multiple readings. All texts can be read differently (Scholes, 1989). Whole-language teachers view research pragmatically, rather than fundamentally—to assess what value a particular study has for their own programs, rather than whether it represents a generalizable truth.

WHOLE LANGUAGE IS SUPPORTED BY RESEARCH

Shapiro (1994) stated, "That educational research should inform our classroom practices is a commonly accepted belief" (p. 434). Authors of whole-language texts have supported their views in reference to theory and research conducted in areas such as reading, emergent literacy, child development, cognitive psychology, writing development, reading and writing relationships, literature-based programs, response to literature, and sociolinguistics (Anderson, 1984; Baskwill & Whitman, 1986, 1988; Bloom, 1989; Butler & Turbill, 1984; Cairney, 1983, 1985a, 1985b; Calkins, 1991; Cambourne, 1988; Cambourne & Turbill, 1988, 1989; Edelsky, Altwerger, & Flores, 1991; Freeman & Freeman, 1992; Froese, 1994; Goodman, 1986a; Goodman, Bird, & Goodman, 1990; Goodman, Goodman, & Hood, 1989; Goodman, Smith, Meredith, & Goodman, 1987; Hancock & Hill, 1987; Harste & Short, 1986; Harste, Short, & Burke, 1988; Harste, Woodward, & Burke, 1984; Heald-Taylor, 1986, 1989; Lamme, 1984; Newman, 1985, 1990, 1992; Oldfather, 1993; Rhodes & Dudley-Marling, 1988; Rigg & Allen, 1989; Ringler & Weber, 1984; Routman, 1988; Smith, 1985, 1988; Stephens, 1991; Strickland & Morrow, 1989; Tovey & Kerber, 1986; Turbill, 1982, 1983; Watson, Burke, & Harste, 1989; Weaver, 1988, 1990; Yatvin, 1991).

Propositional intertexts based on various research studies and theoretical interpretations have been used to design programs for learning disabled students (Farris & Anderson, 1990; Zucker, 1993), young troubled readers (Allen, Michalove, Shockley, & West, 1991), cross-age students (Morrice & Simmons, 1991), ESL students (Freeman, Freeman, & Gonzalez, 1987; Hudelson, 1984), teaching academic content to ESL students (Lim & Watson, 1993), gifted students (Ganapole, 1988), Native-American students (Kasten, 1992), teacher education students (Brazee & Kristo, 1986), inservice teachers (Tchudi, 1992), and students with a record of school failure (Edelsky, Draper, & Smith, 1983). Y. Goodman (1989) noted, "The history of whole language shows that many groups and individuals have made continuous attempts to consider issues such as curriculum; individual differences; social interaction; collaboration; language learning, the relation between teaching, learning, and evaluation; and their influences on the lives of teachers and students" (p. 122). This is a positive view of the research contributions to whole language, and one not shared by others. For instance, Walmsley (1989) noted that, "Donald Graves, Nancie Atwell, Jane Hansen (all of whom have written about 'process-approaches' to reading and writing) have been co-opted into the movement, whether they wanted to or not" (p. 1).

The research that informs different whole-language intertexts is broad, and often not specified. Brazee and Kristo (1986) proposed that, "More and more research now supports a whole language philosophy of evaluation and instruction," and that "learning theory discoveries have confirmed that hands-on learning is the best" (p. 423). On the basis of these propositions, a whole-language program for university-level students is designed. The tendency appears to be that individuals state there is a great deal of research, but do not specify what it is.

However, the whole-language research base is viewed positively by individuals from a variety of backgrounds. McKenna, Robinson, and Miller (1993) noted, "Regarding this translation of philosophy into method, whole language inherits respectable research bases underlying some of the practices that its adherents espouse" (p. 146). Piper (1993) concluded, ". . . it is also the approach to language curriculum that is most consistent with our best understanding of how language acquisition occurs and the most enlightened theories of language" (p. 4). However, K. Goodman (1992a) observed that, "We are in a period when many teachers are producing useful, applicable knowledge while many researchers have locked themselves into a paradigm *de rigueur* that produces little that is useful to teachers" (p. 356; italics original). Stahl, McKenna, and Pagnucco (1994) urged that whole-language instruction needs to be informed by research. Shockley (1993), a teacher whose classroom was observed by Stahl, noted that she did not need to be reminded that research was essential—that she was capable of conducting it herself. McKenna et al. (1993) stated that, "Mainstream researchers are often frustrated by the lack of coherent, universally applicable definitions" (p. 141); and "If whole language varies from teacher to teacher, general definitions and generalizeable conclusions are difficult to make precise" (p. 142). Stahl and Miller (1989) approached this apparent dilemma by concluding: "Therefore, we will refer to the entire range of approaches as *whole language/language experience approaches*" because they are ". . . based on the premise that speaking, listening, writing and reading are interrelated and interdependent" (p. 89; italics original). This approach was criticized by Edelsky (1990), who observed that such a definition ". . . could not distinguish whole language from language experience approaches from activity approaches of the 1950's" (p. 8).

The review by McKenna et al. (1993) identified four major problems in research comparing whole language and basal instruction: (a) whole language is not well defined; (b) the methods and procedures for researching whole language are deemed by critics to be inadequate or inappropriate;

(c) whole-language research is selectively reviewed by its advocates, thereby placing interpreters between teachers and researchers; and (d) whole-language advocates reject research in favor of politics and rhetoric. McKenna et al. established an artificial dichotomy that separates "mainstream researchers" and "whole-language advocates." They stated that, "Mainstream researchers are often frustrated by the lack of coherent, universally applicable definitions" (p. 141). The underlying assumption is that whole-language advocates cannot be mainstream researchers, and that mainstream researchers cannot be whole-language advocates. Further, these authors seemed to believe that there are no coherent definitions of whole language that represent the absolute truth. Therefore, the text implies that there are incoherent definitions that do not represent the absolute truth, and that this makes it difficult for mainstream researchers to draw generalizable conclusions.

Another subtext suggests that mainstream research is valid only when it involves an experimental paradigm, where variables are clearly defined and controlled—a notion that generally deligitimizes research in such disciplines as anthropology and sociology. McKenna et al. approached what they saw as a difficulty defining whole language according to a generalization drawn from studies: ". . . that defined whole language, provided research on whole language programs, or described elementary classroom activities or instructional procedures relating to this term" (Bergeron, 1990, p. 307). Therefore, the definition is a generalization based on the work of two mutually exclusive groups: mainstream researchers and whole-language advocates. It includes views of whole language that would appear, on the basis of the criteria, to be different. In one case, the definitions are incoherent and not universally generalizable; in the other case, they are mainstream research interpretations of definitions that are incoherent and not universally generalizable. The "mainstream" intertext seems to be: instructional programs should be informed by research; the research should be comparative research; whole language is difficult to define because it varies from classroom to classroom; language-experience approach is similar to whole language, and therefore can substitute for whole language in comparative studies; whole-language research is selectively reviewed by its advocates; advocates become interpreters between teachers and researchers; and research is rejected in favor of politics and rhetoric. The whole-language intertext is considerably different.

"The practice of whole language is solidly rooted in scientific research and theory" (K. Goodman, 1989, p. 207). K. Goodman also noted that whole language represents ". . . a new era in which practitioners are informed professionals acting on the basis of an integrated and articulated theory that is consistent with the best scientific research and theories in which it is grounded" (pp. 207–208). He also observed that whole language ". . . cannot be studied or evaluated by reducing what happens in whole-language classrooms to what also happens in skills-based classrooms" (p. 208). In reference to studies focusing on ESL achievement, Edelsky et al. (1981) argued that the language of achievement and proficiency tests ". . . is essentially out-of-context, irrelevant nonsense" (p. 9).

The composite whole-language intertext constructed from these authors' notions appears to be:

1. whole language is supported by and grounded in scientific research;
2. achievement and proficiency tests measure school nonsense;
3. research involving measures of school nonsense is unacceptable;
4. research comparing whole-language instructional programs and other instructional programs is useless;
5. research has direct consequences for schools and schooling; and
6. research should seek to discover literacy learning universals, thereby consequently and subsequently affecting pedagogy.

There is an inconsistency in that the authority of research is both acknowledged and denied. Two opposing camps have been established: the "advocates" and the "mainstreamers." This is an artifical dichotomy, whose views appear intractably opposed. Mainstreamers decry the lack of a "universally applicable" definition, whereas advocates arguably produce hundreds of definitions. Mainstreamers err in believing that whole language is a single concept. Rather, it is an intertext—a family of beliefs instantiated in somewhat different, but related, forms. Both groups recognize that whole language is supported by research. Mainstreamers wish to compare whole language and basal instruction by designing experimental studies—a futile endeavor considering that different whole-language manifestations are the local interpretations of propositional intertexts. Whole language is difficult to define because it is not an "it." Advocates err in suggesting that there are literacy learning universals that research can discover. In both cases, logical positivism is implied (i.e., that results of studies should be generalized to greater populations).

Yin (1989) noted that there are two kinds of research generalizations: statistical-based generalizations on studies meeting basic methodological assumptions, and analytic generalizations of results to broader theories. As local manifestations of a theory or model, whole language is more appropriately studied by such approaches as case study. Despite the problems and limitations, researchers have attempted to compare whole language and basal instruction.

RESEARCH COMPARING WHOLE LANGUAGE
AND BASAL INSTRUCTION

A number of researchers have attempted to compare whole language and basal instruction to test which approach produces the greatest gains in scores on standardized reading tests. McKenna et al. (1993); Palmer et al. (1991); Stahl and Miller (1989); Shapiro (1994); and Stahl et al. (1994), among others, have reviewed such research, and have suggested that different studies produce conflicting results. Palmer et al. reviewed whole-language research according to quality criteria, both quantitative and qualitative. They concluded that whole language has not, in fact, been rigorously tested by empirical research. Stahl and Miller (1989) concluded, "From the data reviewed, it appears that whole language approaches may have an important function early in the process of learning to read, but that as the child's needs shift, they become less effective" (p. 111). This conclusion was criticized because the study included language-experience classrooms (Edelsky, 1990). Stahl and Miller mentioned, but excluded, some of the results of Carrigan's (1986) study because it involved a special population (i.e., Punjabi-speaking South Asians) that favored the basal reading students at the end of first grade, both in writing development and standardized reading scores. Carrigan concluded that the skills-based program taught test-taking skills and basal language. In contrast, the language-experience students had not practiced test-taking skills. Their writing contained more invented spellings and fewer complete sentences, and were less well structured. Canadian Test of Basic Skills (CTBS) scores alone suggest they were behind, whereas a pragmatic evaluation is that they were independently exploring and developing oral and written language naturally.

Moreover, some studies do not involve valid whole-language intertexts, nor do they claim to do so. McKenna et al. (1993) further concluded that, since the publication of Stahl and Miller's (1989) review, two important studies have been conducted (e.g., Byrne & Fielding-Barnsley, 1991; Foorman, Francis, Novy, & Liberman, 1991). These studies suggested, "These studies not only reinforce scepticism about the claims of whole language but exemplify a welcome new tendency among mainstream researchers to target specific claims made on behalf of whole language" (McKenna et al., 1993, p. 145).

The authors concluded that the first study revealed that direct instruction led to greater gains in phonemic knowledge and word recognition than instruction in a more meaning-centered curriculum. The instructional strategies observed in the Byrne and Fielding-Barnsley study are not whole language, even by the definition created by Bergeron (1990), which McKenna et al. suggested is useful. The meaning-centered approach fails as a whole-language intertext because meaning, in this case, is related to the teacher's construction. The activity is not necessarily meaningful because the students are not exploring language; rather, they are being led in an activity that focuses on the meaning of words. McKenna et al. lamented that, ". . . some whole-language adherents do not take seriously the notion of removing the interpreters between teachers and research" (p. 144). Yet they inferred that, "meaning-centered" is a whole-language concept, and that the results of this study ". . . reinforce scepticism about the claims of whole language." They interpreted the study as a "far more constructivist setting," which is not a whole-language setting.

Foorman et al. (1991) studied 80 first-grade subjects in six basal reading programs; three emphasized letter–sound correspondences, and three emphasized words in meaningful contexts (i.e., language experience). The investigators concluded that, for various reasons, "Important as these results sound, conclusions can only be tentative, given the limitations of such analyses" (p. 465). It is predicted that the meaning-centered (less-LS) students will catch up in decoding skills. McKenna et al. suggested that the study tests a code-oriented approach against a "more meaning-centered approach." Meaning-centered approaches are not whole language. This study is not a whole-language study. Stahl et al. (1994) concluded, in general, that the results of studies involving whole language are mixed, with some showing advantages for whole language and others showing disadvantages. They noted that their analyses revealed effect sizes ranging from −.74 to +.75. They concluded that it was not whole language per se that led to the effects, but how whole language was implemented.

McKenna et al. (1993) did not review a study reported in 1991, a long-term study comparing whole language and basal instruction, because it had design problems (S. Stahl, personal communication, December 1994). McCallum, Whitlow, and Moore (1991) reported on a 6-year study, in which a school was organized around two groups: (a) teachers who taught whole language to students from Grades 1 to 6, and (b) teachers who continued to use basal readers. At the end of first grade, the basal students scored significantly higher on all subtests of the CTBS except comprehension. At the end of third grade, the whole-language groups scored significantly higher in comprehension and significantly lower in spelling and word-attack skills. By the end of sixth grade, the whole-language students scored significantly higher on all subtests of the CTBS, except word attack. Because of the high degree of subject mortality of the control group (100%), and the fact that the whole-language students volunteered to be part of the program, possible generalizations are limited.

The study suggests that, for those who believe performance on a standardized test is significant, whole language does take longer to develop the test-taking skills associated with them. Learning the language of standardized tests may be a product of meaningful language learning, which occurs in about the same length of time it takes immigrants from various countries (Collier, 1987; Cummins, 1981) to learn it through traditional skills-based instruction.

Korkeamäki and Dreher (1993) reviewed the research concerning reading in Finnish, arguably the language with the most regular sound–symbol correspondences. Early instruction in Finland is systematic and features slow-paced sound–symbol instruction: ". . . the recommendation is to teach only one letter-sound correspondence per week" (p. 476). The underlying premise is that early decoding should precede comprehension. Korkeamäki and Dreher reported that decoding skill is not enough for the Finnish reader to become independent. Fifty percent of sixth graders have the reading-comprehension skills required to read and comprehend school materials, and 30% of ninth graders cannot comprehend their textbooks. They noted: "Students need to learn the symbol-sound correspondences to decode unfamiliar words, but they need to have many opportunities to interact with print—to read and write purposefully" (p. 481).

A fundamentalist view of the comparative research is that results appear mixed, sometimes favoring whole language and other times favoring skills-based instruction. McKenna et al. (1993) suggested that the role of a research interpreter should not be filled by researchers, but ". . . in their zeal to exclude mainstream researchers from their role as teacher informers, some whole-language proponents appear to have adopted such a role themselves" (p. 144). The following are pragmatic views of a teacher informer.

There is nothing inherently bad about "mainstream" research; however, the way individuals interpret it can be. Experimental research has made positive contributions to science and medicine. Research has helped us understand the pervasive nature of such phenomena as poverty, child abuse, spousal abuse, drug addiction, alcoholism, and school dropout rates. Research also has been consistently accurate in predicting elections in different jurisdictions. When used to compare whole-language and skills-based programs, it reveals quite dramatically that both vary, for multiple reasons, in the way they teach students the skills associated with standardized tests. This is neither a surprising finding, nor a negative finding. Indeed, it has been this author's experience that different students learn different skills best using different strategies.

Teachers who are concerned about test scores because they are crucial within a particular school district or to particular groups of students will have to consider their options carefully. Long-term research suggests that whole-language students surpass their basal schoolmates in the skills required by standardized tests after about 3 or 4 years. It also suggests that long-term emphasis on decoding instruction has detrimental effects on the skills required by standardized comprehension tests.

Some researchers appear to have misinterpreted whole language as advocating a meaning-centered approach. Meaning-centered suggests that meaning exists in some real form in a particular text, and that the teacher's job is to help students discover it (i.e., to discover the truth of the text). This is antithetical to most whole-language intertexts.

Some lament that whole language is difficult to define and that definitions differ. Such findings reveal that whole language is a democratic concept that allows individual interpretation and variation. Whole language is not a concept that is applied universally. Rather, it represents individual applications of different intertexts—it represents local, rather than universal, truth. Ironically, although there is fairly consistent agreement on what basal instruction should include, actual instruction reveals considerable individual modification in classroom applications (Durkin 1978–1979).

The local view of whole language creates difficulty for researchers who wish to discover generalizable truths about it. To study whole-language instruction, researchers construct their own whole-language intertexts (i.e., ones they assume are reliably generalized representations), study the learning going on in classrooms that roughly approximate the parameters of their intertexts, and subsequently add up and average their findings across classrooms effectually masking their individual variations. In this view, whole language is monolithic. The statistics used to describe it are approximations that do not accurately represent any particular instance. The same kind of research reveals that the average state in the United States produces 20,000 tons of pineapples. The kind of research that compares whole-language with skills-based instruction does little to inform instruction locally. To be more reliable and valid, whole-language research should be conducted on a local level, interpretations of which should also be local and pragmatic. For instance, Yin (1989) noted that the use of a case study approach is appropriate when a researcher attempts to make inferences about theory, rather than populations.

Mrs. R. was asked by parents to explain how she knew that her students were learning basic phonics and word-recognition skills. Gunderson and Shapiro (1988) found that Mrs. R.'s students wrote a great deal, and that their independent spelling revealed a developing knowledge of phonics. Shapiro and Gunderson (1988) analyzed the same writing samples, and concluded that students had produced all of the high-frequency vocabulary contained in the typical basal reading series. Gunderson and Shapiro concluded that, ". . . we caution teachers that whole language programs are not easy to implement or maintain" (p. 436). Mrs. R., a pragmatic reader of research, suggested the observation was unfounded—that whole language at the primary level was no more difficult than trying to manage the use of work sheets and workbooks. She also suggested that Gunderson and Shapiro's research clearly showed that students learned phonics and word-recognition skills in her whole-language classroom, and that observations concerning the difficulty of implementation and maintenance were unfounded. Rather, these were a result of researcher misinterpretation of the activities that occurred in the classrooms.

Shapiro (1994) concluded:

> Since 1986 the body of research related to whole-language has grown at a rapid rate. If one scans the convention programs of professional reading associations since that time, this growth is readily apparent. Much of this research, both qualitative and quantitative, indicates that there are many benefits for children who are receiving their literacy instruction in whole-language classrooms. These children become effective readers. Their vocabulary increases, they employ varied strategies in word recognition, their comprehension abilities range from simple literal recall to more sophisticated judgements about authors' intent, they read for pleasure and information, and, perhaps more importantly, they have positive attitudes toward reading. In addition, these children become knowledgeable about the writing process and usually display superior writing ability. (pp. 458–459)

Whole language is supported by research in various disciplines. The research that compares whole language with other pedagogies reveals conflicting results, often depending on the research selected or the researcher's interpretations. The research that seeks to explore whole-language instruction reveals generally positive results.

SUMMARY AND CONCLUSIONS

Walmsley and Adams (1993) concluded that, for teachers, whole language was "tremendously demanding," but counterbalanced by ". . . a growing sense of comfort and confidence in themselves and their program" (p. 273); and that whole language ". . . will always be the philosophy of a dedicated few, rather than the orthodoxy of a (sic) entire school, district, or state" (p. 279). This is a pessimistic view of whole language and its effects on teaching. Whole language will change because of its very nature as intertext. It has been adopted by entire school districts and, in Canada, by entire provinces. "Sales of children's books have quintupled since 1982, and the use of children's rooms in public libraries is skyrocketing" (K. Goodman, 1992a, p. 355). Pearson (1989) predicted, "Unlike the open-school movement of the early 1970s, it is not likely to die at an early age" (p. 231).

Whole language has features that appeal to both advocates and critics. For instance, Pearson (1989) noted, "But never have I witnessed anything like the rapid spread of the whole-language movement" (p. 231). He also stated that, "There are many things I like about whole language; it has succeeded in accomplishing goals that many of us who are not part of the movement have failed to accomplish by using more conventional approaches to reform" (p. 232). Adams (1990) stated that it ". . . is packed with activities for developing phonological awareness, orthographic knowledge, and spelling-sound relations" (p. 422). In the same synthesis, two members of Adams advisory group, Strickland and Cullinan, commented, "We believe that the evidence supports a whole language and integrated language arts approach with some direct instruction, in context, on spelling-to-sound correspondence" (p. 433).

Whole language has changed over the last 10 years as different researchers and theorists have begun to move from single-focus intertexts, those that primarily involve reading (cf. Harste & Burke, 1977), to texts that include composite propositions related to speaking, listening, reading, writing, watching, reader response, literature-based instruction, integrated teaching and learning, and the analysis of knowledge and what's worth knowing (Gunderson, 1993). Whole language evolves as teachers learn from research and practice, and as they become more informed about their own teaching and the whole language occurring in other classrooms, schools, states, and countries. This represents the power of whole language. A whole-language intertext is the representation of a complex, multidimensional, and dynamic model of teaching and learning.

However, there is considerable controversy concerning the nature of whole language. Both proponents and opponents have struggled to define the term *whole language*. This is an unfortunate preoccupation because a particular whole-language incarnation results from the pedagogical implications drawn from a unique propositional intertext—one constructed by an individual teacher on the basis of knowledge and beliefs about learning and teaching. Whole-language intertexts have been constructed by various teachers, and have been used to design and implement programs for widely diverse populations. Whole language is not a philosophy, although particular whole-language intertexts often contain philosophical propositions. It cannot be defined in a traditional fashion.

There is general agreement that whole-language intertexts are informed by research in various areas (e.g., K. Goodman, 1989, 1992a; Pearson, 1989). Although they find the task difficult, some researchers have insisted that whole language be defined and isolated as a single recognizable entity so that it can be compared with other instructional approaches (e.g., McKenna et al., 1993). Others assume that instructional approaches such as language-experience and meaning-centered instruction are equivalent, design studies to compare them with basal instruction, and generalize their findings to whole language (e.g., Stahl & Miller, 1989). Whole language varies from classroom to classroom, and therefore is inappropriately studied by traditional comparative research methodologies.

Some have complained that whole-language advocates interpret research (e.g., McKenna et al., 1993). Such a view suggests that research findings represent truth, except when interpreted by whole-language advocates. A pragmatic view, however, is that searching for the consequences of research findings is appropriate (Peirce; cited in Thayer, 1984) to evaluate the consequences that findings have. In this respect, comparative research shows that a relationship exists between some whole-language instruction and the skills required by standardized reading tests. It suggests that the learning of standardized test skills takes longer to learn in whole-language classes than in basal classrooms—a finding that may have consequences for particular teachers. Research also seems to suggest that systematic phonics instruction is detrimental to performance on standardized reading-comprehension tests in the long term (Korkeamäki & Dreher, 1993), and that whole language results in superior performance on standardized comprehension tests in the long term (McCallum et al., 1991).

Some whole-language theorists propose that research should seek to discover the universals in literacy learning (e.g., Harste, 1993). This view suggests there is an underlying single truth associated with the learning of reading and writing—that reading and writing are the essential epistemological activities of human beings, and that it is liberating. However, literacy is not necessarily liberating (Harman & Edelsky, 1989). Teachers represent the dominant culture. In this sense, the whole-language intertexts they construct represent the dominant view. The multiple voices of students, especially those from diverse cultural groups, are not necessarily represented by the typical whole-language intertext (Delpit, 1988; "Conversation with Lisa Delpit," 1991). The way in which a particular intertext contributes to theory or a general model is best researched by such methodologies as case study.

There is consensus that research should inform instruction, and that teachers should be knowledgeable professionals guided by both theory and research. Teaching is a complex endeavor that faces the hostile realities of financial restraint, decreasing public support, and criticism from many sources. To compound the problem, there is little doubt that the world is changing. "It is widely accepted that knowledge has become the principle force of production over the last few decades" (Lyotard, 1992, p. 140). Lemke (1993) predicted that, because of technology, knowledge and truth will become even more localized. Unfortunately, the use of the computer and other technology reveals serious gender inequities (Butler & Gunderson, 1994). Educators will turn to research for pragmatic answers. A challenge is to decide whether to continue a debate that appears to generate little more than acrimony or to design multiple studies that inform education locally, regionally, and nationally. A researcher's primary role may be to equip teachers with the skills they need to conduct their own research. On a larger scale, it is time to determine what is informative and useful for teachers and state superintendents of education. Teaching and learning in the 21st century will be even more complexly diverse than it is today. Intertexts change in response to research. The question is, Are researchers able to produce research that will account for the diversity and be useful to those who look to it for guidance?

REFERENCES

Adams, M. (1990). *Beginning to read: Thinking and learning about print.* Cambridge, MA: MIT Press.

Allen, J., Michalove, B., Shockley, B., & West, M. (1991). "I'm really worried about Joseph": Reducing the risks of literacy learning. *Reading Teacher, 44*(7), 458–472.

Anderson, G. (1984). *A whole language approach to reading.* New York: University Press of America.

Altwerger, B., Edelsky, C., & Flores, B. M. (1987). Whole language: What's new? *Reading Teacher, 41,* 144–154.

Baskwill, J., & Whitman, P. (1986). *Whole language sourcebook.* Richmond Hill, Ontario: Scholastic-TAB Publications.

Baskwill, J., & Whitman, P. (1988). *Evaluation: Whole language, whole child.* Toronto, Ontario: Scholastic-TAB Publications.

Beaugrande, R., & Dressler, W. (1981). *Introduction to text linguistics.* London: Longman.

de Beaugrande, R. (1980). *Text, discourse and process.* Norwood, NJ: Ablex.

Bergeron, B. S. (1990). What does the term whole language mean? Constructing a definition from the literature. *Journal of Reading Behavior, 22,* 301–329.

Bloome, D. (Ed.). (1989). *The whole story: Natural learning and acquisition of literacy in the classroom.* New York: Scholastic.

Bloome, D., & Egan-Robertson, A. (1993). The social construction of intertextuality in classroom reading and writing lessons. *Reading Research Quarterly, 28*(4), 304–333.

Brazee, P. E., & Kristo, J. V. (1986). Creating a whole language classroom with future teachers. *Reading Teacher, 39*(5), 422–428.

Brown, G., & Yule, G. (1983). *Discourse analysis.* London: Cambridge University Press.

Butler, A., & Turbill, J. (1984). *Towards a reading-writing classroom.* Rosebery, NSW, Australia: Bridge Printery.

Butler, S., & Gunderson, L. (1994). Using a computer in the classroom. In V. Froese (Ed.), *Whole-language: Practice and theory* (pp. 277–309). Scarborough, Ontario: Allyn & Bacon, Canada.

Byrne, B., & Fielding-Barnsley, R. (1991). Evaluation of a program to teach phonemic awareness to young children. *Journal of Educational Psychology, 83*(4), 451–455.

Cairney, T. H. (1983). *Balancing the basics.* Gosford, Australia: Aston Scholastic.

Cairney, T. H. (1985a). Reading and writing: Making connections. In D. Burnes, H. French, & F. Moore (Eds.), *Literacy: Strategies and perspectives* (pp. 29–35). Adelaide: Australian Reading Association.

Cairney, T. H. (1985b). Users, not consumers of language: One class takes control of its own learning. In D. Burnes (Ed.), *Literacy, beginning, developing, maintaining. Proceedings of the 11th Australian Reading Conference* (pp. 1–14). Brisbane, Australia: Australian Reading Conference.

Calkins, L. (1991). *Living between the lines.* Portsmouth, NH: Heinemann.

Cambourne, B. (1988). *The whole story: Natural learning and the acquisition of literacy in the classroom.* Auckland, NZ: Scholastic.

Cambourne, B., & Turbill, J. B. (1988). *From guinea pigs to coresearchers.* Brisbane: Pre-Conference Institute, World Reading Conference.

Cambourne, B., & Turbill, J. B. (1989). *Whole language all day, every day.* New Orleans: Pre-Conference Institute, International Reading Association National Conference.

Cambourne, B., & Turbill, J. (1990). Assessment in whole-language classrooms: Theory into practice. *Elementary School Journal, 90*(3), 337–349.

Carrigan, T. (1986, December). *Reading achievement of grade one students involved in language experience programs vs. basal programs.* Paper presented at the National Reading Conference, Austin, TX.

Chaney, C. (1990). Evaluating the whole language approach to language arts: The pros and cons. *Language, Speech, and Hearing Services in Schools, 21*(4), 244–249.

Cherryholmes, C. H. (1993). Reading research. *Journal of Curriculum Studies, 25*(1), 1–32.

Collier, V. (1987). Age and rate of acquisition of second language for academic purposes. *TESOL Quarterly, 21*(4), 617–641.

Cooter, R. C., Jr., & Flynt, E. S. (1989). Blending whole language and basal reader instruction. *Reading Horizons, 29*(4), 275–282.

Culler, J. (1983). *On deconstruction.* London: Routledge & Kegan Paul.

Cullinan, B. E. (1992). Whole language and children's literature. *Language Arts, 69*(6), 426–430.

Cummins, J. (1981). Age on arrival and immigrant second language learning in Canada: A reassessment. *Applied Linguistics, 2*(2), 132–149.

Delpit, L. D. (1988). The silenced dialogue: Power and pedagogy in educating other people's children. *Harvard Educational Review, 58*(3), 280–298.

A conversation with Lisa Delpit. (1991). *Language Arts, 68,* 541–547.

Derrida, J. (1977). Signature event context. *Glyph, 1,* 172–197.

Derrida, J. (1979). Living on: Border lines. In H. Bloom (Ed.), *Deconstruction and criticism* (pp. 75–175). New York: Seabury.

Dranch, S. A. (1983). Reading through the veiled text: Colette's. *The Pure and the Impure. Contemporary Literature, 24,* 176–189.

Dudley-Marling, C., & Dippo, D. (1991). The language of whole language. *Language Arts, 68*(7), 548–554.

Durkin, D. (1978–1979). What classroom observations reveal about reading comprehension instruction. *Reading Research Quarterly, 14*(4), 481–533.

Early, M., & Gunderson, L. (1993). Linking home, school and community literacy uses. *TESL Canada Journal, 11*(1), 99–111.

Edelsky, C. (1990). Whose agenda is this anyway? A response to McKenna, Robinson, & Miller. *Educational Researcher, 19*(8), 7–11.

Edelsky, C., Altwerger, B., & Flores, B. (1991). *Whole language: What's the difference?* Portsmouth, NH: Heinemann.

Edelsky, C., Draper, K., & Smith, K. (1983). Hookin' em in at the start of school in a "whole language" classroom. *Anthropology & Education Quarterly, 14,* 257–281.

Edelsky, C., Hudelson, S., Flores, B., Barkin, F., Altwerger, B., & Jilbert, K. (1981). Semilingualism and language deficit. *Journal of Applied Linguistics, 4*(1), 1–22.

Edelsky, C., & Smith, K. (1984). Is that writing—or are those marks just a figment of your curriculum? *Language Arts, 61*(1), 24–32.

Farris, P. J. (1989). From basal reader to whole language: Transition tactics. *Reading Horizons, 30*(1), 23–29.

Farris, P. J., & Andersen, C. (1990). Adopting a whole language program for learning disabled students: A case study. *Reading Horizons, 31*(1), 5–13.

Ferguson, P. (1988). Whole language: A global approach to learning. *Instructor, 97*(9), 24–27.

Foorman, B. R., Francis, D. J., Novy, D. M., & Liberman, D. (1991). How letter-sound instruction mediates progress in first-grade reading and spelling. *Journal of Educational Psychology, 83*(4), 456–469.

Foucault, M. (1972). *The archeology of knowledge and the discourse on language* (A. M. S. Smith, Trans.). New York: Pantheon.

Foucault, M. (1974). *The order of things.* London: Tavistock.

Fountas, I. C., & Hannigan, I. L. (1989). Making sense of whole language: The pursuit of informed teaching. *Childhood Education, 65,* 133–137.

Fox, D. (1986). The debate goes on: Systematic phonics vs. whole language. *Journal of Reading, 29*(7), 678–680.

Freeman, D., Freeman, Y., & Gonzalez, R. (1987). Success for LEP students: The Sunnyside Sheltered English Program. *TESOL Quarterly, 21,* 361–367.

Freeman, Y. S., & Freeman, D. (1992). *Whole language for second language learners.* Portsmouth, NH: Heinemann.

French, M. P., Danielson, K. E., Conn, M., Gale, W., Lueck, C., & Manley, M. (1990). Whole language. *Reading Teacher, 43*(4), 348–352.

Froese, V. (Ed.). (1994). *Whole language, practice and theory.* Scarborough, Ontario: Allyn & Bacon, Canada.

Ganopole, S. J. (1988). Reading and writing for the gifted: A whole language perspective. *Roeper Review, 11*(2), 88–92.

Goodman, K. S. (1984–1985). Commentary: On being literate in an age of information. *Journal of Reading, 28,* 388–392.

Goodman, K. S. (1986a). Basal Readers: A call for action. *Language Arts, 63*(4), 358–363.

Goodman, K. S. (1986b). *What's whole in whole language?* Portsmouth, NH: Heinemann.

Goodman, K. S. (1989). Whole-language research: Foundations and development. *Elementary School Journal, 90*(2), 207–221.

Goodman, K. S. (1992a). Why whole language is today's agenda in education. *Language Arts, 69,* 354–363.

Goodman, K. S. (1992b). I didn't found whole language. *Reading Teacher, 46*(3), 188–199.

Goodman, K. S., Bird, L. B., & Goodman, Y. (1990). *The whole language catalog.* Santa Rosa, CA: American School Publishers.

Goodman, K. S., & Goodman, Y. M. (1979). Learning to read is natural. In L. B. Resnick & P. A. Weaver (Eds.), *Theory and practice of early reading* (Vol. 1, pp. 137–154). Hillsdale, NJ: Lawrence Erlbaum Associates.

Goodman, K. S., & Goodman, Y. (1983). Reading and writing relationships: Pragmatic functions. *Language Arts, 60*(5), 590–599.

Goodman, K. S., Goodman, Y., & Hood, W. (1989). *The whole language evaluation book.* Portsmouth, NH: Heinemann.

Goodman, K. S., Shannon, P., Freeman, Y., & Murphy, S. (1988). *Report card on basal readers.* New York: Owen.

Goodman, K. S., Smith, E. B., Meredith, R., & Goodman, Y. (1987). *Language and thinking in school: A whole language curriculum* (3rd ed.). New York: Owen.

Goodman, Y. (1985). Kidwatching: Observing children in the classroom. In A. Jaggar & M. T. Smith-Burke (Eds.), *Observing the language learner* (pp. 9–19). Newark, DE: International Reading Association.

Goodman, Y. (1989). Roots of the whole language movement. *Elementary School Journal, 90*(2), 113–127.

Graves, D. H. (1983). *Writing: Teachers and children at work.* Exeter, NH: Heinemann.

Gunderson, L. (1989). *A whole language primer.* Richmond Hills, Ontario: Scholastic-Tab.

Gunderson, L. (1993, August). *Whole language: Whose voice?* Paper presented at the Whole Language Umbrella Conference, Winnipeg, Manitoba, Canada.

Gunderson, L. (1994). Reading and language development. In V. Froese (Ed.), *Whole language: Practice and theory* (pp. 199–240). Scarborough, Ontario: Allyn & Bacon, Canada.

Gunderson, L., & Shapiro, J. (1988). Whole language instruction: Writing in 1st grade. *Reading Teacher, 41*(4), 430–437.

Haese, K. K. (1991). Putting whole language, literature-based reading into practice. *Wisconsin State Reading Association Journal, 35*(2), 17–21.

Hahn, E. B. (1989). Environmental education. *Reading Psychology, 10*, 89–92.

Hancock, J., & Hill, S. (Eds.). (1987). *Literature-based reading programs at work.* Portsmouth, NH: Heinemann.

Hansen, J. (1982). *When writers read.* Portsmouth, NH: Heinemann.

Harman, S., & Edelsky, C. (1989). The risks of whole language literacy: Alienation and connection. *Language Arts, 66*(4), 392–406.

Harp, B. (1988). When the principal asks, "When you do whole language instruction, how will you keep track of reading and writing skills?" *Reading Teacher, 42*(2), 160–161.

Harste, J. C. (1989). The future of whole language. *Elementary School Journal, 90*(2), 243–249.

Harste, J. C. (1993). Curriculum for the millennium: Putting an edge on learning through inquiry. *Australian Journal of Language and Literacy, 16*(1), 6–22.

Harste, J. C., & Burke, C. L. (1977). A new hypothesis for reading research: Both teaching and learning of reading are theoretically based. In P. D. Pearson (Ed.), *Twenty-sixth yearbook of the National Reading Conference* (pp. 32–40). Clemson, SC: National Reading Conference.

Harste, J. C., Pierce, K., & Cairney, T. H. (1985). *The authoring cycle: A viewing guide.* Portsmouth, NH: Heinemann.

Harste, J. C., & Short, K. G. (1986). *Reading, writing, reasoning: The authoring cycle at work in the classroom.* Portsmouth, NH: Heinemann.

Harste, J. C., Short, K. G., & Burke, C. (1988). *Creating classrooms for authors: The reading-writing connection.* Portsmouth, NH: Heinemann.

Harste, J. C., Woodward, V. A., & Burke, C. L. (1984). *Language stories and literacy lessons.* Portsmouth, NH: Heinemann.

Heald-Taylor, B. G. (1986). *Whole language strategies for E.S.L. students.* Toronto: OISE Press.

Heald-Taylor, B. G. (1989). *Administrator's guide to whole language.* New York: Owens.

Heymsfeld, C. R. (1989). Filling the hole in whole language. *Educational Leadership, 46*(6), 65–68.

Hoffman, J. V. (1992). Leadership in the language arts: Am I whole yet? Are you? *Language Arts, 69*(5), 366–371.

Holdaway, D. (1979). *The foundations of literacy.* Sydney, Australia: Ashton Scholastic.

Hoole, C. (1912). *A new discovery of the old art of teaching school.* Syracuse, NY: C. W. Bardeen. (Original work published 1660)

Hudelson, S. (1984). Kan yu ret an rayt en ingles: Children become literate in English as a second language. *TESOL Quarterly, 18*(2), 221–238.

Hunt, K. (1965). *Grammatical structures written at three grade levels.* Champaign, IL: National Council of Teachers of English.

Johnson, D. W., Johnson, R. T., & Holubec, E. J. (1988). *Cooperation in the classroom.* Edina, MN: Interaction Book Company.

Kasten, W. C. (1992). Bridging the horizon: American Indian beliefs and whole language learning. *Anthropology and Education Quarterly, 23*(2), 108–119.

King, D. F., & Goodman, K. S. (1990). Whole language: Cherishing learners and their language. *Language, Speech, and Hearing Services in Schools, 21*(4), 221–227.

Korkeamäki, R., & Dreher, M. J. (1993). Finland, phonics and whole language: Beginning reading in a regular letter-sound correspondence language. *Language Arts, 70*, 475–482.

Kristeva, J. (1980). *Desire in language: A semiotic approach to literature and art* (T. Gora, A. Jardine, & L. S. Roudiez, Trans.). New York: Columbia University Press.

Lamme, L. L. (1984). *Growing up writing.* Washington, DC: Acropolis.

Lamme, L. L. (1989). Authorship: A key facet of whole language. *Reading Teacher, 42*(9), 704–710.

Lamme, L. L., & Lee, P. (1990). Crossing the moat: From basic skills to whole language in a kindergarten curriculum. *Childhood Education, 66*(5), 295–297.

Lemke, J. (1993, July). *Computers and local knowledge.* Paper presented at the University of British Columbia, Vancouver, Canada.

Lerner, J. W., Cousin, T., & Richeck, M. (1992). Critical issues in learning disabilities: Whole language learning. *Learning Disabilities Research & Practice, 7*(4), 226–230.

Lim, H. L., & Watson, D. J. (1993). Whole language content classes for second-language learners. *Reading Teacher, 46*(5), 384–393.

Lyotard, J. (1992). Answering the questions: What is postmodern? In C. Jencks (Ed.), *The post-modern reader* (pp. 138–150). London: Academy Editions.

Maguire, M. H. (1989). Understanding and implementing a whole-language program in Quebec. *Elementary School Journal, 90*(2), 143–159.

Mather, N. (1992). Whole language reading instruction for students with learning disabilities: Caught in the cross fire. *Learning Disabilities Research & Practice, 7*(2), 87–95.

McCallum, R. D., Whitlow, R. F., & Moore, S. (1991, December). *Standardized tests as measures of achievement in whole language programs: A question of validity.* Paper presented at the National Reading Conference, Palm Springs, CA.

McCaslin, M. M. (1989). Whole language: Theory, instruction, and future implementation. *Elementary School Journal, 90*(2), 223–229.

McKenna, M. C., Robinson, R. D., & Miller, J. W. (1993). Whole language and research: The case for caution. In D. Leu & C. K. Kinzer (Eds.), *Examining central issues in literacy research, theory, and practice* (pp. 141–152). Chicago, IL: National Reading Conference.

Moorman, G. B., Blanton, W. E., & McLaughlin, T. M. (1992). The rhetoric of whole language: Part One and Part Two. *Reading Psychology, 13*(2), iii–xv.

Moorman, G. B., Blanton, W. E., & McLaughlin, T. (1994). The rhetoric of whole language. *Reading Research Quarterly, 29*(4), 309–329.

Morrice, C., & Simmons, M. (1991). Beyond reading buddies: A whole language cross-age program. *Reading Teacher, 44*(8), 572–577.

Morris, V. C., & Pai, Y. (1976). *Philosophy and the American school.* Boston: Houghton Mifflin.

Newman, J. (Ed.). (1985). *Whole language: Theory in use.* Portsmouth, NH: Heinemann.

Newman, J. (Ed.). (1990). *Finding our own way: Teachers exploring their assumptions.* Portsmouth, NH: Heinemann.

Newman, J. (1992). *Interwoven conversations.* Portsmouth, NH: Heinemann.

Norris, J. A., & Damico, J. S. (1990). Whole language in theory and practice: Implications for language intervention. *Language, Speech, and Hearing Services in Schools, 21*(4), 212–220.

Oldfather, P. (1993). What students say about motivating experiences in a whole language classroom. *Reading Teacher, 46*(8), 672–681.

Orr, L. (1986). Intertextuality and the cultural text in recent semiotics. *College English, 48*(8), 811–823.

Pace, G. (1992). Stories of teacher-initiated change from traditional to whole-language literacy instruction. *Elementary School Journal, 92*(4), 461–476.

Pahl, M. M., & Monson, R. J. (1992). In search of whole language: Transforming curriculum and instruction. *Journal of Reading, 35*(7), 518–524.

Palmer, B. M., Gambrell, L. B., & Almasi, J. F. (1991, December). *Whole language research: A methodological analysis.* Paper present at the National Reading Conference, Palm Springs, CA.

Pearson, P. D. (1989). Reading the whole language movement. *Elementary School Journal, 90*(2), 232–241.

Piper, T. (1993). *Language for ALL our children.* Toronto: Maxwell Macmillan Canada.

Reutzel, D. R., & Hollingsworth, P. M. (1988). Whole language and the practitioner. *Academic Therapy, 23*(4), 405–416.

Rhodes, L., & Dudley-Marling, C. (1988). *Readers and writers with a difference: A holistic approach to teaching learning disabled and remedial students.* Portsmouth, NH: Heinemann.

Rich, S. J. (1985a). Restoring power to teachers: The impact of "whole language." *Language Arts, 62*(7), 717–724.

Rich, S. J. (1985b). Whole language: The inner dimension. *English Quarterly, 18*(2), 15–22.

Ridley, L. (1990). Enacting change in elementary school programs: Implementing a whole language perspective. *Reading Teacher, 43*(9), 640–646.

Rigg, P., & Allen, V. G. (Eds.). (1989). *When they don't all speak English: Integrating the ESL student into the regular classroom.* Urbana, IL: National Council of Teachers of English.

Ringler, L. H., & Weber, C. K. (1984). *A language-thinking approach to reading.* New York: Harcourt Brace.

Rorty, R. (1980). *Philosophy and the mirror of nature.* Princeton, NJ: Princeton University Press.

Routman, R. (1988). *Transitions: From literature to literacy.* Portsmouth, NH: Heinemann.

Ruddell, R. B. (1992). A whole language and literature perspective: Creating a meaning-making instructional environment. *Language Arts, 69,* 612–620.

Scholes, R. (1989). *Protocols of reading.* New Haven, CT: Yale University Press.

Shannon, P. (1989). *Broken promises.* Cambridge, MA: Bergin & Garvey.

Shapiro, H. R. (1992). Debatable issues underlying whole-language philosophy: A speech-language pathologist's perspective. *Language, Speech, and Hearing Services in Schools, 23*(4), 308–311.

Shapiro, J. (1994). Research perspectives on whole language. In V. Froese (Ed.), *Whole language: Practice and theory* (pp. 433–470). Scarborough, Ontario: Allyn & Bacon, Canada.

Shapiro, J., & Gunderson, L. (1988). Language experience generated vocabulary vs. basal reader vocabulary at grade one. *Reading Research and Instruction, 27,* 40–46.

Shockley, B. (1993, December). *Discussion of papers by Pressley, Stal & Pagnucco, and Biemeller.* Paper presented at the National Reading Conference, Charleston, SC.

Slaughter, H. B. (1988). Indirect and direct teaching in a whole language program. *Reading Teacher, 42,* 30–34.

Slavin, R. E., Sharan, S., Kagan, S., Hertz-Lazarowitz, R., Webb, C., & Schmuck, R. (Eds.). (1985). *Learning to cooperate, cooperating to learn.* New York: Plenum.

Smith, F. (1985). *Reading without nonsense* (2nd ed.). New York: Teachers College Press.

Smith, F. (1988). *Understanding reading* (4th ed.). Hillsdale, NJ: Lawrence Erlbaum Associates.

Spiegel, D. L. (1989). Content validity of whole language materials. *Reading Teacher, 43*(2), 168–169.

Spiegel, D. L. (1992). Blending whole language and systematic direct instruction. *Reading Teacher, 46*(1), 38–44.

Staab, C. F. (1990). Teacher mediation in one whole literacy classroom. *Reading Teacher, 43*(8), 548–552.

Stahl, S. A., McKenna, M. C., & Pagnucco, J. (1994). The effects of whole language instruction: An update and a reappraisal. *Educational Psychologist, 29,* 175–186.

Stahl, S. A., & Miller, P. D. (1989). Whole language and language experiences approaches for beginning reading: Quantitative synthesis. *Review of Educational Research, 16,* 32–71.

Stanek, L. W. (1991). Whole language for whole kids: An approach for using literature in the classroom. *School Library Journal, 37*(9), 187–189.

Stanovich, K. (1988). Science and learning disabilities. *Journal of Learning Disabilities, 21,* 210–214.

Stephens, D. (1991). *Whole language: A research perspective.* Katonah, NY: Owen.

Stice, C. F., & Bertrand, J. E. (1992). What's going on here? A qualitative examination of grouping patterns in an exemplary whole language classroom. *Reading Horizons, 32*(5), 383–393.

Strickland, D., & Morrow, L. (Eds.). (1989). *Emerging literacy: Young children learn to read and write.* Newark, DE: International Reading Association.

Sumara, D., & Walker, L. (1991). The teacher's role in whole language. *Language Arts, 68*(4), 276–285.

Tchudi, S. (1992). The interdisciplinary island: Whole language, holistic learning and teacher education. *Holistic Education Review, 5*(1), 30–36.

Thayer, H. S. (1984). *Meaning and action: A critical history of pragmatism.* Indianapolis, IN: Hacket.

Thompson, R. A. (1992). A critical perspective on whole language. *Reading Psychology, 13*(2), 131–155.

Tovey, D., & Kerber, J. (Eds.). (1986). *Roles in literacy learning: A new perspective.* Newark, DE: International Reading Association.

Turbill, J. (1982). *No better way to teach writing.* Sydney: PETA.

Turbill, J. (1983). *Now, we want to write.* Sydney: PETA.

Waldon, M. A. (1988). Whole language approach applied. *Reading Psychology, 9*(3), 259–265.

Walmsley, S. A. (1989, December). *Whole language: Definition, issues and concerns.* Paper presented at the National Reading Conference, Austin, TX.

Walmsley, S. A., & Adams, E. L. (1993). Realities of "whole language." *Language Arts, 70,* 272–280.

Watson, D. J. (1989). Defining and describing whole language. *Elementary School Journal, 90*(2), 129–141.

Watson, D. J., Burke, C. L., & Harste, J. C. (1989). *Whole language: Inquiring voices.* New York: Scholastic.

Weaver, C. (1988). *Reading process and practice: From socio-psycholinguistics to whole language.* Portsmouth, NH: Heinemann.

Weaver, C. (1990). *Understanding whole language: From principles to practice.* Portsmouth, NH: Heinemann.

Willinsky, J. (1990). *The new literacy: Redefining reading and writing in the schools.* New York: Routledge & Kegan Paul.

Yatvin, J. (1991). *Developing a whole language program.* Richmond, VA: Virginia State Reading Association.

Yin, R. K. (1989). *Case study research: Design and methods* (rev. ed.). Newbury Park, CA: Sage.

Zucker, C. (1993). Using whole language with students who have language and learning disabilities. *Reading Teacher, 46*(8), 660–681.

CHAPTER ELEVEN

An Emergent-Literacy Perspective on Reading Instruction in Kindergarten

Linda D. Labbo
The University of Georgia, Athens

William H. Teale
University of Illinois at Chicago

Typically, children in the United States learn to read and write conventionally when they are 6 or 7 years of age. But even before children are conventionally literate, they are learning literacy. This learning—the knowledge, strategies, and attitudes that children develop from birth to the time when they can read and write conventionally—has been conceptualized as *emergent literacy* (Sulzby, 1989; Teale & Sulzby, 1986). For many years, first grade in American schools was considered the time during which the teaching of reading began. But today most schools begin formally instructing children in the skills of reading and writing during kindergarten (Durkin, 1987a). As teachers and researchers embrace the developmental philosophy of emergent literacy, which recognizes the not-yet-conventional reading and writing of young children as legitimate and conceptual literacy behaviors, questions persist as to what instruction should look like in an emergent-literacy classroom.

This chapter provides a perspective on the instruction characteristic of a quality emergent-literacy program. In so doing, it draws on relevant research about appropriate ways to teach children to read and write in an emergent-literacy classroom. In the first part of the chapter, we identify general principles that underlie an emergent-literacy approach. These principles set the foundation for the remainder of the chapter, which discusses the typical instructional practices recommended for an emergent-literacy classroom.

PRINCIPLES OF EMERGENT LITERACY AS A MODEL
OF READING INSTRUCTION

It is our contention that, no matter what the age or previous experience of the children, an emergent-literacy approach is appropriate. Thus, all early childhood classrooms should maintain programs that seek to foster children's reading and writing development, rather than waiting until some particular age or level of maturity or development. But to ensure that an emergent-literacy approach is approriate, we believe that any program should adhere to four important principles. These principles relate to the philosophy the teacher adopts in conceptualizing: (a) the purpose of the program, (b) the nature of the literacy learning process in young children, and (c) the role of the teacher in the children's learning. These four principles are as follows:

1. *Literacy is experienced as part of the everyday life and activities of the classroom.* A key emphasis in an emergent-literacy program is creating in children a true desire to read and write (and thus to *learn* to read and write). This desire stems from two interrelated factors. First, literacy needs to be an integral part of children's cultural practices. Literacy is a tool that mediates the wide variety of daily activities of families in a literate society, like that of the United States (Teale, 1986). If children live in contexts where literacy is used to get things done, they grow into literacy. Reading and writing become functional and central parts of the way they go about completing their daily activities. Second, children need to experience the joy of literacy. Reading and writing are inherently interesting activities because of the information, sense of wonder, and communicative opportunities they unlock for children. The desire to engage in reading and writing is a critically important factor to be promoted in an emergent-literacy program.

2. *The teacher views the child learners in the classroom as active constructors of their own literacy knowledge and strategies. Congruently, the teacher sees his or her own role in the promoting of learning as guiding, but not prescribing.* Literacy learning for young children grows mainly out of experiencing literacy in functional and meaningful contexts. The teacher plays a key role in establishing a classroom environment in which children have opportunities to participate in such contexts. The emphasis is on creating a climate that is supportive of learning. But the teacher does not merely create such an environment "out there" and wait for the children to teach themselves. A critical part of the emergent-literacy environment is the teaching that the teacher does. The teacher intervenes in ways that are most supportive of children's learning: creating a situation in which three or four children are in the classroom library together, getting children to collaborate on a writing project, teaching a lesson designed to help children learn a particular reading or writing strategy that would be useful to them, and telling children some piece of information about reading or writing that would be useful.

3. *Different developmental paths into literacy learning are supported.* Research studies on both emergent-reading and emergent-writing development suggest that there is no single developmental progression through which young children go in becoming literate (Sulzby, 1991). For example, we are able to see broad developmental patterns in the forms of writing that young children use, or in their emergent storybook reading strategies (Sulzby, 1985). But the teacher must not create a step-by-step curriculum that presumes that children will learn certain literacy concepts or strategies in a particular sequence or according to a prescribed time frame. There must be flexibility in philosophy, activities, and assessment procedures to accommodate the range of paths children take and strategies children employ in learning to read and write conventionally.

4. *The curriculum offers integrated language arts experiences.* Substantial evidence suggests that listening, speaking, reading, and writing are learned interrelatedly, rather than sequentially, by young children (Teale & Sulzby, 1986). For example, we have clearly seen that early reading and writing strategies build on oral language (Purcell-Gates, 1988), that writing experiences are often related to children's developing decoding knowledge (Clarke, 1988; Ehri, 1979, 1986), and that children's knowledge of reading and literature is internalized (Chomsky, 1972; Cohen, 1968) and put to use when they write (Cullinan, 1987; Cullinan & Galda, 1994; DeFord, 1981). Thus, the emergent-literacy program provides learning/teaching experiences in all of the language arts simultaneously, rather than first concentrating on oral language, then on reading, and finally on writing.

INSTRUCTIONAL PRACTICE
IN AN EMERGENT-LITERACY CLASSROOM

The role of the teacher in the emergent-literacy classroom is to support and facilitate children's literacy development by: (a) embedding literacy in daily classroom routines, (b) creating occasions for children to learn fundamental literacy concepts and strategies, (c) creating opportunities for children to develop literacy strategies and concepts about books through a variety of storybook reading activities, and (d) creating opportunities for children to develop literacy by designing literacy-involving center activities.

Teachers Create Opportunities for Children to Learn
by Embedding Literacy in Daily Classroom Routines

The emergent-literacy classroom is representative of a seamless curriculum in the sense that literacy events are woven throughout the fabric of the day. The language arts of reading, writing, speaking, and listening are viewed as integrated aspects of literacy and integral parts of everyday activities in the classroom. Through this embedded-literacy approach, children have opportunities to develop a basic understanding of the forms and functions of literacy: what written language is like, what it is for, the differences between the written and spoken word, and an appreciation and enjoyment of written language.

Teachers invite children to explore their concepts of what literacy is, and to form hypotheses about how written language works throughout the day by imbuing all facets of the classroom with literacy. The objective is to have literacy function in young children's lives as it does in the lives of adults in a literate society like ours. Adults use written language in the course of daily living routines (e.g., paying bills, reading signs, filling out forms, etc.), entertainment, work, interpersonal communication, as a means of maintaining social relations in their "information networks," and more (Teale, 1986). Emergent-literacy teachers establish a wide variety of ways in which literacy mediates the everyday classroom activities in which children engage.

Demonstrations of Forms and Functions of Literacy Are a Key Part of the Environment. Emergent-literacy teachers create a classroom environment that is rich with opportunities for children to understand literacy as a tool for functioning within a literate culture. When teachers use environmental print to organize centers, label where materials are stored, identify children's cubbies with their names, post procedures and directions at varied centers, or update weather charts and calendars, they demonstrate how literate people use literacy as a tool to organize and accomplish tasks (Neuman & Roskos, 1993; Schickendanz, 1986). Children pursue their daily tasks in this print-rich environment, finding out how useful print can be in meeting their own goals and completing classroom undertakings. For example, in a listening center, a child may refer to printed and/or drawn directions to remember how to operate a tape recorder. During clean-up time in the block center, a child may use signs that show where different types of blocks are stored.

Another example of how emergent-literacy teachers model writing as a source of interesting and useful information is "Morning Message" (Crowell, Kawakami, & Wong, 1986). Morning Message is a lively activity in which the teacher writes on chart paper or the chalkboard a short (one- to three-sentence) message highlighting the day's important, upcoming classroom events. As children observe the teacher in the act of composing the message, they see how print captures and records speech; they learn about written language as a source of daily information (somewhat analogous to the way certain sections of a newspaper function for adults). These opportunities even allow many children to learn about how letters represent speech sounds. Moreover, Morning Message provides a chance for the teacher to engage students in discussing, rereading, adding to, and thinking about the message's content. Consistent modeling of this type can play a powerful role in children's writing development (Birnbaum & Emig, 1983).

Teachers also demonstrate the forms and functions of literacy when they write lists on chart paper of things that need to be done to prepare for an important event or to complete a project. For example, before going on a field trip, the teacher may list: get permission slips signed, make name tags, read about zoo animals, and locate the route from the school to the zoo on a city map. Children come to understand the functional uses of print and lists when they check off completed tasks. There are innumerable ways that emergent-literacy teachers establish classroom routines that demonstrate the functions of literacy for children. When children have opportunities to see the purposeful and meaningful nature of print, they internalize much about its role in society and in their lives.

Invitations for Children to Use the Forms and Functions of Literacy Are Part of the Daily Routine. But merely seeing the uses to which written language is put is not enough; teachers in emergent-literacy classrooms also expect children to *use* reading and writing to negotiate their way through daily or routine activities. Neuman and Roskos (1993) found that children's opportunities for literacy learning were enriched when they were allowed to sign up to participate in activity areas in the classroom, sign up for teacher conferences, or send personal notes on message boards. A classroom post office (Martinez & Teale, 1987) is another example of an activity that creates opportunities for exploring the forms and functions of literacy. When children send letters through the "post office," they compose (through dictation and/or writing) and read (or "read") messages, informally interacting with the teacher or classroom aide. These informal interactions prove to be instrumental in children's literacy development. Teachers respond to children's questions about forms of literacy during teachable moments and in ways that help them gain metalinguistic knowledge, and thus the ability to think and talk about language.

The expectation that young children can write is not an unrealistic one. The emergent-literacy teacher understands that the writing children produce may take varied forms, ranging from drawing to scribbling to printing strings of letters to inventing nonconventional word spellings (Sulzby, 1983, 1989). In other words, in an emergent-literacy classroom, children are not expected to produce the same form of writing, but all children are expected to write. Although the forms of children's writing are often nonconventional, they are vital to their growing concepts about the meaning and stability of print. Because emergent-literacy teachers understand that there are many paths into literacy, they alert children early to the different forms writing may take. They sanction and legitimize children's nonconventional writing attempts by explaining and demonstrating the varied writing children may want to use (Sulzby, 1991).

Even with the classroom focus on allowing children to write in noncon- ventional ways, emergent-literacy teachers create situations that inspire children to want to communicate in legitimate and conventional ways. For example, by asking children to write invitations to a class celebration, the teacher fosters within children a need to create text that is readable by another person. As children write drafts in nonconventional script and ask the teacher to scribe the message in conventional script, they are guided to attend to conventional forms of literacy in meaningful ways. In this context, children do not practice elements of literacy in isolation, but develop literacy concepts and strategies set by the framework of a communicative purpose.

The examples of demonstrations and uses of written language included in this section are not an exhaustive list. However, they do represent some exemplary ways that teachers incorporate literacy events throughout the day. By embedding such literacy events into daily routines, the emergent-literacy teacher builds on research that suggests that many children gain their initial insights into reading and writing by first becoming aware of the functions of literacy (Heath, 1980; Rosen & Rosen, 1973; Taylor, 1983). When children expect print to be meaningful and purposeful, as demonstrated and experienced in their homes and emergent-literacy classrooms, they are likely to have the desire, and the need, to read and write.

Teachers Create Occasions for Children to Learn Fundamental Literacy Concepts and Strategies

When beginning literacy programs are discussed, the conversation often centers around the issue of "basic skills." Almost everyone agrees that a quality early literacy program helps children develop needed knowledge and strategies related to reading comprehension, word recognition, and decoding. The contentious issue is *how* that should happen. When it comes to an emergent-literacy program, there is one additional issue: What is it about decoding that prekindergarten and kindergarten children should be expected to know?

It is our belief that knowledgeable emergent-literacy teachers do not merely structure print-rich environments for young children to wander around in and hope the children pick up important literacy concepts and strategies. Rather, along with establishing the literacy-rich classroom, the teacher also plans certain activities that focus children's attention on specific literacy knowledge and strategies related to important words, letters, and sounds. At the same time, the teacher realizes that these lessons cannot be "skill-and-drill exercises," which treat such learning as if it were not connected to the overall foundation of literacy as meaningful/functional/purposeful activity.

Furthermore, with respect to the issue of what prekindergarten, kindergarten, or first-grade children should be expected to know in regard to the whole issue of decoding, our position is as follows. By the time children finish first grade, they should understand the alphabetic principle and use it in reading.

Of course, not all children will be at this point—there is enormous variation in the normal course of learning. But teachers should aim for this goal.

Researchers from a variety of theoretical and instructional perspectives have addressed the issue of decoding for children of this age. To help readers understand what we are advocating with respect to this potentially divisive issue, we refer to the following conceptions from other scholars in the field of literacy education because we feel it will help clarify our position. By the end of Grade 1, we want children to:

- be at the spelling-sound stage (Juel, 1993)
- use the alphabetic system to make sense of print (Goodman, 1993)
- be at the initial reading, or decoding, stage (Chall, 1983)

This conception also has significant implications for prekindergarten and kindergarten programs. Of course, an emergent-literacy classroom provides opportunities for 4- and 5-year-olds to progress as far as they can in their knowledge of decoding knowledge and strategies. However, by the end of kindergarten, all children should have developed in phonemic awareness to the point where they are able to rhyme, suggest words that begin with the same sound, clap or recognize the number of syllables in a word, and have knowledge of letter names and an understanding that letter–sound relationships exist (Adams, 1990; Cunningham, 1995; Yopp, 1992).

This is a rather lengthy introduction to our discussion of the opportunities emergent-literacy teachers create to help children learn fundamental literacy concepts and strategies. But we feel it is necessary in light of the lengthy and continuing "debate" about what children need to know and how they best learn with respect to these fundamental concepts and strategies. Now we focus on what teachers and children actually do in emergent-literacy classrooms to develop such concepts and strategies.

Invitations for Children to Develop in Comprehending Written Language. Comprehension is discussed in depth in following sections of this chapter, but we initiate discussion of the topic here because we believe that comprehension of written and oral language is pivotal in every part of the overall emergent-literacy curriculum.

When children expect print to be meaningful and purposeful, as demonstrated and experienced in their homes and/or emergent-literacy classrooms, they also come to expect that they will understand written language in many forms. In other words, they know that the marks on the page represent words and ideas that can be understood by themselves and others, and they understand that print serves many personal and social purposes. Pearson and Johnson (1978) submitted that comprehension is more of a process than a product of reading. This cycle of activity involves the reader or listener in a process of interpreting and constructing meaning based on prior knowledge. Teachers support children's growing notions that print is useful and understandable by helping children develop and use basic comprehension skills in a variety of ways.

Teachers may share literature in ways that help children gain insights into reading-comprehension strategies. For example, reading a predictable book and asking children to use the rich context created by the pictures, language, or story patterns to predict what will happen next in the story invites children to use a comprehension strategy that they can use in understanding stories when they read independently. Asking children to discuss their favorite parts of the story, or to retell, reenact, or put a story's sequence of events in order, helps children attend to the content and structure of text (Morrow, 1985; Pellegrini & Galda, 1982). Furthermore, when teachers ask children to write a favorite word from a published book, a life experience story, or a content-area lesson, and then invite children to illustrate the word, share the word with friends, or use the words to generate new stories, they are helping children understand that they can make sense of words and ideas in purposeful ways, as well as helping them building sight-word vocabularies (Ashton-Warner, 1963).

This brief sampling of activities designed to help children learn fundamental comprehension concepts and strategies is by no means meant to provide a definitive list of comprehension instruction strategies. Instead, we hope that it exemplifies the spirit with which comprehension activities are conducted in the emergent-literacy classroom. The teacher does not follow a prescribed curriculum checklist of comprehension skills to be taught. Rather, he or she responds to children's interests and needs, creating interactive situations in which children are supported in learning to think about text in ways that promote their learning of comprehension strategies.

Occasions for Children to Develop Phonemic Awareness, Knowledge of Sound–Symbol Relationships, and Word-Recognition Abilities Are Part of Daily Activities. Researchers have debated whether phonemic awareness is the result or the cause of successful reading development, or both (Lundberg, Frost, & Peterson, 1988). No matter which of these explanations eventually proves the most compelling account of the relationship, emergent-literacy teachers know that young children benefit from engaging in language play that often results in phonemic and phonic awareness. ". . . [P]honemic awareness is an insight into the structure of spoken language, including some ability to manipulate phonemes" (Griffith, Klesius, & Kromrey, 1992, p. 85). Thus, phonemic awareness relates to spoken language. But when orchestrated in ways that allow children to make connections between spoken words and observations of print, phonic awareness (i.e., understanding of the alphabetic and orthographic principles of written language) may also result.

Phonemic awareness is also important because it is a predictor of children's successful literacy development, independent of measures of IQ and vocabulary (Juel, 1988; Rego, 1991), and it is related to children's developing concept of word (Morris, 1981). Winsor and Pearson (1992) found that awareness of phonemes was important in the literacy development of first-grade children who were at risk for failure in reading and writing. The Reading Recovery program (Clay, 1985; Smith-Burke & Jaggar, 1994) demonstrates that instruction can be designed to foster children's phonemic awareness.

The emergent-literacy teacher's objective is not to involve children in isolated skill-and-drill phonemic awareness activities, but to create activities that allow children to explore the sound–symbol relationship in meaningful and often playful ways. Teachers in emergent-literacy classrooms display and share charts of poetry, rhymes, finger plays, jump rope songs, and choral chants. Tracking print, or pointing to the words of rhymes or songs while they are chanted, allows children to gain insights into sounds and symbols. When teachers lead children in rhyming games, word play with riddles, alliterative texts, puns, tongue twisters, and poetry, or when they invite children to clap along with the syllables represented in chants, they help children increase the ability to attend to and manipulate language in ways that promote phonemic awareness.

Yopp (1992) described how young children can be invited to attend to phonemes during group games that involve playful sound-matching activities, sound-isolation activities, blending activities, sound-addition or sound-substitution activities, and segmentation activities. But she cautioned that these types of game-playing activities are meant to supplement other daily activities that involve children with a variety of meaningful print negotiations. Children's involvement in repeated readings of predictable books and their opportunities to write using nonconventional, invented spelling have been found to facilitate phoneme awareness (Clarke, 1988; Winsor & Pearson, 1992). Sulzby (1993) found this to be especially true for low-socioeconomic status (SES) African-American kindergartners and first graders.

Morning Message, an activity mentioned earlier in this chapter, also contributes to children's developing awareness of the sound–symbol relationship. After the children have discussed, reread, and added to the message, the teacher takes time to highlight important words, sounds, and letters. In many cases, the teacher calls on volunteers to circle letters, words, or sounds that they can identify in the message. When children add to the message, the teacher helps them figure out symbols that match the sounds they hear as they dictate their own words.

These and many other opportunities help children hear the constituent sounds that make up language. Eventually, they learn about the relations between letters and sounds, all within a meaningful and purposeful context (Freppon & Dahl, 1991). The teacher's goal is to create activities that are engaging and playful in nature and execution. Thus, children practice phonics-related skills within the larger realm of literacy as a goal-directed activity.

Teachers Create Opportunities for Children to Develop Literacy Strategies and Concepts About Books Through a Variety of Storybook Reading Activities

Emergent-literacy teachers know that a key to children's literacy is their experiences with different kinds of books. Three kinds of interactions with books are important instructional activities for the emergent-literacy classroom: (a) reading books aloud to children; (b) children "reading" (or reading) books on their own; and (c) children engaging in book-related art, drama, music, or writing activities.

Reading Books Aloud to Children

A review of research studies from several decades (Sulzby & Teale, 1991), and a recent meta-analysis of the empirical evidence on parental reading to preschool children (Bus, Van IJzendoorn, & Pellegrini, 1995), concur that reading to young children is significantly and positively associated with their growth in literacy. Storybook reading has been shown to be associated with building background knowledge about different topics and genres, introducing children to subtle differences between oral and book language, and providing children with a model of a fluent reader (Chomsky, 1972; Cohen, 1968; Morrow, 1985). Moreover, daily classroom story readings have been shown to positively influence children's story comprehension (Feitelson, Kita, & Goldstein, 1986). As children watch teachers handle books, they can also come to understand the conventions of books and print, such as directionality of print, front to back, page turning, and even sound–symbol relationships (Clay, 1979; Mason, 1980). Research also suggests that children who have listened to stories since early childhood have greater academic success in school (Applebee, 1978; Durkin, 1966; Heath, 1983; Teale, 1986), and tend to read earlier than those who have not been read to (Hiebert, 1981, 1991; Schickendanz, 1978). Storybook reading can also foster positive attitudes toward reading, which can lead to lifelong reading habits.

The overall significance of parental storybook reading is indicated in the meta-analysis completed by Bus et al. (1995). They analyzed all available quantitative studies ($N = 41$) on the relation between frequency of book reading to preschoolers and outcome measures of language growth, children's emergent literacy, and school reading achievement. Results show that overall effect sizes were medium to strong in each of the areas. From this finding, Bus et al. determined that reading to children was as strong a predictor of language and literacy growth as phonemic awareness.

Emergent-literacy classroom instruction includes frequent read-aloud sessions. When emergent-literacy teachers use the read aloud as an instructional activity, they keep key research results from qualitative studies of storybook reading in mind:

- During storybook time, the discussion and social interaction that surround the words/illustrations of the book are what makes this such a powerful instructional activity (Cochran-Smith, 1984; Martinez & Teale, 1993; Meyer, Stahl, Wardrop, & Linn, 1994; Sulzby & Teale, 1987).
- Teachers have different storybook reading styles; the way in which a teacher reads aloud is related to what children learn from the storybook experience (Dickinson & Keebler, 1989; Dickinson & Smith, 1994; Green, Harker, & Golden, 1986; Teale & Martinez, submitted for publication).
- No matter what storybook reading style a teacher uses, it is important to involve children in storybook reading experiences that present them with a wide variety of text types and topics. It is also helpful to mediate the books in diverse ways to foster a focus on different aspects of literacy knowledge and strategies children need to become capable conventional readers.

Also, emergent-literacy teachers are guided by the collective wisdom of teachers, librarians, children's literature professionals, and storytellers. Such experts' recommendations for how to read aloud effectively to young children are set forth in books (e.g., *For Reading Out Loud!* [Kimmell & Segel, 1988] or *The New Read-Aloud Handbook* [Trelease, 1989]), videos (e.g., *Parents, Kids and Books: The Joys of Reading Together* [Boardman & Teale, 1993] or *Super Story Times: A Guide for Caregivers* [Beginning with Books, 1994]), and textbooks (e.g., Hickman & Cullinan, 1989; Huck, Hepler, & Hickman, 1993). These sources repeatedly advise teachers to: (a) read in engaging ways, (b) share the delight and joy of stories, (c) connect children's experiences with story events, and (d) engage in shared meaning making and collaborative talk. All of this has led to a variety of ways in which storybook reading becomes part of the instructional activities of the emergent-literacy classroom.

Because issues of choice of text type and ways of reading aloud to children overlap, there is no simple taxonomy of different ways of conducting storybook reading in the emergent-literacy classroom. To give readers a sense of the variety of goals served by reading aloud to children, and the various ways in which these goals are achieved, we first outline some general principles for reading aloud as an instructional activity. We then describe briefly the kinds of books and approaches to reading aloud that emergent-literacy teachers frequently use.

Read-Aloud Principle 1: Group Books for Sharing. When children listen to thematically connected books, they have many opportunities to discover connections among varied books, and to make generalizations about genres. Hoffman, Roser, Farest, and Labbo (1992) suggested that a language chart (i.e., a grid of discussion categories written on butcher paper and displayed on the wall) can provide a graphic organizer that helps children discover intertextual connections. For example, grid categories may include: (a) theme or topic features (e.g., humorous books may have a category called "What we thought was funny," or books about flight may have a category called "Things that could fly"), (b) story grammar features (e.g., place, characters, problem, solution), or (c) author/illustrator features (e.g., style or typical subject matter). In a discussion using a language chart, the teacher initially gives an open-ended prompt by asking children to talk about their favorite parts of the story, or asking them to share an experience they have had that is related to the story theme. Next, as each category is discussed, the teacher records children's comments on the chart. Finally, the teacher guides children to look at the chart and see connections across books. Children may note that many of Ezra Jack Keats' stories have characters named Peter and Willie, or that some flying things in the books about flight were made by people and others occurred in nature.

Read-Aloud Principle 2: Share Varied Types of Books. Emergent-literacy teachers know that having a variety of books and genres available allows them to use books for many purposes (Pinnell & McCarrier, 1994). They select and read from many types of literature to: (a) invite children to savor the joys of literature, (b) help them construct rich schema for features of genres, (c) whet their appetites for varied styles of writing, (d) provide information for topics and themes being studied, and (e) create a springboard for varied activities. Big Books, predictable books, folk and fairy tales, realistic fiction, informational/nonfiction books, multicultural books, series books, and poetry all combine to provide children with a rich knowledge base.

Read-Aloud Principle 3: Use Different Approaches/Orientations for Sharing Stories with Children. There are two predominate orientations toward sharing books with young children in a classroom setting: (a) sharing for literary reasons, and (b) sharing to help children learn reading concepts/"skills." When reading aloud for literary reasons, teachers focus primarily on sharing the content of the book with children. Typically, there is discussion before, during, and after reading that emphasizes meaning-making and interpretation of plot, character motivation, and theme. Some teachers, especially if they employ language charts like those discussed earlier (Hoffman et al., 1992), also lead children into discussing issues of writing style, illustration style, or genre characteristics.

When reading aloud to teach children concepts about print (e.g., directionality, differences between pictures and print as a source for reading) or strategies/"skills" (e.g., sight-word recognition, initial consonant decoding), early childhood teachers often use what has come to be known as *shared reading*, or *shared book experience* (Holdaway, 1979). Shared reading typically involves multiple readings of predictable Big Books to (and with) a large group of children. The multiple readings allow children to develop familiarity with the text and eventually to read it emergently on their own (and even engage in dramatic reenactments of it or other responses to it). Also, once the children have been through the book the first time to focus on its content/plot, the teacher feels free to concentrate on concepts or strategies during subsequent readings. A thorough description of shared reading as a teaching technique can be found in Fisher (1991). Our purpose here is not to present the ins and outs of shared reading, but rather to indicate that this approach to reading aloud is a frequently used strategy in emergent-literacy classrooms.

Read-Aloud Principle 4: Provide One-to-One or Small-Group Read-Aloud Experiences for Children Who Need Them. A significant number of children in America's early childhood classrooms come to school with little prior experience of being read to in their home environments (Adams, 1990; Teale, 1986). These children may need more extensive read-aloud experience than can be provided in the typical large-group daily storybook readings characteristic of the emergent-literacy classroom. Morrow (1990) studied benefits of small-group and paired storybook reading. She found that children in small groups asked more questions, predicted story events more frequently, and made more personal connections to stories than did children who participated in whole-class storybook sessions. Thus, there may be children in emergent-literacy classrooms who need more "intensive" storybook reading because they did not hear storybooks at home.

Types of Books and Ways of Sharing Them

Emergent-literacy teachers may invite children to experience different kinds of books in a variety of meaningful ways:

• *Multicultural books.* Books that provide culturally authentic (Bishop, 1992) and insightful stories about a variety of cultural groups are important in emergent-literacy classrooms. Quality multicultural literature offers insights into varied lifestyles and cultural traditions without perpetuating stereotypes

(Kendall, 1983). The multicultural books used include folk literature, fairy tales, contemporary realistic fiction, poetry, and informational books (Truscott & Rickey, 1994). Such books promote children's appreciation of varied cultures, as well as a richer understanding and acceptance of their own and others' cultures. As Ferdman (1990) noted, children become more involved in literacy activities in the classroom when reading and writing reflects and affirms their cultural identity.

- *Big Books.* Readings of Big Books rely on repeated uses of large-sized versions of children's favorite picture storybooks. The book is rested on an easel or chalkboard ledge so that, during storytime, children from any vantage point can see the large type and illustrations. Because all children see the print as the teacher reads, they have the opportunity to gain insights into concepts such as directionality of print, use of punctuation, and the oral/written language connection as the teacher leads them through repeated readings of the same text. These repeated interactions with the text allow the children to develop confidence in reenacting and reading the book (parts of it emergently, parts of it conventionally).

- *Predictable books.* Interactions between adults and children that occur around the sharing of predictable books seem to foster children's responsiveness and attention to language. Features of predictable books, such as repetitive language; rhyming phrases; predictable, sequential episodes within plots; and cumulative story patterns (Tompkins & Hoskisson, 1991) help children understand and predict what the text says, and may even contribute to development of phonemic awareness (Bridge, 1986; Bridge, Winograd, & Haley, 1983; Cullinan, 1989; Heald-Taylor, 1987; Tompkins & Webeler, 1983).

- *Realistic fiction.* Contemporary stories about living in the modern world are also appropriate for read alouds. Depending on the book's theme, it can provide opportunities to explore various lifestyles and face commonplace childhood dilemmas. When realistic stories are told in picture-book format, emergent-literacy teachers call children's attention to both text and pictures because the story is told through the skillful interweaving of print and illustrations (Cullinan & Galda, 1994).

- *Informational/nonfiction books.* Informational books offer an explanation of particular subject matter. The format of the informational book for young children varies from photo essays to picture books. When the teacher brings in a classroom pet, one of the first sources children and teachers turn to find out how to care for the pet is often an informational book written on the conceptual level of young children. One of the most common forms of informational book in the kindergarten classroom is the concept picture book. Many examples of one idea are included in a concept book. Number concepts, or abstract ideas such as shapes, sound, color, or even the alphabet, are included. These provide children the opportunity to build their basic conceptual understandings and enrich their vocabulary.

- *Poetry, song books, and books that play with the sounds of language.* The rhyming found in poetry and song books for young children offers excellent opportunities to promote the development of phonemic awareness. In addition, books that lead children to "tune into" the sounds of words— through alliteration or other similarities or differences in the overall sounds of words—can be important. For example, although children may not fully understand what phrases like ". . . Tinkling tunesters, twangling trillicans/Butterflied and fluttered by the great green trees . . ." (from *17 Kings and 42 Elephants* [Mahy, 1987]) mean, hearing the repeating initial sounds and manipulation of syllables promotes attention to the sounds of language.

Issues to Keep in Mind Regarding the Power of Storybook Reading as an Instructional Activity in the Classroom

We have attempted to explain how teachers can read aloud different kinds of books in a variety of ways to promote children's literacy learning. However, some recent publications have questioned the power of storybook reading to affect young children's language and literacy development. Scarborough and Dobrich (1994) reviewed the empirical research of the past three decades on the effects of parents reading aloud to their preschool children. They examined 20 correlational and 11 intervention studies for the relations between storybook reading experience and (a) literacy achievement during the school years, (b) literacy-related skills prior to school achievement, and (c) oral language skills. Their overall conclusion was that there is a only modest association between reading to preschool children and the children's development of language and literacy skills. In their analysis, storybook reading experience accounted for approximately 8% of the variance in language and literacy development.

Lonigan (1994) and Dunning, Mason, and Stewart (1994) responded to the Scarborough and Dobrich review. They contested the actual magnitude of the relationship (Lonigan contended that the variance accounted for was probably closer to the 14% range), and some of the particulars of Scarborough and Dobrich's conclusions. However, they essentially agreed with the conclusion that the benefits of storybook reading are often overstated.

Other researchers have questioned the utility of storybook reading in the primary classroom. For example, Meyer et al. (1994) found that the amount of time adults spent reading to kindergarten children was negatively correlated with achievement, and that there was no significant relationship between the two in first grade.

We feel that these studies are right to question the rhetoric often used in praise of storybook reading. We can see how teachers and others can get the impression from the literature that all one has to do is bring quality literature into the preschool or primary-grade classroom, read it aloud, and wonderful things will happen to all children's literacy learning. It is not that easy, however. Clearly, reading aloud can only help children learn part of what they need to. There are other critical types of instructional activities that teachers should plan for the classroom besides storybook time.

Nevertheless, we still maintain that read-aloud time can be a powerful instructional activity in the emergent-literacy classroom. There are two keys to making it so. First, teachers should never let storybook reading take the place of other needed instructional experiences. Storybook reading activities should be planned to help children learn the aspects of literacy development that storybook experiences can develop. Second, the quality of the storybook readings that do take place is of paramount importance. Unengaging, mediocre read alouds probably will not help children learn much. As Dickinson and his colleagues (e.g., Beals, DeTemple, & Dickinson, 1994; Dickinson & Keebler, 1989; Dickinson, Hao, & He, 1993) and Martinez and Teale (1993) have shown in their studies, the way in which the readings get done is what really makes the difference. Read alouds are not the magic bullet of early literacy instruction, but they can make a significant contribution to children's learning—if they are well done and thoughtfully used.

Emergent-Storybook Readings: Getting Children Involved in "Reading" (or Reading) Books on Their Own

Emergent-storybook readings are occasions when children read familiar books (books that have previously been read repeatedly to them) in ways that are not yet conventional reading. Children may, among other ways of reading, attend to the illustrations in the book and tell the story, or they may even use a very readinglike intonation to deliver an almost verbatim account of the text. Research indicates that emergent-storybook readings play an important role in the ontogeny of literacy. They offer children opportunities to practice what has been experienced in interactive-storybook reading events and to develop new understandings about features of written language (Sulzby & Teale, 1991). For some children, reenactments even appear to become a primary avenue into conventional reading from print.

Sulzby's (1985) original research into emergent-storybook readings described a classification scheme consisting of 11 reading categories. This scheme appeared to have developmental properties (Sulzby, 1988), and demonstrated children's growing understanding of oral and written language distinctions. Teale, Harris, and Watkins (in preparation) found, in working with teachers, that the following simplification of Sulzby's research tool depicts the major storybook reading concepts and strategies exhibited by preschoolers. Teachers use these to help them see growth and plan appropriate instruction:

What the Child Is Reading	*What the Child Is Doing*
1. Pictures	Label, comment, and/or follow the action—no story formed
2. Pictures	Sounds like telling a story
3. Pictures	Part sounds like telling a story, part sounds like reading a story
4. Pictures	Sounds like reading a story
5. Print	Child may read sight words, track print with finger and reconstruct story from memory, or try to "sound out" words

Emergent-literacy teachers know that there are two keys to getting children to read storybooks emergently: reading certain books aloud repeatedly, and providing children with actual opportunities to read on their own as part of the classroom day. These opportunities come with the availability of two things: (a) reading materials, and (b) a scheduled time during the day when children can use the materials. Thus, emergent-literacy teachers read many books over and over, and they design high-quality libraries into their classrooms.

Classroom Libraries. Much research has shown that a classroom library can play a major role in young children's literacy development. As early as 1969, Bissett discovered that children who had books available in a classroom library interacted with books 50% more than children who did not have immediate access to book collections. Teachers keep design features in mind when setting up a classroom library. They have at least five to eight books per child (Huck, 1976), include books that represent a variety of genres, display books with covers presenting (on open-faced book shelves or by some other means), and include comfortable chairs or pillows in the classroom library (Morrow, 1982; Morrow & Weinstein, 1982). Observations by Martinez and Teale (1988; Teale, Martinez, & McKeown, 1994) in kindergarten classroom libraries showed that open-faced displays of books were especially important, and that children more frequently looked at and read books that had been read aloud by the teacher than books that had not been read during story time. Thus, after books are shared, teachers put them within children's reach.

Scheduled Time for Children's Emergent-Storybook Readings. Teachers know it is important to provide children with time to engage emergent rereadings of favorite storybooks. A time to visit the classroom library in order to engage in self-selected, independent reading is scheduled on a regular basis. Moreover, teachers make visits to the classroom library a part of *every* child's schedule, not just an opportunity for those children who get their "work" done. In other words, emergent literacy teachers see emergent storybook reading in the classroom library as an essential aspect of the work that helps young children become conventionally literate.

Engaging Children in Book-Related Art, Drama, Music, or Writing Activities

In addition to reading aloud and encouraging emergent-storybook reading, teachers in many early childhood classrooms regularly include after-story occasions for children to discuss, draw, or write in response to books, to reenact story events, or to complete varied story-extension assignments. Labbo (1993) found that kindergartners talked about story themes and made life-to-text connections when the story-extension activity was designed to help them consider what they would do in the main character's situation. It is possible that the design of varied response to literature tasks may influence children's engagement with and degree of independent explorations into literacy.

As teachers provide a framework for response to literature activities, they keep several principles in mind. First, they select books that seem to fit the purpose of the literacy lesson. As Martinez and Nash (1993) noted, some books seem to lend themselves to certain kinds of response activities. For example, cumulative tales or problem–solution stories seem particularly well suited for dramatic reenactment. Picture books with vibrant illustrations, such as those by Denise Fleming, Eloise Greenfield, Pat Mora, or Eric Carle, call for children to express their feelings about the story through fingerpainting, creating collages, or drawing with pastels. Second, teachers realize that, to respond to a story, children must be familiar with the story. In these instances, children benefit from multiple readings of the same book. Third, some invitations to respond to books may be open ended and child directed; others may be focused and teacher directed (Labbo, 1993). For example, when a teacher wants to focus children's attention on the patterns of language, as in *Brown Bear, Brown Bear, What Do You See?* (Martin, 1967), he or she might extend the story by asking children to think of a different setting for a story (perhaps a garden), and make a new version of the story by innovating on the language patterns and illustrations (e.g., Pink Worm, Pink Worm what do you see? I see a Yellow Butterfly looking at me).

Hickman (1980, 1981, 1989) defined *response to literature* as an event that occurs in the classroom and involves connections made between children and stories. Three of her categories serve as a guide to organize our thinking about teacher roles described in the sections that follow: (a) supporting drama (e.g., story reenactments, role playing, dramatic improvisations), (b) encouraging children to make story-related art (e.g., pictures, dioramas, paintings, games, displays), and (c) inviting children to write about stories (e.g., summarize, restate, innovate on text). The teacher in the emergent-literacy classroom realizes the importance of these activities in providing opportunities for young children to explore, wonder about, and even invent new conceptual understandings about literacy.

Supporting Dramatic Play in Response to Adult-Authored Stories.
Role playing events of stories often improves children's comprehension of story, enables them to retell more of a story in sequence and include more story details, and fosters children's growing awareness of story structure (Morrow, 1985; Paley, 1981, 1990; Pellegrini, 1983; Pellegrini & Galda, 1982). Story comprehension may be improved through dramatic reenactment: Children are invited to "step in" (Langer, 1990) to a parallel story world and a lived-through experience as they recreate or innovate on dialogue, and experience main characters' problems and attempts to resolve those problems.

When children reenact stories, they internalize the sequence of events and clarify cause and effect. These skills help them develop a story schema and prepare them to understand literature in classroom settings. Teale and Martinez (1989) found that when children engaged in dramatic reenactments of a story before being asked to write about the story, their written products were more sophisticated (as shown by children's use of invented spelling and attention to letter–sound relationships) than when they wrote about a story without benefit of dramatic play.

Thus, emergent-literacy teachers set up situations that encourage children's dramatic reenactments of stories. These occurrences may be informal, impromptu, and spontaneous, through teacher-guided, role-playing sessions that occur immediately after the story has been shared, or they may be carefully arranged occurrences that are conducted in the sociodramatic play center with puppets, costumes, and/or props. In any case, the emergent-literacy teacher is aware of the potential for storybook reenactment to foster children's literacy and literary development.

Supporting Dramatic Play in Response to Child-Authored Stories.
Children benefit from acting out adult-authored stories, as well as from composing and acting out their own stories (Harris-Schmidt & McNamee, 1986; McNamee, 1987). When children serve as authors and actors for original stories, they gain: (a) a sense of the narrative structures and conventions of stories, (b) insights into the literacy skills necessary to accomplish the tasks of writing and acting out original stories, and (c) a sense of audience needs in telling a story well. Because emergent-literacy teachers understand that young children develop these insights over time, and, as Vygotsky (1962)

noted, through social interactions, they become facilitators in the storytelling process. The goal is not to directly "teach" children the skill of narration, but to help them manage a difficult task in meaningful ways. When children are invited to tell and act out original stories, they often have an urge to tell a story, but little initial ability to do so. Therefore, in the initial stages, teachers talk with children about story ideas, ask insightful questions, and record children's dictated dialogue. As children extend and fashion loosely constructed ideas into an organized narrative, they lay a foundation for the thinking processes necessary for independent narration. This socially constructed awareness of story is fine tuned over time until children need less adult support to organize story ideas.

As teachers give children time and support to dramatize and stage original stories, they often observe children adding gestures, inflection, and prosody to the words they have composed. The resulting interplay among audience, actor, and author often results in story revisions and innovations, and thus lays the groundwork for further development of independent narrative thought and function (McNamee, 1987).

Encouraging Story-Related Art. Hubbard's (1989) investigations into children's artwork present the idea that young children use pictorial and linguistic symbol systems to express ideas graphically. Ideas can be communicated through words or images. "Drawing is not just for children who can't write yet fluently, and creating pictures is not just part of rehearsal for real writing. Images at any age are part of the serious business of making meaning—partners with words for communicating our inner designs" (p. 157). When young children draw, they often represent ideas symbolically through pictures (Sulzby, 1983). After analyzing the talk that kindergartners engaged in as they drew or wrote, Dyson (1989) found that children often play within the imagined worlds they create. Young children may also find ways to use a combination of words and pictures to express their feelings or responses to a story (Danielson, 1992; Ernst, 1994).

Children may also gain insights into story structure, sequence of events, recording story dialogue, and attending to visual aspects of print by illustrating story characters or events, arranging their art work on a mural that reflects story sequence, and adding speech balloons (Pinnell & McCarrier, 1994). Labbo (1993) studied the nature of kindergarten children's talk as they work in small groups on accomplishing story activities. Her findings indicate that, as children draw in response to a story, they often live in the world created by the task and, regardless of literacy ability level, are thereby able to understand the main character's point of view. Children may also make connections between their lives and story characters' lives. In light of these findings, it is possible to assume that, when the world of the task simulates or parallels the world of the story, deeper understanding of the story may occur.

Transmediation is a process that involves moving information from one communication system to another (Harste, Wooward, & Burke, 1984) or of generating new meanings and explaining existing meanings. When children are asked to take the role of an artist in responding to a story, they may develop fresh story insights because they are showing what they know in a new way. In Ernst's (1994) view, writing and picturing should go hand in hand as legitimate thinking and symbol systems. Many teachers of young children want to provide sanctioned classroom time for children to explore picturing as a symbolic act, but feel constrained by district guidelines that focus on using classroom time to teach writing and letter formation. By focusing more on how children use art and emergent forms of writing to symbolize their feelings about stories, and less on "covering" the curriculum, the tension that teachers often feel between student choice and teacher direction can be lessened.

An important aspect of art-related story activities that parallels book publishing is exhibiting art. Just as young children need to publish or reenact their favorite written stories, they need to experience the joy involved in preparing for exhibition favorite artworks that tell the story of their feelings. Experiences that allow children to celebrate and acknowledge their own and others' creative efforts foster a desire to produce additional works.

Inviting Story-Related Writing. Pinnell and McCarrier (1994) suggested that many young children who come to school with few literacy experiences benefit from supported, shared writing (McKenzie, 1986) during response to literature tasks. This approach is especially powerful because it allows teachers to demonstrate problem-solving strategies children need to read and write independently. In the Early Literacy Project (Pinnell & McCarrier, 1994), teachers and children "share the pen" in the following five steps: (a) negotiating the composition of text; (b) constructing words through analysis of sounds; (c) using the conventions of print; (d) reading and rereading texts; and (e) searching, checking, and confirming while reading and writing. In many kindergarten classrooms, children are given opportunities to use a story pattern or story rhyming scheme as a template from which to create a new story (Pace, 1991; Teale & Martinez, 1987; Wason-Ellam, 1988). The original story serves as a scaffold, or a dependable format from which to deviate. However, it is important to remember that children in early childhood classrooms can be constrained by story-extension tasks that require them to use story-related rhyming schemes; the original rhyme scheme can become too limiting and require children to struggle to find rhymes that do not match the messages they wish to convey. Thus, writing to a pattern should be used judiciously in an emergent-literacy program. Children can be encouraged to write in many other ways in response to stories; specific ideas can be found in publications by Fisher (1991), McGee and Richgels (1996), and Morrow (1993).

Teachers Create Opportunities for Children
to Develop Literacy by Designing Literacy-Involving
Center Activities

Teachers in emergent-literacy classrooms design centers and interact with children in ways that foster children's literacy development. Teachers encourage children to help each other in centers, conduct informal conferences if children indicate that they need help, and often have the intention to "help the children help themselves" (Allen & Carr, 1989, p. 34). Children may also choose to work independently in centers to pursue individual goals. Therefore, the teacher designs flexible centers that support various opportunities for children to explore literacy.

Sociodramatic Play Center/Thematic Play. Play is valuable for children's cognitive, social, physical, and literacy development (Bruner, 1983; Pellegrini & Galda, 1993). Play situations in the classroom also have the potential to encourage children to explore aspects of literacy in developmentally appropriate ways, both individually and in collaboration with peers or teachers (Isenberg & Jacob, 1983; Morrow, 1990; Neuman & Roskos, 1990, 1992; Roskos, 1988; Schrader, 1988; Teale & Sulzby, 1986; Vukelich, 1990, 1993). Morrow (1990) and Neuman and Roskos (1990) observed that children participate in mutually supportive reading and writing explorations during playtime when literacy materials are included in thematic play areas. Vukelich (1993) found that peers shared what they understood about the meaning of printed messages, the features of writing print, and the functions of print within play settings. Teachers invite children to participate in literacy activities during play, respond to children's literacy efforts during play, and model literacy by briefly engaging in center literacy-related play (Morrow, 1990; Neuman & Roskos, 1990;Vukelich, 1990). Neuman and Roskos (1993) discussed a specific example (i.e., an activity center in an office setting that invites children to explore tools of literacy, create scenarios around office life, and engage in office-related role play). As children play in centers that include literacy tools, they often create ideas that incorporate uses of literacy into their play.

A sociodramatic play center enriched with cultural literacy objects provides opportunities for children to build schema about functions and forms of literacy (Morrow & Rand, 1991). Researchers who have enriched play centers with cultural objects that represent a flower shop or a veterinary office (Morrow, 1990; Neuman & Roskos, 1990; Vukelich, 1989) suggest that, when children enter the microworld created by the teacher, they often role play real-life situations that involve literacy. These scenarios often address themes being addressed in the curriculum. Props and literacy materials provided by teachers often allow children to improvise and create their own scripts. As children play, they create scripts and scenarios that result in simulations that allow them to role play literacy events that occur in the real world. In addition, Neuman and Roskos (1992) found that children often changed the play scenario and engaged in object transformations of literacy props in imaginative ways. For example, cookbooks and scraps of paper became magic directions or descriptive ballet lessons. These self-generated literacy activities often resulted in elaborate and rich play episodes.

The variations on the themes of sociodramatic play centers are limitless. In addition to the examples cited earlier, centers have been organized as a travel agency/airport, space shuttle, restaurant, newspaper office, flower shop, doctor's office, grocery store, shoe store, and beauty shop. Whatever the theme, a variety of print-related props is included.

Teachers Design and Interact with Children in a Writing/Composing Center. Teale and Sulzby (1989) recommended that children be given daily opportunities to write for a variety of reasons and audiences. It is especially important that children have the opportunity to experiment with writing. A writing center can serve as a place where children try things out in writing without having to worry about being "wrong" (Brock & Green, 1992; Spicola & Griffin, 1987). Martinez and Teale (1987) described how to set up, introduce, and operate a writing center. They recommended a well-equipped writing center that includes varied types of paper and writing implements. The center can create an environment that encourages independent and collaborative literacy explorations. When a writing center is available, children may engage in self-sponsored writing that involves (a) writing letters, (b) creating signs for the block center, and (c) writing invitations, get well cards, stories, scripts, and so on. In writing, children often become engrossed in creating multimedia productions that span several days in completion (Paley, 1981). Allen and Carr (1989) noted that writing tables, which foster collaboration, often result in mutually supportive, literacy-related interactions. Children in stable groups who were observed writing over a 5-month period often discussed letters and sounds, and gave advice on how to write words. As children write, they often sort out the alphabetic principle involving the relationship between the letters of writing and the sounds of language. Emergent writing allows children to refine their conceptual understanding of language (Allen & Carr, 1989).

Teachers Design and Interact with Children in a Block Center. The block center offers many opportunities for children to continue explorations about the functions and forms of literacy. The planning and constructing stages of block center play often result in children's decisions to add printed signs as an integral part of a play setting. For example, a busy city street must have a safe place for pretend children to cross, or buildings need to be labeled as hospitals or grocery stores.

Children may also benefit from keeping a record of their block center creations. In some early childhood classrooms, teachers provide a log for constructions. Boys and girls who have spent a great deal of time and effort constructing an object want to record what the object looked like, as well as the time, date, and title of the construction.

Teachers Design and Interact with Children in a Content-Related Center. Emergent-literacy teachers know that part of being a scientist is learning how to observe and record information about experiments. Thus, science centers allow children to sprout seeds or care for a class guinea pig, as well as record observations over time. With the teacher's help, children may also make charts and graphs of class findings. Teachers also display tradebooks related to the science theme or topic of study in the science center. In this way, when children have questions about what they are observing, they have immediate access to sources that may help answer their questions.

Sulzby, Teale, and Kamberelis (1989) observed that kindergarten children need opportunities to write expository text. Topics related to thematic units of study in science or social studies often lend themselves well to organizing knowledge and writing about children's notions about these subjects of study. A central part of content-related centers must be the presence of materials and the time to read and write reports about center experiences.

Teachers Design and Interact with Children in a Computer Center. Computers are becoming more commonplace in elementary schools and early childhood classrooms (Morsund, 1994; Office of Technology Assessment, 1988). Emergent-literacy teachers know that the mere physical presence of a computer in the classroom will not necessarily facilitate children's literacy development. Research on children's use of the computer as a word processor at home (Labbo, 1994) and at school (Cochran-Smith, Kahn, & Paris, 1990; Labbo, 1995; Labbo, Reinking, & McKenna, 1995; Olson & Sulzby, 1991) suggests that the social context created by parents and teachers influences the nature of children's computer-related literacy explorations. When children see adults using the computer to accomplish varied literacy goals in the home or classroom, when adults support children's use of the computer to accomplish children's personal goals, and when adults respond to children's questions about computer operations and composing/writing strategies, children are often able to use features of the computer to think about and explore literacy (Labbo, 1994). Labbo et al. (1995) posited that *how* the teacher guides children to use the computer determines how comfortable children become using the computer as an informal literacy tool to accomplish personal goals. Furthermore, they suggested that the kindergarten and preschool teachers whom they observed during a two-year qualitative study played six roles in successfully incorporating the computer into the classroom culture:

- *Role 1—Seeking Preparation:* Teachers learned how to use the computer by attending computer classes at a local university. One teacher even took the computer home for several weeks and asked her 12-year-old daughter to help her figure out how to use the computer.
- *Role 2—Giving Introductions:* Teachers introduced children to the computer by modeling the functions and forms of computer use by writing class notes, letters, and invitations; composing and drafting stories; or creating signs for the block center.
- *Role 3—Offering Invitations:* Teachers reminded children of the nonconventional, but legitimate, forms of writing they might want to use (e.g., drawing, scribble, letter strings, invented spelling). They did so by displaying on a bulletin board class work that represented various forms of writing, and by including computer printouts of "nonconventionally written" messages created with stamps (icons available on the software program), letter strings, and computer-generated pictures.
- *Role 4—Allowing Explorations:* Teachers gave children time to experience and explore the computer through trial and error. Children worked independently, with peer buddies, with third-grade buddies, with parent volunteers, and with other adults in the classroom.
- *Role 5—Providing Occasions:* Teachers arranged occasions for children to extend their thinking about the functions of computer by taking children on fact-finding field trips to discover how the computer is used in the world of fast food, an insurance office, a book store, or at the hospital emergency room. After a field trip, teachers put the computer into the sociodramatic play center; during play, children continued to refine their understanding of how the computer, and literacy, works in the everyday work world in varied settings.
- *Role 6—Expecting Transformations:* Teachers encouraged and expected children to come up with their own reasons for using the computer. For example, during the bookstore unit, children wanted to design their own calendars and storybooks on the computer so they could sell them in their store. During the play about the hospital, children wanted to use the computer to create prescription forms to make their job as "doctors" and "pharmacists" easier.

It is clear that merely inviting two children to sit together in front of a computer screen and keyboard will not inevitably foster children's collaboration about computer functions or exploration of literacy forms. However, given sanctioned opportunites to explore computer functions and seek their own purposes for using the computer, children in the Labbo et al. (1995) classrooms sought out peers who were expert in either literacy or computer functions to help them solve problems related to accomplishing their goals. Often playful in nature, these interactions seem to be crucial in helping young children capitalize on opportunities for computer-related literacy development.

Thus, the emergent-literacy teacher knows that play is often serious work for young children. The teacher also knows that centers provide the perfect avenue for children's meaningful, intense, and yet playful explorations of literacy. When elements of literacy, literacy props, and literacy-related scenarios are included in centers, children have ample opportunities to put the literacy puzzle together and to build knowledge about the role that literacy plays for the scientist, the florist, the historian, and so on.

CONCLUSION

In this chapter, we have presented a picture of quality emergent-literacy teaching and learning that is appropriate for all young children, regardless of prior experience or background. In the classroom we described, learning about literacy occurs within the context of socially negotiated, collaborative, meaningful activities, in which literacy is a tool that helps accomplish goals (Teale, 1986). Because the teacher views children as active constructors of their own knowledge and strategies, the teacher guides—but does not prescribe or dominate—children's learning. Both teacher-designed instructional activities and children's self-initiated activities in emergent-literacy classrooms enable children to focus on learning strategies used by fluent readers and writers. But the attempt is always to relate the development of these strategies to the acts of reading and writing. We also focused on the key role that literature plays in the emergent-literacy classroom. Children's literature, storybook reading experiences, and responses to literature (including connections through music, art, and drama) form a central core of the instructional activities in an emergent-literacy classroom.

A final feature to note in an emergent-literacy program is activities that involve new technologies, such as computers and multimedia. We single these out here because they will greatly affect the nature of the early childhood literacy learning enterprise in the coming years. Computer-related instructional activities may be just emerging in emergent-literacy classrooms at the present time, but they will be a significant part of becoming literate for young children in the future.

Although we are optimistic about an emergent-literacy program's power to help children, considerable work remains be done for such programs to become the norm as an instructional model for young children. Many early childhood teachers still cling to a reading-readiness approach to instruction, which emphasizes compartmentalized (rather than integrated) instruction and concentrates too much on limited areas such as visual discrimination, auditory discrimination, and letters and sounds. Others feel there is no place for reading or writing instruction in the early childhood classroom because their conception of literacy instruction remains in a skill-based, drill-and-practice/work sheet mentality.

To date, relatively few studies of the emergent-literacy approach have been conducted. Stahl and Miller (1989) compared whole-language and language-experience instruction with traditional, basal reader instruction. They concluded that approaches characteristic of emergent literacy are more effective in kindergarten classrooms than they are in first grade. From a follow-up, quantitative synthesis of comparative studies conducted after the 1989 review, Stahl, McKenna, and Pagnucco (1994) concluded that Stahl and Miller's conclusion still held: Emergent-literacy approaches seemed to be significantly more effective when used in kindergarten. However, both Stahl and Miller and Stahl et al. indicated that their definition of an emergent-literacy approach meant that the teacher paid no systematic attention to developing phonemic awareness or decoding in children. We hope we have clarified that, in our conception of an emergent-literacy classroom, instruction does focus on these aspects, as well as on the conceptual base for reading, comprehension, and attitude toward reading.

A comprehensive research base is needed to understand the role that an emergent-literacy perspective on reading instruction has on young children's literacy development. We recognize the need for more (a) emergent-literacy classroom case studies of the literacy learning of individual children from a variety of backgrounds, (b) ecologically grounded empirical studies of learning in emergent-literacy classroom contexts, and (c) teacher research studies from emergent-literacy classrooms. Additionally, the field needs more work in classrooms to develop quality instructional activities that work for young children (e.g., how to integrate phonemic-awareness activities into curriculum in ways that make sense, rather than as a 20-minute activity that fits a particular time slot).

In certain respects, emergent-literacy research and development is still in its developing stages. But this perspective on classroom reading instruction has much to offer teachers and children. If the next decade provides as much insight into young children's literacy learning and emergent-literacy instructional approaches, we will have much to celebrate: young children who are more capable, confident, and willing readers.

REFERENCES

Adams, M. (1990). *Beginning to read: Thinking and learning about print.* Cambridge, MA: MIT Press.

Allen, J., & Carr, E. (1989). Collaborative learning among kindergarten writers: James learns how to write at school. In J. Allen & J. Mason (Eds.), *Risk makers, risk takers, risk breakers: Reducing the risks for young literacy learners* (pp. 30–47). Portsmouth, NH: Heinemann.

Applebee, A. N. (1978). *The child's concept of story, ages two to seventeen.* Chicago: University of Chicago Press.

Ashton-Warner, S. (1963). *Teacher.* New York: Bantam.

Beals, D E., DeTemple, J. M., & Dickinson, D. K. (1994). Talking and listening that support early literacy development of children from low-income families. In D. K. Dickinson (Ed.), *Bridges to literacy* (pp. 19–42). Cambridge, MA: Basil Blackwell.

Beginning with Books. (Producer). (1994). *Super story times: A guide for caregivers* [videotape]. Pittsburgh, PA: The Carnegie Library of Pittsburgh.

Birnbaum, J., & Emig, J. (1983). Creating minds: Created texts: Writing and reading. In R. Parker & F. Davis (Eds.), *Developing literacy: Young children's use of language* (pp. 87–104). Newark, DE: International Reading Association.

Bishop, R. (1992). Extending multicultural understanding. In B. E. Cullinan (Ed.), *Invitation to read: More children's literature in the reading program* (pp. 80–91). Newark, DE: International Reading Association.

Bissett, D. (1969). *The amount and effect of recreational reading in selected fifth grade classes.* Unpublished doctoral dissertation, Syracuse University, Syracuse, NY.

Boardman, A. (Writer/Producer), & Teale, W. H. (Host/Consultant). (1993). *Parents, kids and books: The joys of reading together* [videotape]. Dallas, TX: KERA Channel 13.

Bridge, C. (1986). Predictable books for beginning readers and writers. In M. Sampson (Ed.), *The pursuit of literacy: Early reading and writing* (pp. 81–96). Dubuque, IA: Kendall/Hunt.

Bridge, C., Winograd, P., & Haley, D. (1983). Using predictable materials vs. preprimers to teach beginning sight words. *The Reading Teacher, 36,* 884–891.

Brock, D., & Green, V. (1992). The influences of social context on kindergarten journal writing. *Journal of Research in Childhood Education, 7,* 5–19.

Bruner, J. (1983). Play, thought, and language. *Peabody Journal of Education, 60*(3), 60–69.

Bus, A., Van IJzendoorn, M., & Pellegrini, A. (1995). Joint book reading makes for success in learning to read: A meta-analysis on intergenerational tramsmission of literacy. *Review of Educational Research, 65,* 1–21.

Chall, J. S. (1983). *Stages of reading development.* New York: McGraw-Hill.

Chomsky, C. (1972). Stages in language development and reading exposure. *Harvard Educational Review, 42,* 1–33.

Clarke, L. (1988). Encouraging invented spelling in first graders' writing: Effects of learning to spell and read. *Research in the Teaching of English, 22,* 281–309.

Clay, M. (1979). *The early detection of reading difficulties.* Portsmouth, NH: Heinemann.

Clay, M. (1985). *The early detection of reading difficulties* (3rd ed.). Portsmouth, NH: Heinemann.

Cochran-Smith, M. (1984). *The making of a reader.* Norwood, NJ: Ablex.

Cochran-Smith, M., Kahn, J., & Paris, L. (1990). Writing with a felicitious tool. *Theory into Practice, 29,* 235–245.

Cohen, D. (1968). The effects of literature on vocabulary and reading achievement. *Elementary English, 45,* 209–213.

Crowell, D., Kawakami, A., & Wong, J. (1986). Emerging literacy: Reading-writing experiences in a kindergarten classroom. *Reading Teacher, 40,* 144–149.

Cullinan, B. (Ed.). (1987). Whole language and children's literature. *Language Arts, 69,* 426–430.

Cullinan, B. (1989). Latching on to literature: Reading initiatives take hold. *School Library Journal, 35*(8), 27–31.

Cullinan, B., & Galda, L. (1994). *Literature and the child.* Orlando, FL: Harcourt Brace.

Cunningham, P. (1995). *Phonics they use: Words for reading and writing* (2nd ed.). New York: HarperCollins.

Danielson, K. (1992). Picture books to use with older students. *Journal of Reading, 35,* 652–654.

DeFord, D. (1981). Literacy: Reading, writing and other essentials. *Language Arts, 58,* 652–658.

Dickinson, D. K., Hao, Z., & He, W. (1993, November). *Book reading: It makes a difference how you do it.* Paper presented at the 83rd annual convention of the National Council of Teachers of English, Pittsburgh, PA.

Dickinson, D. K., & Keebler, R. (1989). Variation in preschool teachers' book reading styles. *Discourse Processes, 12,* 353–376.

Dickinson, D., & Smith, M. (1994). Long-term effects of preschool teachers' book readings on low-income children's vocabulary and story comprehension. *Reading Research Quarterly, 29,* 104–122.

Dunning, D. B., Mason, J. M., & Stewart, J. (1994). Reading to preschoolers: A response to Scarborough and Dobrich and recommendations for future research. *Developmental Review, 14,* 324–339.

Durkin, D. (1966). *Children who read early.* New York: Teacher's College Press.

Durkin, D. (1987). Testing in the kindergarten. *The Reading Teacher, 40,* 766–770.

Dyson, A. (1989). "Once upon a time" reconsidered: The developmental dialectic between function and form. *Written Communication, 6,* 436–462.

Ehri, L. (1979). Linguistic insight: Threshold of reading acquisition. In T. G. Waller & G. E. MacKinnon (Eds.), *Reading research: Advances in theory and practice* (Vol. 1, pp. 63–116). New York: Academic Press.

Ehri, L. (1986). Sources of difficulty in learning to spell and read. In M. L. Wolraich & D. Routh (Eds.), *Advances in development and behavioral pediatrics* (Vol. 7, pp. 121–195). Greenwich, CT: JAI Press.

Ernst, K. (1994). *Picturing learning: Artists & writers in the classroom.* Portsmouth, NH: Heinemann.

Feitelson, D., Kita, B., & Goldstein, Z. (1986). Effects of reading series stories to first graders on their comprehension and use of language. *Research on the Teaching of English, 20,* 339–356.

Ferdman, B. (1990). Literacy and cultural identity. *Harvard Educational Review, 60,* 179–204.

Fisher, B. (1991). *Joyful learning: A whole language kindergarten.* Portsmouth, NH: Heinemann.

Freppon, P., & Dahl, K. (1991). Learning about phonics in a whole language classroom. *Language Arts, 68,* 190–197.

Frith, G., & Mims, A. (1985). Burnout among special education paraprofessionals. *Teaching Exceptional Children, 17,* 225–227.

Goodman, K. (1993). *Phonics phacts.* Portsmouth, NH: Heinemann.

Green, J., Harker, J., & Golden, J. (1986). Lesson construction: Differing views. In G. W. Noblit & W. T. Pink (Eds.), *Schooling in social context: Qualitative studies* (pp. 46–77). Norwood, NJ: Ablex.

Griffith, P., Klesius, J., & Kromrey, J. (1992). The effect of phonemic awareness on the literacy development of first grade children in a traditional or a whole language classroom. *Journal of Research in Childhood Education, 6,* 85–92.

Harris-Schmidt, G., & McNamee, G. D. (1986). Children as authors and actors: Literacy development through "basic activities." *Child Language Teaching and Therapy, 59,* 272–275.

Harste, J., Woodward, V., & Burke, C. (1984). *Language stories and literacy lessons.* Portsmouth, NH: Heinemann.

Heald-Taylor, G. (1987). Predictable literature selections and activities for language arts instruction. *The Reading Teacher, 40,* 6–12.

Heath, S. B. (1980). The functions and uses of literacy. *Journal of Communication, 30,* 123–133.

Heath, S. B. (1983). *Ways with words: Language, life, and work in communities and classrooms.* New York: Cambridge University Press.

Hickman, J. (1980). Children's response to literature: What happens in the classroom. *Language Arts, 57*(5), 524–529.

Hickman, J. (1981). A new perspective on response to literature: Research in an elementary school setting. *Research in the Teaching of English, 15,* 343–354.

Hickman, J., & Cullinan, B. E. (1989). *Children's literature in the classroom: Weaving Charlotte's Web.* Needham Heights, MA: Christopher-Gordon.

Hiebert, E. (1981). Developmental patterns and interrelationships of preschool children's print awareness. *Reading Research Quarterly, 16,* 236–260.

Hiebert, E. (1991). The development of word-level strategies in authentic literacy tasks. *Language Arts, 68,* 234–240.

Hoffman, J., Roser, N., Farest, C., & Labbo, L. (1992). Language charts: A record of story time talk. *Language Arts, 69,* 44–52.

Holdaway, D. (1979). *The foundations of literacy.* Portsmouth, NH: Heinemann.

Hubbard, R. (1989). Inner designs. *Language Arts, 66,* 119–136.

Huck, C. (1976). *Children's literature in the elementary school* (3rd ed.). New York: Holt, Rinehart & Winston.

Huck, C. S., Hepler, S., & Hickman, J. (1993). *Children's literature in the elementary school* (5th ed.). Fort Worth, TX: Harcourt Brace.

Isenberg, J., & Jacob, E. (1983). Literacy and symbolic play: A review of the literature. *Childhood Education, 59,* 272–276.

Juel, C. (1988). Learning to read and write: A longitudinal study of fifty-four children from first through fourth grade. *Journal of Educational Psychology, 80,* 437–447.

Juel, C. (1993). Teaching phonics in the context of integrated language arts. In L. M. Morrow, J. K. Smith, & L. C. Wilkinson (Eds.), *The integrated language arts: Controversy to consensus* (pp. 133–154). Needham, MA: Allyn & Bacon.

Kendall, F. (1983). *Diversity in the classroom.* New York: Teachers College Press.

Kimmell, M., & Segel, E. (1988). *For reading out loud!: A guide to storybooks with children.* New York: Dell.

Labbo, L. (1993). *Negotiating the path between story and young children's literacy development.* Unpublished doctoral dissertation, The University of Texas at Austin.

Labbo, L. (1994, May). *The microcomputer and emergent literacy: A case study of computer-related literacy experiences at home.* Paper presented at the 39th International Reading Association Conference, Toronto, Canada.

Labbo, L. (1995). What am I going to do with the computer they've put in my classroom? *Georgia Journal of Reading, 20,* 14–16.

Labbo, L., Reinking, D., & McKenna, M. (1995, May). *Classroom, computer lab, and living room: Case studies of kindergartners' home and school computer-related literacy experiences.* Paper presented at the 40th International Reading Association Conference, Anaheim, CA.

Langer, R. (1970). Reading interests and school achievement. *Reading Improvement, 7,* 18–19.

Langer, J. (1990). Understanding literature. *Language Arts, 67,* 812–816.

Lehr, S. (1988). The child's developing sense of theme as a response to literature. *Reading Research Quarterly, 23,* 337–357.

Lonigan, C. J. (1994). Reading to preschoolers: Is the emperor really naked? *Developmental Review, 14,* 303–323.

Lundberg, I., Frost, J., & Petersen, O. (1988). Effects of an extensive program for stimulating phonological awareness in preschool children. *Reading Research Quarterly, 23,* 263–284.

Mahy, M. (1987). *17 Kings and 42 Elephants.* Illustrated by P. MacCarthy. New York: Dial.

Martin, B. (1967). *Brown bear, brown bear, what do you see?* Illustrated by E. Carle. New York: Holt, Rinehart & Winston.

Martinez, M., & Nash, M. (1993). Bookalogues: Families and communities. *Language Arts, 70,* 678–685.

Martinez, M., & Teale, W. (1987). The ins and outs of a kindergarten writing program. *The Reading Teacher, 40*(4), 444–450.

Martinez, M., & Teale, W. (1988). Reading in a kindergarten classroom library. *The Reading Teacher, 41,* 568–573.

Martinez, M., & Teale, W. (1993). Teacher storybook reading style: A comparison of six teachers. *Research in the Teaching of English, 27,* 175–199.

Mason, J. (1980). When do children begin to read: An exploration of four year old children's letter and word reading competencies. *Reading Research Quarterly, 15,* 203–221.

McGee, L., & Richgels, D. (1996). *Literacy's beginnings: Supporting young readers and writers* (2nd ed.). Boston, MA: Allyn & Bacon.

McKenzie, M. (1986). *Journeys into literacy.* Hudderson, England: Schofield & Sims, Ltd.

McNamee, G. D. (1987). The social origins of narrative skills. In M. Hickmann (Ed.), *Social and functional approaches to language and thought* (pp. 287–304). New York: Academic Press.

Meyer, L., Stahl, S., Wardrop, J., & Linn, R. (1994). Effects of reading storybooks aloud to children. *The Journal of Educational Research, 88,* 69–85.

Morris, D. (1981). Concept of word: A developmental phenonenon in the beginning reading and writing process. *Language Arts, 58,* 659–668.

Morrow, L. (1982). Relationships between literature programs, library corner designs, and children's use of literature. *Journal of Educational Research, 75,* 334–339.

Morrow, L. (1985). Retelling stories: A strategy for improving young children's comprehension, concept of story structure and oral language complexity. *The Elementary School Journal, 85,* 647–661.

Morrow, L. (1990). Preparing the classroom environment to promote literacy during play. *Early Childhood Research Quarterly, 21,* 330–346.

Morrow, L. (1993). *Literacy development in the early years: Helping children read and write* (2nd ed.). Boston, MA: Allyn & Bacon.

Morrow, L., & Rand, M. (1991). Promoting literacy during play by designing early childhood classroom environments. *The Reading Teacher, 44,* 396–402.

Morrow, L., & Weinstein, C. (1982). Increasing children's use of literature through program and physical design changes. *The Elementary School Journal, 83,* 131–137.

Morsund, D. (1994). Editor's message: Technology education in the home. *The Computing Teacher, 21*(5), 4.

Neuman, S., & Roskos, K. (1990). Play, print and purpose: Enriching play environments for literacy development. *The Reading Teacher, 44,* 214–221.

Neuman, S., & Roskos, K. (1992). Literacy objects as cultural tools: Effects on children's literacy behaviors in play. *Reading Research Quarterly, 27,* 202–225.

Neuman, S., & Roskos, K. (1993). Access to print for children of poverty: Differential effects of adult mediation and literacy-enriched play settings on environmental and functional print tasks. *American Educational Research Journal, 30,* 95–122.

Office of Technology Assessment, Congress of the United States (1988). *Power on!: New tools for teaching and learning.* Washington, DC: Author.

Olson, K., & Sulzby, E. (1991). The computer as a social/physical environment in emergent literacy. In J. Zutell & S. McCormick (Eds.), *Learner factors/teacher factors: Issues in literacy research and instruction. Fortieth Yearbook* (pp. 111–118). Chicago, IL: National Reading Conference.

Olson, M., & Griffith, P. (1993). Phonological awareness: The what, why, and how. *Reading & Writing Quarterly: Overcoming Learning Difficulties, 9*(4), 351–360.

Pace, G. (1991). When teachers use literature for literacy instruction: Ways that constrain, ways that free. *Language Arts, 68,* 12–25.

Paley, V. (1981). *Wally's stories: Conversations in the kindergarten.* Cambridge, MA: Harvard University Press.

Paley, V. (1990). *The boy who would be a helicopter: The uses of storytelling in the classroom.* Cambridge, MA: Harvard University Press.

Pearson, P. D., & Johnson, D. D. (1978). *Teaching reading comprehension.* New York: Holt, Rinehart & Winston.

Pelligrini, A. (1983). Saying what you mean: Using play to teach "literate language." *Language Arts, 60,* 380–384.

Pellegrini, A., & Galda, L. (1982). The effects of thematic fantasy play training on the development of children's story comprehension. *American Educational Research Journal, 19,* 443–452.

Pellegrini, A., & Galda, L. (1993). Ten years after: A reexamination of symbolic play and literacy research. *Reading Research Quarterly, 28,* 163–175.

Pinnell, G., & McCarrier, A. (1994). Interactive writing: A transition tool for assisting children in learning to read and write. In E. H. Hiebert & B. Taylor (Eds.), *Getting reading right from the start* (pp. 149–170). Boston: Allyn & Bacon.

Purcell-Gates, V. (1988). Lexical and syntactic knowledge of written narrative held by well-read-to kindergartners and second graders. *Research in the Teaching of English, 22,* 128–160.

Rego, L. (1991). The role of early linguistic awareness in children's reading and spelling. *Dissertation Abstracts International, 53,* 1391A. (University Microfilms No. BRD-96830)

Rosen, H., & Rosen, C. (1973). *The language of primary school children.* London: Penguin.

Roskos, K. (1988). Literacy at work in play. *The Reading Teacher, 41,* 562–567.

Scarborough, H. S., & Dobrich, W. (1994). On the efficacy of reading to preschoolers. *Developmental Review, 14,* 245–302.

Schickendanz, J. (1978). "Please read that story again!" Exploring relationships between story reading and learning to read. *Young Children, 33*(5), 48–55.

Schickendanz, J. (1986). *More than the ABC's: The early stages of reading and writing.* Washington, DC: National Association for the Education of Young Children.

Schrader, C. (1988). Written language use within the context of young children's symbolic play. *Early Childhood Research Quarterly, 4,* 225–244.

Smith-Burke, T., & Jaggar, M. (1994). Implementing reading recovery in New York: Insights from the first two years. In E. Hiebert & B. Taylor (Eds.), *Getting reading right from the start: Effective early literacy interventions* (pp 63–84). Boston: Allyn & Bacon.

Spicola, R., & Griffin, M. (1987). What happens when kindergarten children write. *Reading Education in Texas, 3,* 53–58.

Stahl, S. A., McKenna, M. C., & Pagnucco, J. R. (1994). The effects of whole langaue instruction: An update and a reappraisal. *Educational Psychologist, 29,* 175–186.

Stahl, S. A., & Miller, P. D. (1989). Whole language and language experience approaches for beginning reading: A qualitative research synthesis. *Review of Educational Research, 59,* 87–119.

Sulzby, E. (1983, September). *Beginning readers' developing knowledges about written language* (Final report to the National Institute of Education [NIE-G-80-0176]). Evanston, IL: Northwestern University Press.

Sulzby, E. (1985). Children's emergent reading of favorite storybooks: A developmental study. *Reading Research Quarterly, 20,* 458–481.

Sulzby, E. (1988). *Emergent literacy with and without the computer: A part of project CEIL, Computers In Early Literacy* (A proposal to the Spencer Foundation). Ann Arbor, MI: University of Michigan Press.

Sulzby, E. (1989). Assessment of writing and of children's language while writing. In L. Morrow & J. Smith (Eds.), *The role of assessment and measurement in early literacy instruction* (pp. 83–109). Englewood Cliffs, NJ: Prentice-Hall.

Sulzby, E. (1991). *Emergent literacy. Teaching Reading: Strategies from Successful Classrooms, a six part national teacher training video series.* Urbana, IL: Center for the Study of Reading.

Sulzby, E. (1993). Repeated readings of literature and low socioeconomic status black kindergartners and first graders. *Reading and Writing Quarterly: Overcoming Learning Difficulties, 9,* 183–196.

Sulzby, E., & Teale, W. H. (1987). *Young children's storybook reading: Longitudinal study of parent-child interaction and children's independent functioning* (Final report to The Spencer Foundation). Ann Arbor, MI: University of Michigan Press.

Sulzby, E., & Teale, W. H. (1991). Emergent literacy. In R. Barr, M. Kamil, P. Mosenthal, & P. Perason (Eds.), *Handbook of reading research* (Vol. II, pp. 727–757). New York: Longman.

Sulzby, E., Teale, W., & Kamberelis, G. (1989). Emergent writing in the classroom: Home and school connections. In D. Strickland & L. Morrow (Eds.), *Emerging literacy: Young children learn to read and write* (pp. 63–79). Newark, DE: International Reading Association.

Taylor, D. (1983). *Family literacy.* Exeter, NH: Heinemann.

Teale, W. H. (1986). Home background and young children's literacy development. In W. H. Teale & E. Sulzby (Eds.), *Emergent literacy: Writing and reading* (pp. 173–206). Norwood, NJ: Ablex.

Teale, W. H., Harris, L., & Watkins, D. (in preparation). *The emergent literacy assessment toolkit.*

Teale, W. H., & Martinez, M. G. (1989). Connecting writing: Fostering emergent literacy in kindergarten children. In J. Mason (Ed.), *Reading and writing connections* (pp. 177–198). Boston: Allyn & Bacon.

Teale, W. H., & Martinez, M. G. (submitted for publication). *The relation between storybook reading style and kindergartners' story comprehension.*

Teale, W. H., Martinez, M. G., & McKeown, T. (1994). *Kindergarten children's reading choices and behaviors in three classroom libraries.* Unpublished raw data.

Teale, W., & Sulzby, E. (1986). *Emergent literacy: Writing and reading.* Norwood, NJ: Ablex.

Teale, W., & Sulzby, E. (1989). Emergent literacy: New perspectives. In D. Strickland & L. Morrow (Eds.), *Emerging literacy: Young children learn to read and write* (pp. 1–15). Newark, DE: International Reading Association.

Tompkins, G., & Hoskisson, K. (1991). *Language arts: Content and teaching strategies.* New York: Macmillan.

Tompkins, G., & Webeler, M. (1983). What will happen next? Using predictable books with young children. *The Reading Teacher, 36,* 498–502.

Trelease, J. (1989). *The new read-aloud handbook* (2nd ed.). New York: Penguin.

Truscott, D., & Rickey, M. (1994). Multicultural/multiethnic children's literature: Familiarity, availability, and use in classrooms and libraries. In C. Kinzer & D. Leu (Eds.), *Forty-third yearbook of the National Reading Conference* (pp. 190–199). Chicago, IL: National Reading Conference.

Vukelich, C. (1989, December). *Materials and modeling: Promoting literacy during play.* Paper presented at the National Reading Conference, Austin, TX.

Vukelich, C. (1990, December). *Adult modelling in literacy-enriched play settings: Its influence on young children's understanding of print.* Paper presented at the meeting of the National Reading Conference, Miami, FL.

Vukelich, C. (1993). Play: A context for exploring the functions, features and meaning of writing with peers. *Language Arts, 70,* 386–391.

Vygotsky, L. (1962). *Thought and language.* Cambridge, MA: MIT Press.

Vygotsky, L. (1978). *Mind in society: The development of higher psychological processes.* Cambridge, MA: Harvard University Press.

Wason-Ellam, L. (1988). Making literary connections. *Canadian Journal of English Language Arts, 11,* 47–54.

Winsor, P., & Pearson, P. D. (1992). *Children at risk: Their phonemic awareness development in holistic instruction* (Tech. Rep. No. 143). Urbana, IL: Center for the Study of Reading.

Yopp, H. (1992). Developing phonemic awareness in young children. *The Reading Teacher, 45,* 696–703.

Zarrillo, J. (1989). Teacher's interpretations of literature-based reading. *The Reading Teacher, 43,* 22–28.

CHAPTER TWELVE

Reading Instruction in an Integrated Language Perspective: Collaborative Interaction in Classroom Curriculum Genres

Christine C. Pappas
University of Illinois at Chicago

An integrated language perspective rests on three major interrelated principles that stress a particular view of the nature of learners, language, and knowledge (Pappas, Kiefer, & Levstik, 1995). *Learners* are seen as active meaning-makers who are continuously interpreting and making sense of the world based on what they have already learned and the knowledge they have already constructed and reconstructed. *Language* is the major system by which meanings are communicated and expressed in our social world. Because language serves a multitude of social purposes, texts (oral and written) are realized in various ways, by various linguistic patterns or registers. Thus, language can be understood only in relation to the social contexts in which it is being used, and it is learned only through actual use—as part of human activity. *Knowledge* is organized and constructed by individual learners through social interaction. It is built-up mental representations that are constantly changing, hence it is always tentative and provisional. Because knowledge is not a static, absolute, "out-there" object, but is instead a process of knowing or coming to know, it is always affected by our culture, existing social circumstances, the historical moment, and so forth.

To depict how these three conceptions of learners, language, and knowledge constitute or realize an integrated language view of reading instruction, the chapter is organized into three major sections. The first section outlines a genre approach to language and language teaching-learning on which the integrated language perspective rests. It talks about the vast heterogeneity of written texts—there are many ways to read, for different purposes, in different social contexts—and then examines the implications of what this means for learning to read. The concept of genre is also applied in the latter part of this section by characterizing the situated participant structures of regular classroom activities as *curriculum genres*. Because learners in an integrated language perspective are seen as active meaning-makers constructing and reconstructing their own knowledge within various social contexts, issues of teacher control, power, and authority in teaching reading have to be made problematic. A rationale is presented for why a collaborative style of teaching is an essential feature of the integrated language perspective and how such an approach fosters collaborative classroom discourse between teacher and students and among students in various literacy curriculum genres.

This discussion, then, sets the stage for the second section where reading instruction within thematic units is more specifically addressed. Thematic units, a core characteristic of the perspective, are seen as long-term curricular plans developed by teachers so that students can have many opportunities to be engaged in student-initiated inquiries that integrate reading with writing, talk, and the various curricular areas. Thematic units enable students to view disciplines as cultural frames or ways of thinking, and at the same time provide opportunities for them to understand the linkages and inter-relatedness between disciplines. The latter part of this section provides examples from a JOURNEYS thematic unit to illustrate how a teacher organized curriculum to promote such interdisciplinary understandings. Two curriculum genres—*Literature Circle* and *Teacher-Led Reading Aloud*—are highlighted to show how this teacher attempted to take on a collaborative style of teaching by sharing power with her students in reading instruction.

In the last section, the chapter's main threads are brought together to consider future research avenues from an integrated language perspective. It addresses the role of genre in the struggles and tensions inherent in developing collaborative styles of teaching for diverse student populations.

A GENRE APPROACH TO LANGUAGE AND LANGUAGE TEACHING–LEARNING

Genre and Learning to Read

Many may recognize the term *genre* from their memories of English literature courses, where it is common to speak of various literary genres (e.g., novels, plays, short stories, sonnets, odes, etc.). Genre is used here to include these types of texts, but it also encompasses much more, for it stresses a functional view of language and language learning. Bakhtin's (1986) influential essay entitled "The Problem of Speech Genres" offers a useful introduction to such a stance:

All the diverse areas of human activity involve the use of language. Quite understandably, the nature and forms of this use are just as diverse as the areas of human activity. . . . Language is realized in the form of individual concrete utterances (oral and written) by participants in the various areas of human activity. The utterances reflect the specific conditions and goals of each such area not only through their content (thematic) and linguistic style, that is, the selection of the lexical, phraseological, and grammatical resources of the language, but above all through their compositional structure. All three of these aspects—thematic content, style, and compositional structure—are inseparably linked to the *whole* of the utterance and are equally determined by the specific nature of the particular sphere of communication. Each separate utterance is individual, of course, but each sphere in which language is used develops its *relatively stable types* of these utterances. These we may call *speech genres*. (p. 60; italics original)

The argument here is that there is an extreme heterogeneity of genres—both oral and written—because the spheres of human activity in which genres function in life are of a boundless, limitless number. *Culture* can be seen as an integrated body of the total set of meanings available to a community; it is a semiotic potential or resource that "includes the ways of doing, ways of being, *and* ways of saying" (Hasan, 1985, p. 99; italics added).

Genres are text types (I use *text* throughout this chapter as a gloss for Bakhtin's term *utterance*) that reflect a culture's ways of saying. They are abstractions of people's prior knowledge of both their direct experiences of life and its activities and their verbal (oral and written) experiences and encounters (Swales, 1990). Texts, then, are social processes; they are generic manifestations of the culture that they, in many ways, constitute (Fairclough, 1992; Halliday & Martin, 1993; Kress, 1993). Genres are what Wertsch (1991) called the diverse items that make up a cultural *tool kit* (i.e., the mediational means available to humans to enable them to act, understand, and be understood). Any speaker, reader, or writer must select among generic forms—a multitude of paths that have been experienced and built up from previous contextualized use. As Bakhtin (1986) argued, the fact that we are able to communicate at all is due to genres:

We learn to cast our speech [or writing] in generic forms and, when hearing [or reading] others' speech, we guess its genre from the very first words; we predict a certain length (that is, the approximate length of the speech whole) and a certain compositional structure; we foresee the end; that is, from the very beginning we have a sense of the speech whole. . . . If speech genres did not exist and we had not mastered them, if we had to originate them during the speech [speaking, listening, reading, or writing] process and construct each [text] at will for the first time, speech communication would be almost impossible. (p. 79)

Because cultural activities are socially structured (i.e., having a particular sequence of actions, etc.), the texts or genres related to, or being used by way of performing these activities, are also structured (Hasan, 1995; Lemke, 1990; Martin, 1992). Thus, in Bakhtin's words, genres are forms that inter-relate "thematic content, style, and compositional structure" as a whole; they reflect certain organizational patterns or "shapes" of discourse that are used to make meaning.

Genres, spoken or written, have two characteristics that, at first glance, appear to be contradictory. First, genres are stable. They have fixed elements or patterns: A story is organized differently than an essay, which, in turn, is different from a recipe. These different genres are stable because they do certain jobs in our culture. We can choose from this system of language, this range of genres, to communicate our intentions and meanings.

Although they are stable, genres always involve change. They change because we put together various available options from different genres in a different way or borrow elements or features from different genres in new, novel ways; we create new genres. Because we frequently have new language goals or purposes to be accomplished in everyday life, aspects of the patterns of genres are altered. Genres are evolved and evolving systems.

The generic characteristics of stability and change lead to predictable and creative texts. A particular text is always a new, creative instance of some genre. At the same time, it is always predictable, being in some sense "old hat" for its users. In other words, genres are inherited social forms, but they are also historical processes and entities that change and merge (Fairclough, 1992; Slevin, 1992).

Thus, the relationship between text and social context is a dialectic, symbiotic one: "[a] text *is created* by its context . . . [and] it also *creates* that context" (Halliday, 1994, p. 199; italics original). A particular text realizes the specific conditions of a context of situation, while it contributes to or construes the context (Fairclough, 1992; Halliday & Hasan, 1985; Halliday & Martin, 1993; Hasan, 1995; Nystrand, 1987).

This may be apparent for spoken language contexts, but it also holds for the use of written texts. Indeed, a genre approach argues against the notion that written texts are somehow "autonomous" (Olson, 1977, 1991) or instances of timeless "decontextualized" language. Instead, a genre approach contends that both oral and written texts are contextualized, although in different ways (Cazden, 1992; Halliday, 1985, 1987; Halliday & Hasan, 1985; Nystrand, 1986, 1987; Nystrand & Wiemelt, 1991). Spoken texts are typically contextualized, in large part, with respect to features of the actual physical situations in which participants find themselves. Written texts might be seen as being "decontextualized" from such physical situations at the context of use (Nystrand, 1986), in that readers cannot usually rely on these settings as resources for understanding. However, written texts are usually constructed for a context of eventual use (Nystrand, 1986), and thus are contextualized in terms of what Cazden (1992) called the "contexts of the mind."

Written texts are "contextualized first in the mind of the writer and then recontextualized in the minds of readers" (p. 148).

Because of this (re)contextualization, the meaning of written texts is just as interactive as the meaning of spoken texts (Halliday, 1978). That is, written texts also involve exchanges of meaning—a dialogue (Bakhtin, 1981, 1986) or reciprocity (Nystrand, 1986, 1987; Nystrand & Wiemelt, 1991) occurs between readers and writers. However, this does not imply that meaning in written texts is relative or indeterminate. On the contrary, both writers and readers are constrained by: (a) their shared cultural values; (b) the genres they know and use; (c) the ways they balance their respective intentions and needs; and (d) expectations about the particular texts they compose or interpret. On each side of the reading–writing process—indeed in any use of language—there exists an intrapersonal *voice*—Bahktin's (1981, 1986) term for the "speaking consciousness." For this reason, texts always express a point of view or enact particular values. Moreover, because we acquire genres through hearing or reading others' utterances, and because these genres are marked with the voices of those prior contexts, there is *conflict* in this process (Cazden, 1992). In Bakhtin's (1981) words, "[Language] is populated—overpopulated—with the intentions of others. Expropriating it, forcing it to submit to one's own intentions and accents, is a difficult and complicated process" (p. 294).

Thus, learning to read (and write) is learning and creating the various written genres of the culture. That is, children's developing communicative competence consists of their growing abilities to command a repertoire of genres—oral and written (Cazden, 1992; Christie, 1990; Daiute, 1993; Hymes, 1987; Pappas, 1991a, 1993a, 1993b). The view here is that children are capable of this challenge. They are proficient semioticians: They are adept in constructing and assigning meanings in their culture (Halliday, 1975, 1978; Newkirk, 1989; Pappas, 1993b). Consequently, a curriculum must be organized to promote such literate sense-making; it must provide opportunities for students to read and write a range of written genres for a variety of meaningful purposes.

Curriculum Genres: The Importance of Collaborative Teaching Styles in Reading Instruction

During a typical school day, a range of instructional routines are enacted in classrooms through different shifts of social-semiotic relationships. These shifts are encoded in behaviorial patterns, as well as through changing, corresponding linguistic patterns to express these various classroom meanings (Bloome & Bailey, 1992; Bloome & Egan-Robertson, 1993; Green, Kantor, & Rogers, 1991; Santa Barbara Classroom Discourse Group, 1992). Using a term suggested by Christie (1987, 1993), I have called these demarcated event/participant routines *curriculum genres* (Pappas, 1990, 1991b, 1993c, in press). Particular curriculum genres are particular activity structures (i.e., each curriculum genre represents a socially recognizable sequence of actions that realizes particular meanings or purposes for teachers and students in the overall classroom curriculum). Thus, a curriculum genre as an "action genre" is analogous to Bakhtin's (1986) idea of "speech genre," which was discussed in the beginning of the chapter (see also Wells, 1994, for a similar slant on classroom genres).

Believing that knowledge is constructed by learners, teachers in integrated language classrooms constantly struggle to develop curriculum genres that are collaborative in nature. They attempt to build on students' diversity so that reading and writing, and the curriculum in general, are more connected to students' real lives. Making reading and writing more personally meaningful, and making the processes of the formation of literacy powerful for students, is what Willinsky (1990) called the New Literacy. Moreover, this stance means that the literacy activity is turned over to the student learner in important ways. In Willinsky's words:

> The New Literacy programs are intent on altering the meaning of . . . classroom work. . . . [T]he shift involves increasing the students' control over the text and its meaning. But to shift this meaning of literacy also necessarily alters the relationship between teacher and student. The teacher, as an authority of what needs to be known and done, begins to turn over more of this responsibility to the student and to the meaning that comes from somewhere within the student's work with literacy. In these terms, then, the New Literacy proposal is to reshape the *work* of the classroom around a different form of reading and writing. The moral, psychological, and social worth of this literacy begins with the form of literacy in this fashion clearly entails redefining the role the relationship of teacher and student. (p. 7)

Thus, Willinsky has argued that teachers also evaluate the everyday instructional patterns of interactions they have with their students in terms of control, power, and authority.

The teaching–learning relationship promoted here is not one of transmission and reception, which is characteristic of many traditional classrooms, but is realized through collaborative interaction. As such, it also questions an individualistic conception of learning by emphasizing that learning activities take place not within individuals, but in transactions between them (Wells, 1994; Wells & Chang-Wells, 1992). Thus, it reflects a sociocultural theory based on Vygotsky's view of learning, which has been extended by others (Vygotsky, 1962, 1978; see also Moll, 1990; Newman, Griffin, & Cole, 1989; Wertsch, 1985, 1989, 1991). That is, there is a "recognition of the interdependence of individual and society, as each creates and is created by the other" (Wells & Chang-Wells, 1992, p. 29).

From such a perspective, the teaching–learning relationship represents the coconstruction of meaning and knowledge, in which the teacher shares his or her expertise to guide and assist learners in the *zone of proximal development* (i.e., where the teacher responds to learners' own intentions and understandings, but beyond their current level of unaided performance) so that students are empowered to construct new knowledge and manage tasks on their own. As Kreisberg (1992) articulated, power relationships in education are *power with* (not *power over*) so that "[t]he themes of voice, synergy, synergistic community, balance of assertiveness and openness, . . . assertive mutuality, co-agency, integration, dialogue, and shared decision making are expressed in the classroom" (pp. 193–194).

Because most of the processes of school teaching–learning are encoded in language (Cazden, 1986, 1988; Christie, 1987, 1989; Edwards & Mercer, 1987; Lemke, 1985a, 1990; Wells, 1994; Young, 1992), much of the classroom discourse in integrated classrooms is collaborative in nature as well. Thus, this kind of talk is quite different from the talk found in traditional, transmission-oriented classrooms. In the latter, talk is dominated by teacher questions, typically termed *pseudoquestions*—ones for which the teacher already knows the answers (Edwards & Mercer, 1987; Ramirez, 1988; Shuy, 1988; Young, 1992). These questions are frequently embedded in a characteristic initiate-respond-evalute (IRE) talk structure that is controlled by the teacher (Cazden, 1988; Edwards & Mercer, 1987; Lemke, 1990; Sinclair & Coulthard, 1975; Young, 1992). In this IRE pattern, the teacher *initiates* a sequence or interaction by calling a child to respond; the nominated child *responds* to the initiation or question posed by the teacher; finally, the teacher *evaluates* what the child has said before calling on the next child. In integrated language classrooms, teachers try to implement alternatives to IRE patterns. They attempt to develop curriculum genres for teaching reading that realize New Literacy ideas or collaborative interaction, so as to give students more control of their own literacy learning.

THEMATIC UNITS AS A MEANS FOR INTEGRATING READING ACROSS THE CURRICULUM

The use of a thematic unit—a broadly based topic of study that consists of worthwhile and interesting content—is a critical component of an integrated language approach (Pappas et al., 1995). These units enable teachers to allow for and promote authentic language use in the classroom: They provide many opportunities for children to use language for a range of purposes (i.e., to use a range of genres). Students participate in various experiences of their choice to develop the sustained and deliberative attention to particular topics across the curriculum that makes systematic learning possible

(Wells, 1986; Wells & Chang-Wells, 1992). In doing so, they begin to see that various disciplines (e.g., history, economics, and the other areas of the social studies; arithmetic, geometry, and other domains of mathematics; biology, chemistry, physics, and other subject matter of the sciences; etc.) are all different ways of knowing.

Disciplines or content areas represent particular cultural frames (i.e., ways of sense-making), and members participating in these distinctive domains have constructed certain types of vocabulary and discourse (i.e., genres) by which to express their meanings to others involved in the various disciplines (Cope & Kalantzis, 1990; Geertz, 1983; Halliday & Martin, 1993; Lemke, 1990; Martin, 1990; Mousley & Marks, 1991). Thus, thematic units enable students to make and understand these discipline-domain distinctions, but counter the perception that these disciplinary distinctions are delineations. Real-life problems are complex and have to be tackled by drawing on knowledge from many disciplines. The units' central themes provide coherence by emphasizing linkages and identifying relationships among disciplines. Thus, an integrated, interdisciplinary view of knowledge and curriculum shows the particular relevancy of the specific disciplines, and demonstrates to students the strength of each discipline perspective in a connected way (Jacobs, 1989). The organizing center, theme, or "hub" of thematic units promotes this connection, thereby helping children learn the "parts" of the disciplines better. As a result, students get a "metaconceptual bonus—a 'powerful idea,' a cross-cutting idea, a perspective on perspective taking, a dimension of experience" (Ackerman, 1989, p. 29), which is of great educational value.

Because of its emphasis on constructivism, student-directed inquiry is at the core of children's learning in an integrated language perspective (Pappas et al., 1995; Perkins, 1989). The concepts and relationships that span and connect disciplines in thematic units, and provide coherence also offer students a range of topics (i.e., invitations) for in-depth study. This means that, although the focus of this book is on reading instruction, reading in an integrated language perspective cannot be conceived of as an isolated process or activity, an end in and of itself, but as one of the important tools and means to support such inquiry and learning. Thus, when children learn to read or use written texts across the curriculum in thematic units, they acquire the conventions of the various genres related to the different "ways of knowing" of particular disciplines.

An Example: A JOURNEYS Thematic Unit

The instructional reading approach of the integrated language perspective is best illustrated by showing how it is implemented in a particular thematic unit. The examples provided here are drawn from a thematic prototype for a second- and third-grade family grouping (Pappas et al., 1995). The unit, entitled "JOURNEYS THROUGH TIME AND SPACE," was developed to meet several needs and interests that the teacher, Dehea Munioz, saw in her school and classroom. First, a brief descriptive brush stroke of the unit is presented. Second, a more in-depth look is taken at two particular curriculum genres, which have been chosen to portray the collaborative nature of reading instruction employed. These are typical of the ways in which the teacher has turned over responsibility and meaning in literacy to the students in her instruction (Willinsky, 1990).

Dehea had several purposes for developing the JOURNEYS unit. First, because she has been a cross-cultural traveler, Dehea wanted her students to learn to see themselves as world citizens, interested in cross-cultural travel and welcoming people from different backgrounds. In addition, she wanted to exploit that many of her students had already moved a number of times: Some were recent immigrants from Southeast Asia; others had lived in several regions of the United States, or simply moved about in their own community. Thus, journeys were part of their lives.

Second, Dehea knew from parent conferences and children's comments that many of her students had experienced hostility because of their cultural differences. Consequently, she believed that the journeys theme would allow her—at the early elementary level—to work on the process of developing a multicultural/cross-cultural perspective, which was a school goal and a real issue for her students. (The school housed a "magnet" program that emphasized cross-cultural and multiculural studies, and drew students from all over the city and from various sociocultural and economic backgrounds.)

Finally, when she examined the school's curriculum guide, Dehea noted that the science curriculum required her to deal with certain aspects of physical and biological science; the social studies curriculum called for a study of neighborhoods and communities of the past and present, with an emphasis on human interaction with the environment. She was sure she could easily incorporate these topics into her JOURNEYS unit (see Fig. 12.1 for the WEB of the unit, which lists and organizes book resources, as well as potential activities and inquiries for her students).

Dehea thought about and planned for most of the books and many of the activities beforehand, but several additions and modifications were made by the children during the course of the unit. As Fig. 12.1 illustrates, the JOURNEYS unit includes a few major areas (e.g., Human Journeys, Imaginary Journeys, and Nature's Journeys), as well as many subthemes. For example, the larger topic of Human Journeys incorporates "Immigration to North America," "Historic Journeys in the United States," "Journeys Toward Growth and Understanding," and so forth. The larger topic of Nature Journeys has four types of "migrations" to explore—"Plant," "Animal," "Astronomical," and "Geological." There are also other subthemes to study—"Language Travels,"

Immigration to North America

THE LAND I LOST
ELLIS ISLAND: LAND OF HOPE
ELLIS ISLAND: LAND OF HOPE
HECTOR LIVES IN THE UNITED STATES NOW
THE LONG WAY TO A NEW LAND
IMMIGRANT GIRL
MY GRANDMOTHER'S JOURNEY
ALL THE LIGHTS IN THE NIGHT
A PEDDLER'S DREAM
WATCH THE STARS COME OUT
MAKING A NEW HOME IN AMERICA
I HATE ENGLISH
TO BE A SLAVE
HOW MANY DAYS TO AMERICA?
A BOOK OF AMERICANS
IMMIGRANT KIDS
WHEN AFRICA WAS HOME
HELLO, MY NAME IS SCRAMBLED EGGS
EMMA'S DRAGON HUNT
GRAB HANDS AND RUN
HOANG ANH: A VIETNAMESE-AMERICAN BOY

Survey: Why do people move?
Chart: Places class members have lived or visited.
Use a variety of maps to locate foreign place-names
used in the United States
Storyteller: Stories with African roots
Interview new immigrants:
What brought you here?
What is most strange in new country?
What is most missed from old country?
Comparison Chart*: Different immigrant groups and
why they came.
Discuss difference between voluntary and involuntary
Immigration.
Have a multicultural fair: Share what has been learned
about the people who come to America and the
native peoples who lived here first. Make and share
ethnic foods, art, crafts, dance and music.

Journeys Toward Growth and Understanding

GRANDPA'S FACE
NATHANIEL TALKING
MARIA TERESA
TURTLE KNOWS YOUR NAME
HOW DOES IT FEEL TO GROW OLD?
UNDER THE SUNDAY TREE
ALL THE COLORS OF THE RACE
THE CROSSROADS
NOT SO FAST, SONGOLOLO
YOUNG MARTIN'S PROMISE
VIVA MEXICO
AMAZING GRACE
WORKING COTTON
MIRETTE ON THE HIGH WIRE

K-W-L*: What is a journey?
Interview: people of different ages
What is the best thing about being your age?
What can you do now that you couldn't do before?
What would you like to do that you can't do easily at this age?
Classroom meetings: Plan for the class's progress on theme, deal
with interpersonal and management issues.
Current events time. Discuss current issues that concern children.
Display news items, pictures, etc. about current issues.
Write letters of concern about issues of importance.
Compare different kinds of work in community and in other parts
of the world (i.e., Crossroads).
What kinds of work require travel? Begin bulletin board to display
student findings.
Read biographies and compare types of personal journeys.
Make collage of things important to own journeys.
Make a life line showing important things you have learned to do
and some challenges you have faced over time.

Getting There

FREIGHT TRAIN
ROUND TRIP
AIRPORT
BICYCLE MAN
LIFE ON A BARGE
THE ERIE CANAL
INCREDIBLE CROSS-SECTIONS
HOT AIR HENRY
SCHOOL BUS
FLYING
JONATHAN AND HIS MOMMY
FILL IT UP
THE WAY THINGS WORK
THE SECRET LIFE OF HARDWARE
TRUCKER
TRUCK SONG
CARS AND HOW THEY GO

Mechanical connections. Study how simple and
compound machines used for household gadgets and
tools work. Chart the national origins and organize by
continent or region.
How would the history of the world be different if air
travel (or cars, etc.) did not exist?
Design a new way to travel, using what you know about
simple and compound machines. Make a cross section
of your invention.
Read maps to plot routes around the community.
Take a "Jonathan and Mommy" walk.
Use maps to plan a field trip.
Follow maps to explore the school or neighborhood.
Take a trip on a bus, train, or boat.
Design paper airplanes that can glide, do loops, etc.
Do clay boats activity: Design boat that can carry the
most cargo.
How much travel do you do in one day?
Categorize and chart types and purposes for travel.
Visit airport or other transporation center.
Make model city. Plan for transporation, as well as
other services. What would make your city a good
place to visit?
Make a collage of different ways to travel.
Goods travel, too. Make a list of all the places your
clothes came from (check tags).
The world in a chocolate bar. Where do all the
ingredients in a candy bar come from? Locate on map.

HUMAN JOURNEYS

IMAGINERY JOURNEYS

Migrations of First Peoples

THE PEOPLE SHALL CONTINUE
THE GIRL WHO LOVED WILD HORSES
THE MUD PONY
BABY RATTLESNAKE
KEEPERS OF THE EARTH
KEEPERS OF THE ANIMALS

Map movement of native people from your area.
Video: section of Scott Momaday on Onondaga Nation.
Discuss: Why do the people of the Six Nations call themselves a separate nation?
Mural comparing life in three different nations.
Compare Native American journey stories with those from other cultures.

Historic Journeys in the United States

ARMINTA'S PAINT BOX
AURORA MEANS DAWN
AUNT HARRIET'S UNDERGROUND RAILROAD IN THE SKY
CASSIES JOURNEY
DEATH OF THE IRON HORSE
JOSHUA'S WESTWARD JOURNAL
THE JOSEPHINA QUILT STORY
FOLLOW THE DRINKING GOURD
DAKOTA DUGOUT
SARAH, PLAIN AND TALL
JOURNEY CAKE, HO

Visit a historic site. Use trip book to collect data on life at that site, why people came there.
People moving in the past:
Make time line of U.S. migrations.
If you were going west, what would you most want to take with you? If you were Native American, what would you want to say to these new people?
What if . . . ? activity:
What if Native Americans and European Americans had settled their differences peacefully?
Classroom museum: Create displays that show historic journeys.
Plan a frontier community: Give students picture map of area. What resources can you use? What kind of job will you need in your town? Make an ad for your town to attract new people.
Make a model of a Native American community (select group from your area, or near neighbor). Show how people used the natural resources.

Magical and Fantasic Journeys

THE WRETCHED STONE
THE MYSTERIES OF HARRISON BURDOCK
POSSUM MAGIC
MIRANDY AND BROTHER WIND
JUNE 29, 1999
ALADDIN AND THE ENCHANTED LAMP
THE FOOL OF THE WORLD AND THE FLYING SHIP
THE MAGIC HORSE
AIRMAIL TO THE MOON
ANNO'S JOURNEY
TRAVELING TO TONDO
SHEEP ON A SHIP
THE TREK
MOLASSES FLOOD
WHERE THE WILD THINGS ARE

Make a list of magical elements in stories.
Make a museum of literary quests.
Compare quests in book with those in popular children's films.
Write "What happened next . . ." after reading one of the magical journey stories.
Using Possum Magic as a model, write a version for another culture.
Make a collection of time travel books.
What foods would you eat and where would you go?
Draw a picture of a time you would like to visit. Who would you be? What would you like to do? Find out as much as you can about the time you have selected and share your findings with class.
"When are you?" Identify time clues in pictures.

Journeys in Traditional Literature

WHEN SCHLEMIEL WHEN TO WARSAW
EAST OF THE SUN AND WEST OF THE MOON
ANANSI THE SPIDER
THREE JOVIAL HUNTSMEN
THE PEOPLE COULD FLY
GREEK MYTHS
SUNDIATA
HER SEVEN BROTHERS
TAM LIN
SUN
FLIGHT
LEGENDS OF JOURNEYS
THE THREE BEARS AND 15 OTHER STORIES

Locate culture of origin for each story and mark on world map.
Make a story map based on one of the literary journeys.
Compile a list of travelers and their reasons for travel.
Display*: When . . . travels, it is because . . . Study illustrations. What do they tell about the time and place in the story?
Create a cartoon strip of a journey tale.
Write: If I were a story traveler . . .
Put on the Interact musical version of Goldilocks.

FIG. 12.1. (Continued)

293

Journeys in Art, Music, and Movement

I SPY
LINNEA IN MONET'S GARDEN
DRAWING FROM NATURE: DRAWING LIFE IN MOTION
THE TURN ABOUT, THINK ABOUT, LOOK ABOUT BOOK
WALK TOGETHER CHILDREN: BLACK AMERICAN SPIRITUALS
A VERY YOUNG DANCER

Use *The Turn About . . .* book, and create own turn about pictures.
Analyze art: How do artists get their work to "move"? Use art in children's books, as well as that of other visual artists. Look at art from all over the world.
Make art that moves. Try making mobiles, using line alone to imply motion.
Listen to journey music (e.g., "Four Seasons," "The Moldau," "Grand Canyon Suite," "Peter and the Wolf"). What makes the music "journey"?
Collect sounds of movement. Use tape recorders and record sounds of movement (footsteps, cars, wind blowing, etc.).
Make a symphony of natural movement sounds.
Make a mural of a journey using techniques studied in other artists' work.
Put "journey" poetry to music, or do Choral Readings*.
Listen to recordings of different types of vocal music. What types of journeys are found in songs?
Turn a journey story or poem into dance.
Learn movement that will make you healthier. Plan a fitness journey.
Make a fitness path on the school grounds or plan an obstacle course in the gym.

Out-of-this-World Journeys

FLYING TO THE MOON AND OTHER STRANGE PLACES
FIRST TRAVEL GUIDE TO THE MOON
MY TRIP TO ALPHA I
THE FORGOTTEN DOOR
THE SNOW QUEEN
THE SEARCH FOR DELICIOUS
PETER PAN
JUNE 29, 1999

Create a cross-cultural space colony.
How many miles? Find out how many miles it is to different parts of the solar system. Place these "astronomical" numbers on large strips of paper around the room.
Make a time line of space travel.
Plan for the future. What should NASA tackle next? Write to NASA to find out what their plans are.
Write stories about future space journeys.
Study alternative worlds in literature. What do they have in common?
Which might you want to visit?
Dramatize scenes from favorite fantasies.
Make a literature guide for fantasy. What are the characteristics of different types of fantasy? How are journeys used in these books?

Language Travels

TALK ABOUT ENGLISH
BEN'S TRUMPET
TAKE MY WORD FOR IT
MARMS IN THE MARMALADE

Collect words from other languages that have become part of English.
On world map, place names on their country of origin.
Collect slang words and regional variations, and make a dictionary of slang or regionalisms. Where did these words come from? Why don't they stay around very long? Make a Graffiti Wall* to collect new words as they are found.
Collect language used for specific activities: athletics, music, etc.
Study the "language" of art and music: How have sounds and images journeyed around the world?
Collect travel words, and put on Graffiti Wall*.

Numerical Journeys

ANNO'S COUNTING HOUSE
WORLD OF WONDERS: A TRIP THROUGH NUMBERS
MAPS AND GLOBES

Work the problems in Anno's Counting House.
Create a different journey with number problems.
Present children with a mathematical quest. Follow math clues to complete quest.
Work on reading astronomical numbers.
Cooking math.
How numbers grow: addition and multiplication.
Are we there yet? Calculating mileage on maps.

Geological Migrations

ROCKS AND MINERALS
VOLCANO
VILLAGE OF ROUND AND SQUARE HOUSES
HOW TO DIG A HOLE TO THE OTHER SIDE OF THE EARTH
FOLLOW THE WATER BROOK TO OCEAN
WATER'S WAY
THE MAGIC SCHOOL BUS AT THE WATERWORKS

Field trip to stream/creek. Find evidence that rocks and soil have moved. Take photos for exhibit.
Use sand table to observe erosion by wind and water.
Make mural of cause and effect: How volcano, earthquake, water change how the earth looks.
Walking trip to collect evidence that earth and rock have moved or been moved.
Class book: *Earth Movers.*
Use globe to look for evidence of continental shifts.
How does the earth's movement change people's lives? Small group report.
Field trip to water treatment plant.

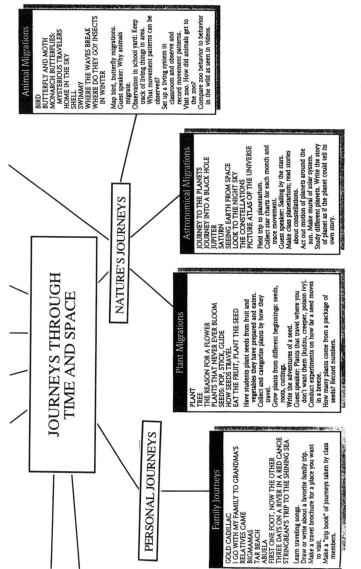

JOURNEYS THROUGH TIME AND SPACE

NATURE'S JOURNEYS

PERSONAL JOURNEYS

Animal Migrations

BIRD
BUTTERFLY AND MOTH
MONARCH BUTTERFLIES:
    MYSTERIOUS TRAVELERS
HOME IN THE SKY
SHELL
SWIMMY
WHERE THE WAVES BREAK
WHERE DO THEY GO? INSECTS
    IN WINTER

Map bird, butterfly migrations.
Guest speaker: Why animals
    migrate.
Observation in school yard: Keep
    track of living things in area.
    What movement patterns can be
    observed?
Set up a living system in
    classroom and observe and
    record movement patterns.
Visit zoo. How did animals get to
    the zoo?
Compare zoo behavior to behavior
    in the wild as seen in videos.

Astronomical Migrations

JOURNEY TO THE PLANETS
JOURNEY INTO A BLACK HOLE
JUPITER
SATURN
SEEING EARTH FROM SPACE
LOOK TO THE NIGHT SKY
THE CONSTELLATIONS
PICTURE ATLAS OF THE UNIVERSE

Field trip to planetarium.
Collect star charts for each month and
    trace movement.
Guest speaker: Sailing by the stars.
Make class planetarium; read stories
    about constellations.
Act out motion of planets around the
    sun. Make mural of solar system.
Study different planets. Write the story
    of planet as if the planet could tell its
    own story.

Plant Migrations

PLANT
TREE
THE REASON FOR A FLOWER
PLANTS THAT NEVER EVER BLOOM
SEEDS: POP, STICK, GLIDE
EAT THE FRUIT, PLANT THE SEED

Have students plant seeds from fruit and
    vegetables they have prepared and eaten.
Collect and categorize plants by how they
    travel.
Grow plants from different beginnings: seeds,
    roots, cuttings.
Write the adventures of a seed.
Guest speaker: Plants that travel where you
    don't want them (kudzu, creeper, poison ivy).
Conduct experiments on how far a seed moves
    in a breeze.
How many plants come from a package of
    seeds? Record numbers.

Family Journeys

GOLD CADILLAC
I GO WITH MY FAMILY TO GRANDMA'S
RELATIVES CAME
BIGMAMAS
TAR BEACH
ABUELA
FIRST ONE FOOT, NOW THE OTHER
THREE DAYS ON A RIVER IN A RED CANOE
STRINGBEAN'S TRIP TO THE SHINING SEA

Learn traveling songs.
Draw or write about a favorite family trip.
Make a travel brochure for a place you want
    to visit.
Make a "trip book" of journeys taken by class
    members.

FIG. 12.1. Dehea Munioz's second/third grade JOURNEYS thematic unit. From Pappas, Kiefer, and Levstik (1995). Reprinted with permission of Longman Publishers.

"Numerical Journeys," "Journeys in Art, Music, and Movement," and so on. Thus, a review of Fig. 12.1 shows that Dehea provided books from a range of genres to support a variety of invitations or choices for inquiry within and across disciplines. In doing so, Dehea enabled her students many opportunities to use and integrate reading with writing (and speaking and listening, too).

Dehea organized the school day to support this integration and inquiry: She provided ample time slots for whole-class, small-group, and individual work (see Table 12.1 for her weekly schedule; Pappas et al., 1995).

This chapter focuses on two curriculum genres enacted during the first day of the unit (see Pappas et al., 1995, for more details about the unit). The first curriculum genre, Literature Circle (sometimes called Response Group), occurred around 10:45 a.m. as part of the morning Integrated Work Time. The second curriculum genre, Teacher-Led Reading Aloud, happened twice in the afternoon, first as part of Book Sharing at 1:00 p.m. and then later at 2:45 p.m., the period right before dismissal.

Before and after these two curriculum genres, several activities and experiences during this first day helped launch many ideas and topics related to the journeys theme. For example, during the Group Time at 8:10 a.m., Dehea called the children to a center where a terrarium containing a coccoon

TABLE 12.1
Weekly Schedule, Dehea Munioz's
Second/Third Grade Family-Grouped Class

Time	Monday	Tuesday	Wednesday	Thursday	Friday
7:30	Teacher preparation time.				
8:00	Children arrive, put away coats, prepare lunch count, and take attendnce.				
8:10	Group time. Initiating activity—sets stage for individual and small-group activities for the day. Plans for the day are discussed.				
8:30	Physical education	Art	Health	Music	Library
9:30	Recess				
9:45	Integrated work time. Children work in small groups or individually. Teacher works with small groups or has individual conferences. Time flexible.				
11:15	Math				
12:00	Lunch and outdoor play.				
1:00	Book sharing. Teacher reads a book aloud. Several children talk about the books they have been reading.				
1:30	Integrated work time. Children continue work time, or teacher works with whole class.				
2:15	Group sharing. Children report on their group work. Teacher may conduct lesson on relevant topics.				
2:45	Read Aloud* or SSR*. Teacher reads aloud or everyone engages in SSR*.				
3:00	Cleanup and dismissal.				

Note. From Pappas, Kiefer, and Levstik (1995). Reprinted with permission of Longman Publishers.

on a leafy branch had been placed, along with books (mostly informational ones) and activity cards (open-ended questions on butterflies and moths). She asked the children to describe what they observed in the terrarium as she recorded their comments on chart paper under the heading of "Observations." She sometimes stopped to further clarify whether a child's response was really an observation (something we can test with our senses) or an inference (something we think our observations mean), listing those latter ideas under "Inferences."

During Physical Education period, her students also engaged in movement and music experiences related to the journeys theme. At the beginning of the morning Integrated Work Time, right before Literature Circle, she had the children brainstorm their ideas of JOURNEYS, as she wrote them down on a class WEB. She also asked questions to point them in other directions: journeys they have taken that may have changed them; journeys that were fun; journeys that moved them to another place to live. Moreover, she asked if they knew people who go on many journeys or who might have interesting stories to tell. She reminded them that they could add to the WEB as new ideas came up. Here is where she explained more specifically that the unit would involve activities connected to journeys, and would help them think about journeys in new ways. She summarized some of these activities and introduced several of the books with the journeys theme. Then after Literature Circle, students calculated various distances in the classroom and school, and from school and home during Math Time; in the afternoon Intergrated Work Time, between the two Read-Aloud sessions, children in small groups investigated place names in different regions of the United States, and related them to where they came from in various countries in the world.

Thus, the two curriculum genres to be considered next were embedded within an already intellectually rich curricular context, which would lead to even more meaningful and worthwhile inquiry on a variety of topics around the JOURNEYS theme. Literature Circle is a student-led curriculum genre where students in small groups discuss the literature they have read. In contrast, Teacher-Led Reading Aloud is a whole-class curriculum genre where the teacher reads to, and discusses with, students various books on the journeys theme. Both examples described here rely on the "Human Journeys" macrotheme depicted in Fig. 12.1, which is also the area in which Dehea planned her own teacher research during the unit.

Dehea was interested in several issues. First, she wanted to know more about the impact of "culturally conscious" books (i.e., literature that speaks from inside a culture, not just about a culture) on her students. Consequently, she planned to study how these texts affected her students by analyzing their response journals and classroom discussions. Second, Dehea decided to look at the impact of planned reflection based on multiple exposures to different cultures. She believed that children needed to reflect on what they had experienced, and they needed enough experience—more than one, simple exposure—to appreciate both cultural universals (i.e., elements of culture common to all people and nations, such as food, language, arts, recreation, beliefs, etc.) and cultural differences (i.e., the variety of manners, myths, and customs that develop around cultural universals). She felt that the response journals and classroom discussions would also help her understand how her students' reflections might change as they had regular cross-cultural/multicultural experiences.

In addition, she chose to focus more carefully on five children by monitoring their responses, both in their journals and in other written and oral work. The five children she selected, three boys and two girls, appeared to be having difficulty with cultural differences. Two were children whose parents had expressed their concern to Dehea regarding intolerance directed at their children in the community. The other three were children who seemed to have a tendency to stereotype in many of their cross-cultural/multicultural interactions. Thus, Dehea thought that in-depth cases studies of their reactions across time would also provide useful evidence of the impact of the thematic unit's cross-cultural/multicultural component.

Literature Circle Curriculum Genre. Dehea grouped sets of books around several themes (again, refer to Fig. 12.1)—"Out-of-This-World Journeys," "Magical and Fantastic Journeys," "Getting There," and "Journeys Toward Growth and Understanding." On the first day of the unit, as part of the first Integrated Work Time and after she and her students covered the unit's overview and developed a class WEB, she briefly explained the basic theme of each group of books, and then asked for volunteers for each. During the unit, students were to read most of these books. Dehea planned to monitor and study her students' responses to the books from the "Journeys Toward Growth and Understanding" set as part of her teacher research.

Students looked through the book selections, and then each chose one to read silently. She asked children to work together in groups of three or four. When they were finished with their books, they were to take turns telling each other about the books. As each person spoke, children were asked to think about how their books were similar and different. Based on this discussion, the students were to construct categories for a comparison chart (see Pappas et al., 1995, for a description of this type of activity). This small-group work constituted an enactment of what this classroom called Literature Circle. They did not always read different books and then tell about them, nor did they always end up extending the discussion by creating a comparison chart as a group product. However, students became accustomed to this routine's fundamental purpose and interactional pattern— namely, to share and analyze together in a small group their interpretations of the books they read.

Three children who volunteered to read books from the "Journeys Toward Growth and Understanding" are our focus here. Latoya and Joseph, two second-grade African-American students, read *Working Cotton* (Williams, 1992) and *At the Crossroads* (Isadora, 1991), respectively. Trans, a Vietnamese-American third grader, read *Not So Fast Songololo* (Daly, 1985). When they finished reading their books (during Sustained Silent Reading [SSR], another frequent curriculum genre in integrated language classrooms), they found a corner table to begin their discussion. They had already written down some responses to their books in their Learning Logs (see Pappas et al., 1995, for information about this type of journal) before they sat down to meet.

Latoya volunteered to tell about her story first. She told Joseph and Trans that it was about a little girl, Selan, who went with her family early in the morning on a bus to a cotton field, and how the family—Mamma, Daddy, two older sisters, Ruise and Jesmarie, and the baby-sister, Leanne—spent the whole day picking the cotton. Latoya, flipping through the book to identify the names of the family members, had trouble with how to pronounce Selan and Ruise. Latoya turned the book around, pointing to the names in the text, and asked, "How do you think we should say these names?" Trans and Joseph took a look and together agreed on how to say them. Then, Latoya returned to her retelling of the book. She told how the story is centered around Selan helping her mother by picking cotton for her mother to put in her sack. Selan wishes she could either be with her mother and the baby or have her own sack like her older sisters. The family eats lunch in the field, and then at evening, when it is amost dark, they go back on the bus.

Layota said, "I had two favorite parts. I liked the part where it talked about how fast her daddy picked the cotton—here let me read it 'cause it's short." As Latoya read that page, Trans tried to see if he could "pick" cotton like the father. Joseph and Latoya both laughed because Trans' "picking" efforts seemed very jerky, rather than the book's description of "smooth and fast." "The second part I liked," Latoya continued, "was towards the end when her daddy found a cotton flower, which he said was to bring them luck." Joseph then asked if Latoya liked the whole book. She said that she did, and thought she'd like to work with her family like Selan, but wasn't sure she wanted to do it every day because it looked like lots of hard work, and Selan had no time to play with the other kids in the field.

Then Joseph told about his book, *At the Crossroads*. "This is about some kids from Africa, I think, who are waiting for their fathers who have been away for a long time working in the mines. They wait and wait at the crossroads and finally the fathers come home early in the morning." Joseph added that, "That's the part I liked best because they were so happy they played music and sang as they marched home."

At this point, Dehea, who had earlier placed a tape recorder with the group (the students were quite used to having part of classroom talk taped by Dehea), stopped by to check the tape in the recorder, to see how things were going in the group, and to remind them to note down how the books seemed similar so they could come up with their comparison chart categories. Joseph asked, "Should we begin to do this after the second book, or should we wait till Trans tells about his book?" Dehea told them that either would be okay, and that they could decide that on their own as she moved to monitor how another Literature Circle group was progressing.

Trans turned to Latoya and Joseph, and asked what they should do. Latoya thought they should begin talking about possible similarities after Joseph was done, and then add or change things after Trans reported. The other two agreed, and Joseph quickly finished his turn by telling about how the book was about how really happy the kids were because their dads are coming home, how they got ready for it by making music instruments out of stuff they found around their places, and how everybody in the town joined in by singing and dancing. "Okay," said Joseph, "Now, what are things that are alike in the two books?" Within a short time, they agreed that both had to do with families, that the characters were all Black people. "What else?" Joseph asked. "Well," Trans remarked, "I haven't gotten to tell my story yet, but my book had those things, too. I wonder if we should also have a 'setting' category, but I don't know where my story happened cause there is a different word used for money." Trans looked through the book, found the spot, and read, " 'How much are those red tackies in the window?' asks Gogo. 'Four rands,' the man replies." "Are 'rands' like 'dollars'?" Joseph asked. "We might have to ask Ms. Munioz to see if she knows where this took place or how we could find out." Latoya, looking at the page Trans just read, also brought up, "What are 'tackies'—his red sneakers?" Trans nodded affirmatively, and then noted that he thought that the spelling of "tryes" on a car on that page also was not like how we spell it. That might be a clue to where the setting is. "You know," said Trans, "maybe we could make a category on different or odd words—or names—'cause the kid in this book has a funny name—'Songololo.' "

The group decided to consider that after Trans had his turn. He told that his book was about this boy, whose name is Shepard, but is called Songololo by his granny, and his trip to the city with his granny, who is named Gogo. Trans related how Shepard helped Gogo, who is old and has to use a cane to walk, cross the streets, and how at the end she buys him new shoes—tackies. Trans reported that that was his favorite part of the book because Shepard had really wanted those new shoes. Then they reviewed the three books to find interesting words/names. They agreed on the names Zola, Sipho, and Nomsa from the *Crossroads* book, and Latoya suggested that they could put down some of the "Black talk" in the *Cotton* book. "This author used talk like mine—see this 'be' here in 'Sometime I still be sleep' on this first page." Because such wording was not in the other books, they agreed to put that down in the category. Latoya also thought that some of the names might be added—"I've never heard of the names Ruise, Selan, and Jesmarie, have you?"

They finished their work by noting what they decided on—they also included a category of favorite parts—and chose Trans to report their work to the teacher because he had to ask for her help on his book's setting. After getting feedback from Dehea, this group planned to meet the next day during Integrated Work Time to create their comparison chart.

Teacher-Led Reading-Aloud Curriculum Genre. As already indicated, Dehea scheduled two Teacher-Led Reading-Aloud sessions each day (see Table 12.1). At 1:00 p.m., right after lunch and outdoor play, Book Sharing occurred, the first part of which was where Dehea read aloud to the whole class. After her reading, students volunteered sharing other books they were reading, including books they wrote themselves. Thus, the Reading-Aloud Curriculum Genre was part of the larger Book Sharing Curriculum Genre.

The other reading-aloud session was the fifteen minutes at the end of the day. Actually, instead of Dehea reading aloud, this period could also be a period of SSR. Dehea's reading aloud was especially frequent in the beginning weeks of the unit (or at other times when she wanted to initiate new topics or subthemes during the unit). She read aloud more so she could introduce the range of books and genres that would be available for her students to read, and also to inform them as to the kinds of inquiry that would be possible for them to pursue. As children made their own choices and began to read more to support their individual and small-group inquiries, this period became their own time to read.

During the first Teacher-Led Reading-Aloud session on the first day of the unit, Dehea read the short introduction and the first story from *The Land I Lost* (a chapter book found under "Immigration to North America"—see Fig. 12.1; Nhuong, 1982). As the introduction explained, these are autobiographical stories that Nhuong wrote based on his memories of growing up in a small hamlet in the central highlands of Vietnam before the war. Dehea taped this session because the discussion around this and other books in the unit was part of her study of her curriculuar emphasis to develop cross-cultural/multicultural understandings in her students.

Although the discussions in this curriculum genre were "teacher-led," Dehea worked hard to make her reading-aloud sessions collaborative. She looked up periodically to see if her students wanted to offer a comment or question. She and her students had previously set up a rule that it was not necessary to raise their hands to speak during read-aloud time unless it seemed that more than one person wanted to speak at the same time. At that time, they raised their hands, and then Dehea acknowledged them and indicated the order of their turns.

Thus, this kind of interaction was quite different from many traditional classrooms, where the classroom discourse is characterized by the strict teacher-dominated IRE talk structure described in the preceding section. The aim in such an IRE structure is to treat a text solely as a series of bits of information to be correctly recalled by children, and to have them dutifully conform to the teacher's agenda, with little opportunity to express their own reactions to the text (Oyler, 1993; Wells & Chang-Wells, 1992; see also Dickinson & Smith, 1994; Martinez & Teale, 1993, for recent reviews and accounts of studies on book reading in classrooms.)

Thus, Dehea's classroom talk in the Teacher-Led Reading-Aloud Curriculum Genre reflected an alternative to these IRE patterns. She fostered student initiations—places where students interrupted her reading or initiated discussion to give their reactions to what had been read. Consequently, as Dehea read the first story, "Tank, the Water Buffalo," from the book, children were very interested in Tank and offered many comments about him, such as "He roars like a lion I bet" and "I think he's called Tank 'cause he is as big as a tank." When the text recounted a day when a young bull from a nearby hamlet enters Tanks's territory and challenges his authority, children stopped Dehea's reading to suggest predictions as to what was going to happen. One child said, "Ah oh, there's going to be fight." Another responded to him by proposing, "Maybe he'll just roar at him and shoo him away." This was also an instance of cross-discussion (Lemke, 1990), where students talked directly to each other without teacher mediation, which is another feature of the kind of collaborative talk that occurred when Dehea read aloud. Because Dehea validated these predictions by telling her students that "these are all good ideas—let's see what's going to happen," she further encouraged their future motivation to share their transactions with texts with their classmates.

Dehea loved these student-initiated transactions to the book because she was interested in understanding her students' understandings. She believed that they provided some of the best evidence to assess children's responses to the ideas in the book and the concepts to be examined and studied in the thematic unit. However, this does not mean that she failed to ask her own questions or offer her own ideas as another participant in this grand conversation about the book (Eeds & Wells, 1989). She asked questions of clarification or justification (i.e., asking children to rephrase or elaborate on their comments that might be unclear or ambiguous), she offered predictions of her own or other comments aside from those introduced by her students, and she answered questions children posed but could not seem to answer themselves.

She also asked questions about the text that her students might not have considered on their own. For example, because there is an educational goal in the unit to study the topic of human interaction with the environment, after this first story was read and all of her students offered their own questions and comments about it, Dehea asked children to relate what they had learned so far about what life was like in this small hamlet near the jungle in Vietnam. Children talked about how "it rained a lot for part of the time," that "they really lived with animals, much more so than just having pets," and that "they hunted a lot for food because they didn't have shops nearby." Because they did not mention it, Dehea asked them, "Do you remember about their houses? I thought they were interesting." At this prompt, children talked about the houses being bamboo with roofs made of coconut leaves, and there was an extended discussion of the need for the trenches around their houses and the movable "monkey bridges" that they pulled up at night to keep them safe.

At the end of the read-aloud discussion, Dehea told the children that there were several copies of this book available if they wanted to finish reading for their inquiries. This discussion also provided an opportunity to tell them that a student's parents would be coming to class to talk about their childhoods in Vietnam (i.e., Trans' parents). Because of the many Vietnamese immigrants living in the community, this is a culture with whom the children can have multiple contacts, which are mediated by discussion and further study.

As already noted, there was a second enactment of the Teacher-Led Reading-Aloud Curriculum Genre on this first day of the unit. Here Dehea read *I Hate English!* (Levine, 1989), another book listed under "Immigration to North America" in Fig. 12.1. This picture storybook concerns a young girl, Mei Mei, who is a recent immigrant to New York's Chinatown from Hong Kong. At her school, everything is in English. Although she can understand much of what she hears there, she refuses to speak it. Finally, due to the efforts of an English as Second Language (ESL) teacher, Mei Mei overcomes her negative feelings about English.

The children were uncommonly quiet during the reading of the book, but a vigorous discussion ensued after the reading was done and Dehea asked the students, "What do you think?" Most of the children's comments indicated empathy for Mei Mei, especially when the story related that she was afraid she might lose something if she spoke in English instead of Chinese, her native language. One of the boys (Joseph from the Literature Circle) asked two of the Latina girls in the classroom, Sonia and Maria, who had come to the United States from Mexico during their kindergarten year and who were bilingual speakers, if they felt like Mei Mei when they began to learn English. Sonia nodded affirmatively, but said it was only for a short time. Maria indicated that, "I didn't feel that way at all 'cause I came to live here with my cousins and they could already speak English. I wanted so much to be able to play with them that I really tried hard to learn it." Dehea responded that she thought it was interesting that Sonia and Maria had different feelings about this. She suggested that this might be a good inquiry for the class to do as part of the unit—surveying family, friends, and even other kids or teachers in other classes who speak English as a second language to find out how it was for them. Because most of the students seemed to like the idea, and the school bell for the end of the day had rung, Dehea said that they would make more definite decisions about it the next day.

Summary

Only a "glimmer" of the kinds of reading instruction in an integrated-language perspective can be covered in this chapter. Obviously, the JOURNEYS thematic unit provided many more reading activities and experiences for students than the two curriculum genres highlighted here, which were chosen to emphasize the collaborative nature of reading instruction in the perspective. This does not mean that all of these other reading experiences are so collaborative. For example, Dehea had frequent, short minilessons (another curriculum genre), where she was more directive in teaching some reading strategy that she saw her students needed, or when she guided them to learn how to be responsible in small-group work or learn how to share and analyze texts as part of their inquiries in the unit. The "results" of these teacher-directed reading activities were seen in the Literature Circle example provided. The children applied a strategy to decide on a reasonable placeholder for names they have trouble decoding or pronouncing. They also showed that they knew how to take turns in retelling books and sharing what they liked about these books in small groups, as well as how to study texts for similarities and differences to construct comparison charts.

In addition, the examples here involve students reading mostly narrative texts/genres, and they mostly center on social studies content. However, a review of the WEB in Fig. 12.1 and the brief description of the rest of the first day in the beginning of this section indicate that students would also be reading texts from a range of genres as part of their inquiries in other curricular areas. For example, science content was a focus in subsequent days as a follow-up to their introductory observations/inferences regarding the cocoon in the terrarium, and students read lots of information books on butterflies and moths to study these animals' "journeys" of migration. Moreover, many students who were intrigued by the animals mentioned in *The Land I Lost* read aloud (e.g., wild hogs, horse snakes, otters, eels, and other water creatures) decided to find out more about them by reading many informational texts on them. In other words, reading a variety of genres in the JOURNEYS unit occurred across the curriculum.

NEW RESEARCH DIRECTIONS:
UNDERSTANDING GENRES IN A DIVERSE SOCIETY

As indicated at the onset of this chapter, the integrated language perspective relies on three principles about learners, language, and knowledge. Drawing on these principles, two major interrelated threads, both having to do with genre, have been woven throughout this chapter on reading instruction, and both suggest opportunities for future research regarding reading instruction in the perspective.

The first thread emphasized that children need to read a range of written genres to develop communicative competence. Using thematic units, teachers like Dehea assemble a variety of good children's literature to support student-initiated inquiry around worthwhile content or themes that span and connect the curricular disciplines, and thereby make this learning possible. One important research trend would be to investigate more specifically students' literacy development in such an integrated sense-making enterprise. That is, how do children learn to understand written genres—an overarching goal of reading instruction—by using these diverse texts for reflective, in-depth inquiry on a range of topics? This involves documenting the kinds of intertextuality—the juxtaposing of texts (oral and written) that are socially constructed by students and the teacher (Bloome & Bailey, 1992; Bloome & Egan-Robertson, 1993; Lemke 1985b; Santa Barbara Classroom Discourse Group, 1992)—to be found within and between enactments of various curriculum genres, and in and across thematic units during a school year. Certainly, Dehea's intentional, systematic inquiry (Cochran-Smith & Lytle, 1993) on her students' oral and written responses to culturally conscience books, and their multiple reflections on other cross-cultural/multicultural experiences in the unit are good examples of one aspect of such an examination.

However, any research enterprise must acknowledge the prominence that talk plays in classroom communities of inquirers as children simultaneously learn language and learn through language (Halliday, 1993; Wells, 1986, 1994; Wells & Chang-Wells, 1992). The two curriculum genres presented here attempted to depict two typical ways that reading instruction is realized in integrated-language classrooms. But what was stressed in these two routines were the collaborative nature of the teaching–learning processes at work and how collaborative talk fostered the coconstruction of meanings among participants. In the Teacher-Led Reading-Aloud Curriculum Genre, although Dehea had certain educational goals to be accomplished, students had ample opportunities to share their interpretations and reactions to the two books she read that day. This enabled her to follow up on their initiations and ideas and to build on and extend them in a manner that is contingently responsive to the meanings they were constructing (Pappas et al.,

1995; Wells, 1986, 1994; Wells & Chang-Wells, 1992). In the Literature Circle Curriculum Genre, because Dehea dropped in only briefly at the group that day, most of the semiotic mediation via talk was done by peers. However, her assistance was seen more on the next day, when she met the group as they created their comparison chart. It was in this discussion that she was able to support students' creative attempts to make connections and find novel solutions to problems that arose in the activity.

In each case, what is critical in these curriculum genres is the way contributions by both students and the teacher are part of a continuing dialogue, for which they all have joint responsibility. Language is significant in the production, maintenance, and change of social relations of power in society in general (Fairclough, 1989, 1992). Thus, any transformation of language as an integral part of school reform to promote social justice is an enormous challenge. Because transmission-oriented curriculum, with its corresponding teacher-dominated discourse patterns, has been and still is such a strong educational tradition, it is an ongoing struggle for teachers to shift the locus of power so as to hear and respond to the voices of students who come from many ethnolinguistic backgrounds (Pappas, 1993c). How such collaborative interaction gets accomplished in the processes of language and literacy education in a diverse society is a second important avenue for future research. Alternative, non-IRE classroom discourse strategies that change participation status will need to be explored by teachers to support learning in various curriculum genres (O'Connor & Michaels, 1993; Pappas 1993c; Pappas et al., 1995). This again will entail a scrutiny of the kinds of intertextuality that are offered, acknowledged, and negotiated between students and teacher in this collaborative interaction.

REFERENCES

Ackerman, D. B. (1989). Intellectual and practical criteria for successful curriculum integration. In H. H. Jacobs (Ed.), *Interdisciplinary curriculum: Design and implementation* (pp. 25–37). Alexandria, VA: Association for Supervision and Curriculum Development.

Bakhtin, M. M. (1981). *The dialogic imagination.* Austin: University of Texas Press.

Bakhtin, M. M. (1986). *Speech genres and other late essays.* Austin: University of Texas Press.

Bloome, D., & Bailey, F. (1992). Studying language and literacy through events, particularity, and intertextuality. In R. Beach, J. Green, M. Kamil, & T. Shanahan (Eds.), *Multiple disciplinary perspectives on language and literacy research* (pp. 181–210). Urbana, IL: National Conference on Research in English.

Bloome, D., & Egan-Robertson, A. (1993). The social construction of intertextuality in classroom reading and writing lessons. *Reading Research Quarterly, 28,* 305–333.

Cazden, C. B. (1986). Classroom discourse. In M. C. Wittrock (Ed.), *Handbook of research on teaching* (3rd ed., pp. 432–463). New York: Macmillan.

Cazden, C. B. (1988). *Classroom discourse: The language of teaching and learning.* Portsmouth, NH: Heinemann.

Cazden, C. B. (1992). *Whole language plus: Essays on literacy in the United States and New Zealand.* New York: Teachers College Press.

Christie, F. (1987). The morning news genre: Using a functional grammar to illuminate educational issues. *Australian Review of Applied Linguistics, 10,* 182–198.

Christie, F. (1989). Language development in education. In R. Hasan & J. R. Martin (Eds.), *Language development: Learning language, learning culture* (pp. 152–198). Norwood, NJ: Ablex.

Christie, F. (1990). The changing face of literacy. In F. Christie (Ed.), *Literacy for a changing world* (pp. 1–25). Victoria, Australia: Australian Council for Educational Research.

Christie, F. (1993). Curriculum genres: Planning of effective teaching. In B. Cope & M. Kalantzis (Eds.), *The powers of literacy: A genre approach to teaching writing* (pp. 154–178). Pittsburgh, PA: University of Pittsburgh Press.

Cochran-Smith, M., & Lytle, S. L. (1993). *Inside/outside: Teacher research and knowledge.* New York: Teachers College Press.

Cope, B., & Kalantzis, M. (1990). Literacy in the social sciences. In F. Christie (Ed.), *Literacy for a changing world* (pp. 118–142). Victoria, Australia: Australian Council for Educational Research.

Daiute, C. (1993). Youth genres and literacy: Links between sociocultural and developmental theories. *Language Arts, 70,* 402–416.

Daly, N. (1985). *Not so fast Songololo.* London: Penguin.

Dickinson, D. K., & Smith, M. A. (1994). Long-term effects of preschool teachers' book readings on low-income children's vocabulary and story comprehension. *Reading Research Quarterly, 29,* 104–122.

Edwards, D., & Mercer, N. (1987). *Common knowledge: The development of understanding in the classroom.* London: Routledge.

Eeds, M., & Wells, D. (1989). Grand conversations: An exploration of meaning construction in literature study groups. *Research in the Teaching of English, 23,* 4–29.

Fairclough, N. (1989). *Language and power.* London: Longman.

Fairclough, N. (1992). *Discourse and social change.* Cambridge, England: Polity Press.

Green, J. L., Kantor, R. M., & Rogers, T. (1991). Exploring the complexity of language and learning in classroom contexts. In L. Idol & B. F. Jones (Eds.), *Educational values and cognitive instruction: Implications for reform* (pp. 333–364). Hillsdale, NJ: Lawrence Erlbaum Associates.

Halliday, M. A. K. (1975). *Learning to mean: Explorations in the development of language.* London: Edward Arnold.

Halliday, M. A. K. (1978). *Language as a social semiotic: The social interpretation of language and meaning.* London: Edward Arnold.

Halliday, M. A. K. (1985). *Spoken and written language.* Victoria, Australia: Deakin University Press.

Halliday, M. A. K. (1987). Spoken and written modes of meaning. In R. Horowitz & S. J. Samuels (Eds.), *Comprehending oral and written language* (pp. 55–82). San Diego, CA: Academic Press.

Halliday, M. A. K. (1993). Towards a language-based theory of learning. *Linguistics and Education, 5,* 93–116.

Halliday, M. A. K. (1994). "So you say 'pass' . . . thank you muchly." In A. D. Grimshaw (Ed.), *What's going on here? Complementary studies of professional talk. Volume two of the multiple analysis project* (pp. 175–229). Norwood, NJ: Ablex.

Halliday, M. A. K., & Hasan, R. (1985). *Language, context, and text: Aspects of language in a social-semiotic perspective.* Victoria, Australia: Deakin University Press.

Halliday, M. A. K., & Martin, J. (1993). *Writing science: Literacy and discursive power.* Pittsburgh, PA: University of Pittsburgh Press.

Hasan, R. (1985). The identity of the text. In M. A. K. Halliday & R. Hasan (Eds.), *Language, context, and text: Aspects of language in a social-semiotic perspective* (pp. 97–116). Victoria, Australia: Deakin University Press.

Hasan, R. (1995). The conception of context in text. In P. H. Fries & M. Gregory (Eds.), *Discourse in society: Systemic functional perspectives* (pp. 183–283). Norwood, NJ: Ablex.

Hymes, D. (1987). Communicative competence. In H. von U. Ammon, N. Dittmar, & K. J. Mattheier (Eds.), *Sociolinguistics: An international handbook of the science of language and society* (pp. 219–229). New York: deGruyter.

Isadora, R. (1991). *At the crossroads.* New York: Greenwillows.

Jacobs, H. H. (1989). The growing need for interdisciplinary curriculum content. In H. H. Jacobs (Ed.), *Interdisciplinary curriculum: Design and implementation* (pp. 1–11). Alexandria, VA: Association for Supervision and Curriculum Development.

Kreisberg, S. (1992). *Transforming power: Domination, empowerment, and education.* Albany: State University of New York Press.

Kress, G. (1993). Genre as social process. In B. Cope & M. Kalantzis (Eds.), *The powers of literacy: A genre approach to teaching writing* (pp. 22–37). Pittsburgh, PA: University of Pittsburgh Press.

Lemke, J. L. (1985a). *Using language in the classroom.* Victoria, Australia: Deakin University Press.

Lemke, J. L. (1985b). Ideology, intertextuality and the notion of register. In J. Benson & W. Greaves (Eds.), *Systemic perspectives in discourse* (pp. 275–294). Norwood, NJ: Ablex.

Lemke, J. L. (1990). *Talking science: Language, learning, and values.* Norwood, NJ: Ablex.

Levine, E. (1989). *I hate English!* Illustrated by S. Bjorkman. New York: Scholastic.

Martin, J. M. (1990). Literacy in science: Learning to handle text as technology. In F. Christie (Ed.), *Literacy for a changing world* (pp. 79–117). Victoria, Australia: Australian Council for Educational Research.

Martin, J. M. (1992). *English text: System and structure.* Philadelphia, PA: John Benjamins.

Martinez, M., & Teale, W. (1993). Teacher storybook reading style: A comparison of six teachers. *Research in the Teaching of English, 27,* 175–199.

Moll, L. C. (Ed.). (1990). *Vygotsky and education: Instructional implications and applications of sociohistorical psychology.* Cambridge, England: Cambridge University Press.

Mousley, J., & Marks, G. (1991). *Discourses in mathematics.* Victoria, Australia: Deakin University Press.

Newkirk, T. (1989). *More than stories: The range of children's writing.* Portsmouth, NH: Heinemann.

Newman, D. P., Griffin, P., & Cole, M. (1989). *The construction zone: Working for cognitive change in school.* Cambridge, England: Cambridge University Press.

Nhuong, H. Q. (1982). *The land I lost.* Illustrated by V. Mai. New York: HarperCollins.

Nystrand, M. (1986). *The structure of written communication: Studies in reciprocity between writers and readers.* Orlando, FL: Academic Press.

Nystrand, M. (1987). The role of context in written communication. In R. Horowitz & S. J. Samuels (Eds.), *Comprehending oral and written language* (pp. 197–213). San Diego, CA: Academic Press.

Nystrand, M., & Wiemelt, J. (1991). When is a text explicit? Formalist and dialogical conceptions. *Text, 11,* 25–41.

O'Connor, M. C., & Michaels, S. (1993). Aligning academic task and participation status through revoicing: Analysis of a classroom discourse strategy. *Anthropology and Education Quarterly, 24,* 318–335.

Olson, D. R. (1977). From utterance to text: The bias of language in speech and writing. *Harvard Educational Review, 47,* 257–281.

Olson, D. R. (1991). Children's understanding of interpretation and the autonomy of written texts. *Text, 11,* 3–23.

Oyler, C. J. (1993). *Sharing authority in an urban first grade: Becoming literate, becoming bold.* Unpublished doctoral dissertation, University of Illinois, Chicago, IL.

Pappas, C. C. (1990, July). *The reading-aloud curriculum genre: Exploring text and teacher variation.* Paper presented at the 17th International Systemic Congress, Stirling, Scotland.

Pappas, C. C. (1991a). Fostering full access to literacy by including information books. *Language Arts, 68,* 440–462.

Pappas, C. C. (1991b, April). *The reading-aloud curriculum genre: Book genre and teacher variation.* Paper presented at the annual meeting of the American Educational Research Association, Chicago, IL.

Pappas, C. C. (1993a). Is narrative primary? Some insights from kindergarteners' pretend readings of stories and information books. *JRB: A Journal of Literacy, 25,* 97–129.

Pappas, C. C. (1993b). Questioning our ideologies about narrative and learning: Response to Egan. *Linguistics and Education, 5,* 157–164.

Pappas, C. C. (1993c). *Urban teachers' struggles in sharing power with their students: Exploring changes in literacy currriculum genres.* Unpublished manuscript, University of Illinois, Chicago, IL.

Pappas, C. C. (in press). *Learning written genres: A socio-semiotic perspective.* Cresskill, NJ: Hampton Press.

Pappas, C. C., Kiefer, B. Z., & Levstik, L. S. (1995). *An integrated language perspective in the elementary school: Theory into action* (2nd ed.). White Plains, NY: Longman.

Perkins, D. N. (1989). Selecting fertile themes for integrated learning. In H. H. Jacobs (Ed.), *Interdisciplinary curriculum: Design and implementation* (pp. 25–37). Alexandria, VA: Association for Supervision and Curriculum Development.

Ramirez, A. (1988). Analyzing speech acts. In J. L. Green & J. O. Harker (Eds.), *Multiple perspective analyses of classroom discourse* (pp. 135–163). Norwood, NJ: Ablex.

Santa Barbara Classroom Discourse Group [Dixon, C., de la Cruz, E., Green, J., Lin, L., & Brandts, L.]. (1992). Do you see what we see? The referential and intertextual nature of classroom life. *Journal of Classroom Interaction, 27,* 29–36.

Shuy, R. (1988). Identifying dimensions of classroom language. In J. L. Green & J. O. Harker (Eds.), *Multiple perspective analyses of classroom discourse* (pp. 115–134). Norwood, NJ: Ablex.

Sinclair, J. M., & Coulthard, R. M. (1975). *Towards an analysis of discourse.* London: Oxford University Press.

Slevin, J. F. (1992). Genre as a social institution. In J. Trimmer & T. Warnock (Eds.), *Understanding others: Cultural and cross–cultural studies and the teaching of literature* (pp. 16–34). Urbana, IL: National Council of the Teachers of English.

Swales, J. M. (1990). *Genre analysis: English in academic and research settings.* Cambridge, England: Cambridge University Press.

Vygotsky, L. S. (1962). *Thought and language.* Cambridge, MA: MIT Press.

Vygotsky, L. S. (1978). *Mind in society: The development of higher psychological processes.* Cambridge, England: Cambridge University Press

Wells, G. (1986). *The meaning makers: Children learning language and using language to learn.* Portsmouth, NH: Heinemann.

Wells, G. (1994, April). *Discourse as tool in the activity of learning and teaching.* Paper presented at the American Educational Research Association, New Orleans, LA.

Wells, G., & Chang-Wells, G. L. (1992). *Constructing knowledge together: Classrooms as centers of inquiry and literacy.* Portsmouth, NH: Heinemann.

Wertsch, J. V. (1985). *Vygotsky and the social formation of mind.* Cambridge, England: Cambridge University Press.

Wertsch, J. V. (1989). A sociocultural approach to mind. In W. Damon (Ed.), *Child development today and tomorrow* (pp. 14–33). San Francisco, CA: Jossey-Bass.

Wertsch, J. V. (1991). *Voices of the mind: A sociocultural approach to mediated action*. Cambridge, MA: Harvard University Press.

Williams, S. A. (1992). *Working cotton*. Illustrated by C. Byard. San Diego, CA: Harcourt Brace.

Willinsky, J. (1990). *The new literacy: Redefining reading and writing in the schools*. New York: Routledge.

Young, R. (1992). *Critical theory and classroom talk*. Clevedon, England: Multilingual Matters.

CHAPTER THIRTEEN

Response-Based Reading Instruction in the Elementary Grades

Lee Galda
The University of Georgia, Athens

Sherry Guice
State University of New York at Albany

If you were able to look into the mind of a reader, you would see that reader busily engaged in an evolving dialogue with a text, a dialogue in which the reader's life experience helps shape the meaning that the words on the page are guiding. This is the view of reading that reader-response theory posits, and this view of reading influences response-based instruction. Response theory depicts reading as *transactional, temporal, social,* and *transformational.*

A RESPONSE-BASED VIEW OF THE READING PROCESS

The idea that reading is transactional was proposed by Louise Rosenblatt in her 1938 seminal work, *Literature as Exploration* (reprinted in 1968, 1970, 1979, and 1983) and developed in a later book, *The Reader, the Text, the Poem: The Transactional Theory of the Literary Work* (Rosenblatt, 1978), in which she argues that meaning is co-constructed by reader and text. A reader brings knowledge and predispositions to bear on the words on the page; the text guides the reader through the words on the page and together they produce a work of art that is called a poem, a story, or a novel. This work of art exists only when a reader is reading a text; a text is merely inert words without a reader. The knowledge and experience that a reader brings to a text is not simply content knowledge, such as that argued by schema theory (Anderson & Pearson, 1984), but also knowledge of form, structure, and

311

style (Purves, 1991). Further, reader preferences, expectations, and experience with varied types of text also influence the making of meaning. It is because reading is transactional that we can read the same books but have very different interpretations of those books. While reading *Charlotte's Web* (White, 1952) one reader may think that Templeton helped Charlotte save Wilbur because Templeton was nicer than he seemed; another may think that he simply was greedy. Both may be right according to their own created meaning.

Readers read in different ways for different purposes, adopting a stance towards a text that shapes the way they read. Stance is both signaled by a text and determined by a reader's experience. Even preschool children begin to differentiate between texts that are true and not true, between books that help you do things (such as how-to books) and books that are fun to read and think about, no matter how impossible the ideas may seem. Rosenblatt (1978), Britton (1970), Langer (1990a, 1990b), and others (see, e.g., Cox & Many, 1992) argue that these different kinds of texts necessitate different kinds of reading. Although there are differences in terminology and details among these scholars, the general argument is the same. For the sake of clarity we use Rosenblatt's terminology.

Some texts, such as recipes, directions, reports, and other forms of expository writing, signal readers to focus on the referential, to "carry away" meaning from the text (Rosenblatt, 1978), meaning that can be used to get things done in the world (Britton, 1970). This kind of reading is *efferent reading*, where the primary purpose behind the reading is gathering information of some kind. The other kind of reading, *aesthetic reading*, is focused on the experiential, reading done for the experience that it provides (Rosenblatt, 1978). While attention to referential elements are necessarily part of this kind of reading, the reader is more concerned with the developing whole, with the unity of the work, than with developing knowledge or determining action (Purves, 1991). This kind of reading is signaled by poems, stories, novels and, as Scholes (1989) would argue, other aesthetic texts such as visual art and music. Aesthetic reading is not to get some information with which to operate in the real world, but to live through an experience. Although one could read *Charlotte's Web* for information about spiders, the more appropriate way to read is for immersing oneself in the story.

Readers create experiences and build knowledge as they read over time, beginning at one time and place and ending at another. As they read the text they are constantly building meaning, meaning which is constructed from the experiences of the readers and guided by the flow of the words on the page. Meaning is developed, changed, and abandoned as the text unfolds in time and readers respond to the guidance of the text (Benton, 1983; Iser, 1978; J. Langer, 1990a). As we read we call upon what we know of the actual world to help us make meaning from the text. As this meaning develops we alter it to incorporate new ideas that the text triggers; finishing a book brings us to a new understanding of the beginning.

J. Langer's (1990a) research strongly suggests that as readers read they do at least four things. Readers begin by entering the text or, as Langer puts it, "being out and stepping in" the "envisionment." This involves using prior knowledge and textual cues (surface features) to begin to build an understanding of a text. Readers can be immersed in the text, developing meaning as they read, or "being in and moving through." They might also stop to reflect on life as they read, stepping back and rethinking what one knows (p. 244). Readers also move out of the meaning they are building and evaluate both their experience of reading and the content of their understanding, judging text and reading process in relation to other texts and experiences. This Langer calls "stepping out and objectifying the experience." These stances (as she terms them) are fluid, and readers move through them as they read. Using their skill as readers and their past experience, readers employ these processes recursively while responding to the constraints and demands of the text.

Whether they are reading efferently or aesthetically, readers adopt these stances (J. Langer, 1990a). However, their overall orientation differs depending on their purpose. Efferent reading is oriented toward understanding the point of the text, organizing a growing understanding of the text in terms of the topic under consideration. Aesthetic reading, on the other hand, encompasses both organizing new understandings in relation to the developing story world, or whole, *and* developing multiple possibilities for meaning, going beyond the information given (Langer, 1990a).

This meaning, although fueled by the reader's own life experiences, is both individual and intensely social in part because the construction of meaning is guided by the text. Texts are language, and "this quality of language—essentially social yet always individually internalized—makes the literary experience something both shared and uniquely personal" (Rosenblatt, 1978, p. 53). Individuals construct their personal meanings as they read. These meanings are shared with others and become part of a socially constructed interpretation of a text. Fish's (1980) notion of the interpretive community explains the construction of meaning among groups of like-minded people. However, it does not account for the individual's rejection or elaboration of socially constructed meaning. Steig's work (1989) suggests that readers retain their individual meaning and not only enhance their own understanding as they share, but also shape both the group's meaning and that of individuals within the group. We test, alter, and enlarge our constructed meaning as we talk about texts with others, or respond through writing, acting, singing, or drawing. As we share our personal meaning with others, their own responses to the text and to our interpretations become part of our experience and thus of our responses. The meaning we make of *Charlotte's Web* contains ideas and images of all those with whom we have talked about the book.

The text itself, as language, provides the opportunity for idiosyncratic meaning while also promoting shared meaning. We may all have unique experiences and feelings, but we mediate those experiences and feelings through language, and language is a socially constructed system. We share referents within our language, and thus there is always some amount of shared meaning. At the most basic, denotative level, *Charlotte's Web* is not a book about anything we want it to be about. It is a fantasy narrative about how a loving spider saves the life of her friend, a pig. The larger meaning, to some degree idiosyncratic to each reader, is that which is socially negotiated and shared.

The social, temporal, and transactional nature of the act of reading generates the possibility of reading being transformational. Just as reading is an act of transforming words into meaning, reading an aesthetic text allows readers the possibility of transforming themselves as well. Aesthetic reading offers readers a "virtual" experience (S. Langer, 1957), the opportunity to experience lives that they will never live. Harding (1937, 1968) and Britton (1970) argue that because this kind of experience is not connected to direct action in the real world, readers have an opportunity for contemplation not often available during real world experiences. Reading aesthetically allows readers to experience, contemplate, and evaluate the values, attitudes, and emotions present in the created story, building not only their own storehouse of experiences, but also their own value systems. The luxury of thinking without the necessity of action makes the aesthetic experience one that allows readers to bring texts into their lives in a manner that helps them define and shape their lives (Britton, 1970; Scholes, 1989). Thus aesthetic reading makes possible a transformational experience whenever a reader picks up a book. Whether looking at mirrors of ourselves or through windows into the lives of others, our experience during aesthetic reading allows us the opportunity to reconstruct ourselves.

This view of reading, then, and especially of aesthetic reading, positions reading as a constructive act in which readers, with guidance from the words on the page, compose meaning as they read. This meaning both shapes and is shaped by other texts—those we have read and those we have lived. Scholes (1989) argues that we construct the texts (stories) of our lives in much the same fashion as we construct the stories that we read. Our virtual and actual experiences mutually inform and influence each other. All that we have experienced, including the virtual experiences that we have through literature, becomes text. New texts are meaningful to us when we link them with previously constructed texts, both actual and virtual. Reading becomes a constructive, intertextual activity given meaning by its relation to our lives (Scholes, 1989).

RESEARCH SUPPORT FOR A RESPONSE-BASED
VIEW OF READING

One important strand of research that has implications for classroom practice is that which investigates stance and its effect on reading. This research documents how stance influences the construction of meaning during reading and how stance is shaped by teaching practices.

Stance and the Construction of Meaning

The stance a reader takes toward a text influences the experience that reader has while reading. If, for example, you were to pick up a cookbook to find a recipe for something to cook for dinner tonight, you would read the recipes looking for information such as amount of preparation time (Can I fit this in between work and dinner time?), ease of preparation (Do I feel like doing all of this work?), necessary ingredients (Do I have everything I need or will I have to stop at the grocery story?), and actual effect (Are my children going to like this or is it all going to go into the compost?). In efferent reading like this you are focused on real world concerns, on the outcome of your using the recipe to produce dinner.

On the other hand, you could pick up the same cookbook and read it for the experience of reading it. Thoughts about form (What pretty typeface/illustrations/layout.), structure (I like having these pasta recipes separated into "hot" and "cold."), and content (Boy, does this sound delicious.) appear and disappear, but little or no time is given to thoughts of a practical nature.

The first kind of reading ends with the reader in the kitchen cooking dinner; the second ends with the reader curled up with the book enjoying possibilities. The first is primarily efferent reading, the second primarily aesthetic.

Rosenblatt (1978, 1991) and others argue that while all texts can be read primarily (although not completely) from either stance, a piece of literature is best read from an aesthetic stance. It is only from an aesthetic stance that readers can realize the potential in the literary text. If a reader reads a story or poem focusing on referential elements (What are the metaphors? What is the structure of this plot? How does this line scan?) then the reader loses the opportunity to engage in the emotional experience of the text. Simply put, if the emotional experience of a literary text does not come first, then the reading of that text is arid, incomplete, and lacking in power; the transformational potential inherent in reading literature is unrealized.

This does not mean that referential elements are never considered. Rather, these concerns are a secondary focus. We read first for the experience and then think about that experience in terms of our lives and the text: Why did we respond as we did? What happened in our lives that caused this?

What other texts have we read that informed our reading of this one? What has the author done with language that shaped our construction of meaning?

Reading aesthetically involves contemplating the text as a whole, an author's vision of reality as it might be, an exploration of alternatives. Being able to do this seems to be related to development. Applebee (1978) and Galda (1982, 1990) present evidence to support the idea that as children develop their aesthetic stance changes. Applebee (1978) examined the responses of children from ages 2 to 17 and found that the change in the attitudes, conventions, and organization of their responses reflected the general trends in development described by Piaget (1970). Young children are aesthetic by nature, effortlessly combining the world of the senses and the world of the imagination. For them, story and life are part of the same fabric. As children develop, they begin to separate story and poem from life. Sometimes this results in difficulty in accepting authors' views of alternative realities, with children insisting on a close correspondence between life as they know it and texts as they read them. As they read and develop over time, the ability to entertain the alternate realities posed by multiple texts increases (Applebee, 1978; Galda, 1982, 1990).

Galda (1990) found that children's evaluative statements about realistic fiction became increasingly analytic from fourth to eighth grade. Their responses to fantasy, a less preferred and more difficult genre, developed more slowly and were much less analytic.

Stance and Teaching

This development, of course, does not occur in a vacuum but rather is the result of multiple reading experiences. What teachers do with texts has a lot to do with how their students' experience them. In his research that explores response in many different cultures, Purves (1973, 1981) reports that there is a correspondence between the way teachers prefer to respond and the way their students prefer to respond that increases with age. In a comparative study of students' preferred responses to literature in 10 countries, Purves found that American students learn to look for morals in the literature they read because teachers teach them to do so. Elementary grade students are interested in pursuing a variety of questions after reading a piece of literature, but across the high school years students become more and more fixed in the efferent pursuit of a moral.

Other research continues to support Purves' conclusion while documenting in detail the ways in which teachers' stances influence the stances of their students (e.g., Cox & Many, 1992; Hade, 1989; Many & Cox, 1992). Studies like these point out the strong effect that teachers have on their students' becoming aesthetic readers. The structure of literature events, the kinds of questions teachers ask, and the stances they demonstrate all influence the way in which children approach the books they read.

Research on Children and Classrooms

Reader-response theory and research are not focused on *how* children *learn* to read, but rather on *how they develop as engaged readers*. Rather than focusing on the strategies that children use to comprehend text, reader-response research examines the ways in which children connect life and text as they learn to enjoy and appreciate the literature that they read. In response-based teaching specific practices vary across classrooms, although there are certain conditions that are essential to encourage children's development as readers. Martinez and Roser (1991) suggest that

> classrooms where responses to literature thrive seem to be characterized by teachers' valuing of responses as the crux of literacy growth. Valuing of response in the classroom is evident when teachers (a) provide opportunities for response, (b) provide response models, and (c) receive children's responses (in all their diversity). (p. 652)

Response-based teaching relies on the presence of many texts, an abundance of time to read, and the opportunity to read and respond in the company of others (Galda, 1988; Teale & Martinez, 1988). Students are active and questioning and teachers are skilled fellow-readers rather than the source of definitive knowledge (Hade, 1991; O'Brien, 1991). These conditions should exist to enhance children's responses to books and their construction of meaning.

GOALS OF A RESPONSE-BASED CURRICULUM

A response-based curriculum seeks to retain and sustain the inherent joy in reading, recognizing that engaged readers are good readers. Focusing on the responses of readers rather than the individual texts, teachers recognize the transactional and social nature of reading and help readers explore their own responses, recognize diversity, and explore similarities and differences in their responses (Purves, Rogers, & Soter, 1990). Building on children's delight and involvement in reading, a second goal is to develop children's awareness of how texts work, helping children learn about language and its use through reading. A third goal reflects the transformational potential in literature; teachers help children learn about themselves and others, and about their worlds through the reading they do.

> The vicarious experiences that are possible with fiction, the emotional expansion that is possible with poetry, and the exposure to information . . . that is possible with nonfiction all increase children's knowledge of themselves and

their worlds. And this increased knowledge widens children's horizons and makes even more learning possible. (Cullinan & Galda, 1994, p. 41)

Promoting individual, meaningful transactions with texts results in the development of engaged readers. From this engagement other things flow, as children learn about rhetorical and literary aspects of texts, learn how to be strategic readers, and learn about themselves and others.

The Role of the Teacher

In response-based instruction the teacher is an experienced, strategic reader who demonstrates effective reading and responding, provides texts from which to choose and time to read them, and encourages students to engage in a dialogue about what is read, making intertextual connections as well as explicit connections with their own lives.

Connecting text to life and life to text anchors reading to our most fundamental experience of self. Cochran-Smith (1994) documents how one preschool teacher helped her students make these explicit connections during read aloud time, and many others have described ways in which teachers can validate students' connections between what they read and how they live (e.g., Short & Pierce, 1990). The teacher Cochran-Smith observed asked questions and made comments that encouraged her students to understand the books they were reading in terms of what they had already experienced in their lives; a book about a new puppy would be explicitly connected to the new puppies that class members have. She also encouraged them to understand things that happened to them in their lives by connecting them to stories; feeling jealous when a sibling is born would be explicitly connected to the many new baby stories that had been read. These connections between texts and life are part, Scholes (1989) argues, of a larger intertextuality in which all texts (life, art, music, drama, literature, and so on) are connected, one to the other, through the constructive activity of the reader.

Teachers facilitate an understanding of individual response and intertextual/experiential connections with the questions they ask. Open-ended questions that ask for new ideas, as opposed to closed questions that seek already known information, encourage students to explore and develop their own construction of meaning, and understand the personal connections they have with a text. Discussions that begin with the personal, in which students compare responses, often evolve into comparisons of texts and rhetorical/literary analyses. Eeds and Wells (1990), in describing the "grand conversations" that students and teachers can have about books, show how authentic dialogues about literature result in increased connection with texts as well as an increase in knowledge about literature and how it works. When discussing personal responses, students and teachers not only think about and elaborate on their responses to what they read, they also consider the texts they have read in light of the techniques of the author. For example, if readers identify closely with a character, then discussions about that character often lead to discussions of techniques of characterization that enabled the author to create such a memorable character.

Langer (1990b) suggests one way to frame instruction that can be used to evaluate various response-based classroom practices: ". . . instruction (in the form of scaffolding) helps support and extend students' understandings of the text they have read, not the teacher's perception of the right response" (p. 816). Teachers model active meaning making through their attitudes, their reading practices, and what they say about reading while supporting, but not constricting, their students' responses.

The Role of the Student

Because response is at once personal and intensely social, students must actively pursue their individual interests and desires while exploring, with their fellow readers, the nature of meaning, the hypotheses about life and literature they construct, and the experience of reading. In response-based classrooms students generate much of the activity that occurs, pursuing interests and shaping experience in the construction of new knowledge about themselves, each other, the texts they read, and the domain of literature. Students read and respond to what they read. Teachers provide opportunities for students to construct knowledge through many and varied encounters with different texts in a variety of social contexts.

Classroom Practice

Response-based instruction is not simply the presence of many books and lots of time spent reading them, but also includes strategy instruction, the study of rhetorical concerns, and the study of a body of texts as well. While the focus is on children's imaginative engagement with the books they read and the responses that they express, it both leads to and is embedded in instruction involving basic comprehension strategies for both aesthetic and efferent reading. Learning to read and to understand what is read enhances children's aesthetic encounters with books. Likewise, learning about authorial techniques enhances children's aesthetic appreciation of the books they read. With aesthetic engagement as a base, teachers provide instruction that will increase their students' expertise as readers and responders.

There are many ways to implement this instruction, including focusing on core books which the whole class has experienced (either reading individually or being read to), developing literature units that involve small groups of students working intensively with one or more texts, and encouraging individual, self-paced reading. Sometimes instruction is led by the teacher, other times it is student-led. Sometimes the books are selected by the teacher, other times they are student-selected (Hiebert & Colt, 1989; Zarrillo, 1989). Because response-based instruction is based first of all on the responses of the students rather than the dictates of a curriculum it looks different in different classrooms.

All readers need a book-rich, supportive classroom community where they are free to read and respond to books. What constitutes such an environment for reading and interpreting books? One way to think about instruction from a response-based stance in both early and middle grade classrooms is to consider various *physical, intellectual,* and *practical* conditions that can enhance children's responses to literature.

Physical Conditions. Physical aspects of the classroom can enhance the opportunities for reading and responding. Print-rich environments invite readers to look at, read, and respond to books. This means that classroom libraries include, first and foremost, many books from all genres of literature, a range of difficulty levels, and a range of perspectives; 400–500 books are not too many (Huck, Hepler, & Hickman, 1993). Response-based classrooms also include a variety of appropriate formats for presenting books to children: big books, poems on charts, student-authored books, multiple copies of titles, and more. Books are displayed throughout the classroom and displays are frequently changed by teachers and children. Such classrooms include space for reading corners or nooks that entice children to read in comfortable positions (Morrow, 1982); comfortable readers rarely read sitting at desks. Further, response-based classrooms contain a variety of art and writing materials so that children can illustrate, write, and create responses to books in a variety of ways (Morrow, 1990; Strickland & Morrow, 1989).

Intellectual Conditions. Perhaps the most important feature of teaching from a response-based stance is the intellectual character of the classroom. Teachers set the intellectual tone of classrooms. We know, for example, that all readers benefit from hearing stories (Cullinan, 1992; Feitelson, Kita, & Goldstein, 1986; Simpson, 1986). Teachers demonstrate both fluent reading and the love of books by frequently sharing a variety of stories, poems, novels, and articles. The intellectual character of a response-based classroom is further enriched by a teacher who considers all children's responses valid and models ways to think about literature through open-ended, thoughtful discussions. Intellectual access is enhanced when children have ample opportunities to seek advice about books from knowledgeable peers and expert teachers. Similarly, children learn to select ways to express responses to books that are meaningful and increase their understanding of the books they read.

Practical Conditions. Of course, just having books to read and an intellectual atmosphere for response is not enough. Teachers also make decisions concerning how best to organize instruction to promote children's responses to books; they make practical, instructional decisions that ensure this by confronting organizational dilemmas that arise when teaching from a response-based stance.

One dilemma is time. How much time do readers need? In the past our students were spending as little as 7–15 minutes a day in silent reading in their classrooms (Anderson, Hiebert, Scott, & Wilkinson, 1985), and yet we know that silent reading is directly related to reading achievement and growth (Anderson, Fielding, & Wilson, 1988). The argument is thus: Time spent reading for pleasure (rather than to be tested) results in happy readers, who spend more time reading which makes them better readers, who spend even more time reading. And so the cycle continues.

The amount of time to be allocated for reading is dependent on several factors including the age of the children, the school schedule, and the unique character of a given group of children. Response-based teachers generally squeeze as much time for browsing through books, reading, and responding to books as they possibly can from the school day. Further, they consider reading and responding time as part of the entire curriculum, not just part of reading/language arts or sustained silent reading.

Another dilemma is how teachers can organize for instruction that enhances children's opportunities to read and respond to books. One recent suggestion is to consider organizing for reading in three ways: independent reading, shared reading, and/or whole group instruction (Galda, Cullinan, & Strickland, 1993; Huck et al., 1993). Independent reading is a necessary part of all response-based instruction for children of all ages; teachers' decisions concerning whole and group instruction should be based on the needs of children. Having the whole class read a particular book, for example, may not best meet the needs of some groups of children because of the sheer range of children's reading abilities, interests, and rates.

Teachers also decide what response-based activities most benefit their children. This is a difficult instructional decision since teaching and learning interactions reveal to children the teachers' concept of text meaning and how one goes about transacting with texts. For example, teachers may overtly state that they value individuals' multiple text meanings, while inadvertently guiding students toward agreeing on one text meaning. Applebee (1990) found that although teachers across the nation professed that they base language arts instruction on reader-response theory, classroom observations revealed that, in the majority of cases, children's personal responses were elicited as motivational introductions to discussions devoted to reaching *the* meaning of the text rather than celebrating the diverse range of meanings found in most situations. However, there are some successful classroom practices for both early and middle grade children that promote the natural range and diversity of children's responses to books.

Successful Classroom Practices in Early Literacy

Young children's literacy development is enhanced by participating in various response-based activities. Hearing, reading, and responding to stories orally and through writing enhances children's vocabulary (Cohen, 1968; Feitelson et al., 1986; Pappas, 1993), comprehension of stories (Adams & Collins, 1979; Stein & Glenn, 1979), positive feelings about books and reading (Mendoza, 1985; Morrow, 1992), and writing skills (Kelly, 1990; Smith, 1983). Teachers have a great influence on children's responses to books; in fact, research suggests that even the way teachers read aloud affects children's responses (Dickinson & Keebler, 1989; Martinez & Teale, 1993; Roser & Martinez, 1985).

Recent research indicates that young children benefit from the opportunity to hear and read stories repeatedly. Repeated experience with texts seems to enrich and broaden the complexity of responses of young children (Jacque, 1993; Kiefer, 1983; Martinez & Roser, 1985; Trousdale & Harris, 1993; Yarden, 1988). This research suggests that teachers plan for opportunities for repeated readings of the same title by rereading favorite stories to children and by presenting stories in various formats, such as reading big books, providing multiple copies of titles for independent reading, and providing access to stories through taped books. Further, teachers demonstrate various meaning-making strategies, including letter and word-level decoding strategies, as they share books with children.

Young children's responses to books are also broadened when they talk to their peers. Hickman (1979, 1981) found that children talk to exchange information about texts by reading together, sharing stories, retelling stories, and commenting on their ideas about stories. Thus, a successful response-based approach includes regularly scheduled time for children to talk about books among themselves and in groups in literature circles, arranged by both the teacher and the children, that serve a variety of response purposes (see Short & Pierce, 1990).

Young children spontaneously respond to books physically by play acting, clapping, singing, chanting, and moving (Hickman, 1981). Research has further suggested that children's recall and comprehension of stories is enhanced by dramatic activity (Pelligrini & Galda, 1982). Teachers capitalize on children's inclinations to respond physically to stories by encouraging dramatic play and story enactments that are initiated and directed by the children (Martinez, 1993). In classrooms with young children, drama centers filled with various props offer children opportunities for spontaneous story reenactment. (We are not suggesting formal productions of published plays.

Huck et al. [1993] warn that elaborate, and often stressful, play productions detract from the process of making meaning.) Teachers can further promote dramatic responses to literature by encouraging groups of children to present stories through informal performances, readers' theater, puppetry, role playing characters, and choral readings (see Stewig & Buege, 1994).

Children also respond to books in artistic modes. Hickman (1981) observed children designing board games about books and drawing pictures to express their responses. For very young children writing and drawing are inseparable (Dyson, 1986a, 1986b; Ferreiro & Teberosky, 1982). Thus, young children regularly respond to books in written forms such as journals, letters to teachers and communications to peers, either with or without the use of words, and through various artistic modes. Some possibilities for expressing meaning through art include constructing maps and murals; illustrating settings, characters, moods, and themes; and utilizing various materials and styles of artistic expression, such as collage, drawing, sculpting, finger painting, and other techniques.

Hickman (1981) observed young children writing about literature and using literature as a model for their writing. Response journals serve as places where children can record their thoughts about books, and they can take many forms ranging from private diaries to dialogue journals to class notebooks. Response journals, however, are not intended as an exercise or as a substitute for a workbook. They can be misused. For example, teachers in a longitudinal study at The Center for the Learning and Teaching of Literature reported using response journals to "make" children read and to "check their comprehension" (Johnston, Guice, Baker, Malone, & Michelson, 1993). Teachers who work from a response-based view of reading carefully consider how and why they have children write responses. Children need to write responses to express and reflect on text meaning, not prove to their teacher that they have read. Children's meaning making is also enhanced when they write about books for a variety of reasons directed toward a variety of audiences. Providing children with opportunities to express thoughts about books and stories through letters, notes, poetry, reports, timelines, questions, advertisements, and continuations or changes of the story helps them develop their ideas about books.

Successful Classroom Practices in Middle Grades

Although middle-grade children benefit from many of the same classroom practices as do younger children, their social and emotional needs are different. Middle-grade children need a different sort of teacher direction. McClure's research (1990) suggests that fifth and sixth graders respond well to supportive teachers who promote divergent thinking, give honest feedback, and model their own thought processes and difficulties.

Middle-grade children have also had more experiences with books, print, and the media than their younger peers. Thus, they have clearly defined text preferences (Purves & Beach, 1972). Middle-grade readers especially need the freedom to explore those interests by being allowed to select from a range of books. Allowing students some choice in their selection of texts can also help to accommodate the needs of all readers. Teachers can influence students' book selection by regularly reading aloud to them and exposing them to titles through book talks, casual summaries of books intended to entice readers. However, at this age, peers seem to have even greater influence on book selection. Hepler and Hickman (1982) found that middle-grade children help one another decide what to read. Middle-grade children also encourage friends to read the same books so that they may discuss them together (Guice, 1991). Middle-grade children naturally talk among themselves to help one another select texts in a response-based classroom.

Research indicates that middle-grade readers' responses are enriched by talking informally with peers and formal discussion. Shanklin and Rhodes (1989) suggest that verbal interaction actually enhances comprehension. Eeds and Wells (1989) determined that in a fifth-grade classroom the teacher and children "built meaning by working together" (p. 26) in literature discussion groups by talking about interesting points and negotiating meaning through conversation. Children also construct meaning as they talk to one another without the presence of an adult (Hepler & Hickman, 1982; McClure, 1985) and as they write, read, select books, and respond to books through drama and art (Guice, 1992). However, Langer (1990b) believes that secondary students' interpretations of books are best enriched when they are supported in discussions reflecting real questions about books that have been modeled by knowledgeable teachers. This seems to be true of middle-grade students as well. Further, middle-grade children benefit from learning different interpretive literary models. Temple and Collins (1992) present a variety of interpretive models for teachers and readers to experiment with, ranging from archetypal heroes to psychoanalytic interpretive strategies. A variety of opportunities to talk spontaneously about books with peers and to participate in organized, but flexible, literature discussion groups helps middle-grade children develop their responses to the books they read.

Unlike their younger peers, middle-grade children are less likely to respond to books physically (Hickman, 1981). Thus, the role of dramatic activities in response-based classrooms is less clear cut. Research on the effect of dramatic activity on the responses of middle-grade children is mixed. Some children find dramatic expression very threatening and participate only because they are required to (Guice, 1992); however, it has been suggested that some middle-grade readers may benefit from opportunities to respond to books through drama (Burke, 1980; Kardash & Wright, 1987;

Weston, 1993). Middle-grade children's concept of story can be enhanced by various student-directed, oral and dramatic response activities organized around group, cooperative planning: mock trials, readers' theatre, choral readings, role playing, debates, and reenactment. Middle graders may also benefit from the opportunity to re-experience these responses by viewing and analyzing videotapes.

Although it is common to find children in classrooms responding to books through various artistic modes, little research has been conducted on the effect of drawing, painting, or constructing on middle-grade children's responses to literature. In one of the few studies that explore this question, Cox (1991) suggested that middle-grade children's written responses were enhanced when they drew pictures after reading individual chapters. For those who choose to, responding artistically can only broaden children's interpretations of books (Bartelo, 1990).

As children become older, their responses to books become more interpretive, analytic, and complex (e.g., Applebee, 1978; Cullinan, Harwood, & Galda, 1983; Pillar, 1983). Middle-grade children, especially, benefit from the thinking about books that writing generates; writing helps children sharpen and refine their responses to books (Golden & Handloff, 1993; Hancock, 1992; Smith, 1982; Vardell, 1983). Response-based teachers are careful not to intrude upon children's individual responses by routinely limiting children to assigned times, topics, and lengths for writing. At the same time, they help students broaden their responses to books through thought-provoking written response activities. There are unlimited forms written responses can take ranging from the variations in response journals to written conversations (Harste, Short, & Burke, 1988) to reports, letters (Atwell, 1987), reviews, poems, advertisements, questions, character sketches, and different story versions. These forms can serve to enhance the children's construction of text meaning through writing.

RESEARCH AND PRACTICE IN THE FUTURE

Little has been reported on research in response to literature with children who have difficulties reading. Do readers who have difficulties respond differently than more able readers? Are there developmental trends in struggling readers' responses to books? What instructional practices can best empower struggling readers with a love of literature and enhance the way they express their responses to books?

Much of the research in response to literature has been conducted in classrooms with middle-class children. The instructional implications of this research are often adopted by educators who teach children from a range of ethnic and socioeconomic backgrounds. Instruction is often based on the assumption that children have had the range of experiences in reading and responding to books that is most common in middle-class families. How different cultural literacies, values, discourse patterns, and family or community backgrounds affect response and classroom practice is only beginning to be explored.

Several researchers and theorists have advocated an approach to classroom organization that has three levels of reading: core books read by everyone, group books, and individual books. We need more systematic inquiries into the implications of this instructional organization. How does this approach affect the responses of children of various reading abilities, habits, and interests?

Another line of research on response to literature concentrates on the analysis of children's response journals. Consequently, there are myriad suggestions for teachers in practitioner journals on how to enhance children's responses. Although there has been quite a bit of research on teachers' questions, we still wonder how teachers' questions shape children's written responses. What is the effect of teacher directions on children's written responses? How can we invite children to respond individually to books and at the same time encourage more complexity in written responses? Likewise, we might consider how the process of visual expression, such as drawing, influences reader–text transactions, especially among older students. What are the pedagogical implications of having children respond to books in artistic modes?

Perhaps most important to consider is how teachers decide what is best for their given group of children. Considering the limited time often allotted for language arts/reading instruction, how do teachers make informed decisions concerning the range of possibilities available to them through a response-centered curriculum? How does instruction in such classrooms affect children's interpretations of books?

IDEAL RESPONSE-BASED INSTRUCTION IN REAL CLASSROOMS

Focusing instruction on the transactions between readers and texts encourages children to develop a lifelong love for books and reading. We have presented a range of reasons for considering teaching reading from a response-based stance. We have also presented a range of instructional possibilities from which to choose. However, the most important aspect of teaching from a response-based stance is maintaining the sanctity of the reader-text relationship, while at the same time enhancing children's awareness of literature and their own range of responses to literature. A focus on achieving this balance is what characterizes instruction in successful response-based classrooms.

If you were able to look into an ideal response-based classroom, you would see children in a supportive, intellectual environment reading real books for real reasons and responding to those books in ways that are meaningful to them.

REFERENCES

Adams, M. J., & Collins, A. (1979). A schema-theoretic view of reading. In R. Freedle (Ed.), *New directions in discourse processing.* Norwood, NJ: Ablex.

Anderson, R. C., Fielding, L. G., & Wilson, P. T. (1988). Growth in reading and how children spend their time outside of school. *Reading Research Quarterly, 23,* 285–304.

Anderson, R. C., Hiebert, E. H., Scott, J. A., & Wilkinson, I. A. (1985). *Becoming a nation of readers: The report of the commission on reading.* Washington, DC: The National Institute of Education.

Anderson, R. C., & Pearson, P. D. (1984). *A schema-theoretic view of basic processes in reading comprehension* (Tech. Rep. No. 306). Urbana, IL: Center for the Study of Reading, University of Illinois.

Applebee, A. N. (1978). *The child's concept of story.* Chicago: University of Chicago Press.

Applebee, A. N. (1990). *Literature instruction in American Schools* (Report Series 1.4). Albany, NY: Center for the Learning and Teaching of Literature, State University of New York at Albany.

Atwell, N. (1987). *In the middle: Writing, reading and learning with adolescents.* Portsmouth, NH: Heinemann.

Bartelo, D. M. (1990). The linkages across listening, speaking, reading, drawing, and writing. *Reading Improvement, 27*(3), 162–172.

Benton, M. (1983). Secondary worlds. *Journal of Research and Development in Education, 16*(3), 68–75.

Britton, J. (1970). *Language and learning.* London: Allen Lane, Penguin Press.

Burke, J. J. (1980). The effect of creative dramatics on the attitudes and reading abilities of seventh grade students. *Dissertation Abstracts International, 41*(12), 4887A.

Cochran-Smith, M. (1984). *The making of a reader.* Norwood, NJ: Ablex.

Cohen, D. (1968). The effect of literature on vocabulary and reading. *Elementary English, 45,* 209–213.

Cox, B. (1991). A picture is worth a thousand worksheets. *Journal of Reading, 35*(3), 244–245.

Cox, C., & Many, J. (1992). Toward an understanding of the aesthetic response to literature. *Language Arts, 69*(19), 28–33.

Cullinan, B. (1992). *Read to me: Raising kids who love to read.* New York: Scholastic.

Cullinan, B., & Galda, L. (1994). *Literature and the child* (3rd ed.). Fort Worth, TX: Harcourt Brace.

Cullinan, B., Harwood, K., & Galda, L. (1983). The reader and the story: Comprehension and response. *Journal of Research and Development in Education, 16,* 29–37.

Dickinson, D., & Keebler, R. (1989). Variations in preschool teachers' storybook reading styles. *Discourse Processes, 12,* 353–376.

Dyson, A. H. (1986a). The imaginary worlds of childhood: A multimedia presentation. *Language Arts, 63*(8), 799–808.

Dyson, A. H. (1986b). Transitions and Tensions: Interrelationship between the drawing, talking, and dictating of young children. *Research in the Teaching of English, 20*(4), 370–409.

Eeds, M., & Wells, D. (1989). Grand conversations: An exploration of meaning construction in literature study groups. *Research in the Teaching of English, 23,* 4–29.

Eeds, M., & Wells, D. (1990). *Grand conversations: Literature groups in action.* New York: Scholastic.

Feitelson, D., Kita, B., & Goldstein, Z. (1986). Effects of listening to series stories on first graders' comprehension and use of language. *Research in the Teaching of English, 60,* 339–356.

Ferreiro, E., & Teberosky, A. (1982). *Literacy before schooling.* Exeter, NH: Heinemann.

Fish, S. E. (1980). *Is there a text in this class? The authority of interpretive communities.* Cambridge, MA: Harvard University Press.

Galda, L. (1982). Assuming the spectator stance: An examination of the responses of three young readers. *Research in the Teaching of English, 16*(1), 1–20.

Galda, L. (1988). Readers, texts, contexts: A response-based view of literature in the classroom. *The New Advocate, 1*(2), 92–101.

Galda, L. (1990). A longitudinal study of the spectator stance as a function of age and genre. *Research in the Teaching of English, 24*(3), 261–278.

Galda, L., Cullinan, B. E., & Strickland, D. S. (1993). *Language, literacy, and the child.* New York: Harcourt Brace Javanovich.

Golden, J. M., & Handloff, E. (1993). Responding to literature through journal writing. In K. Holland, R. Hungerford, & S. Ernst (Eds.), *Journeying: Children responding to literature* (pp. 175–186). Portsmouth, NH: Heinemann.

Guice, S. (1991). *Sixth graders as a community of readers: An interpretive case study from the emic perspective.* Unpublished doctoral dissertation, The University of Georgia.

Guice, S. (1992, December). *Readers, texts, and contexts in a sixth-grade community of readers.* Paper presented at the annual meeting of the National Reading Conference, San Antonio.

Hade, D. D. (1989, April). *The stances and literary interpretations of second and third grade children and their teacher.* Paper presented at the American Educational Research Association, San Francisco.

Hade, D. D. (1991). Being literary in a literature-based classroom. *Children's Literature in Education, 22*(1), 1–17.

Hancock, M. R. (1992). Literature response journal: Insights beyond the printed page. *Language Arts, 69*(1), 36–42.

Harding, D. W. (1937). The role of the onlooker. *Scrutiny, 6,* 247–258.

Harding, D. W. (1968). Response to literature: The report of the study group. In J. R. Squire (Ed.), *Response to Literature.* Urbana, IL: National Council of Teachers of English.

Harste, J., Short, K., & Burke, C. (1988). *Creating classrooms for authors: The reading–writing connection.* Portsmouth, NH: Heinemann.

Hepler, S., & Hickman, J. (1982). "The book was okay. I love you"—Social aspects of response to literature. *Theory into Practice, 21,* 278–283.

Hickman, J. (1979). *Response to literature in a school environment, grades K through 5.* Unpublished doctoral dissertation, The Ohio State University.

Hickman, J. (1981). A new perspective on response to literature: Research in an elementary school setting. *Research in the Teaching of English, 15,* 343–354.

Hiebert, E. H., & Colt, J. (1989). Patterns of literature-based reading instruction. *The Reading Teacher, 43,* 14–20.

Huck, C. S., Hepler, S., & Hickman, J. (1993). *Children's literature in the elementary school* (5th ed.). New York: Holt, Rinehart, Winston.

Iser, W. (1978). *The act of reading: A theory of aesthetic response.* Baltimore: The Johns Hopkins University Press.

Jacque, D. G. (1993). The judge comes to kindergarten. In K. Holland, R. Hungerford, & S. Ernst (Eds.), *Journeying: Children responding to literature* (pp. 43–53). Portsmouth, NH: Heinemann.

Johnston, P., Guice, S., Baker, K., Malone, J., & Michelson, N. (1993, April). *Assessment of teaching and learning in "literature-based" classrooms.* Paper presented at the annual meeting of the American Educational Research Association, Atlanta.

Kardash, C. A. M., & Wright, L. (1987). Does creative drama benefit elementary school students: A meta-analysis. *Youth Theater Journal, 2*(1), 11–18.

Keifer, B. (1983). The responses of children in a combination first/second grade classroom to picture books in a variety of artistic styles. *Journal of Research and Development in Education, 16*, 14–20.

Kelly, P. R. (1990). Guiding young students' response to literature. *The Reading Teacher, 43*(7), 464–470.

Langer, J. A. (1990a). The process of understanding: Reading for literary and informative purposes. *Research in the Teaching of English, 24*(3), 229–260.

Langer, J. A. (1990b). Understanding literature. *Language Arts, 67,* 812–816.

Langer, S. K. (1957). *Philosophy in a new key: A study in the symbolism of reason, rite, and art* (3rd ed.). Cambridge, MA: Harvard University Press.

Many, J., & Cox, C. (1992). *Reader stance and literary understanding: Exploring the theories, research, and practice.* Norwood, NJ: Ablex.

Martinez, M. (1993). Motivating dramatic story reenactment. *The Reading Teacher, 46*(8), 682–688.

Martinez, M., & Roser, N. (1985). Read it again: The value of repeated readings during storytime. *The Reading Teacher, 38,* 782–786.

Martinez, M. G., & Roser, N. L. (1991). Children's responses to literature. In J. Flood, J. M. Jensen, D. Lapp, & J. Squire (Eds.), *Handbook of Research on Teaching the English Language Arts* (pp. 643–654). New York: Macmillan.

Martinez, M. G., & Teale, W. H. (1993). Teacher storybook reading style: A comparison of six teachers. *Research in the Teaching of English, 27*(2), 175–199.

McClure, A. A. (1990). *Sunrises and songs: Reading and writing poetry in an elementary classroom.* Portsmouth, NH: Heinemann.

Mendoza, A. (1985). Reading to children: Their preferences. *The Reading Teacher, 38,* 522–527.

Morrow, L. M. (1982). Relationships between literature programs, library corner designs, and children's use of literature. *Journal of Educational Research, 75*(6), 339–344.

Morrow, L. M. (1990). Preparing the classroom environment to promote literacy during play. *Early Childhood Research Quarterly, 5*(4), 537–554.

Morrow, L. M. (1992). The impact of a literature-based program on literacy achievement, use of literature, and attitudes of children from minority backgrounds. *Reading Research Quarterly, 27*(3), 249–275.

O'Brien, K. L. (1991). A look at one successful literature program. *The New Advocate, 4*(2), 113–123.

Pappas, C. C. (1993). Is narrative "primary"? Some insights from kindergartners' pretend readings of stories and informational books. *Journal of Reading Behavior, 25*(1), 97–129.

Pellegrini, A. D., & Galda, L. (1982). The effects of thematic-fantasy play training on the development of children's story comprehension. *American Educational Research Journal, 19,* 443–452.

Piaget, J. (1970). Piaget's theory. In P. Mussen (Ed.), *Carmichael's manual of child psychology* (Vol. 1, pp. 703–732). New York: Wiley.

Pillar, A. C. (1983). Aspects of moral judgement in response to fables. *Journal of Research and Development in Education, 16,* 39–46.

Purves, A. C. (1973). *Literature education in ten countries: An empirical study: International studies in evaluation.* Stockholm: Almqvist and Wiksell.

Purves, A. C. (1981). *Achievement in reading and literature: The United States in international perspective.* Urbana, IL: National Council of Teachers of English.

Purves, A. C. (1991). The school subject literature. In J. Flood, J. M. Jensen, D. Lapp, & J. R. Squire (Eds.), *Handbook of research on teaching the English language arts* (pp. 674–680). New York: Macmillan.

Purves, A. C., & Beach, R. (1972). *Literature and the reader: Research in response to literature, reading interest, and the teaching of literature.* Urbana, IL: National Council of Teachers of English.

Purves, A. C., Rogers, T., & Soter, A. O. (1990). *How porcupines make love II: Teaching a response-centered literature curriculum.* New York: Longman.

Rosenblatt, L. M. (1976). *Literature as exploration.* New York: Noble & Noble. (Original work published in 1938)

Rosenblatt, L. M. (1978). *The reader, the text, the poem: The transactional theory of the literary work.* Carbondale, IL: Southern Illinois University Press.

Rosenblatt, L. M. (1991). Literature—S.O.S.! *Language Arts, 78*(6), 444–448.

Roser, N., & Martinez, M. (1985). Roles adults play in preschoolers' response to literature. *Language Arts, 52*, 485–490.

Scholes, R. E. (1989). *Protocols of reading.* New Haven, CT: Yale University Press.

Shanklin, N. L., & Rhodes, L. K. (1989). Comprehension instruction as sharing and extending. *The Reading Teacher, 42*(7), 496–500.

Short, K. G., & Pierce, K. M. (1990). *Talking about books: Creating literate communities.* Portsmouth, NH: Heinemann.

Simpson, M. K. (1986). A teacher's gift: Oral reading and the reading response journal. *Journal of Reading, 30*(1), 45–50.

Smith, F. (1983). Reading like a writer. *Language Arts, 60*, 558–567.

Smith, L. R. (1982). Sixth graders write about reading literature. *Language Arts, 54*(4), 357–362.

Steig, M. (1989). *Stories of reading: Subjectivity and literary understanding.* Baltimore: The Johns Hopkins University Press.

Stein, N. L., & Glenn, C. G. (1979). An analysis of story comprehension in elementary school children. In R. O. Freedle (Ed.), *Advances in discourse processes (Vol. 2): New directions in discourse processing* (pp. 53–120). Norwood, NJ: Ablex.

Stewig, J. W., & Buege, C. (1994). *Dramatizing literature in whole language classrooms* (2nd ed.). New York: Teachers College Press.

Strickland, D. S., & Morrow, L. M. (1989). Environments rich in print promote literacy behavior during play. *The Reading Teacher, 43*(2), 178–179.

Teale, W. H., & Martinez, M. G. (1988). Getting on the right road to reading: Bringing books and young children together in the classroom. *Young Children, 44*(1), 10–15.

Temple, C., & Collins, P. (1992). *Stories and readers: New perspectives on literature in the elementary classroom.* Norwood, MA: Christopher-Gordon.

Trousdale, A. N., & Harris, V. J. (1993). Missing links in literary response: Group interpretation of literature. *Children's Literature in Education, 24*(3), 195–207.

Vardell, S. M. (1983). Reading, writing, and mystery stories. *English Journal, 72*(8), 47–51.

Weston, L. H. (1993). The evolution of response through discussion, drama, writing, and art in fourth grade. In K. Holland, R. Hungerford, & S. Ernst (Eds.), *Journeying: Children responding to literature* (pp. 137–150). Portsmouth, NH: Heinemann.

Yarden, D. (1988). Understanding stories through repeated read-alouds: How many does it take? *The Reading Teacher, 41*(6), 556–561.

Zarrillo, J. (1989). Teachers' interpretations of literature-based reading. *The Reading Teacher, 43*(1), 22–28.

CHAPTER FOURTEEN

Beyond Individual Response: Toward a Dialogical Approach to Literature Instruction

Mark A. Faust
The University of Georgia, Athens

In 1983, midway through my career as a high school English teacher, I made two important discoveries—one theoretical in nature, the other grounded in my teaching practice. A summer of graduate study focused on reader-response theory had introduced me to new questions and concerns about the role of the reader in producing literary understanding. Uncertain about how these new ideas might influence my stance as a teacher, I turned to an unanticipated and practical source of assistance—my students. One afternoon, as a chorus of voices in my eleventh-grade American Literature class renewed their request to be allowed, for once, to "just read," instead of "analyzing" a text in class, I invited an explanation of exactly what it was they believed would be preferable to what we had been doing. Perhaps the fact that my invitation received a coherent response should not have surprised me, but surprised I was when, in essence, my students told me: "We want more time to read; we want to talk about ideas *we* think are important; we want answers to questions *we* raise." My job? "Tell us when our answers are wrong and let us know if we miss anything, but only if it really matters." Although I was confused about the role assigned to me, how could I not be impressed by the clarity of these requests?

During the ensuing years, I gradually revised my approach to teaching so that I placed more emphasis on guiding students toward feeling a sense of ownership over their experiences as readers. As students clearly became more engaged and involved, I gradually became convinced that producing literary criticism of one form or another may not be the most sensible goal

331

for many teenage readers of literature. Nonetheless, I struggled to imagine legitimate alternatives to the teacher-led discussions and essay writing that had been staples in my repertoire of teaching strategies. Considering my background as an English major in college and graduate school, perhaps it was inevitable that the way I interpreted my role resulted in a kind of "seesaw" effect. Either my students' (reader-oriented) voices or my (text-oriented) voice would prevail in the classroom, with me, more often than not, claiming the last word in order to "balance" their "personal" responses with the more "academic" perspectives I believed it was my responsibility to provide.

In this chapter, I discuss new developments in response-oriented theory that have created realistic options for literature teachers who wish to avoid this uncomfortable position of being caught between two extremes (i.e., teachers who do not wish their students habitually to settle for unexamined, uncritical responses, and yet who want to avoid prematurely dwelling on terminology and concepts that might be inappropriate for young readers). Common to all of these options is an emphasis on creating opportunities for dialogue to occur, on writing, speaking, and listening as potentially integral aspects of reading experiences.

Increasingly over the past 10 years, response-oriented theorists/researchers have emphasized the sociocultural dimensions of literary understanding (Applebee, 1992; Beach, 1993; Bloome, 1985; Purves, 1993; Rosenblatt, 1986). Drawing on these and other sources, I present a view of literature instruction that stresses the value of helping all readers become more self-aware about their own experiences with literature while seeking to understand the experiences of others. Then I describe ways that classroom teachers can create opportunities for students to reflect as they read, to share their reflections with others, and, generally speaking, to *make something* of their experiences with literary texts.

THE READER AND THE TEXT: A DILEMMA

I was so taken by my students' distinction between "just reading" and "analyzing" because their explanation resonated with the distinction between "reader-based" and "text-based" literary theory, which I was beginning to explore at that point in my career. Despite being cautioned by several colleagues about the danger of being "taken in" by "lazy kids," I persisted in trying to honor my students' request without wholly discrediting myself as their teacher. In place of the usual assign, quiz, discuss, write, test pattern (Sheridan, 1991), which I had used to structure my classes for years, I experimented with methods aimed at encouraging and supporting my students as readers rather than critics (Benton & Fox, 1986). Some of these methods are described in the latter portion of this chapter, where I focus on aspects of what, in my view, would be an ideal approach to literature instruction at the secondary level. First, I revisit my initial encounter with reader-response theory, and then discuss ways in which this theory is becoming increasingly "dialogical."

As indicated previously, the initial impact of reader-response theory on my teaching was not wholly positive insofar as it pinned me on the horns of a dilemma. Once I was persuaded by the ground-breaking work of theorists such as Holland (1975), Culler (1975), Bleich (1978) Iser (1978), and Fish (1980)—to believe that a work of literature remains inert and powerless until it is brought to life in the minds of readers, and that the process whereby literature is brought to life is inseparable from whatever meaning it can be said to possess—I could no longer be satisfied with merely talking about literature with my students without first acknowledging their experiences as readers. This is where I ran into difficulty. My initial attempts at listening to my students' unguided responses resulted in writing and discussion that had precious little to do with the critically approved interpretations that, for me, accounted for why we were reading literature in the first place. Yet I did not know how to intervene without silencing my students as readers, and consequently forcing them to rely on me to guide them toward more "academic," and therefore "valid," responses. Either I communicated to the young readers in my class that a text is little more than an ink blot inviting them to explore the scope of their imaginations, or I became an authority figure in effect dictating what they should experience as readers.

One way to understand my situation would be to point out that my teaching suffered the effects of a false dichotomy subtly endorsed by reader-response theorists writing in the 1970s, who were anxious to dissociate their work from that of more mainstream, text-based, literary theory. In an effort to shift attention from texts as objective entities to the subjective experiences of readers, response-oriented theorists tended to leave intact not only a dichotomous view of texts and readers, but a number of other value-laden assumptions concerning the purposes for reading and studying literature inherited from their more text-oriented forebears. For instance, early reader-response theorists tended to share with mainstream theorists a belief that the overriding aim of literary study is the production of comprehensive and defensible interpretations (Tompkins, 1980). Closely linked with this belief is an assumption that competent readers ultimately should produce approximate, if not complete, consensus concerning the interpretation of particular texts. Another important shared assumption is that the reading process can be accounted for solely in terms of singular experiences involving individual readers and texts.

As response-oriented theory has evolved in recent years, largely as a result of research involving actual readers, the previously mentioned assumptions about reading and literature instruction that overlap with mainstream theory and practice are rapidly fading from view. It is possible now to talk about readers and texts without being drawn into stale and counterproductive arguments about whether meaning is "subjective" or "objective" (of course, it is both and neither). It is possible now to talk about reading as a communal activity without invoking the quasimystical elitism passed down from the New Critics to contemporary advocates of "cultural literacy" (e.g., Hirsch, Bennett). "Today," wrote Hansson (1992), "readers are recognized for the role they play in the production of meanings and values in and around literary works. These readers are no longer implied readers, ideal readers, or other kinds of imagined readers—they are real readers" (p. 135). And real readers are real people with diverse backgrounds, interests, concerns, and purposes for reading literature.

Now that researchers are attending to what actual readers are saying about what happens when they read literature and what makes this a valuable experience for them, it has become apparent, as Hansson pointed out, that we require nothing less than "a partly new language for the description, analysis, evaluation, and teaching of literature—a language which does justice to the reader's role in the production of meanings and values in literature" (p. 143). Recent research involving actual readers, scholarship exploring the potential impact of cultural diversity on literature instruction, and newly developed social constructionist arguments concerning the making and sharing of knowledge all support Hansson's claim—that we need to account for reading as a meaning-making process.

RESEARCH SUPPORT FOR A DIALOGICAL APPROACH TO LITERATURE INSTRUCTION

Although some earlier studies focused on responses made by actual readers who were not also literary critics (Purves, 1968; Squire, 1964), the past 10 years have produced a marked increase in research aimed at generating a truly reader-based understanding of literary response (Beach, 1993). One strand of this activity is typified by the work of de Beaugrande (1985), who wrote, "though it is useful to see how a *professional expert* reader depicts his or her own activities when processing a literary text, such depictions can be only one small part of the total empirical domain. We need to focus much more on how *ordinary* readers negotiate a text" (1985, p. 1). Promising to focus on ordinary readers, de Beaugrande asserted, "we must always bear in mind that the text exists only as an *event*: the written artifact is not a 'text' in the communicative sense until someone performs an action upon it" (pp. 1–2). In his research, de Beaugrande tape-recorded students' thinking aloud after each of two readings of a poem. His examination of these transcripts led to "a broad, provisional classification of the typical operations students performed" (p. 9), which indeed recognizes important features of the students' experiences as readers.

The "typical operations" de Beaugrande noted are: hedging ("signalling that statements are provisional, inexact, or uncertain"), paraphrasing, normalizing ("bringing the content of a passage closer to the respondent's own everyday discourse"), citing, key word association, and generalizing (pp. 9–16). These findings are interesting: they suggest that readers typically draw on and orchestrate a variety of strategies. Nonetheless, as Kintgen (1986) noted, taxonomies of response strategies tend to overlook the organic, narrative aspect of reading events: "We must . . . confront not merely the problems posed by identifying the mental structures readers use, but more importantly, the mysteries of how they make use of these mental structures, how and why they make choices and behave as they do in constructing interpretations" (p. 93).

In his own research involving graduate English students, Kintgen (1983) focused on how an individual reader's "horizon of expectations" (or stance) imposes a narrative structure on the way he or she selects from a range of mental operations, of which 24 are identified. Kintgen's research underscored his point that a reader's expectations necessarily will interact with one another and evolve during the course of a reading event, which makes it nearly impossible to foresee in detail how a particular reader will engage with a particular text, even if one knows something about the prior knowledge and background of experience that reader will bring to his or her reading. A number of key studies have corroborated this finding, as researchers have sought to develop a language for describing what happens during reading events (Benton & Fox, 1986; Benton, Teasey, Bell, & Hurst, 1988; Blake & Lunn, 1986; Cox & Many, 1992; Dias, 1987; Langer, 1990; Protherough, 1986; Thomson, 1987). Although their terminology varies, these researchers have clearly encouraged us to look at readers of literature as active cocreators of meaning.

At the same time, by focusing exclusively on the private, individual responses of readers, the researchers tended to disregard the social dimensions of reading literature, which others, such as Bloome (1985), Hynds (1989), and Golden (1992), have argued are critical if we are ever to achieve a complete portrait of the potentialities inherent in literary understanding. Ultimately, they argued, a reader's lived-through experience with a literary text should be viewed as more than a product of individual choice and inclination. For instance, Bloome (1985) suggested that the social context in which reading takes place always "influences how students will interact with and interpret a text" (p. 135). He went on to point out that reading needs to be viewed as a cultural activity involving "shared ways of acting, valuing, feeling, believing, and thinking" (p. 136). Attending to these factors, which have been ignored by mainstream, text-based literary theory, requires that "educators look at reading events in a new way—in terms of reading as a social process" (p. 140).

Drawing on the ideas of Bakhtin (1981, 1986), Hunt and Vipond (1992) developed a view of "point-driven" reading that describes the most rewarding experiences people have with literary texts. This view is similar to what others, drawing from the same source, have referred to as *dialogic reading* (Bialotosky, 1989; Holquist, 1990; Patterson, 1985). It has evolved for them from being focused on "the notion of a 'point' as a specific, unitary—and perhaps unproblematic—phenomenon that a story might in some sense 'have' " to requiring that it be thought of as "a process of establishing relationships between people by means of texts" (p. 79). Hunt and Vipond underscored the "most important" of their theoretical assumptions—namely, "that reading is a transaction between reader and text, shaped by situation" (p. 82)—when they asserted that "point-driven" or "dialogic" reading should be viewed as "a form of social interaction" (p. 83).

Therefore, "point-driven" or "dialogic" reading is motivated by a reader's active participation in what Bakhtin (1986) referred to as a "concrete situation of speech communication" (pp. 83–84). According to Hunt and Vipond:

> The most important single fact about a "concrete situation of speech communication" is that it is socially constructed. When the situation affords it, a reader or listener takes a text as an utterance, it becomes a move in a dialogue. If the reader sees the text as an utterance in one dialogue, the reader will tend to expect certain kinds of things from it; if it is seen as a move in another, quite different dialogue, the reader will expect different things from it. In other words, what a given reader does is affected as much by how that reader sees the text as framed by an ongoing dialogue as it is by anything we may be able to identify as "text characteristics." And it is what the reader does that determines the shape of the most fundamental kinds of connections or inferences that will be constructed on the basis of the text. In brief, what that reader does will be profoundly influenced by how she or he constructs the situation and the text's role in it. (pp. 84–85)

Simply by inviting students to see themselves as participants in an ongoing dialogue with others around a specific text, Hunt and Vipond witnessed a way of reading that failed to arise as a result of other experimental methodologies. Rather than present texts as "stimulus materials that readers used to complete various tasks," Hunt and Vipond offered texts to readers as "occasions for response" in conversation with an interviewer. The ease with which students adopted a dialogic stance underscores the crucial "importance of how the text is framed. . . . In order that texts be taken as utterances they must be embedded in concrete situations that support dialogue" (p. 86).

During the course of a collaborative research project, Harold Vine and I (Vine & Faust, 1993) found unexpected support for a dialogical view of the reading process. Like the researchers mentioned earlier, we gathered data based on the private, individual experiences of readers. However, interpreting that data led us to conclude that empowered, engaged reading is essentially dialogical in ways we did not anticipate. Our data consisted of 288 readings of a single poem gathered from readers ranging in age from 11 to 50. The readers were requested to respond in writing using a method we devised, which enabled us to make inferences about their meaning-making. Each reader was invited to read the poem three times during a single sitting, and to write from memory in between each reading. In addition, each reader was asked to reflect in writing on how his or her experience with this particular text evolved over three readings. Initially, we hoped to identify clear developmental patterns across age differences and over multiple readings. Over time, this hope faded as we became fascinated by the enormous variety of ways in which our readers "constructed situations," which included a role for the printed text of the poem. Although the developmental patterns we expected never materialized for us—at times it felt as if we had solicited 288 utterly unique readings—we discovered that we could compare and contrast the experiences of readers often differing in age who clearly were engaged readers of the poem. As was the case for Hunt and Vipond, the focus of our research shifted from trying to describe what happens during individual reading events to asking what it might mean to read in an engaged way.

Our findings indicate that engaged readers use a process of sensing and making sense of situations to generate a lived-through experience with a literary text. We also found that our readers who clearly were reading in an engaged way were profoundly influenced by particular and varying concerns aroused during their reading. Generally speaking, these concerns emerged in the form of questions aimed at clarifying a particular social situation. A third factor we found to be common among our engaged readers was a tendency toward self-awareness (of processes being used) and other-awareness (author, implied author, narrator, fictional characters, and/or other readers or potential readers). The clear presence and significance of a dialogical stance in what our engaged readers wrote, despite the individualistic bias of our research design, makes us now wish we had created conditions more conducive to looking at reading as a social process.

Reading in an engaged way may be equally a matter of attending to oneself and others as it is a matter of paying close attention to printed texts. This theory is beginning to stand out in research on reader response (Purves, 1993). Nowhere is this more evident than in the increasing compatibility between reader-response theory and scholarship, which specifically addresses problems and possibilities that arise when teachers develop programs of literature instruction that recognize cultural and other sources of diversity (see Hurlbert & Samuel, 1992; Trimmer & Warnock, 1992). Paradoxically, our becoming more sensitive to the uniqueness of individual reading events has opened the door to the recognition that, just as there are different kinds of texts, there also are different kinds of readers. To fully account for similarities and differences in the experiences reported by individual readers requires sensitivity to the latter as much as to the former. A dialogical approach to literature instruction calls on teachers to recognize the value in developing students' understanding of themselves and the cultural communities in which they live (Newell & Durst, 1993). The notion that literature (somehow) contains timeless and universal truths, which it is the reader's job to recover, is gradually being replaced by a view of reading as conversational, driven by twin goals of intra- and interpersonal dialogue, and cultural and cross-cultural understanding.

SOCIAL CONSTRUCTIONISM AND THE FUTURE OF LITERATURE INSTRUCTION

In setting out to describe "the larger process within which writers and readers coexist and mutually define themselves," Clark (1990) typified a growing number of response-oriented scholars and researchers who are calling for recognition and understanding of the social dimensions of reading. Tierney (1990) pointed to increased interest in what he referred to as "situation-based cognition," from which perspective the experience of reading literature may be described as a "place" where things happen between people, rather than as a procedure for decoding messages:

> For researchers and others who enjoy looking into the windows of the reader's mind, I hope our explorations have just begun and that our awe for what readers do remains intact. Above all, I see reading as a place where readers discover and reflect upon themselves—who they are and what matters. They do so as they develop intimate relationships with authors and characters, participate in events, journey into different times, make discoveries, solve mysteries, celebrate or share in joy or disaster, and are moved to voice opinions, and sometimes even to revolt. (p. 41)

Tierney's emphasis on the situatedness of reading experience is supported by social constructionist arguments concerning the situatedness of knowledge in general. Increasingly, social constructionism is being linked to descriptions of reading and writing processes (Beach, 1990; Smith, 1992), as well as to calls for reform in the way literature is taught in schools (Applebee, 1992; Johnston, 1993; Purves, 1993).

According to Bruffee (1986), "A social constructionist position in any discipline assumes that entities we normally call reality, knowledge, thought, facts, texts, selves, and so on are constructs generated by communities of like minded peers" (p. 774). This epistemological assumption is the cornerstone of a new way of thinking about thinking, which promises to liberate us from long-standing problems associated with dualistic thinking (Gergen, 1985). Scholars in a variety of fields are now exploring the possibility that, as Gergen put it, "knowledge is not something people possess somewhere in their heads, but rather, something people do together" (p. 270). By calling into question objective foundations for knowledge, this line of reasoning appears to undermine what we have come to accept as the "scientific method." Gergen argued against the necessity of this conclusion:

> Constructionism offers no foundational rules of warrant and in this sense is relativistic. However, this does not mean that "anything goes." Because of the inherent dependency of knowledge systems on communities of shared intelligibility, scientific activity will always be governed in large measure by normative rules. However, constructionism does invite the practitioners to view these rules as historically and culturally situated—thus subject to critique and transformation. There is stability of understanding without the stultification of foundationalism. (p. 273)

Constructionism informs the work of scholars representing a variety of disciplines, who have revolutionized our understanding of knowledge production as a culturally situated phenomenon (Bruner, 1990; Geertz, 1983; Kuhn, 1962; Rorty, 1979; Scholes, 1989).

This work holds important implications for literature instruction because it liberates teachers from feeling compelled to determine whether particular meaning statements are located "in the text" or "in the reader." From a constructionist perspective, the answer to this familiar dilemma will always be both and neither because writers and readers will be understood as cocreators of a situation that will be interpreted as meaningful in different ways by different people. A constructionist perspective allows that literary understanding, which is generally assumed to involve the explication of printed texts, may instead be thought of in terms of building communities. Rather than as a "timeless" artifact containing "universal truths," we may now approach a literary text as a special opportunity to imagine possible worlds inhabited by people like and unlike ourselves, and including writers as well as other readers. Constructionism and dialogism are complementary concepts that have reoriented my view of literature instruction from one that demanded me to be concerned about doing justice to texts to one that allows me to be more concerned about the quality of my students' experiences as readers and persons. How constructionism and dialogism might inform classroom practice is the focus of the remainder of this chapter.

CLASSROOM PRACTICES
THAT SUPPORT DIALOGICAL READING

The dilemma I spoke about earlier disappeared for me as a teacher when I stopped referring exclusively to critically approved interpretations to plan lessons and evaluate the quality of my students' experiences with literature. Instead, I found myself creating conditions that supported dialogue, encouraged students to explore their own purposes for reading, and helped them situate themselves, socially and culturally, as readers. Distancing myself from philosophic arguments concerning the status of texts enabled me to take seriously questions about the role of reading in the lives of the teenagers who attended my classes every day. Of course, I cannot offer a recipe for producing engaged readers, but I can highlight aspects of my own dialogical approach to literature instruction, which consists of three strands: engaging, enhancing, and evaluating. Although there is a linear dimension to these strands, each is best viewed as a particular focus of inquiry that, together with the other two, may be used by teachers to orchestrate whatever specific objectives they have decided are most appropriate for their students at a particular time.

The goal of engaging is to enable students to read a text as rapidly and naturally as possible for the purpose of sensing and beginning to make sense of situations through articulating their first impressions. The goal of enhancing is to enable students to realize their questions and concerns with the work, and to explore one or more of those questions and concerns by rereading all or portions of the text (and related texts where appropriate) for the purpose of extending and refining their awareness of how they and others may be situated as readers of that text. The goal of evaluating is to enable students to review their enhanced senses of the work—their explorations of self and others—and to reflect on their successes and frustrations, their meaning-making processes, and their next steps for reading and learning.

As a classroom teacher, I would not hesitate to share what I was learning at the time about how reading experience may evolve over time (developmentally) and in time (as an event). A high priority for me would be helping students to see themselves as readers, and to reflect on how their experiences with reading had evolved during their lifetimes. Equally important would be the goal of helping young readers to articulate what they and their peers presently are able to do with texts. A dialogical approach to literature instruction teaches students to be aware that evoking a text is a selective process—that, as in everyday life, the situations readers imagine must remain open to question. Students also learn to respect that what concerns them as human beings necessarily will influence what kind of reader they will be, what books they will find engaging, and what stances they will adopt during the course of particular reading events. At the same time, they learn to respect that others' concerns may, and probably will, differ from their own. In such an environment, students become accustomed to the notion that the point of reading need not be to comprehend a final, best interpretation. Rather, they learn to respect multiple points of view as they learn to accept responsibility for their role in determining how and for what purposes they will read.

The practices I highlight here are not intended to be prescriptive. Rather, they are meant to be suggestive of the kinds of experiences an "ideal" curriculum based on dialogism could offer to students. To begin, I underscore three aspects that together distinguish a dialogical approach to literature instruction from all others. First, it encourages students to respect their own and others' first impressions with a text as it encourages them to respect that reading experience evolves over time and in time. Second, it encourages students to be self-aware about their purposes, questions, and concerns as readers. Third, it encourages students to respect the social dimensions of reading so that they become accustomed to imagining how persons with differing backgrounds of experience might read the same text. In principle, the "content" of a response-based curriculum is determined not by what writers have done, but by what writers and readers do together. Instead of expecting texts to function as "containers" of meaning, students learn to approach reading dialogically—as "a process of establishing relationships with people by means of texts" (Hunt & Vipond, 1992, p. 79).

Classroom Talk

Purves, Soter, and Rogers (1991) began their useful description of a "response-centered classroom" with a simple, but powerful, claim: "In a response-centered classroom, teachers and students really listen to each other" (p. 76). Adding that, in such classrooms, "feelings are shared and authority is shared," they described a situation in which "ideas can be revised based on what other people say and do" (p. 76). The extent to which students really listen to each other and help each other to think aloud about their reading is an indication of how well their teacher has succeeded in creating conditions that support dialogue. What are those conditions? Purves et al. suggested that teachers obtain audio- or videotapes of their classes:

> Listen and watch. What role do you play in the discussion? What kinds of questions do you ask? . . . What do you do if someone doesn't raise his or her hand right away? What role do students play? . . . Do you say something between each student's utterance? Are you constantly evaluating student responses? Do the students ever talk to each other (about literature)? What are you signalling to students about how to read literature? Do you have a sense of how *the students* responded to the text? (pp. 82–83)

In classrooms where students expect reading to be an occasion for dialogue, an alert, knowledgeable teacher may be able to discern what is motivating students to respond as they do. Making time for students to engage in informal, exploratory talk in small groups, and being patient with apparent digressions and inefficiency, can lead to important revelations about how students are "working together to construct a reading of a story" (Sandman, 1991, p. 9). Knowing when to hold back and when to participate in "nurturing conversations" (Hynds, 1991), wherein "meanings and interpretations are shared, negotiated, and changed from reader to reader" (p. 177), will be a central concern for teachers who care about building classroom communities that bridge the connections between life and literature.

In-Process Reflection

Students who know their responses are valued, and who expect to listen and be listened to can benefit from a variety of open-ended procedures for "becoming mindful" of their experiences as readers (Durrant, Goodwin, & Watson, 1990). Marking passages and making jot notes while reading ("post-it notes" are useful when students are reading books they do not own), thinking aloud on paper or audiotape during or after reading, and composing brief letters to other readers of the same text are all easy ways to generate power and a sense of ownership. In a very direct way, students are made aware of their own process of selective attention (Pradl, 1987), as well as that "thoughtful reading is rarely a matter of flashy insight. More often it is a gradual, groping process" (Wolf, 1988). Thomson (1987) believed teachers should to encourage and legitimize simpler forms of writing that acknowledge a reader's first impressions with a text. He suggested various types of "column notes" that prompt students to record such things as "commentary, speculation, and relevant autobiography" (p. 277). Informal talk and ungraded reflective note making can consume large amounts of class time. However, this time is well spent when it helps students and their teachers grow into more thoughtful, self-aware readers who are "wide awake" to possibilities in literature and life (Calkins, 1991).

Responding With Questions

Leggo (1991) observed that, "[o]ne of the most prevalent weaknesses of students' responses to poetry is the persistent tendency to closure" (p. 58). He went on to describe his own successful attempts at developing "reading strategies that defer closure and promote openness" (p. 58). In addition to the generative experiences already described as "classroom talk" and "in-process reflection," Leggo advocated inviting "readers to pose their initial responses in the form of questions, lists, and lists of questions which do not need to be ordered or categorized" (p. 58). In most situations where students do not readily respond with questions even when invited to do so, I have found that simply directing students' attention to their own first impressions, so as to help them recognize their own implicit questions, is often enough to get them started. Other strategies are to provide students with generic open-ended questions (e.g., What makes sense to you? What were you reminded of as you read this story? What do you care about as you read this poem?), and to model a questioning stance in sharing one's own responses in class (Newkirk, 1984).

The point here is that students need to generate their own questions. Young readers need to experience the power that derives from creating what Hynds called (1992) *challenging questions*:

> Challenging questions are those that lead students to direct their responses to each other, rather than to the teacher alone—questions that encourage variety, diversity, and even idiosyncrasy, rather than conformity of response. Such questions allow literary themes and ideas to interact and coalesce, rather than to fragment and disintegrate; they nurture self-assured interpretation, rather than blind dependence on teachers or study guides. (pp. 96–97)

Once students accept that their questions will become the basis for class discussion, they are ready to learn more about the questioning process (Rogers, Green, & Nussbaum, 1990). How do questions work? What makes some questions more powerful and engaging than others? How and why might readers revise their initial questions? What do our questions reveal about how we read? Focusing on the questioning process can empower students to use questions on their own as a means to sustain and enhance their experiences with literature. Focusing on the questioning process also provides teachers with opportunities to make students aware of multiple ways of reading any text. Dialogical teaching involves using questions both to listen to what students are saying about their reading as well as to open up new lines of inquiry students may not be aware of, but may be ready to take into consideration.

In-Role Speaking and Writing

Reflecting on my own early experiences with eliciting student responses leads me to concur with Thomson (1987)—that "the activities of reading literature and discussing it with others are not sufficient of themselves to ensure that students will extend and refine their understanding of themselves and of other people and the human condition" (p. 135). Teenagers all too easily embrace the notion that similarities and differences among readings do not really matter—that, because "everyone has their own opinion," there's no point in going further than granting everyone an opportunity to "say what they think." This notion evaporates when students are convinced that learning about themselves and making meaningful connections with others may be legitimate purposes for reading in a setting that supports dialogue.

A powerful alternative to focusing exclusively on questions is to have students situate themselves as readers by attempting to imagine how others—including the implied author, fictional characters, and other readers—could be situated with regard to a particular text. Thomson underscored the power of verbal and written role playing to encourage self- and other-awareness.

> Once a person begins to improvise action and words around a fictional scene or character, she begins to give that character life from within herself, to the considerable increase of her own understanding and involvement. Paradoxically, it is by entering further into *ourselves*, by drawing on our own affective resources, that we come to empathize with others. . . . Once we speak our feelings directly, instead of merely talking about them or writing about them, things do start to happen—feelings are stirred up and insights can occur. (p 136)

In-role speaking and writing requires students to imagine what it might be like to experience a particular situation from multiple perspectives. Activities of this type (O'Neill & Lambert, 1982) support the overall goal of response-based teaching, which is to promote dialogical reading and provide a direct means of combating legitimate fears that arise whenever the necessarily subjective nature of reading experience is recognized. Along with sharing first impressions in small-group settings, discussing the outcomes of in-process reflection, and developing powerful questions, opportunities for in-role talk and writing will increase the likelihood that students will develop the capacity to be responsible and responsive readers.

Extended Writing

The power of extended writing to help students sustain and enhance their experiences with literature is well documented (Probst, 1988). In contrast to traditional approaches to literature instruction, which require students to produce "display texts" (Bloome, 1985) for grading purposes, a dialogical approach calls for a wide array of writing possibilities. Britton's (1982) functional model of writing purposes is a useful reference here because its three categories encompass the whole range of these possibilities. The *expressive* mode defines a kind of focused, generative writing that invites students to sustain a particular train of thought without concerning themselves with matters of structure or mechanics. Journals, readers' notebooks, and learning logs are exemplary venues for gathering expressive writing, and provide powerful ways to extend the outcomes of classroom talk, in-process reflection, and questioning.

Expressive writing also may serve as a gateway to other forms of writing, which thereby remain connected with the purposes, questions, and concerns of students (Newell & Durst, 1993). In addition, Britton identified two broad purposes for composing more formal responses to literature. Students who respond to stories and poems in kind with imaginative creations of their own are said to be operating in the *poetic* mode. Students who explain or otherwise account for their reading in order to be informative are said to be operating in the *transactional* mode. Writing their responses down can bring students' own situations as readers into focus and prepare them to imagine how other readers (or potential readers) and writers are situated. Furthermore, sharing their written responses enables students to experience meaning-making from the writer's, as well as the reader's, perspectives.

Framing Conversations

A common misconception I repeatedly encounter in my work with student teachers is that a dialogical approach to teaching and learning results in something like an "open classroom," in which students "mingle" and "rap" in an environment virtually uncontrolled by external sources of authority. In time, I am able to convince most that whatever might be said for or against it, an "open classroom" bears almost no relation to what I mean when I talk about students feeling a sense of ownership as they develop the ability to take responsibility for their own and each others' learning. Teachers and students have important roles to perform when transforming their classroom into a community of readers and writers (Foster, 1994).

To focus on reading and writing as social processes, teachers need, in Gilbert's (1991) words, to "denaturalize . . . classroom and reading practices" (p. 209).

> [When] writing and reading are conceptualized as social activities, then the conditions of production and the conditions of interpretation of texts can be described as social and cultural practices: as observable, knowable, possible. Writing/speaking (the production of texts) and reading/listening (the interpretation of texts) can then be seen as integrally related to a discursive site. (pp. 206–207)

A dialogical approach calls for teachers and students to discuss what it means to read in an engaged, responsive way. More than that, it calls for discussions about why, where, and for whom this kind of reading might be valuable. O'Neill (1990) asserted that "classroom strategies which foreground ways in which texts and readings are constructed may be more helpful to students learning to read, than promoting a notion that response to text is fundamentally idiosyncratically grounded in personal experience" (p. 92). Such discussions, especially when they are tied to actual reading events, tend to frame students' personal evocations by bringing to light the different stances governing their responses. Whether teachers intervene from the outset by selecting texts and designing activities, or whether they wait and judiciously respond to what students say or write on their own, the point is to frame classroom conversation so that students begin to see themselves and others as coauthors of their experiences as readers. Inviting students to situate themselves as readers can be the basis for enabling them to "transform themselves and their world" (Roemer, 1987).

Probst (1992) asserted that a literature class should be structured so that students and teachers "will recognize the potential in literary experience for learning about ourselves, about those who surround us, about the myriad of factors that contribute to the making of meaning, and about the rich reservoir of strategies by which we might make sense of life and texts" (p. 76). These are important goals for our time, in which the need for communication and collaboration is particularly urgent. A successful democracy demands more than tolerance from its citizens (Pradl, 1990); it demands the kind of understanding that makes possible the peaceful negotiation of differences. Our young people must learn how to listen to themselves and others as they develop ways of understanding personal and cultural diversity. They need to learn how to read in the broadest sense of the word (Slevin, 1992). A dialogical approach to literature instruction can make a significant contribution toward preparing future generations to live in a world where diversity and conflicts of interest can no longer be safely ignored.

REFERENCES

Applebee, A. (1992). The background for reform. In J. Langer (Ed.), *Literature instruction: A focus on student response* (pp. 1–18). Urbana, IL: National Council of Teachers of English.

Bakhtin, M. (1981). *The dialogic imagination.* Austin: University of Texas Press.

Bakhtin, M. (1986). *Speech genres and other late essays.* Austin: University of Texas Press.

Beach, R. (1990). New directions in research on response to literature. In E. Farrell & J. Squire (Eds.), *Transactions with literature* (pp. 65–77). Urbana, IL: National Council of Teachers of English.

Beach, R. (1993). *Reader response theories.* Urbana, IL: National Council of Teachers of English.

Benton, M., & Fox, G. (1986). *Teaching literature: Nine to fourteen.* Oxford, England: Oxford University Press.

Benton M., Teasey, J., Bell, R., & Hurst, K. (1988). *Young readers responding to poems.* London: Routledge.

Bialotosky, D. (1989). Dialogic criticism. In G. D. Atkins & L. Morrow (Eds.), *Contemporary literary theory.* Amherst, MA: University of Massachusetts Press.

Blake, R., & Lunn, A. (1986). Responding to poetry: High school students read poetry. *English Journal, 75*(2), 68–73.

Bleich, D. (1978). *Subjective criticism.* Baltimore: Johns Hopkins University Press.

Bloome, D. (1985). Reading as a social process. *Language Arts, 62*(2), 134–142.

Britton, J. (1982). *Prospect and retrospect.* Upper Montclair, NJ: Boynton & Cook.

Bruffee, K. (1986). Social construction, language, and the authority of knowledge: A bibliographic essay. *College English, 48*(8), 773–790.

Bruner, J. (1990). *Acts of meaning.* Cambridge, MA: Harvard University Press.

Calkins, L. (1991). *Living between the lines.* Portsmouth, NH: Heinemann.

Clark, G. (1990). *Dialogue, dialectic, and conversation.* Carbondale, IL: Southern Illinois University Press.

Cox, C., & Many, J. (1992). Toward an understanding of the aesthetic response to literature. *Language Arts, 69,* 28–33.

Culler, J. (1975). *Structuralist poetics.* Ithaca, NY: Cornell University Press.

de Beaugrande, R. (1985). Poetry and the ordinary reader: A study of immediate responses. *Empirical Studies of the Arts, 3*(1), 1–21.

Diaz, P. (1987). *Making sense of poetry: Patterns in the process.* Ottowa: Canadian Council of Teachers of English.

Durrant, C., Goodwin, L., & Watson, K. (1990, December). Encouraging young readers to reflect on their processes of response: Can it be done, Is it worth doing? *English Education,* 211–219.

Fish, S. (1980). *Is there a text in this class?* Cambridge, MA: Harvard University Press.

Foster, H. (1994). *Crossing over: Whole language in secondary classrooms.* New York: Harcourt Brace.

Geertz, C. (1983). *Local knowledge: Further essays in interpretive anthropology.* New York: Basic Books.

Gergen, K. (1985, March). The social constructionist movement in modern psychology. *American Psychologist,* 266–275.

Gilbert, P. (1991, December). From voice to text: Reconsidering writing and reading in the English classroom. *English Education,* 195–211.

Golden, J. (1992). Inquiries into the nature and construction of literary texts: Theory and method. In R. Beach, J. Green, M. Kamil, & T. Shanahan (Eds.), *Multidisciplinary perspectives on literacy research* (pp. 275–292). Urbana, IL: National Council of Teachers of English.

Hansson, G. (1992). Readers responding—and then? *Research in the Teaching of English, 26*(2), 135–148.

Holland, N. (1975). *Five readers reading.* New Haven, CT: Yale University Press.

Holquist, M. (1990). *Dialogism: Bakhtin and his world.* New Haven, CT: Yale University Press.

Hunt, R., & Vipond, D. (1992). First, catch the rabbit: Methodological imperative and the dramatization of dialogic reading. In R. Beach, J. Green, M. Kamil, & I. Shanahan (Eds.), *Multidisciplinary perspectives on literacy research* (pp. 69–89). Urbana, IL: National Council of Teachers of English.

Hurlbert, C. M., & Totten, S. (Eds.). (1992). *Social issues in the English classroom.* Urbana, IL: National Council of Teachers of English.

Hynds, S. (1989). Bringing life to literature and literature to life: Social constructs and contexts of four adolescent readers. *Research in the Teaching of English, 23*(1), 30–61.

Hynds, S. (1992). Challenging questions in the teaching of literature. In J. Langer (Ed.), *Literature instruction: A focus on student response* (pp. 78–100). Urbana, IL: National Council of Teachers of English.

Iser, W. (1978). *The act of reading.* Baltimore: Johns Hopkins University Press.

Johnston, P. (1993). Assessment and literate "development." *The Reading Teacher, 46*(5), 428–429.

Kintgen, E. (1983). *The perception of poetry.* Bloomington, IN: Indiana University Press.

Kintgen, E. (1986). Expectations and processes in reading poetic narratives. *Empirical Studies of the Arts, 4*(1), 79–95.

Kuhn, T. (1962). *The structure of scientific revolutions.* Chicago: University of Chicago Press.

Langer, J. (1990). The process of understanding: Reading for literary and informative purposes. *Research in the Teaching of English, 24*(3), 229–260.

Leggo, C. (1991, November). The reader as problem-maker: Responding to a poem with questions. *English Journal,* 58–60.

Newell, G., & Durst, R. (Eds.). (1993). *Exploring texts: The role of discussion and writing in the teaching of literature.* Norwood, MA: Christopher Gordon.

Newkirk, T. (1984). Looking for trouble: A way to unmask our readings. *College English, 46*(8), 756–766.

O'Neill, C., & Lambert, A. (1982). *Drama structures.* London: Hutchinson.

O'Neill, M. (1990). Molesting the text: Promoting resistant readings. In M. Hayhoe & S. Parker (Eds.), *Reading and response.* Philadelphia: Milton Keynes.

Patterson, D. (1985). Mikhail Bakhtin and the dialogical dimensions of the novel. *Journal of Aesthetics and Art Criticism, 44,* 131–140.

Pradl, G. (1987). Close encounters of the first kind: Teaching the poem at the point of utterance. *English Journal, 76*(2), 45–51.

Pradl, G. (1990). Reading literature in a democracy: The challenge of Louise Rosenblatt. In J. Clifford (Ed.), *The experience of reading: Louise Rosenblatt and reader-response theory* (pp. 23–46). Portsmouth, NH: Heinemann.

Probst, R. (1988). *Response and analysis.* Portsmouth, NH: Heinemann.

Probst, R. (1992). Five kinds of literary knowing. In J. Langer (Ed.), *Literature instruction: A focus on student response* (pp. 54–77). Urbana, IL: National Council of Teachers of English.

Protherough, R. (1986). How children describe their reading of stories. In V. Lee (Ed.), *English literature in schools* (pp. 278–290). Philadelphia: Milton Keynes.

Purves, A., with V. Rippere. (1968). *Elements of writing about a literary work: A study of response to literature.* Urbana, IL: National Council of Teachers of English.

Purves, A., Soter, A., & Rogers, T. (1991). *How porcupines make love: II.* Boston: Longman.

Purves, A. (1993). Toward a reevaluation of reader response and school literature. *Language Arts, 70,* 348–361.

Roemer, M. (1987). Which reader's response? *College English, 49*(8), 911–921.

Rogers, T., Green, J., & Nussbaum, N. (1990). Asking questions about questions. In S. Hynds & D. Rubin (Eds.), *Perspectives on talk and learning* (pp. 73–90). Urbana, IL: National Council of Teachers of English.

Rorty, R. (1979). *Philosophy and the mirror of nature.* Princeton, NJ: Princeton University Press.

Rosenblatt, L. (1986). The literary transaction. In P. Demers (Ed.), *The creating word* (pp. 66–85). London: Macmillan.

Sandman, J. (1991). When are they going to get to the point? Listening to peer group discussions in an introductory literature class. *The English Record, 41*(4), 7–12.

Scholes, R. (1989). *Protocols of reading.* New Haven, CT: Yale University Press.

Sheridan, D. (1991). Changing business as usual: Reader response in the classroom. *College English, 53*(7), 804–814.

Slevin, J. (1992). Genre as a social insitution. In J. Trimmer & T. Warnock (Eds.), *Understanding others: Cultural and cross-cultural studies and the teaching of literature* (pp. 16–34). Urbana, IL: National Council of Teachers of English.

Smith, R. (1992). Hymes, Rorty, and the social rhetorical construction of meaning. *College English, 54*(2), 138–158.

Squire, J. (1964). *The responses of adolescents while reading four short stories.* Urbana, IL: National Council of Teachers of English.

Thomson, J. (1987). *Understanding teenagers' reading.* New York: Nichols.

Tierney, R. (1990, March). Redefining reading comprehension. *Educational Leadership,* 37–42.

Tompkins, J. (1980). The reader in history: The changing shape of literary response. In J. Tompkins (Ed.), *Reader response criticism* (pp. 211–232). Baltimore: Johns Hopkins University Press.

Trimmer, J., & Warnock, T. (1992). *Understanding others: Cultural and Cross-cultural studies and the teaching of literature.* Urbana, IL: National Council of Teachers of English.

Vine, H., & Faust, M. (1993). *Situating readers: Students making meaning of literature.* Urbana, IL: National Council of Teachers of English.

Wolf, D. (1988). *Reading reconsidered: Literature and literacy in high school.* New York: College Board Publications.

CHAPTER FIFTEEN

Powerful Models or Powerful Teachers? An Argument for Teacher-as-Entrepreneur

Gerald G. Duffy
Whitworth College

This chapter argues for empowering teachers to be in charge of their own literacy instruction. It does not favor any particular instructional model; in fact, I argue that under certain circumstances instructional models inhibit teachers' ability to take charge of their instruction. I base my position in my experience and research, which convince me that (a) while explicit instruction of literacy within life-like situations is essential, no instructional model is superior to all others, and (b) the best literacy instruction is provided by independent, enterprising, entrepreneurial teachers who view instructional models as ideas to be adapted rather than as tenets to be followed. Consequently, the question I ask is not "Which instructional model should teachers use?" but, rather, "What should we teach teachers about how to use instructional models?"

BACKGROUND

I base my argument in 39 years of working in classrooms as a teacher, teacher educator and researcher. During that time, I have seen relatively few teachers depart from traditional lock-step instruction to create life-like contexts for learning literacy. Nor are my observations unique. A wide range of research findings result in similar conclusions (see, for instance, Cohen, 1988; Cuban, 1984; Durkin, 1978–1979; Elmore & McLaughlin, 1989).

There are good reasons for this situation. Not the least of these is the difficulties of managing modern classrooms. Classrooms are complex places in the best of times; with recent changes in society, they are now much more complex than they were 40 years ago. As a result, teachers work harder than ever before, and find it difficult to generate life-like literacy situations in the midst of this complexity.

But part of the problem rests with the way we teach teachers to use instructional models. Because their work is so hard, teachers are easy prey for those who promise to simplify their work. Literacy educators often imply simple solutions by urging that a particular instructional model be followed faithfully. In doing so, instructional power is attributed to the model, and teachers are left feeling (as many have said to me over the years) that "the people who wrote this [model] know more than I do." In so saying, teachers abdicate to the model the responsibility for the success or failure of literacy instruction in their classrooms.

I came to this conclusion over many years. As a young classroom teacher in the late 1950s, I found myself debating between the progressive education passions of my teachers college professors and the "back-to-basics" pressure which began with Sputnik. I resolved early on that, to be effective, I would need to create my own model which incorporated both views.

Once I became a teacher educator, I urged my student teachers to similarly assume control of their instruction. It was not long, however, before I realized that, for many, this was not easy to do. I frequently observed my student teachers, for instance, applying my advice in technically correct but senseless ways rather than thoughtfully combining ideas to fit the students and the goal at hand. Consequently, when I became involved in the mid-1970s with the Institute for Research on Teaching (IRT) at Michigan State University, I was concerned about teachers who mindlessly followed prescriptions. Hoping to find a thoughtful kind of literacy instruction (Duffy, 1988; Duffy & Roehler, 1981), my colleagues and I focused on whether teachers made differential teaching decisions based on thoughtful analysis of reading. However, after hundreds of classroom observations over four years, it was clear that most teachers decided what to do by reference to prescriptions from distant authority and not by thoughtful reference to conceptions of literacy (Duffy & Anderson, 1984). We called what we saw "repeated exposure" (Duffy & Roehler, 1982) because teachers repeatedly required students to "cover" what an authority said to cover, rather than inventing their own explanations and learning situations.

So in 1980, we began another longitudinal study, this time focusing on what happens when teachers invent their own explanations. However, even though the experiment confirmed that student outcomes improve when teachers create explicit explanations of mental processes (Duffy, Roehler, Sivan, et al., 1987), the same kind of dichotomy emerged: that is, some experimental group teachers combined our advice with other ideas and created rich, applicable situations which made literacy real to kids; others followed our advice narrowly and created shallow, technically accurate explanations possessing neither spirit nor substance (Duffy, Roehler, & Rackliffe, 1986).

Once again, we were face-to-face with differences in teacher mindfulness. Some teachers were in charge of their instruction; others passively followed directions. I began to consider whether the problem lay in the way we teach teachers and, as a result, I initiated a 4-year study of the teacher education process while working with in-service teachers in rural Michigan (Duffy, 1993, 1994). Again, results reinforced how difficult it is for teachers to break from whatever instructional model is being promoted. Many really believed they were not supposed to tamper with the instructional model, paralyzed by the belief that the "experts" cannot be contradicted. The most effective teachers, however, rejected the belief that their job was to follow authority (whether it was me or a distant author of an instructional model or authors of materials they were using) and embraced the concept that the best instruction was an invention of *their* minds. Two kinds of inventions characterized their work: one, they invented life-like literacy experiences as a context for student learning and, second, they invented their own instructional models, adapting and combining principles from several instructional models.

As a result, I now argue that power must lie with teachers, not with instructional models. The crucial challenge is not to identify the best instructional model but, rather, to put teachers in cognitive control of the models they choose to use. Consequently, my professional energies as director of an alternative teacher education program at Whitworth College for the past 4 years have been focused on how the teacher education process can be modified to create such teachers.

EXAMPLES OF ENTREPRENEURIAL TEACHERS IN ACTION

A person is not literate until literacy skills are applied to one's life. For example, one is not literate in history until past events help us understand the problems facing President Clinton; one is not literate in science until knowledge of physics can be used to sail a boat; one is not a literate reader of poetry until a poet's words enrich our view of the world. The test of being literate is active use of language in pursuit of some real-world end.

Developing this kind of literacy is our biggest challenge. Because genuine literacy is embedded in real-world activity, the best literacy teachers invent occasions for students to use literacy in pursuit of such ends. Because such situations are nonstandard, unconventional, and counter to our past experience about what students do in school, such teachers must be thoughtful opportunists who create situations where students can experience real literacy, despite prevailing practices, mandates or directives. I call these kinds of teachers "entrepreneurial."

Consider, for instance, how Cathi, one of my student teachers, was entrepreneurial in inventing a life-like learning situation for her kindergartners:

> Cathi had established a connection with a teacher in Hawaii, and had arranged for that teacher's students to send Cathi's kindergartners pictures of what Hawaiian children do in the winter. These pictures were the focus of much talk about the difference between Spokane winters and Hawaiian winters. Then Cathi asked her kindergartners whether they would like to help the Hawaiian children learn what Spokane was like. She gave each kindergartner a postcard of Spokane and the name of one Hawaiian child. Within the situation of writing to the Hawaiian children, Cathi taught a very explicit lesson on how to write a post card, including where to put the greeting, where to sign your name, and so on.

Cathi put creation of a life-like learning situation ahead of following prevailing practices and mandates. As a result, Cathi's students probably began to build a belief that literacy is communication. In contrast, if Cathi had followed the prescribed model in that classroom, students would have labeled parts of a post card on a work sheet and kindergartners would have probably concluded that post card writing was artificial.

Another student teacher, in a fourth grade, similarly created a life-like situation as a context for genuine literacy:

> George wanted his students to learn to respect the environment and to take active roles in protecting the environment. When faced with teaching a required chapter on ecology, George used the building of a new subdivision in the neighborhood as the focus of the study. The driving question he posed for students was, "What can we do to ensure that our environment is protected when these new houses are built?" He obtained the covenants for the subdivision and reviewed them with the students. Students learned strategies for comprehension and applied them as they read about and discussed ecological relationships and how the subdivision's covenants should be revised so that these relationships would be preserved and the environment protected. They then rewrote the subdivision's covenants accordingly, invited the developer to the classroom, and argued that he should change the covenants of the development in specific ways in order to preserve the environment.

By embedding instruction within the context of a problem relevant to the students, George made learning comprehension strategies a sensible and worthwhile thing to do. As a result, students probably concluded that being strategic about comprehension was important because it helped them make a difference in their world.

Similarly, consider how Joe put his sixth graders in position to believe that study skills are worth learning:

> Joe wanted his students to become independent, creative individuals, but the sixth-grade curriculum mandated the teaching of study skills. He could have followed the model embedded in the mandated materials. But, instead, he tried to figure out a way to situate study skills in activity that would provide students with life-like opportunities to do what literate people do. A conversation with students about which kinds of architecture is "best" led students to choose sides, some favoring classical architecture, some favoring modern, and so on. Capitalizing on this interest, Joe involved his students in researching their favored kind of architecture, with the goal of having a culminating debate about which type of architecture was best. In the lesson I observed, Joe was soliciting from students the questions they wanted to answer and the resources they could access. In subsequent lessons, he provided explicit study skill instruction that students applied when locating and organizing information for the debate.

Like Cathi and George, Joe rejected standard practices associated with the mandated instructional model. Instead, he assumed cognitive control, searching for a situation that would make a traditionally dry school task genuinely useful. As a result, it is likely that Joe's students believe study skills are important tools, rather than busywork with no real use.

Similar instruction occurs in high schools. For example, consider Alan, a high school English teacher:

> Alan was told that he had to teach a grammar unit, complete with identifying parts of speech, sentence structure, etc. Rather than following the teacher's guide and the instructional model embedded there, Alan started by searching for a life-like situation. Ultimately, he involved students in producing a radio broadcast for the school's radio station. In producing the show, the students had to write a script for what they would say about the news, sports, and other items. Within the framework of preparing the script, Alan provided explicit instruction in grammar, which students applied as they wrote scripts for the broadcast.

Alan was proactive in searching for a unique and life-like way to situate grammar instruction. Because students were actually doing a real radio broadcast, clear writing (and correct grammar) was important. As a result, his students perceived grammar to be important and worth learning.

What counts in these examples is that each teacher invented for students life-like experiences in literacy use. Clusters of such life-like experiences create what Nespor (1987) calls "richly detailed episodic memories" which, in turn, result in a *system* of beliefs about what it means to *be* literate.

I rarely see teachers who provide their students with the clusters of experience which build beliefs about being literate. We know that some exist (see, for instance, Allington & Cunningham, 1996; Brown, 1991; Cunningham & Allington, 1994). However, we are a long way from having enough of them.

CONDITIONS ESSENTIAL TO BEING
AN ENTREPRENEURIAL TEACHER

My 4 years at Whitworth College have focused on what we need to do to develop more such teachers. It seems that at least five conditions must exist.

An Expectation Must Be Set

First, a different expectation must be set for teachers. Instead of implying that one *follows* a specific instructional model, teachers must be authorized to adapt instructional models to the situation, and to invent learning situations which captivate students.

When teacher educators and staff developers set the expectation that teachers invent instruction by responding to students' interests and needs and by adapting models to these situations, it is the teachers who are in charge. *They* own instruction, so they take responsibility for it. If, on the other hand, a particular instructional model is pushed, the message often is that teachers are to emulate the model "owned by" a distant expert. Teachers subjugate themselves to the model and hesitate to strike out on their own in an opportunistic way.

What concerns me here is that the psychology implicit in promoting models makes teachers into disciples rather than thinkers. Consider two currently popular reading programs: Reading Recovery and Project Read. Both programs have merit; neither sets out to disempower teachers. However, once you are "trained" to be a Reading Recovery teacher or a Project Read teacher, the expectation is that you will teach the way you were trained to do it. That is, you will use the instructional model embedded in the program. If instruction succeeds, it is because the right program was used. The teacher is identified not as a good literacy teacher but as a "Reading Recovery teacher" or a "Project Read teacher." Power is in the program, not in the mind of the teacher.

Because of the pressures of modern classroom teaching, many teachers are susceptible to suggestions to "follow" a model. If we are to create entrepreneurial teachers, we must set a counter expectation—that all models, all programs and all literacy educators have well-conceived ideas, but that good instruction is not a simple matter of "doing what they said to do." It is, instead, a matter of embedding those ideas in a life-like context, combining together elements of several instructional models if that is what it takes to achieve the desired outcome. In sum, instructional models are resources to be adapted, not scripts to be followed.

Entrepreneurial Teachers Must Have a Vision

One reason why some teachers are susceptible to passively following models and programs is that they lack a passionate vision of their own. Consequently, we have learned that vision is a second necessary condition of entrepreneurial teaching.

Vision usually takes the form of an ultimate outcome for schooling—what the teacher believes students should ultimately become. It is always personal in three ways. First, it reflects the teacher's personal values and beliefs. Second, it reflects the teacher's particular perspective on society's needs in future decades. Third, it reflects the teacher's perspective on what is important about literacy. Because the teacher's ideas and values are a priority, the teacher gains dignity. It is such dignity which sets professional teachers apart from technicians. Technicians follow the directions of others, content to assign to those others the responsibility for deciding what students should become because they have no passionate vision of their own. Professional teachers, in contrast, have a vision. They see teaching as a calling—and as a moral act. They know what impact they want to have. They teach in order to develop that outcome in students, and they refuse to abdicate their professional right to do so.

Entrepreneurial Teachers Base Instruction in Why

It is not easy to promote ultimate outcomes in classrooms which, by their very nature, are artificial environments. We have learned that for our teachers to do so they must learn to think in terms of *why* something is being learned.

This means thinking in terms of knowledge types (Paris, Lipson & Wixson, 1983). When I get ready to teach, for instance, I think not only about *what* I want to teach (declarative knowledge) and *how* it works (procedural knowledge) but, also, *when, why,* and *under what circumstances* it will be used (conditional knowledge). Because I want students to learn to *be* literate, I cannot just teach them *about* literacy. I must think about when and why the language learning I am about to teach would be useful, and then I must invent a situation in which students use it that way in the act of being literate.

If teachers think first about *why* students need a particular learning, they are less likely to mindlessly follow directives and are more likely to create genuine literacy opportunities for students.

Entrepreneurial Teachers Invent Life-Like Learning Situations

The point has already been made that invention of life-like learning situations is central to entrepreneurial teaching. However, inventing these situations is very difficult for teachers to do.

Two concepts are helpful in teaching teachers to invent such situations. First, the concept of "situated cognition" (see Brown, Collins, & Duguid, 1989; Leinhardt, 1988; Resnick, 1987) helps teachers understand how to situate learning in the context of real-world tasks. Second, the concept of "authentic" learning helps teachers develop tasks that "represent the kind of work literate individuals would do of their own free will (unfettered by an authority figure to control their behavior)" (Pearson, 1989, p. 231). We illustrate these concepts by using generic examples such as teaching compass use in the context of a hike in the woods. When situated that way, students tend to learn compasses well because compasses are really used when you take a hike in the woods—the task is authentic.

We help teachers operationalize the idea of creating life-like situations by encouraging them to do unit teaching—project-based instruction—in which the culminating project itself is life-like. Originally developed in the 1930s as part of the progressive education movement and recently revisited by educators (Blumenfeld, Soloway, Marx, Krajcik, Guzdial, & Palincsar, 1991), units are relatively long-term, rooted in students' desire to answer a life-like question and culminated with a resolution of the question. Basic skills taught during a unit are perceived to be useful because they are applied in completing the culminating project. Alan's high school grammar unit is a good example, as is George's ecology unit. Both involved compelling projects that served as vehicles for applying basic skills in immediately useful ways.

Other recently observed examples of life-like projects include second graders reading expository text about weather (and learning related reading strategies) because the culminating activity was the local TV weatherman doing a broadcast from their classroom; third graders reading children's literature (and learning associated reading strategies) as part of a project to distribute paperback books to foster homes; fourth graders reading expository and narrative text about Native Americans (and learning associated letter writing skills) because they were writing to the governor about injustices done to local Native Americans; and resource room students reading expository text about bird houses (and learning basic comprehension strategies) because they needed to build and sell bird houses to raise money for their end-of-year party.

Because these projects were life-like, students were motivated. For instance, Alan reported that he "couldn't get students to stop working" on the high school grammar unit. But the real power of units is that students see the *use* of what they are learning. As Doyle (1983), Winne (1985), and Blumenfeld, Mergendoller, and Swartout (1987) describe, academic work situated in important activity causes students to learn to value its use while academic work taught with a focus on passing a test focuses them only on getting a grade.

Creating life-like learning situations is very subtle, however. It is easy to be fooled by interesting-looking activity which, upon closer examination, is not life-like at all. For instance, when I watched Dean teach division to third graders, he had his students divide groups of beans into smaller groups, using manipulatives in accordance with the instructional model he had been taught to use. But postlesson student interviews revealed that his students saw no reason for learning division (except, of course, for the obligatory but vague "it will help us when we grow up"). This is because Dean thought about using manipulatives, but did not provide a life-like use for division. From the students' perspective, division was superfluous because they were not going to use the beans once they were divided. However, if (as one possible example) Dean had taught division within the context of dividing animal crackers equally among the students as part of a birthday treat, students might have seen the sense of learning to divide.

The same principle applies to literacy. When we see students reading literature books, for example, we tend to assume that instruction is authentic. In reality, however, literature-based reading instruction can be just as boring as basal text instruction. To be really effective, students need to read literature within a context they perceive to be compellingly life-like. Anything short of this still smacks of "school work" and is often perceived as having no relevance to life.

Similarly, "fun" instruction does not suffice. The teacher who has her students make papier mâché models of story characters has students who think they are having fun, but those students do not see language learning as useful or important because they are not using language to achieve important ends (Duffy, 1993).

What we have learned is that unless we work hard at teaching teachers to create life-like literacy situations, they will fall back on following prescriptions or on "fun" activities which have no life-like applications. Situated learning and unit structures help break teachers out of this mold.

Entrepreneurial Teachers Use Many Models

Although many teacher education programs favor a particular instructional model to the exclusion of others, our experience tells us that entrepreneurial teachers must know about many models, and must create from these models a model of their own. In doing so, the criterion is a coherent combination of concepts—that is, the student teacher must combine elements of various instructional models in a logically consistent way and convincingly justify how the invented model promotes the desired vision for students.

Our students do this in all phases of our program. When learning classroom management, students create their own management plan by selecting from the various available management models; when learning classroom organizational strategies, students create their own plan by selecting from various grouping plans; and, of course, when learning about literacy instruction, students create their own instructional model from the total set of literacy models. By presenting models in this way, we reinforce the concept central to entrepreneurial teaching: that instructional power lies in the minds of teachers who tailor instruction to the students and to the vision they have for students.

Entrepreneurial Teachers Do "On-the-Fly" Decision Making

Of all the things we have learned about developing entrepreneurial teachers, perhaps none is more important than emphasizing from the start that good teaching is a complex, ambiguous balancing act. Teachers work in a perpetually changing context in which decisions are often made spontaneously. To be effective, they must embrace such spontaneity, understand that there are no simple solutions, and accept the ambiguity that comes with wrestling with dilemmas.

This is particularly relevant to literacy, where much energy is devoted to convincing teachers to "adopt" one or another program, theory, model, or philosophy, or to play a particular role in the classroom, or to employ a particular set of materials. One often gets the impression that there is a single "right way" and all other ways are "wrong." We see this repeatedly in the ongoing bloodletting between the instructional model embedded in whole language and the one embedded in direct instruction (for the most recent of these arguments, see Smith, Reyna, & Brainerd, 1993, and Smith, 1993).

In practice, however, there are no panaceas. The best teachers never follow a single program, theory, model, or philosophy, nor do they play a single role or employ one set of materials to the exclusion of others. Instead, the best teachers draw thoughtfully from various sources, play many roles, and use many techniques and materials in a manner which I have previously labeled "conceptual selectivity" (Duffy, 1991). For instance, good teachers may use KWL (Ogle, 1986) on one day; mental modeling (Duffy, Roehler, & Herrmann, 1988) on another day, reciprocal teaching (Palincsar & Brown, 1984) on another day, and Slavin's cooperative grouping (Slavin, 1987) on yet another day. Similarly, it is not unusual to see the same teacher using basal textbooks one day, literature books on another, various kinds of expository text on another and workbooks on another; or to be using language experience ideas one day and systematic phonics on another; or to be using whole language ideas one day and direct instruction ideas another. In short, the best teachers are in intellectual control, drawing on a variety of options and selecting appropriate adaptations depending on the situation.

Teachers can learn to do this if teaching is presented from the very beginning as a complex and ambiguous act. They must have no illusions about finding easy answers, and must be prepared to thread their way through each day with a combination of quick thinking and tolerance for ambiguity, with directional guidance coming from a firm vision of what students should become. In short, they need to be entrepreneurial.

DEVELOPING ENTREPRENEURIAL TEACHERS

Prevailing teacher education practices do not always promote entrepreneurial teachers. To the contrary, many programs promote "teacher-proof" materials or programs that teachers are "trained" to follow; or promote one instructional model or philosophy to the exclusion of others; or present teacher educators as gurus whose recommendations cannot be modified. The result is that too many teachers see themselves as followers to be directed. Such teacher education programs cause Apple (1983) to talk about the "de-skilling" of teachers and Cuban (1984) to suggest that teachers' "brittle compliance" impedes reform agendas.

But even when the intent is to develop entrepreneurial teachers, the task is not easy. Unlike children who come to school with limited conceptual models and rudimentary belief systems about literacy, prospective teachers come to teacher education with firmly established beliefs about teaching. Having themselves spent thousands of hours as students, prospective teachers are what Pajares (1992) calls "insiders" who have already created a powerful belief system about teaching. And because they were, for the most part, successful as students, they often see nothing wrong with current schooling. They do not question traditional curriculum and instruction—because they did well with it, they believe it must be good. In short, they see no need for change.

This phenomenon often results in new teachers who perpetuate the status quo. To combat this, my colleagues and I at Whitworth consciously set out to break our prospective teachers from their own experience as students (Buchmann, 1989). We want them to replace their old beliefs about lock-step teaching with a belief that the instructional activity that organizes instruction is invented by teachers and their students.

We begin with their vision, insisting that our students think long and hard about society, the changing nature of schools and what, under those circumstances, they want for their students. We work hard at getting them to think about conditional knowledge and how conditional knowledge about specific curricular goals connects with their vision for students. And we set a strong expectation that growth and change is a constant in the life of a professional teacher.

At the heart of our efforts are the field experience and the research requirement. In the field, our prospective teachers are placed with mentor teachers who themselves think of teaching as an entrepreneurial enterprise, and our student teachers teach in that classroom from the day the school doors open in the fall until they close in the summer. Teacher education courses are closely coordinated with what is going on in the field, and a premium is placed on fluid preactive and interactive decision making, creation of life-like learning situations and adaptive use of multiple instructional models.

Regarding research, study of one's own practice as a classroom teacher is a major part of the program. Guided by the "teacher-as-researcher" concept (Richardson, 1994; Santa & Santa, 1995), our teachers learn to ask questions about their work and to use qualitative research methods to inquire about those questions. Mentor teachers become actively involved in this research, helping their neophytes while also getting smarter about their own instructional practices in the process. We see it as another way to develop independent teachers; that is, we use research, self-study and respect for careful analysis of classroom events as another way to be "in charge" as a teacher.

Our goal is to replace old beliefs with a new conception. By putting our prospective teachers in charge of their own vision, by helping them think about curriculum in terms of conditional knowledge, by insisting that life-like activity is part of their responsibility and not someone else's, by encouraging them to be conceptually selective when thinking about models and when making "on the fly" instructional decisions, and by making self-study a routine component of daily teaching, we hope to develop teachers who are in charge of their own instruction and who can, therefore, serve children better.

However, what we are attempting is hard. All our students start out by fighting us. Like children who are anxious about the performance-grade exchange upon which the system is based (Doyle, 1983), many prospective teachers resist authentic situations and higher-level thinking, and negotiate instead for less complexity and less ambiguity. The refrain early on is "What do you really want here?" and they are not reassured when told, "Your own thinking." They want explicit directions that ensure a grade of A—they do not want to be out there where they have to be creative.

Similarly, a few of our student teachers cannot adapt to the demands of entrepreneurial teaching. One who is now engaged in very traditional teaching blames *us* because we "did not teach her how to teach." What she means, of course, is that we did not give her a prescription to follow. Instead, we gave her multiple models and many principles and expected her to synthesize these together into her own personal model.

Professors in the program also face difficulties. A common difficulty is the tension between teaching teachers to be entrepreneurial while simultaneously preparing them to "talk the talk" with hiring personnel who often expect teachers to follow district mandates. Another is the difficulty in allowing prospective teachers to develop visions and conceptions which, while uniquely theirs, conflict with ours.

And, of course, we do not have universal agreement among our mentors regarding what prospective teachers need to be doing in the field. A few believe neophytes cannot be entrepreneurial; others think being entrepreneurial means leaving the prospective teacher totally alone and going for coffee.

But, despite the difficulties, we persist. We believe that teachers who do their own thinking will provide qualitatively better instruction than teachers who passively follow models or materials.

CONCLUSION

The answer to the title question—"Powerful Models or Powerful Teachers?"—is, of course, "Both." Thoughtful instructional models are essential to help us think analytically about teaching; creative teachers are essential to educate an increasingly difficult clientele.

But, on the whole, I fear that teachers are often set up to follow a particular instructional model rather than being taught to thoughtfully combine models according to the demands of the instructional situation. This, I believe, is part of the reason why we see fewer creative classroom teachers of literacy than we would like.

Consequently, this chapter is designed to stimulate thought about how instructional models should be presented to teachers. It argues for helping teachers see models as tools to be adapted, not as panaceas to be adopted, and it encourages literacy educators to be as careful about the messages they send teachers about how to *use* models as they are about describing the content of models. As such, this chapter is a plea for more thought about how to teach teachers, not a plea for less thought about instructional models.

REFERENCES

Allington, R., & Cunningham, P. (1996). *Schools that work*. New York: Harper Collins.

Apple, M. (1983). Curricular reform and the logic of technical control. In M. Apple & L. Weiss (Eds.), *Ideology and practice in schooling* (pp. 143–166). Philadelphia: Temple University Press.

Blumenfeld, P., Mergendoller, J., & Swartout, D. (1987). Task as a heuristic for understanding student learning and motivation. *Journal of Curriculum Studies, 19*, 135–148.

Blumenfeld, P., Soloway, E., Marx, R., Krajcik, J., Guzdial, M., & Palincsar, A. (1991). Motivating project-based learning: Sustaining the doing, supporting the learning. *Educational Psychologist, 26*, 369–398.

Brown, R. (1991). *Schools of thought.* San Francisco: Jossey-Bass.

Brown, S., Collins, A., & Duguid, P. (1989). Situated cognition and the culture of learning. *Educational Researcher, 18*, 32–42.

Buchmann, M. (1989). Breaking from experience in teacher education: When is it necessary? How is it possible? *Oxford Review of Education, 15*, 181–195.

Cohen, D. (1988). *Teaching practice: Plus ca change* (Issue Paper 88-3). National Center for Research on Teacher Education. East Lansing: Michigan State University.

Cuban, L. (1984). *How teachers taught, 1890–1980.* New York: Longman.

Cunningham, P., & Allington, R. (1994). *Classrooms that work.* New York: Harper Collins.

Doyle, W. (1983). Academic work. *Review of Educational Research, 53*, 159–199.

Duffy, G. (1988). From turn-taking to sense-making: Broadening the concept of reading teacher effectiveness. *Journal of Educational Research, 76*, 134–139.

Duffy, G. (1991). What counts in teacher education? Dilemmas in empowering teachers. In J. Zutell & C. McCormick (Eds.), *Learning factors/teacher factors: Literacy research and instruction* (pp. 1–18). 40th Yearbook of the National Reading Conference. Chicago: National Reading Conference.

Duffy, G. (1993). Teachers' progress toward becoming expert strategy teachers. *Elementary School Journal, 94*(2), 109–120.

Duffy, G. (1994). How teachers think of themselves: A key to mindfulness. In J. Mangieri & C. Collins (Eds.), *Creating powerful thinking in teachers and students: Diverse perspectives* (pp. 3–25). Fort Worth: Holt, Rinehart & Winston.

Duffy, G., & Anderson, L. (1984). Teachers' theoretical orientations and the real classroom. *Reading Psychology, 5*, 97–104.

Duffy, G., & Roehler, L. (1981). Classroom teaching is more than opportunity to learn. *Journal of Teacher Education, 32*, 7–13.

Duffy, G., & Roehler, L. (1982). The illusion of instruction. *Reading Research Quarterly, 17*, 438–445.

Duffy, G., Roehler, L., & Herrmann, B. (1988). Modeling mental processes helps poor readers become strategic readers. *The Reading Teacher, 41*, 762–767.

Duffy, G., Roehler, L., & Rackliffe, G. (1986). How teachers' instructional talk influences students' understanding of lesson content. *Elementary School Journal, 87*, 3–16.

Duffy, G., Roehler, L., Sivan, E., Rackliffe, G., Book, C., Meloth, M., Vavrus, L., Wesselman, R., Putnam, J., & Bassiri, D. (1987). Effects of explaining the reasoning associated with using reading strategies. *Reading Research Quarterly, 22*, 347–368.

Durkin, D. (1978–1979). What classroom observation reveals about reading comprehension instruction. *Reading Research Quarterly, 14*, 481–533.

Elmore, R., & McLaughlin, M. (1988). *Steady work.* Santa Monica, CA: Rand.

Leinhardt, G. (1988). Situated knowledge and expertise in teaching. In J. Calderhead (Ed.), *Teachers' professional learning* (pp. 147–168). London: Palmer Press.

Nespor, J. (1987). The role of beliefs in the practice of teaching. *Journal of Curriculum Studies, 19*, 317–328.

Ogle, D. (1986). K-W-L: A teaching model that develops active reading of expository text. *The Reading Teacher, 39*, 564–570.

Pajares, M. F. (1992). Teachers' beliefs and educational research: Cleaning up a messy construct. *Review of Educational Research, 62*, 307–332.

Palincsar, A., & Brown, A. (1984). Reciprocal teaching of comprehension-fostering and monitoring activities. *Cognition and Instruction, 1*, 117–175.

Paris, S., Lipson, M., & Wixson, K. (1983). Becoming a strategic reader. *Contemporary Educational Psychology, 8*, 293–316.

Pearson, P. D. (1989). Reading the whole language movement. *Elementary School Journal, 90,* 231–242.

Resnick, L. (1987). Learning in school and out. *Educational Researcher, 16,* 13–20.

Richardson, V. (1994). Conducting research on practice. *Educational Researcher, 23*(5), 5–10.

Santa, C., & Santa, J. (1995). Critical issues: Teacher as researcher. *Journal of Reading Behavior: A Journal of Literacy, 27*(3).

Slavin, R. (1987). Cooperative learning: Where behavioral and humanistic approaches to classroom motivation meet. *Elementary School Journal, 88,* 29–37.

Smith, F. (1993). The never-ending confrontation. *Phi Delta Kappan, 74,* 411–412.

Smith, K., Reyna, V., & Brainerd, C. (1993). The debate continues. *Phi Delta Kappan, 74,* 407–410.

Winne, P. (1985). Steps toward promoting cognitive achievements. *Elementary School Journal, 85,* 673–693.

Author Index

A

Abbott, J., 41, 57
Ackerman, D. B., 290, 306
Adams, A., 73, 79
Adams, E. L., 238, 247
Adams, M. J., 14, 15, 17, 26, 70, 79, 209, 217, 222, 237, 239, 241, 253, 261, 275
Allen, J., 222, 230, 241, 270, 271, 275
Allen, V. G., 222, 230, 246
Allington, R. L., 192, 199, 210, 215, 217, 356, 363, 364
Almasi, J. F., 212, 220, 221, 234, 245
Altwerger, B., 6, 27, 214, 218, 222, 230, 233, 241, 242
Alvermann, D. E., 87, 105, 204, 217
Amanti, C., 209, 219
Ames, C., 134, 135, 143, 145, 157
Anders, P. L., 37, 44, 56, 58
Andersen, C., 222, 242
Anderson, G., 222, 230, 241
Anderson, L. M., 92, 99, 100, 102, 103, 106, 352, 364
Anderson, R. B., 64, 84
Anderson, R. C., 9, 26, 59, 79, 133, 136, 150, 153, 157, 158, 208, 217, 311, 321, 327
Anderson, V., 94, 105
Anthony, H. M., 92, 99, 100, 102, 103, 106
Apple, M., 361, 363
Applebee, A. N., 184, 199, 210, 217, 258, 276, 316, 321, 325, 327, 332, 338, 346

B

Archer, J., 134, 145, 157
Argyris, C., 35, 52, 53, 56
Armbruster, B. B., 70, 79
Ashton-Warner, S., 256, 276
Askov, E., 8, 24, 28
Atwell, N., 325, 327
Au, K. H., 153, 157, 163, 179, 189, 190, 191, 194, 195, 196, 197, 200, 210, 212, 216, 218
Austin, M. C., 1, 26

B

Bacmeister, R., 191, 200
Bailey, F., 287, 305, 306
Baker, C. D., 20, 26
Baker, K., 323, 328
Baker, S., 71, 74, 79, 83, 84
Bakhtin, M. M., 284, 285, 287, 288, 306, 336, 346
Baldwin, R. S., 16, 29
Barkin, F., 233, 242
Barr, R., 210, 218
Bartelo, D. M., 325, 327
Bartine, D. E., 24, 26
Baskwill, J., 222, 230, 241
Bassiri, D., 352, 364
Baumann, J. F., 59, 66, 72, 79, 83, 91, 105, 151, 157, 212, 218
Beach, R., 324, 329, 332, 334, 338, 346
Beals, D. E., 264, 276
Becker, W. C., 63, 64, 65, 66, 67, 79, 80, 81
Beed, P. L., 154, 157
Bell, R., 335, 346

Subject Index

A

Academic tasks, 85-86, 288, 359
Accelerated progress, 76, 164, 167
Adaptive models, 210
Aesthetic reading, 13, 22-23, 191, 268, 312-316
Assessment, 112, 115, 117, 123, 144, 190, 235-236, 251
Assisted performance, 208
Attitudes, 143, 355
Authenticity, 7, 353-354, 358
Author's chair, 7, 119, 121
Automaticity, 14, 17, 115, 136

B

Bank Street Model, 65
Basal readers, 8, 14, 21, 115-117, 275, 360
Beginning reading, 74, 110, 112-115, 122-123, 161-179, 249-281
Behaviorism, 2, 8, 42
Benchmark School, 4, 131-159
Big Books, 7, 193-194 , 260, 262
Book introductions, 176
Book reports, 115, 117

C

Case study research, 233
Center for the Learning and Teaching of Literature, 323
Changing established beliefs, 361-362
Checklists, 99-100

Child-centered curriculum, 7, 63, 75
Choices in book selection, 266, 274, 312, 324
Classroom environment, 250-254
Classroom libraries, 265-266
Classroom management, 41, 43, 50, 53, 360
Classroom post office, 253
Code differences, 185, 187
Code structures, 45-46, 55
Cognitive apprenticeship, 4-6, 9-11, 15, 203-204, 207, 211
Cognitive control, 355
Cognitive processes, 204-205
Cognitive strategies, 85-106, 131-133, 151-152, 211
Cognitive Strategy Instruction In Writing, 87, 92, 99-100, 102-103
Collaboration, 271, 273-274
Collaborative reading, 214
Collaborative writing, 119, 164-165, 169, 170, 174-176
Comprehension, 109-110, 113, 115, 117, 122-123, 254-256, 258
Computer-assisted instruction, 74, 78, 240, 272-274
Concepts about print, 6, 19, 113, 163, 176, 179, 258, 261-262, 269
Conceptual knowledge, 32, 42, 133
Conceptual models, 32
    of professional practice, 32-35, 38
    of Teaching, see models of teaching
Conditional knowledge, 211, 357
Construction of meaning, 208, 316-317, 324